The Birth of Classical Europe

THE PENGUIN HISTORY OF EUROPE

General Editor: David Cannadine

*already published

SIMON PRICE AND
PETER THONEMANN

The Birth of Classical Europe

A History from Troy to Augustine

VIKING

VIKING
Published by the Penguin Group
Penguin Group (USA) Inc., 375 Hudson Street,
New York, New York 10014, U.S.A.
Penguin Group (Canada), 90 Eglinton Avenue East, Suite 700,
Toronto, Ontario, Canada M4P 2Y3
(a division of Pearson Penguin Canada Inc.)
Penguin Books Ltd, 80 Strand, London WC2R 0RL, England
Penguin Ireland, 25 St. Stephen's Green, Dublin 2, Ireland
(a division of Penguin Books Ltd)
Penguin Books Australia Ltd, 250 Camberwell Road, Camberwell,
Victoria 3124, Australia
(a division of Pearson Australia Group Pty Ltd)
Penguin Books India Pvt Ltd, 11 Community Centre, Panchsheel Park,
New Delhi – 110 017, India
Penguin Group (NZ), 67 Apollo Drive, Rosedale, North Shore 0632,
New Zealand (a division of Pearson New Zealand Ltd)
Penguin Books (South Africa) (Pty) Ltd, 24 Sturdee Avenue,
Rosebank, Johannesburg 2196, South Africa

Penguin Books Ltd, Registered Offices:
80 Strand, London WC2R 0RL, England

First American edition
Published in 2011 by Viking Penguin,
a member of Penguin Group (USA) Inc.

1 3 5 7 9 10 8 6 4 2

Copyright © Simon Price and Peter Thonemann, 2010
All rights reserved

Illustration credits appear on pages vi-xii.

LIBRARY OF CONGRESS CATALOGING IN PUBLICATION DATA

Price, S.R.F.
The birth of classical Europe : a history from Troy to Augustine / Simon Price and Peter Thonemann.
p. cm.
Includes bibliographical references and index.
ISBN 978-0-670-02247-2
1. Europe—History—To 476. 2. Europe—Civilization—Greek influences. 3. Europe—Civilization—
Roman influences. 4. Civilization, Classical. I. Thonemann, Peter. II. Title.
D80.P73 2011
938—dc22
2010034578

Printed in the United States of America

Contents

List of Figures

List of Maps

List of Plates

1. Grandstand fresco from Knossos. Height: 0.32 m. From Sir Arthur Evans, *The Palace of Minos* (London: Macmillan, 1921–36), vol. 3, pl. XVI, facing p. 47.

2. Restoration drawing by Piet de Jong of Grave Circle A at Mycenae. From *Annual of the British School at Athens*, 25 (1921–3), pl. 18.

3. Fresco from palace at Pylos. Height 0.61 m. Photo: Courtesy of The Department of Classics, University of Cincinnati.

4. Diver investigating bronze ingots on Uluburun wreck. Photo: Institute of Nautical Archaeology.

5. Drawing of section of relief of the pharaoh Ramesses III defeating the Sea Peoples. Height (of section illustrated): 4.22 m. From H. H. Nelson (ed.), *Medinet Habu*, vol. 1: *Earlier Historical Records of Ramses III* (Chicago: University of Chicago Press, 1930), pl. 37 (central section).

6. Macmillan aryballos (perfume bottle), British Museum (inv. GR 1889.4–18.1). Height: 6.8 cm. Photo: © The Trustees of the British Museum. All rights reserved.

7. Gold pendant from woman's grave in Toumba monument, Lefkandi. Diameter of disc: *c.* 3.5 cm. Photo: Ian Cartwright. Courtesy of Irene Lemos.

8. Necklace of faience figurines in Egyptian style, Lefkandi. Height: *c.* 14 cm. Photo: Ian Cartwright. Courtesy of Irene Lemos.

9. Peplos Korē, Acropolis Museum, Athens (inv. 679). Height: 1.20 m. Photo: AICT/Allan T. Kohl.

10. Cast of Peplos Korē, Museum of Classical Archaeology, Cambridge. Photo: Museum of Classical Archaeology, Cambridge.

11. Harmodius and Aristogeiton. This reconstruction is based on Roman marble copies of the bronze original. University of Rome: Museo dei Gessi. Height: 1.95 m. Photo: Deutsches Archäologisches Institut, Rome, Schwanke, Neg. 1984.3297.

12. Metope no. 27 from south side of Parthenon, British Museum, London. Height: 1.20 m. Photo: Peter Thonemann.

13. Reconstruction of the queen's tomb at Vix, in Musée du Châtillonnais, Châtillon-sur-Seine. Photo: © MSM 65502 Vic-en-Bigorre.

14. Bibracte (Mont Beuvray) seen from the air. Photo: © René Goguey/Recherches d'Archéologie Aérienne. Courtesy: Vincent Guichard.

15. Celtic shield from the Thames at Battersea. Height: 0.78 m. British Museum (inv. P&EE 1857.7-15.1). Photo: © The Trustees of the British Museum. All rights reserved.

16. Statue of a dying Gaul, Capitoline Museum, Rome (inv. 747). Length: 1.85 m. Photo: AICT/Allan T. Kohl.

17. Dama del Cerro de los Santos. Height: 1.35 m. Museo Arqueológico Nacional, Madrid (inv. 3500). Photo: Museo Arqueológico Nacional, Madrid.

18. Carthage. Reconstruction of the military harbour. Watercolour, undated, by Peter Connolly after drawings by H. R. Hurst and S. C. Gibson. © Peter Connolly through akg-images. Photo (5TU–K1–Y3–1–B): akg-images/Peter Connolly.

19. Landscape and changing settlements of Sphakia, south-west Crete. Photo: Lucia Nixon.

20. Centuriation 100 km south of Carthage, in territory of Hadrumetum. From André Caillemer and R. Chevallier, 'Die römische Limitation in Tunesien', *Germania*, 35 (1957), pp. 45–54, pl. 8.1. Photo: Institut géographique national.

21. Submarine view of the Madrague de Giens wreck, first century BC. Photo (1986d02525): © CNRS Photothèque/Chêne, Antoine.

22. View of Palmyra from the Arab Fort, looking south-east. Photo: Lucia Nixon.

23. Procession of the imperial family on the Ara Pacis, Rome. Height: 1.55 m. Photo: AICT/Allan T. Kohl.

24. *Boadicea and her Daughters* by Thomas Thornycroft, London. Photo: Peter Thonemann.

25. View of the Sebasteion, Aphrodisias. Photo: Peter Thonemann.

26. The Porta Nigra, Trier. Photo: AICT/Allan T. Kohl.

27. Relief lamp perhaps from Egypt. Louvre, Paris (inv. Ca 661). Height: 12.5 cm. First century BC/first century AD. Photo: © 2005 RMN/Hervé Lewandowski.

28. Illustration of Aeneas leaving Dido from the Vatican Virgil (Vatican lat. 3225, fo. 39ᵛ). Photo: © Copyright of the Vatican Library (Biblioteca Apostolica Vaticana).

29. Mosaic of Europa and the Bull, Lullingstone. Width: *c.* 2.44 m. Photo: English Heritage.

30. Church of St Simeon, Qala'at Siman, Syria. Photo: Elizabeth Nixon.

31. Coins:

    (*a*) Alexander the Great, on silver coin (tetradrachm) of Lysimachus (*c.* 2.8 cm.), obverse, 297/6-282/1 BC. Ashmolean Museum, HCR7601 (= *Sylloge Nummorum Graecorum Ashmolean*, no. 3723 = *AHFC* (Christopher J. Howgego, *Ancient History from Coins* (London: Routledge, 1995)), pl. 6, no. 56). Photo: Ashmolean Museum, University of Oxford.

    (*b*) Gold coin (stater) of Flamininus, obverse, 196 BC. M. H. Crawford, *Coinage of the Roman Republic* (Cambridge: Cambridge University Press, 1974), p.544, no. 548/1a. British Museum, London. Photo: © The Trustees of the British Museum. All rights reserved.

    (*c*) Silver coin (denarius) of Italian rebels, reverse, *c.* 90 BC. H. A. Grueber, *Coins of the Roman Republic in the British Museum* (London: Longmans, 1910), II.327, no. 18. British Museum, London. Photo: © The Trustees of the British Museum. All rights reserved.

    (*d*) Silver coin (tetradrachm) of Mithradates (*c.* 2.9 cm.), obverse,

89/8 BC. Ashmolean Museum, HCR8002 (= *AHFC*, pl. 6, no. 57). Photo: Ashmolean Museum, University of Oxford.

(*e*) Silver coin (denarius) of Augustus (*c.* 2 cm), reverse, *c.* 19 BC. Ashmolean Museum, HCR7897 (= *AHFC*, pl. 13, no. 115). Photo: Ashmolean Museum, University of Oxford.

(*f*) Silver coin (tetradrachm) of Jewish rebels (*c.* 2.8 cm), obverse, AD 134/5. Ashmolean Museum, HCR6354 (= *AHFC*, pl. 19, no. 159). Photo: Ashmolean Museum, University of Oxford.

Acknowledgements

We are most grateful to those who have read individual chapters, or even the whole book: Michael Crawford; John Day; Peter Hainsworth; Irene Lemos; Elizabeth Nixon; Lucia Nixon, whose influence on the book is pervasive; Miranda Nixon; John North; Cynthia Shelmerdine; Philip Thonemann; Sarah Thonemann; and Roger Tomlin.

We are indebted to those who have helped us with excursuses on uses of the classical past: Lucy Bailey; Helen Barr; Nicholas Cole; John Day; Michael Dobson; Peter Hainsworth; Clive Holmes; Marie-Chantal Killeen; Bernard O'Donoghue; Nicholas Shrimpton; and Jennifer Yee.

In the gathering of images for figures and plates, we are equally indebted to numerous people: William Van Andringa; John Baines; Maureen Basedow; Henry Hurst; Irene Lemos; Simon Loseby; Elizabeth Nixon; Lucia Nixon; Miranda Nixon; Damian Robinson; Eduardo Sánchez-Moreno; Bert Smith; Cyrielle Thomas; Andrew Wilson; Greg Woolf; and others who helped us with illustrations that in the end could not be included in this book. We are also grateful to Aneurin Ellis-Evans for composing the index. The extract from 'The Ruin' on pp. 333–4 is from *Three Old English Elegies*, edited by R. F. Leslie (Exeter: University of Exeter Press, new edition, 1988).

Finally, we would like to record the splendidly harmonious and good-humoured nature of the collaboration between the two of us.

Oxford
July 2009

The Birth of Classical Europe

Introduction

In October 2005 a huge steel, bronze and glass sculpture was unveiled outside the seat of the European Parliament in Strasbourg. The sculpture, donated to the European Parliament by the town of Agios Nikolaos on Crete, depicts the mythological princess Europa, cast in bronze, riding on the back of a steel and glass bull. Once upon a time (or so the story goes), the god Zeus fell in love with a beautiful girl named Europa. In order to gain her affections, Zeus turned himself into a magnificent bull, and carried her on his back across the sea to Crete. According to some accounts, one of their three sons was a certain Minos, who became king of Crete. So the Strasbourg sculpture acts as a elegant symbol for the place of Crete in the history of Europe: since Europa later gave her name to the continent of Europe, the Minoan civilization on Crete marks the true beginning of European history.

The viewer of the Strasbourg statue of Europa and the bull is offered a neat definition of 'Classical' Europe: a region named after a figure in Greek mythology (Europa), whose son Minos gave his name to the region's first great civilization. There is, of course, some truth in this cosy modern take on the story, but the tale will bear a little closer examination. The Strasbourg statue of Europa is far removed from the Greek and Roman versions of the story.

The story of Europa and the bull was well known in the ancient Greek world. The rape of Europa is mentioned in the earliest surviving work of Greek literature (Homer's *Iliad*), and is commonly depicted in Greek art, on painted vases and in sculpture. It is thus a good example of a Panhellenic myth, a story known in different parts of the Greek world, and told for a variety of different reasons. The most striking local telling of the story comes, once again, from Crete. Here, coins minted by various Cretan cities between the fifth and third centuries BC feature Europa.

Sometimes they show her being carried on the back of the bull, but sometimes they show her lying under a plane tree. It was apparently beneath this plane tree that Europa and Zeus first lay together. The city of Gortyn was particularly successful in asserting its claim to the story and the tree itself became a notable landmark there. In the Roman period the tree was celebrated for never losing its leaves, and cuttings from it were used to propagate clones in other parts of Crete. In other words, the Gortynians asserted a special place for themselves in the wider Greek world by laying claim to this famous Panhellenic myth. It was right here in Gortyn, underneath this actual tree, that Zeus had made Europa pregnant with Minos and his brothers. This claim should no doubt be understood as part of Gortyn's long-standing rivalry with the nearby cities of Knossos and Phaistos. If Gortyn was the true site of the passion of Zeus and Europa, then Knossos and Phaistos were the losers. This account should warn us that the Greeks did not regard their myths as 'mythical', as fairy stories, but as tales of a remote past which could be rooted in real places and things. This local version of the tale is still popular among tourist guides at the site of Gortyn, who point out a particular huge tree as the very one under which Europa lay in the arms of Zeus.

The story of Europa was also popular among Roman writers. In his *Metamorphoses*, the Latin poet Ovid recounts how Europa, the daughter of the king of Tyre in Phoenicia, was out playing with her young female friends on the seashore. Zeus had fallen in love with her, and wanted to seduce her. So he transformed himself into a magnificent bull, and joined the herd of bullocks that he had arranged to be grazing by the sea. Europa fell for the splendid animal, and after a while climbed onto its back. The bull then bore the frightened young woman across the sea to Crete. Here he resumed his own form. Ovid's telling of the story is a world apart from the local myths of Gortyn, Knossos and Phaistos. It is a 'floating', deracinated version, privileging no one place on Crete over any other, which simply forms an elegant (and slightly allusive) episode in the sequence of transformations that constitutes his *Metamorphoses*. And precisely because it is so deracinated, it was Ovid's account of this, and other myths, which achieved canonical status in the Renaissance and afterwards. It is the Ovidian version that inspired paintings by artists like Titian and Rembrandt.

The spin that makes this myth emblematic of European civilization is very recent indeed. In antiquity, the myth does not bear this meaning. The region of Europe is hardly ever personified in antiquity; it was only in the nineteenth century that the continent regularly came to be personified in the form of Europa on the bull. The connection between the Minoan civilization of Crete and the origins of Europe is also a modern one. The Greeks simply regarded Minos as one of several early rulers of Crete, not as the founder of a primordial civilization. Although the Strasbourg statue of Europa and the bull is based on a story dating back at least to the eighth century BC, its cultural significance is intimately tied to the particular political circumstances of the early twenty-first century AD.

This history of Classical Europe will travel from the so-called Minoan civilization of Crete to the later Roman empire, from the middle of the second millennium BC to the fourth and early fifth centuries AD. Although our geographical canvas stretches from Scotland to the Nile valley, and from the Atlantic coast of Portugal to the mountains of Armenia, we have not tried to present a full history of all the area now counted as 'Europe'. At the centre of our canvas stand the ancient peoples of the northern Mediterranean basin, the Greeks and the Romans. For this we make no apology: the principal long-term developments in this period were driven by the people of the Aegean sea, the southern Balkans and the Italian peninsula. The nine chapters of this book are structured chronologically, because analysis of history has to go hand in hand with understanding the flow of events. We have tried to avoid presenting a timeless account of 'the Greek view of X', or 'the Roman view of Y': there is no such thing as *the* ancient myth of Europa. Even very general ideas are rooted in particular circumstances and events.

Histories have to begin somewhere, and this one begins rather earlier than most accounts of the Classical world. (The Date Chart at the end of this book provides a concise summary of the key dates.) We begin with the age of the Minoan and Mycenaean palaces on Crete and in mainland Greece. We look, too, at relations with their neighbours in the eastern Aegean and beyond, placing special emphasis on Troy, in north-western Asia Minor. In Chapters 2 and 3, we expand our horizons westwards, to take in the whole of the central Mediterranean world. We examine the period of turmoil that followed the collapse of the palaces (the so-called Dark Age), and the emergence of the first Greek and Italic city-states. Chapters 4 and 5 then take the history of the Greeks through the Classical era and into the Hellenistic age, when the culture of the Greek city-state spread far beyond its Aegean homelands into the heart of Asia. Chapters 6 and 7 return to the Italian peninsula, moving from the founding of the Roman Republic to the growth of the Roman *imperium* overseas, culminating with the breakdown of Republican institutions, and the transition from Republic to Empire. Chapter 8 is occupied by an in-depth analysis of the workings of the Roman empire. Finally, in Chapter 9, we examine the transformation of the imperial system in the fourth century AD, the increasing impact of Christianity on the empire, and the changing attitudes of the period towards 'classical' culture. St Augustine's attempts to reconcile Christian culture with the 'Classical' inheritance of Rome form an appropriate conclusion to the book (and also a starting point for the next volume in this series).

The geographical scope of the book, therefore, varies over time. Each chapter begins with a brief exposition of its context and compass, and offers some account of the extent of the area under consideration. The main part of the chapter includes discussion of the characteristics of the state in that period. Was the state a palace, a city-state, a monarchy? How large was it? Did the area have a single centre, or was it multi-centred? What sort of settlement hierarchy was there? What sorts of connections were there between the area and the outside world? The obvious storm-centres of Greek and Roman history (Knossos, Sparta, Athens, Macedon, Rome) will receive due treatment, but a number of other, less well-known places will also appear repeatedly in the course of the book: cities like Massilia (modern Marseilles), Carthage and Miletus, and regions like Sphakia in south-west Crete, Lycia in south-west Turkey and the island of Cyprus.

Although our story does proceed in roughly chronological order, we have tried to offer something more than a mere narrative history of the ancient world. Instead, we have aimed to explore, in a series of different contexts, three main themes.

The first and overarching theme is 'memory'. This book offers (among other things) a historical study of memory, which does not draw a simple line between the 'true' and the 'false' memory claims of the past. All history is an act of remembering, an attempt by the historian to preserve the memory of the past by putting it on record (as the Greek historian Herodotus says in his opening sentence). There are other possible justifications for the study of history, but this one is surely basic, our moral duty to recall the past, and to oppose those who rewrite the past for unsavoury ends. But the historian cannot (or should not) claim to be the simple guardian of objective truth. History is, at least in part, a constructed artefact, the product of intellectual, social and political pressures. This is not to suggest that memory and history are the same thing. History makes claims for truth which are defensible because of the disciplines and rigour of history. The narratives of history are differently constructed from those of memory. But there are also similarities between memory and history. Neither memory nor history provides an innocent account of past events: both create their own versions of the past, and both are products of their own time. The interest in studying memory in the past is that it places centre stage the self-understandings of particular peoples, and so gets us closer to understanding their world. Study of memory ought to place us closer to the mind-sets of people in the past; it should help to prevent us from advancing anachronistic interpretations of the period, and make it possible for us to see how the choices people make relate to their own view of their past.

As we shall see, the Greeks and Romans had a very different sense of the past from that of the modern historian. For example, we know (or think we know) that the end of the Mycenaean civilization in Greece *c.* 1200 BC was followed by a 400-year 'Dark Age'. The earliest Greek city-states, which began to emerge in the eighth century BC, owed nothing to the culture and institutions of the Mycenaean palaces; the eighth-century Greeks began with a 'slate wiped clean'. However, the Greeks themselves preserved no collective memory of a centuries-long 'Dark Age'. The Greeks of the seventh and sixth centuries BC believed that their present-day city-states were the direct successors of the palace-states of the remote past (including the period of the Trojan War). We are now able to say with some certainty that the Greeks were, empirically, wrong: this ancient model of continuity between the 'heroic age' and the present day is not a true historical chronology, but a 'chronology of desire'. Nonetheless, this Greek 'chronology of desire' has to be taken seriously. What the Greeks thought about their past (whether true or not) was central to Greek self-definition. The development of Greek society between the seventh and fourth centuries BC was driven not by what *we* know about their early history, but by what *they* thought they knew.

This book therefore aims to take seriously the question of how people in the past saw themselves in relation to their own past. It offers, in other words, a set of 'rolling pasts'.

The theme of 'memory' can also be explored in another way. While trying to show what the Greeks and Romans made of their own past, we also want to explore the kinds of uses that people in more recent periods have made of antiquity. For example, the contested cultural identity of Macedon in the fourth century (was it Greek or not?) has become inextricably entangled with the current political controversies about the cultural identity of that region, and about the nomenclature of the former Yugoslav Republic of Macedonia. And why was it that Josiah Wedgwood named his factory 'Etruria'? Why has 'Boadicea' proved to be so potent a symbol of British national identity? These examples will be presented as inset boxes, so as not to break up the flow of the main narrative. Our own uses (and abuses) of the classical past are part of the web of connections that links us to 'Classical Europe'.

One final aspect of the theme of memory is the definition of certain moments, places or monuments as 'classical'. For historians today, one such privileged moment is 'Classical Athens', Athens of the fifth and fourth centuries BC. But when and why was it so regarded? Was Classical Athens regarded as 'Classical' already in antiquity? By whom? Virgil has held a privileged position as a 'Classical' author since the Middle Ages (after all, he was Dante's guide to hell). Was this true also under the Roman empire?

The second major theme of this book is that of communal identity. Uses of the past are one way in which communal identities are defined, but they are not the only way. This book explores the changing ways in which the peoples of Europe defined themselves in antiquity: civic, ethnic, regional, cultural and linguistic. We pay particularly close attention to the multiple cultural identities of the peoples of the Roman empire, including Greeks, Jews and Christians. Did the Roman empire try to foster a specifically Roman identity among its subjects? Did it succeed? Many of Rome's subjects certainly borrowed Roman ways (the process commonly known as 'Romanization'), but these borrowings took widely different forms in different parts of the empire. We shall see that the 'Romanization' of the western Roman provinces in the first three centuries AD led to a widespread obliteration of historical memory; the inhabitants of Roman Gaul or Britain became, in a real and powerful sense, 'peoples without history'. By contrast, in the eastern provinces of the empire, the memory of the Classical Greek past was not just preserved but actively privileged (and encouraged by the Roman imperial state). Other minority groups founded their communal identity on their shared religious beliefs; we focus in particular on Jews and Christians, considering both their views of each other and their differing perceptions of the past, and also their views of the contemporary world.

The book's third theme is spatial (and conceptual). If part of the theme of memory concerns changing definitions of what counts as 'Classical', part of this theme is an analysis of changing ideas about what 'Europe' was. As a result of the expansion of the European Union between 2004 and 2007 (from 14 to 27 members), the outer borders of 'Europe' have come to seem disconcertingly fluid. It is quite possible that, in a decade's time, Europe will share a border with modern Iran. Nonetheless, and particularly in western Europe, many people retain an underlying sense of the natural boundaries of 'old Europe', the Europe of the earlier European Union. But of course even this 'old Europe' is not a natural but a historical and cultural construct. At various points in this book we shall explore when and how 'Europe' was defined in antiquity, from its initial definition as being different from 'Asia' (that is, the area east of the Hellespont, and ruled by the Persians), to the new spatial interests created by a Roman empire stretching from Scotland to the Euphrates. In the time period covered by this book, the centre or centres of the 'civilized' world changed in location, and the boundaries of that world were differently defined, often by natural features such as seas, rivers and mountains.

Throughout the book, we have tried to give some sense of the sizes of settlements, which vary enormously from period to period, and region to region. Where possible we have given precise areas of sites, rather than vague and rather meaningless terms like 'small' or 'large'. The unit of area we have used is the normal modern archaeological unit, the hectare (that is, 10,000 square metres, or a square with sides of 100 metres). In order to get a feel for the size of a hectare, it is helpful to know that a soccer pitch is roughly 1 hectare, and an American football field is just under half a hectare. If you prefer to think in terms of acres, double the number of hectares (or, to be more precise, multiply by 2.5).

It is also helpful to have some modern comparisons in mind for larger areas. For example, Windsor Castle covers just over 10 hectares (26 acres), while Paris within the Boulevard Périphérique is 9,470 hectares.

There is no one solution to how to deal with Greek names. We have treated them in three ways. The most common names, like Athens or Corinth, have an established English form. The next most common, like Menelaus or Ithaca, are in a Latinate form, while rare names, like Keos or Peparethos, retain their Greek forms. 'Heracles' is used for the Greek name of the deity, and 'Hercules' for the Latin.

I

The Aegean World: Minoans, Mycenaeans and Trojans: *c.* 1750–1100 BC

In the beginning, there was Troy and the Trojan War, made famous in European history by the two epic poems ascribed to Homer, the *Iliad* and the *Odyssey*. According to these poems, the Trojan War began when Helen, wife of Menelaus, king of Sparta, was abducted by Paris, a prince of Troy. The *Iliad* tells the story of the anger of the Greek warrior Achilles at Troy; the *Odyssey* recounts the adventures of Odysseus on his way home from Troy to the island of Ithaca. We see these two epics as largely fictional stories, but these and later memories of the Trojan War were of fundamental importance within antiquity and beyond. Greeks, Romans and others found their origins in the events surrounding the Trojan War, the founding acts of European history. Before looking at the later importance of the Trojan War, we need to understand the period in which these later tales are set, the period of the palaces in Crete and mainland Greece.

Heinrich Schliemann, born in 1822 in what is now northern Germany, had the beginnings of a classical education, but then moved into business, making money from various ventures, including the Californian gold rush. He later claimed that his father had inspired him with stories from Homer, and that at the age of 8 he had decided that one day he would excavate the site of Troy. These claims are probably part of the rich fantasy life Schliemann created for himself. But from his late thirties or early forties he was able to live on his accumulated wealth, and travelled widely for pleasure. In 1868, when he was 46, he visited Greece and Turkey, and the following year he published a book, *Ithaka, the Peloponnese and Troy*, in which he argued that Troy was to be found at Hisarlık, in north-west Turkey, near the mouth of the Dardanelles, contrary to the prevailing view which located Troy at the nearby site of Pınarbaşı. This argument was based in part on the work by a British archaeologist Frank

Calvert, who had been excavating the site for the previous five years. Schliemann was determined to dig there himself, and in 1871, with the help of Calvert, he started the excavations that made him famous. Schliemann's excavation techniques were poor, even by the standards of his time, as he simply dug through all the nine layers, including the layer near the bottom (Level II) that he believed to be Homer's Troy, the city of King Priam. He is also accused of planting evidence, or at least of being extremely slack in his recording of the finds. But he did publish a book on the site, *Troy and her Ruins*, in 1875, and returned to dig there again on several other occasions. Despite all the criticisms levelled at Schliemann at the time and subsequently, his work, and his publicizing of it, did succeed in establishing Hisarlık in the modern imagination as Homer's Troy. Schliemann also dug at other 'Homeric' sites. In 1876, he excavated in the Peloponnese at Mycenae, the home of Agamemnon, and on the island of Ithaca, off the north-west coast of Greece, at what he believed to be Odysseus' palace.

Despite serious flaws in Schliemann's arguments and evidence, he was responsible for two great achievements. First, chronological. In the early nineteenth century, most western Europeans assumed that the story of the Trojan War had no historical basis whatsoever, and was just a myth. Educated people still believed that the account of the world's creation given in Genesis was literally true. In the seventeenth century Archbishop Ussher had determined that the world was created in 4004 BC, and there was no obvious place in his generally accepted account for complex societies in the Aegean earlier than the fifth century BC. It is hard for us today to imagine a view of the past in which time started so recently, a world without a human past stretching backwards for countless millennia: *Homo sapiens* is attested from about 130,000 years ago, and our more remote ancestor, *Homo habilis*, from about 2.5 million years ago. By the mid-nineteenth century geologists had already argued for a much longer history for the world. Schliemann revealed once and for all that there was an important 'time before' in the Aegean – a prehistoric period, lasting a thousand years or more, with its own complex societies, complete with large-scale monuments and long-distance connections. His second achievement was more technical. He came to realize that monuments alone were not enough for dating these newly discovered stretches of time, and that pottery, with its durability as a material matched to the changing styles of fabric, shape and pattern, could furnish a way of constructing an accurate relative chronology. Sequences of pottery, dated in relative terms, with some absolute pegs, are to this day the basis of archaeological chronologies.

Another great figure in the establishment of our present views about the early Aegean was Sir Arthur Evans, responsible for the excavation of Knossos on Crete. While Schliemann had been driven by his reading of Homer, Evans was in search of early forms of writing. Arthur Evans (1851–1941) was born into a well-to-do family; his father was an eminent archaeologist and collector. After taking a degree in modern history at Oxford, Evans travelled widely in northern and eastern Europe. In 1877 he became Balkan correspondent for the *Manchester Guardian*. When he married Margaret Freeman the following year, he and his wife set up house in Ragusa (modern Dubrovnik) on the Dalmatian coast. In 1883 they went to Greece, where they met Schliemann and heard about his work at Mycenae and other Mycenaean sites. When Evans became Keeper of the Ashmolean Museum (Oxford) in 1884 he announced that his goals were to broaden archaeology beyond the Classical period, and to collect and display a wider variety of ancient material.

It was not until 1894 that Evans made his momentous first visit to Crete. He had become interested in Aegean writing systems, through collecting engraved gems and seals for the Ashmolean. He visited the site of Knossos, and proposed to the local Cretan Archaeological Council that he would buy the land and excavate the site himself, hoping to discover there new evidence on early writing. Knossos was already known to be a rich archaeological site. In 1739 the British traveller Richard Pococke had seen the (scanty) standing remains, and in 1878 Minos Kalokairinos, from the nearby city of Herakleion, had dug trenches in what was later identified as the west wing of the palace, identifying the remains as those of the ancient Labyrinth, home of the Minotaur. Schliemann too had wanted to dig at Knossos and had made some soundings there in the 1880s. He had obtained an excavation permit from the Turkish authorities in Crete, but had not been able to make a suitable financial arrangement with the landowner.

In Evans's case it was the political situation on Crete that prevented the start of his own work at Knossos. The Cretans were waging a War of Independence against the Ottoman Turks. The Turks left the island in 1898 and a new, autonomous Cretan government was established. By early 1900 Evans had acquired both the Knossos site and an excavation permit, and started work on 23 March. By this time he had already realized from the finds that had come his way that the culture of prehistoric Crete was different from that of the Mycenaean mainland, so different as to be 'non-Hellenic', in his eyes. He had therefore borrowed the name of Minos, son of Europa and Zeus and king of Crete, and created the term 'Minoan' to describe early Cretan culture. What Evans found at Knossos confirmed this view. The monumental structure, which he called the Palace of Minos, with its elegant architecture; the bright, exuberant wall-paintings and pottery; the 'engraved tablets' in a script that came to be called Linear B: all these were different from anything that had been seen before. The excavations lasted for five years (1900–1905), and the results were published in the six beautiful volumes of *The Palace of Minos* (1921–36).

It is easy to criticize Evans now, and indeed he was wrong about some important issues. He could never accept that the relationship between Minoan Crete and the Mycenaean mainland changed from Minoan cultural pre-eminence of the Aegean to Mycenaean pre-eminence on Crete, and he made mistakes in some of the restorations he undertook at Knossos, although restorations were necessary, not least because, most unusually, he had discovered multi-storey structures, which had to be made safe for further excavation and for visitors. Evans remains the major figure in the prehistoric archaeology of Crete, for his vision and for his determination to bring the results of his work into the public arena. He died heartbroken in 1941, in the mistaken belief that the German invaders of Crete had destroyed Knossos, but in fact the Germans had taken great care to protect the site. The pre-eminent historical importance of Knossos was firmly established throughout Europe.

Knossos and the rest of Crete in what is known as the Second Palace period, which began around 1750 BC, forms the starting point for this book. After a period of considerable prosperity and success for the island between the seventeenth and early fifteenth centuries, numerous sites were violently destroyed around 1430 BC. Around this time, the first Mycenaeans from the Greek mainland arrived on Crete. It would be too simplistic to see the coming of the Mycenaeans as a straightforward conquest of the island; rather, the new arrivals seem to have employed a combination of force, blending and collaboration with the existing Minoan elites. In the late fifteenth and fourteenth centuries, Knossos emerged as the main administrative centre of the island, with a new language of administration (Greek). The Mycenaean period on the mainland and on Crete was marked by further prosperity. But by 1100 BC, the end-point of this chapter, the palatial organization of the mainland and Crete had ceased to operate, and far-reaching social and political changes occurred. In the Second Palace period all roads had led to Knossos, but by 1100 BC that was no longer the case. The Aegean world had fragmented.

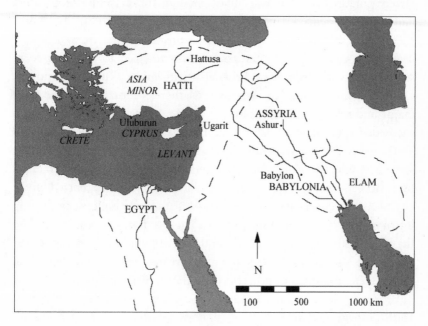

Map 1. The major Near Eastern states, c. 1220 BC.

We should not over-emphasize the importance of the palatial civilizations on Crete and in mainland Greece in the mid-second millennium BC. The Minoan and Mycenaean palace-states lay on the outer western fringe of a wider world of immeasurably more powerful and sophisticated Near Eastern states. Around 1500 BC the dominant power in the Near East was the kingdom of Egypt to the south. The Middle Kingdom (2116–1795 BC) had been replaced, after an Intermediate period (1795–1540 BC), by the New Kingdom (1550–1070 BC). The Middle Kingdom had been a period of stability in Egypt, with a secure frontier with Nubia (modern Ethiopia) to the south. During the Intermediate period, Egypt was ruled by a foreign dynasty, the Hyksos, with wide diplomatic and trading connections, but exercising only fragile control over the whole country. With the expulsion of the Hyksos dynasty and the establishment of the New Kingdom *c.* 1550 BC, Egypt was reunified, extending from Nubia in the south to somewhere in Palestine to the north-east, more than 1,200 kilometres as the crow flies.

At the same time, the rest of the Near East was home to a number of competing states. During the turbulent years of the usurping Hyksos Dynasty in Egypt, central Asia Minor (modern Turkey) and Mesopotamia had also experienced a period of disruption and anarchy. Over three generations, starting around 1590 BC, urbanism had declined to its lowest level for 1,500 years. Human society was reduced to small, insecure settlements, with little or no broader organization. Out of this power-vacuum, from around 1500 BC onwards, there eventually emerged three major and relatively stable states. In Lower Mesopotamia, the Kassites succeeded in taking over Babylonia, the area of the lower Euphrates and Tigris rivers. Their extraordinarily long-lived dynasty ruled this area for some 400 years. In Upper Mesopotamia, an Assyrian kingdom emerged by 1400 BC. The Assyrians, originally a small principality centred on the city of Ashur (covering some 50 hectares), gradually built themselves up into a major Near Eastern superpower. The Assyrian state encroached on the Kassite kingdom to its south, and spread far to the north and west (some 700 kilometres north–south at its greatest extent). Finally, the old Hittite state reasserted its power in central Anatolia, entering a new phase of prosperity from around 1420 to 1200 BC, centred on its huge capital Hattusa (near modern Boğazköy), in north-central Anatolia. During this period the site was enlarged to cover 180 hectares, enclosed within monumental walls; palace complexes were built; and a special religious area was established in the upper city, with no fewer than thirty temples. From here the Hittite state controlled central Anatolia, and by around 1220 BC it had come to dominate a vast area, stretching from the Aegean coast of Anatolia in the west, towards an eastern border with the Assyrian kingdom on the Euphrates, and a southern border with Egypt in Palestine (some 1,000 kilometres east–west and north–south). It was one of the major players in the Near East in the second half of the second millennium, and had active diplomatic relations with the Aegean world.

These great Near Eastern empires of the second half of the second millennium BC shared many modern-looking institutions. Egypt, Babylonia and Assyria were territorial states, ruled from a centre. Egypt had been a territorial state for the past 1,500 years, but in Babylonia and Assyria, formerly independent cities lost their autonomy and formed parts of the new, wider state. By contrast, the Hittite kingdom was based more on the loyalty of vassal princes than on the wholesale incorporation of dependent cities. The ruling dynasties legitimated their positions through claims to historical precedent, and through construction of dynastic lineages. The states formed part of a common international system, and engaged in extensive diplomatic and trading connections with each other. For example, there survive copies of 350 letters sent between the Egyptian pharaoh Akhenaten (1353–1335 BC) and rulers outside Egypt (the so-called Amarna Letters). Most were sent by Akhenaten to his vassals in Syria-Palestine, but about forty were sent to or were received from rulers whom he treated as his peers, the 'Great Kings', who addressed each other as 'brothers'. These 'Great Kings' included the rulers of Babylonia, Assyria and the Hittites, as well as other, lesser states whose favour the Egyptians required. Diplomacy included, when necessary, treaties between the different principalities, which spelled out in precise detail the

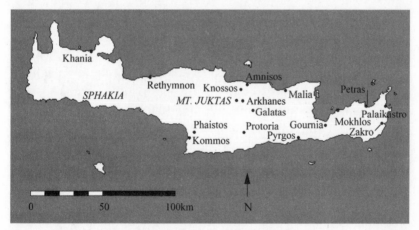

Map 2. Crete in the Second Palace period. The possible palaces are: Arkhanes; Galatas; Khania; Knossos; Kommos?; Malia; Palaikastro?; Petras, Phaistos; Protoria?; Rethymnon?; Zakro.

boundaries between them. The internal workings of the states were highly centralized, with a very strong focus on the king as the central symbol of the state. The populations owed service to the king, in the form of taxes (for example, flocks, grain or silver) and labour (for public works or military service). In the Assyrian kingdom, the laws regulated many aspects of private life. In specifying, for example, the penalties which could legally be exacted of an adulterous wife and her lover, the laws created a communal framework which sought to control private vendettas. In comparison to these advanced states of the Near East, the Mycenaean and Minoan palatial societies of the Aegean were pretty small players.

The Aegean world consists of Crete in the south, the Greek mainland up at least as far as Volos (in ancient Thessaly), and some of the southern Aegean islands. The island of Crete was dominated by a series of at least seven palaces. Knossos, excavated by Evans, is the most famous. It and Phaistos were indeed the two largest ones, but ten other palaces, all marked on Map 2, are known or conjectured. The list depends on the precise requirements for qualification as a palace.

Minos and Atlantis

Evans's excavation of Knossos generated widespread interest in Minos. Evans himself argued that his work demonstrated the substantial truth of later Greek myth: Minos was a real person, whose palace was the Labyrinth of later myth, and whose sport of bull-leaping was the origin of the Minotaur story. One scholar in *The Times* of 1909 brought in Plato's account of the lost kingdom of Atlantis, a mighty power in the Atlantic that made an unsuccessful expedition against Europe and Asia, only to be overwhelmed by natural disaster and sink into the waves. He argued that this legend was based on misunderstood Egyptian records of Minoan Crete. This type of argument has proved distressingly appealing to subsequent searchers for Atlantis: more recent archaeologists have attempted to link Atlantis with the ending of Minoan power, and the eruption of the Santorini volcano (for the redating of this eruption, see below, p. 27), and have even placed Atlantis at Troy. More recently, in 2004 Atlantis was 'discovered' off Cyprus, and in 2009, thanks to Google Earth, in the Atlantic off the west coast of Africa. The ordinary reader of Plato finds these repeated attempts to uncover 'the truth' behind Plato's quite casual little story very odd.

Partly as a result of the excavation of Knossos, twentieth-century artists drew much inspiration from Cretan myths, treating old themes in a distinctively modern fashion. For example, in 1919–20 images of

Europa and the bull by the German artist Lovis Corinth explored the then topical theme of the sexual awakening of the young girl. Other Cretan myths also proved fertile for artists. During the 1930s Pablo Picasso became obsessed with ideas of the Minotaur, stimulated in part by Spanish bullfighting, but also by the bullfighting fresco found at Knossos. Picasso went on to explore the themes of sexuality and violent death in a series of drawings and prints, including *Minotauromachie* (1935), regarded by some as the greatest graphic work of the twentieth century.

The site of Knossos lies some 5 kilometres from the north coast of Crete, south-east of modern Herakleion. The palace of the mid-second millennium BC had important predecessors on the same site. There had been significant settlement here during the third millennium BC, including a substantial structure on the same alignment as that of the later palaces.

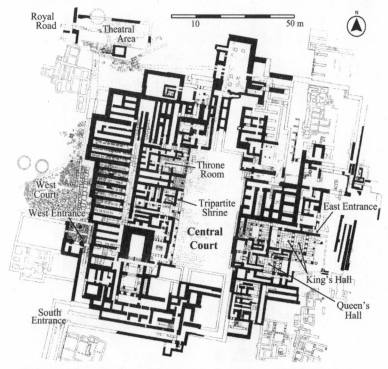

Figure 1. Plan of palace of Knossos in the mid-second millennium BC.

The First Palace, a large monumental complex, was built soon after 1900 BC, but destroyed by an earthquake *c.* 1700 BC. The Second Palace was built *c.* 1700 BC, on much the same lines as the First Palace, but in its turn was destroyed *c.* 1430 BC (see Figure 1). It was much used as the setting for ritual activities, by both women and men. These activities probably included the performance of bull-leaping, a ritual of great importance to the palace. The palace was approached from the north-west, via a stepped structure which may have been used to receive visitors, into the West Court, facing the west façade of the palace. From here a complex of corridors, with lavish frescos, led to the Central Court. This court was a large open area (50 × 25 metres), used for ceremonial purposes. Courts of this kind are defining characteristics of all the Cretan palaces. An antechamber off the Central Court led to the Throne Room; nearby was a shrine (the Tripartite Shrine), and two pillar crypts, small dark rooms believed to have ritual significance (Plate 1).

The residential quarter was set in the south-east part of the palace, with clever architectural features to maximize indirect light and air, and

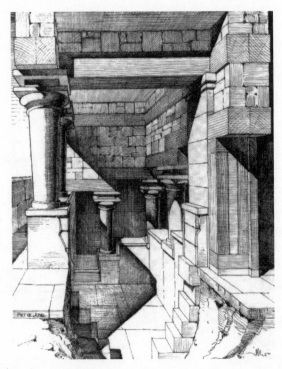

Figure 2. Restoration drawing of part of the Palace of Knossos, by Piet de Jong.

indoor plumbing (see Figure 2). Evans, the excavator of the site, thought that women and men lived separately: he assigned a larger set of rooms to men, the King's Hall, and a smaller set to women, the Queen's Hall. Evans's assumptions about gender survive in the modern names for these rooms, but there is no evidence for segregated living quarters. Indeed, it may be that this whole area, like that to the west of the Central Court, was used for ceremonial purposes. The palace also had substantial storerooms, with huge storage jars to hold wine or olive oil, and a workshop for the production of luxury vessels that were made from stone imported from the Greek mainland. In the Second Palace period, the palace was surrounded by clusters of separate residential buildings. Overall, the settlement surrounding the palace covered about 67 hectares. The houses varied in size and complexity, but the grandest ones reproduced a number of architectural features seen in the palace itself.

The ten or so palaces on Crete in the middle of the second millennium BC formed a network of centres, covering much of the island. They had common architectural features, and similar functions. Though the other palaces are smaller than Knossos and Phaistos, it seems that the states were more or less equal. They transferred goods between each other, and presumably also interacted in other ways. Ranking below the palaces was a system of subordinate settlements, which imitated the palaces in various ways. The town at Gournia included a main building that in one phase partially enclosed the settlement's main square, making it like a palatial central court. Throughout the island there were also numerous 'villas', free-standing buildings with architectural features derived from the palace repertoire. They are less sophisticated than the palaces, and lack even miniature central courts, but they share the palatial style of stone-cutting and room design. The 'villas' and palaces formed part of a single political and economic system.

This system, however, did not incorporate all parts of Crete. The palaces and 'villas' are concentrated in the central and eastern part of the island, with a westward extension along the north coast as far as Khania. The west and south-west parts seem not to have been within the orbit of the palaces' organization of the production of goods. The region of modern Sphakia is a good example of this. Forming part of the south-western part of the island, due south of Khania, Sphakia had few reflections of the palaces. In the western and central parts of Sphakia, which are cut off from the north coast by the White Mountains, settlements

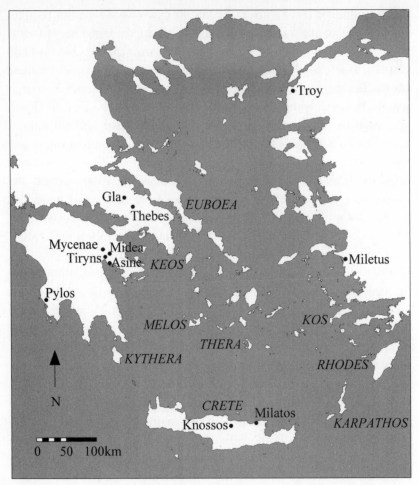

Map 3. The Aegean *c.* 1400 BC.

were modest both in scale and in artefacts. Only in eastern Sphakia, where a large coastal plain was open to coastal connections from palaces in central Crete, were things different (Plate 19). Settlements were larger in scale, with some signs of the palatial architectural repertoire.

Palaces also developed on the Greek mainland, but at a rather later date than on Crete. There was a long process of evolution from scattered chiefdoms (common in the earlier second millennium BC) towards more centralized states. The architectural development of the palaces is poorly understood, but soon after 1400 BC palaces were in operation at Mycenae, Tiryns, Pylos and Thebes. The palaces acquired a standard pattern, rather different from that found on Crete. At Pylos, the best-preserved mainland palatial site, the palace was modest in size (less than half a hectare), but complex in organization (see Figure 3). The fourteenth-century palace at Pylos seems to have imitated Minoan palace architecture, but the surviving palace of 1300–1200 BC is quite different from the Cretan palaces. It was entered through an elaborate gateway, with perhaps a guardhouse on one side, and a records room on the other, to process incoming and outgoing goods. From there one could pass through one court and a vestibule into the so-called megaron. The megaron was a rectangular room with four columns surrounding a central, circular hearth, with a lantern or clerestory above, and a throne set against one wall. The megaron was one of the defining characteristics of the mainland

Figure 3. Plan of the palace at Pylos. The heavy lines indicate walls certainly attested; the hollow lines indicate walls not well preserved. 1: gateway; 2: guard-house; 3: records rooms; 4: courtyard; 5: vestibule; 6: megaron; 7: pantries and storerooms; 8: smaller megaron; 9: megaron in South-west building; 10: court for feasting; 11: area for feasting.

palaces, also found in the earlier palaces at Mycenae and Tiryns. Decorated with splendid frescos, the megaron was the key setting for ceremonial. It was surrounded by pantries and storerooms. From the court, one could also reach a smaller version of the main megaron, with adjacent bedroom and bathroom. Communal feasts were probably held in two places: for the elite in the open area between the South-west and the main building, outside another megaron, and for ordinary people in the open area in front of the palace.

The palaces at Mycenae, Tiryns and Thebes, on outcrops rising from the plain, were surrounded by elaborate fortifications (Plate 2). There were also other major fortified citadels at, for example, Midea, Asine and Gla. At Gla, an outcrop was surrounded by very thick walls, constructed of enormous stones. The huge walls enclosed a large area, some 24 hectares, making this the largest Mycenaean fortress. In the middle was a rectilinear enclosure (covering 4 hectares), with some widely separated buildings.

For us, the palaces on Crete and the Greek mainland in the middle of the second millennium BC mark the beginnings of Greek history. The Minoans and Mycenaeans, however, did not conceive themselves as part of a 'young' civilization; rather, they stood at the end of a long continuum, stretching far back into the prehistoric past. The lavish fresco decoration of the palace at Pylos is especially interesting. The megaron in the South-west building was decorated with scenes of warriors in Mycenaean armour defeating men dressed in animal skins. Though the armour (helmets, swords and greaves) is common in depictions of soldiers, the scenes seem not to be depictions of contemporary warfare. The boar's-tusk helmets worn by some of the warriors were already old-fashioned in this period; as the Mycenaean warriors are all bare-chested and their opponents are not in realistic dress, the fighting is probably set in the remote, 'heroic' past. The megaron in the main palace is even more striking. The frescos on the walls of the megaron depict huge animals and human figures, with heraldic lions and griffins on either side of the throne; at one end of the megaron was an outdoor banqueting scene, with at least four men seated at tables, and, processing in from the vestibule to the megaron, a procession of men and women leading a bull to sacrifice. The dominant figure in the banqueting scene was a bard with a lyre, seated on a multi-coloured rock, possibly singing the heroic deeds of the past (Plate 3). The frescos of the Pylos megaron clearly had narrative significance to their original viewers. We cannot tell whether the frescos depict specific or generic scenes, but we can certainly imagine an audience listening to the bard's songs about the Mycenaeans' own heroic past.

The importance of the past in Mycenaean society emerges particularly clearly from the remarkable shaft graves of Grave Circle A at Mycenae (Plate 2). The graves were found by Schliemann in 1876, and their fantastic contents were proclaimed by him as typically Mycenaean. Five of the burials had gold face-masks, and incredibly rich grave goods. Overjoyed, Schliemann sent a telegram to the king of Greece: 'With great joy I announce to Your Majesty that I have discovered the tombs which the tradition proclaimed by Pausanias indicates to be the graves of Agamemnon, Cassandra, Eurymedon and their companions, all slain at a banquet by Clytemnestra and her lover Aegisthus.' In fact, it is now clear that these graves date to about 1700–1600 BC, and are thus much older than the surviving palace at Mycenae, and also much older than the conventional date of the Trojan War. But after 1300 BC, when the fortification wall was extended to the south-west, increasing the area of the acropolis by over a third, and the Lion Gate was built, Grave Circle A received special treatment. Other parts of the surrounding cemetery were built over, but the six shaft graves were preserved. A massive new retaining wall was constructed, perhaps on a foundation contemporary with the original graves, creating a much higher ground level. Round it was built an elaborate circular parapet, entered from near the new Lion Gate. Within it, some of the original tombstones were brought up to the new ground level, and reorientated. The rulers of Mycenae after 1300 BC were presenting themselves as the rightful heirs of the rulers buried in the much older shaft graves.

The palaces on the Greek mainland stood at the centre of complex local systems. They were surrounded by substantial settlements, the size of small towns: at Pylos the associated settlement covered some 20 hectares, at Mycenae 32 hectares. As on Crete, the mainland palaces formed a multi-centred system. The separate palaces are similar to each other, but seemingly not dependent on any one single palace. Within each palace there was one supreme figure, the *wanax*, who presumably had overall authority in internal decision-making and in external diplomacy. Beneath him was the 'leader of the people', second in command to the *wanax*, and beneath him 'nobles', 'companions', 'officials', along with 'mayors' and 'vice-mayors' of the districts of the state. Some of these officials belonged to the central palace administration, others to the local administration out in the territory controlled by each individual palace. One set of these local officials was called *basileis*. Their authority perhaps rested on kinship, and predated the palace system; it is probably for this reason that the *basileis* (unlike the rest of these officials) survived the collapse of the palatial system. The *basileis* were involved in supervising local craft production. On one occasion, they were listed alongside the 'leader of the people', and so must be more than mere foremen, but the title rose in stature in the aftermath of the palatial system, coming to mean 'noble' and even 'king' (below, p. 49).

The political and military roles of this hierarchy are not clear to us, but the state certainly had considerable authority in economic matters. Unlike the Minoan palaces, the mainland palaces did not store goods centrally, but they did record and track agricultural goods produced elsewhere. They did not have much control over the production of agricultural staples, but they did oversee the production of some items, for example flax for the linen industry, and for these commodities they monitored the actual industrial processes. Much of the concern of the state was with internal redistribution of goods, but prestige goods like perfumed oil were widely exchanged abroad, probably in return for metals, spices and ivory, which the state needed to import. Though they are architecturally different from Cretan palaces, the mainland palaces performed the same functions: ceremonies, administration, recording of production of agricultural goods, storage of luxury items, and the manufacture of some products.

The palaces also had consequences for the extent to which the elite memorialized their ancestors. On the mainland, before the development of the palaces, local elites had displayed their wealth and power in the commemoration of their dead. The characteristic Mycenaean burial places were the 'tholos' and chamber tombs. Particularly impressive architecturally are the tholoi, mostly found in the Peloponnese, which consisted of long entrance-ways leading to circular, vaulted chambers rising to a point. The name tholos means 'beehive', since ancient beehives were of exactly this shape. A good example is the 'Treasury of Atreus' at Mycenae, part of the entrance façade of which is in the British Museum. In the palatial period, the number of tholoi in use declined, and they became concentrated round the palaces. It seems that members of the palatial elite chose to concentrate their resources in the vicinity of the palaces. On Crete in the Second Palace period there is very little evidence for burials at all, in contrast to the preceding and following periods. The palaces perhaps so dominated society that there was no room for memorializing the dead of individual families.

The relation between Crete and the mainland is not just a matter of similarities and differences. Around 1430 BC, many sites on Crete and also Minoan sites on the islands north of Crete were destroyed by fire, though not necessarily all at the same time. How to account for this phenomenon has been much debated. It used to be popular to claim that the eruption of the volcano on Santorini (ancient Thera), leading to a huge tsunami, caused these destructions. This claim was never plausible historically (why did damage on Crete not get repaired?), and some seismologists do not believe in the tsunami theory at all (how could the collapse of the north-west part of Santorini generate a tsunami travelling to the south-east?). In any case, the latest dating of the eruption of the volcano, based on radiocarbon analysis of a piece of buried olive wood, places it back in the late seventeenth century BC. The eruption of Santorini is now securely dated two hundred years before the destruction of the palaces.

The other main explanation for the destruction around 1430 BC used to be in terms of a takeover of the island by Mycenaean invaders from the mainland. Sites, or parts of sites, associated with the palatial administration seem to have been especially targeted. For example, at Pyrgos, the villa, but not the adjacent town, was burned. There are also some signs of terrible violence. At Mokhlos bodies were not buried, and at Knossos it seems that the flesh of dead children was eaten, perhaps because of siege conditions. We do not know for sure who was behind these destructions, but the current view is that an explanation in terms of Mycenaean invaders is too simple. Knossos under the Mycenaeans did come to dominate Crete for a time, but the Mycenaeans probably collaborated with, and intermarried with, local Minoan elites.

Knossos itself did not escape the general destruction at this time, but unlike other Minoan palaces, it was immediately rebuilt. The palace at Knossos soon became the main administrative centre on Crete for the Mycenaeans. The new palatial administration made use of at least four geographical regions, with a fifth linking Knossos to two local major sanctuary sites, to which we shall return. The four regions extended from at least Khania in the west to perhaps the western edge of the Lasithi plateau in eastern Crete. Within the areas controlled by Knossos, subsidiary regional centres, both palaces and villas, continued to exist. For example, Phaistos, once an independent palace, continues to be mentioned in the post-1430 documents from Knossos; however, to all appearances the Phaistos palace was no longer capable of operating independently. Despite some elements of continuity, Cretan culture and art was hugely disrupted after the takeover: the language of administration changed, as we shall see shortly; buildings centred on courts were no longer built; the characteristic architectural features of palace-style buildings ended; and a large range of luxury objects, for example relief frescos, stone bull's-head drinking vessels, and three-dimensional objects in ivory, ceased to be produced. It was not until the thirteenth century (1300–1200 BC) that the dominance of the island by Knossos ended, and Minoan identity asserted itself once again.

The palaces on Crete were bigger than those on the Greek mainland, but both were much smaller than the contemporary Near Eastern palaces of the mid-second millennium BC. Compare Mycenae (palace of only 1 hectare within a citadel of nearly 4 hectares) and Knossos (palace of 2 hectares) with Hattusa (no less than 180 hectares within the fortifications). This fundamental difference of scale has significant implications for the degree of complexity of the Cretan and mainland palatial systems. Unlike the states in the Near East, they did not develop written law-codes, or employ writing in complex and varied contexts. But the Cretan and mainland palaces did use writing in certain restricted contexts.

Writing began on Crete just before and during the period of the First Palaces. The idea was probably derived from the Near East, but the forms used were local inventions. The first script, known as 'Cretan hieroglyphic' (misleadingly, because it bears no resemblance to Egyptian hieroglyphic), was used to record numbers of commodities. 'Cretan hieroglyphic' was limited geographically to the centres at Knossos and Malia, but another script, Linear A, developed in southern Crete in the period of the Second Palaces. It was used throughout the island and beyond. Linear A was a more complex script than 'Cretan hieroglyphic': it had more signs, more linear shapes (hence its name), a range of signs for syllables, things and numbers. It too was used to record commodities, both on clay tablets, seals and pottery, but it was also used in other contexts; for example, it was inscribed on religious objects to record palatial dedications. It is still not clear whether the scripts of 'Cretan hieroglyphic' and Linear A

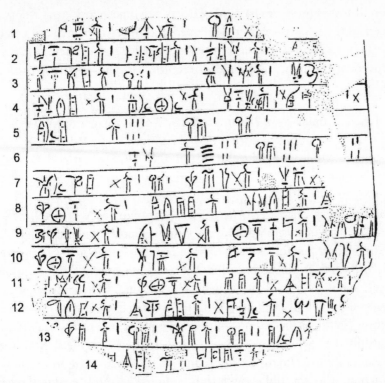

Figure 4. Linear B tablet from Knossos (now in the Ashmolean Museum, Oxford).

represented the same language, two different languages, or different dialects of the same language. Whatever language or languages these might have been, we are confident that they were not Greek.

With the arrival of Mycenaeans on Crete, the system of writing changed. The script known as Linear B certainly originated on Crete, where it was used for exclusively administrative purposes. Far more Linear B than Linear A survives on Crete, mostly from Knossos, but also from Khania in the west. The Mycenaeans took the new script back with them to the Greek mainland. Clay tablets incised in Linear B are found in the palaces of Pylos, Tiryns, Mycenae and Thebes, and inscribed sealings at Midea. As on Crete, Linear B was used on the mainland solely for administrative purposes.

Linear B borrowed up to two-thirds of its signs from Linear A, but simplified them and added new ones. Its use was restricted to administrative purposes, and it was written almost entirely on clay, whether incised on tablets, or painted on transport jars. For example, a tablet from Knossos preserves parts of two lists of women working at Knossos (see Figure 4). Such lists were compiled in order to keep track of palace workers, and also to calculate the rations needed to feed them, and their dependent children. At the end of the first list, lines 4–6, we read the following:

> Line 4: Woman from Phaistos X WOMAN 1. Philagra X WOMAN
> 1. *18–to-no, daughter WOMAN 2 X. wi-so WOMAN 1 X
> Line 5: Women from e-ra WOMAN 7. Girl 1, Boy 1
> Line 6: Total WOMAN 45 Girls 5, Boys 4.

The lists have a simple form: a name, the sign for WOMAN, and a number. The 'X's were added, very faintly, after the unfired clay tablet had dried, presumably as each woman or group of women was checked off by the palace official or scribe. The women are designated in various ways. Some are named individually, like Philagra. Others are named or grouped by their place of origin, like the woman from Phaistos (in south-central Crete), or the seven women from *e-ra*, located somewhere else in central Crete. Some women have young children with them, who were presumably too young to work. But one woman, *18–to-no*, has a daughter, who was old enough to be counted as another adult woman (incidentally, '*18' signifies a sign whose phonetic value has not yet been determined). The indented line 6 gives the total of the first list, forty-five women with their children, five girls and four boys. The partially preserved first list gives records for only twenty-odd women plus one girl and two boys, so it is clear that quite a big piece is missing from the top of the tablet. This meticulous form of listing people or commodities is typical of the Linear B tablets.

The Linear B script represented a different language from Linear A. Before the Second World War scholars could not read Linear B, but were united in their belief that it did not represent Greek; scholars are similarly united today in respect of Linear A, though this time on good grounds. But in 1952, an outsider to the discipline, Michael Ventris, succeeded in decoding Linear B, and proved that it did indeed represent the Greek language. For example, in the Linear B document just quoted, almost every word is known also in later Greek: 'daughter' (*tu*; abbreviation for later Greek *thugater*); 'girl' (*ko-wa*; later Greek: *korē*); 'boy' (*ko-wo*; later Greek: *kouros*). The Linear B tablets and painted transport jars are thus inscribed in Greek, more than four hundred years before the next surviving Greek writing.

The proof that the Mycenaeans on the mainland and on Crete used, and presumably spoke, Greek is a major link between this part of the second millennium BC and later Classical antiquity, though it is a real question how many Cretans actually learned to speak Greek during this period. But Linear B also demonstrates the differences between the palatial culture and what followed. Writing was very restricted in this period, and Linear B was more restricted in its use than Linear A. The script of Linear B was developed for list-making, and was not extended to write more discursive (let alone literary) texts. It was limited to the palaces and their bureaucratic administration. Because it was not deeply rooted in society, once the palaces ended, writing also disappeared.

In addition, Linear B was not a major medium of memory; as at Pylos and Mycenae, there were other ways of memorializing the past. Even in terms of list-making, the Linear B tablets were intended to have limited lives. The texts were written on clay tablets, which were then dried in the shade. They were kept for no more than a year, and then the clay could be recycled, which is why texts sometimes record carry-over information about debts from the previous year. Only in cases where these annual records were accidentally fired when the building storing them was destroyed do they survive. The Linear B tablets are therefore not parts of permanent archives. In this respect, they differ from the records of the Egyptians, Assyrians and Hittites. Those peoples did have permanent archives, with copies of royal correspondence, treaties and royal annals. They also displayed some texts publically in prominent locations, something that is entirely unknown in Mycenaean Crete or Greece.

The palaces of Crete and the Greek mainland, though they eventually came to be linked by common administrative practices and language, had developed along separate paths. There were some common practices, and in the end a broadly common identity, but also important differences between the two cultures. These differences are most clearly visible in the context of religious practices. On Crete during the Second Palace period rituals seem to have been organized by the palaces. In place of the monumental religious buildings found in the contemporary Near East, on Crete worship in this period centred on the palaces themselves and on peak sanctuaries. Several rooms in the palace at Knossos are said

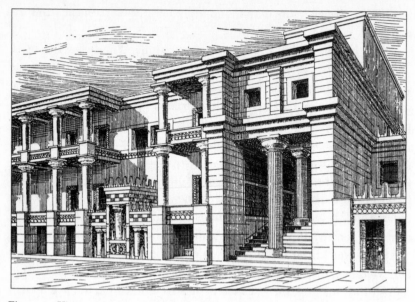

Figure 5. Knossos: reconstruction drawing of Tripartite Shrine on west side of Central Court.

to have had ritual functions, but the arguments are speculative, and only two rooms, the so-called Tripartite Shrine (see Figure 5) and the Shrine of the Double Axes, were certainly used for cult activity. Much of the equipment used for cult was portable, which may mean that there were few permanently designated places for rituals, and hence little in the way of cult architecture. Peak sanctuaries and sacred caves were the other key component in the palatial religious system. The 'peaks', medium-level hilltops, were visible from each other, and formed a hierarchy of local and regional sanctuaries. For Knossos, the peak sanctuary on the lower of the two ridge-tops of Mt. Juktas was especially important. From the palace there was a fine view south to the peaks at the end of the valley in which Knossos lies. A Minoan road took worshippers the 6 kilometres along the valley up to Mt. Juktas. The site itself, approached via a grand ramp and surrounded by an impressive circuit wall, consisted of open terraces, an altar with offering tables, and modest subsidiary rooms built into the hillside. Another major cult site for Knossos was the cave of Eileithyia at Amnisos, 5 kilometres north-east of Knossos, which was the location for rituals and the making of offerings. The offerings at Amnisos, and at other caves, were much the same as those made at peak sanctuaries, which underlines the unity of the palatial religious system.

The religious system on the mainland was rather different. The Mycenaeans borrowed some religious symbols from Crete, but did not have peak or cave sanctuaries, nor other external religious sites linked to palatial centres. At the palace centres, as on Crete, religious architecture was modest. At Mycenae, most of the cult centre, just south of Grave Circle A, was built immediately after the construction of the new fortification wall. It consisted of a complex of rooms, which are architecturally unremarkable, but with clear ritual features inside. For example, one shrine had in the centre a low rectangular dais, perhaps for libations (see Figure 6). On a raised platform at the far end of the room was a figurine, probably of a female deity, with a small offering table in front. To the left, a window offered a view of exposed natural rock, which must have been significant, linking the cult to this particular spot. To the right, a flight of steps led to an upper room, in which were stored numerous clay figures, probably representing worshippers. The whole complex, with its images of the goddess and her worshippers, has no parallels anywhere on Crete.

The gods worshipped on Crete and the mainland can be given names only when we have the evidence of Linear B, and only rarely is it possible to link the name of a deity to a particular place. The Linear B tablets give us names of deities familiar from later periods (such as Zeus, Hera,

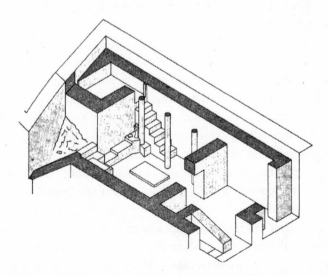

Figure 6. Isometric view of the shrine room at Mycenae, viewed from the southwest. The main room measures 5.1 × 4.3 metres.

Poseidon and Dionysus), and they may have been important deities, but the tablets also give the names of other deities not known later, such as Potnia ('Mistress') and Diwia (the female version of Zeus). The group of deities worshipped varied from state to state. At Pylos, for example, one Linear B tablet records the religious rituals for a particular month, the location of the ceremonies, the offerings and personnel involved, and the deities who received the offerings. Overall, the tablet lists eight people, who may be 'sacristans', and thirteen gold vessels, probably heirloom drinking vessels used annually in the rituals; these rituals took place both in the main palatial religious area, and in four or five other sanctuaries outside Pylos. Potnia, worshipped in the main religious area, was the principal deity in the rituals on this tablet, but other deities were also worshipped: 'The Lady of the Tresses' and 'The Cattle-like Lady' in the sanctuary of Poseidon (a major deity at Pylos); Zeus, Hera, Drimios 'son of Zeus', and Hermes Areias; more minor deities like Iphimedeia and Diwia; and also lesser beings, 'The Thrice-Hero' and 'The House-Master'. Pylos clearly had a highly complex pantheon, with deities of different importance, receiving a regular cycle of worship.

It is tempting to stress the familiar names in this list, Zeus, Hera, Poseidon and Hermes, to point out that the religious system had both male and female deities, and male and female priests, and thus to claim a strong degree of continuity between the Bronze Age and the later Greek pantheon. But to succumb to this temptation would be a mistake. Point-for-point comparisons between Bronze Age and Classical religions ignore systemic differences between the religious systems of the two periods. The two religious systems are embedded in entirely different social and political settings, and even the similarity of some names does not imply that those deities have the same meanings in both periods. Talk of 'continuity' implies that deities were simply passed down the generations. This is to put things the wrong way round. Later generations took up names and practices that they knew of from the past, but adapted them to their own purposes, constructing their own new religious system for a changed world.

Some modern interpretations have emphasized the differences between the cultures of the Minoans and the Mycenaeans. Minoan civilization is often characterized as peaceful, without violent internal conflict, and the Minoans as carefree, happy and natural. By contrast, the Mycenaeans are regarded as dour and bellicose, their alleged invasion of Crete shattering the earlier peaceful idyll. Onto this schematic contrast another distinction is sometimes overlaid. The Minoans, for all their agreeable qualities, were foreign to us, not speaking Greek, while the Greek-speaking Mycenaeans are often seen as early Europeans. In fact, this polarity between the Minoans and the Mycenaeans is largely arbitrary, and the overlay of the European/non-European dichotomy deeply unhelpful. The Minoan language might be Indo-European (we do not know), and the Minoans and the Mycenaeans had much in common, especially in their external relations, overseas settlements, diplomatic contacts, and trading patterns. All three of these interrelated contexts show that we should not draw a simple contrast between Crete and the mainland.

Contacts between Crete and the islands to the north of Crete became intense in the First Palace period. Exchange between the two areas had considerable impact on the local populations of the Aegean islands, whose elites sought to emulate Cretan products. The trading exchanges were facilitated by the creation of overseas settlements of Minoans, principally on the islands of Thera, Melos and Keos. In the Second Palace period, the size and number of such settlements increased significantly. There were important sites to the north-west of Crete: on the island of Kythera, which had its own Minoan peak sanctuary, from which Crete is easily visible; on the islands north-east of Crete, Karpathos, Rhodes and Kos; and at Miletus on the coast of Asia Minor. In some cases, the previous population of the sites continued to live there, with a small admixture of Cretans; in others, the settlements were new creations in previously uninhabited parts of these long-settled regions. The site of Miletus is especially interesting. In the First Palace period, a handful of foreign merchants from Crete settled at an earlier town on the site of Miletus. In the Second Palace period, the nature of the Minoan presence at the site changed radically. The material culture of the site at Miletus in this period was predominantly Minoan: 85–95 per cent of the locally produced domestic pottery is of Minoan types. A sanctuary of Minoan type was constructed, with a mudbrick altar, and the Linear A script was in use, being incised on locally produced pottery before firing. It is clear that in this period many Minoans were living at the site of Miletus, in a colony with its own specifically Minoan organization. It was probably in this period that the site was first given the name 'Miletus'; the Minoan settlers probably brought the name of the settlement with them from the town of Milatos on Crete.

This pattern of overseas settlements in the Aegean changed after the Mycenaean arrival in Crete. Minoan influence on the southern Aegean islands was replaced by a strong Mycenaean influence. At Miletus as at other similar sites, the Minoan period ended in destruction, and was replaced by a Mycenaean settlement. Most of the pottery, both imported and locally produced, follows Mycenaean patterns; even more significantly, houses and tombs were also of Mycenaean type, and there is evidence for Mycenaean-style rituals. A zone of Mycenaean settlements extended down the Anatolian coast south from Miletus, and into the offshore islands, especially Rhodes.

Both Crete and the Greek mainland had important diplomatic and other relations with contemporary Near Eastern states throughout the period covered in this chapter. In both the First and Second Palace periods, Crete was in close contact with Egypt. Wall-paintings of the second half of the sixteenth century BC from the royal palace at Tell el'Dab'a in the Nile Delta are very Minoan-looking, in style, technique and subject matter. The scenes show various Minoan motifs, including youths in Minoan dress, who may be engaged in the characteristic Cretan practice of bull-leaping. The importation of Minoan iconography points to close ties between Crete and Egypt at the start of the Egyptian New Kingdom period. In the fifteenth century, two noble tombs at Thebes, then the capital of Egypt, offer depictions of people called 'Keftiu' wearing Minoan dress and carrying metal or stone vessels of Minoan type, including a bull's-head drinking cup, and models of whole bulls. These people must be Cretan ambassadors presenting lavish gifts to the Egyptians. It has even been suggested that in earlier paintings Keftiu look more Minoan, in later ones more Mycenaean.

The Hittites too had relations with the peoples of the Aegean. From the fifteenth century BC, the Hittite king was aware of 'the Ahhiyawa', a plural noun that referred to a neighbouring people in the west. The identification of the Ahhiyawa has been much disputed, but recently published Hittite texts now make it clear that the Ahhiyawa not only lay to the west of the Hittites, but were actually overseas. It is thus safe to identify them with the 'Achaeans', the Homeric name for the Greeks. In the thirteenth century, the Ahhiyawa began to assume some importance for the Hittite king. Hattusili III (1267–1237 BC) was attempting to restore order to the western part of Anatolia. A rebellious Hittite subject, Piyamaradu, had fled from Hattusili to Milawanda (Miletus), which was outside Hittite control, but under the indirect control of the king of the Ahhiyawa. Hattusili entered Milawanda in pursuit of Piyamaradu, asking the local ruler to hand the rebel over to him. But Piyamaradu fled by boat to take further refuge in Ahhiyawan territory, from which he continued to conduct raids on Hittite lands. Hattusili's campaign had failed, and he wrote to the king of the Ahhiwaya, addressing him as brother, asking for his help in ending Piyamaradu's activities. Given that we regard the Mycenaean states as a series of competing polities, it is striking that Hattusili regards the ruler of just one of them as the Ahhiyawa king. It is possible that the person concerned was the ruler of Thebes in central Greece (not to be confused with Thebes in Egypt). Thebes is known from Linear B tablets to have controlled not only the surrounding region of central Greece (the region later known as Boeotia), but also much of the large island of Euboea to the east. (This Boeotian connection may also account for a surprising concentration of Boeotian place names later attested in the area around Miletus.) The ruler of Thebes seems to have succeeded in promoting himself in the eyes of Hattusili as *the* Achaean king. Hattusili's successor, Tudhaliya IV (1237–1209 BC), also campaigned in western Anatolia: he invaded the land of Milawanda, possibly destroying the settlement at Miletus, and installed an ally as overlord of this area. Tudhaliya referred to the kings whom he regarded as his peers: 'the kings who are of equal rank to me, the king of Egypt, the king of Babylonia, the king of Assyria and the king of Ahhiyawa'. The scribe erased the reference to the king of Ahhiyawa, perhaps because of the Achaean king's loss of authority following Tudhaliya's actions in western Anatolia.

The common thread between Minoan and Mycenaean settlements overseas and the evidence for their relations with the Egyptians and Hittite kingdoms in the mid-second millennium BC is trade. From Crete, there were three main trade routes: to the north-west, via Kythera to the southern Peloponnese; to the north, via Thera, Melos and Keos, to the copper and silver mines in Attica; and to the north-east, via Karpathos and Rhodes, to Anatolia, and then eastwards to Cyprus and the Levant (the region of modern Syria, Lebanon, Israel and Jordan). It is no accident that the Minoan settlements discussed above were all located along these three routes. After the Mycenaeans arrived on Crete, Mycenaean trade took over from Minoan. The principal routes changed after 1300 BC, but the Mycenaeans, like the Minoans, had extensive interests in Anatolia and in Cyprus and the Levant.

The nature of trade in this period is seen most vividly in the evidence from a ship that foundered off Uluburun on the south coast of Anatolia not long before 1300 BC, and was excavated underwater from 1984 to 1994 (Plate 4). The ship, 15–16 metres long, was on its way west, having started in the Levant, perhaps at Ugarit, the largest international trading state in the region, sited just north of modern Lattakia in Syria. It was carrying an incredibly rich cargo: no fewer than 490 ingots of raw copper from Cyprus, weighing 10 tonnes, and about 120 ingots and fragments of tin, from somewhere else in the Near East, weighing another tonne. The copper ingots were of poor quality, being thin and brittle, but the metals would have produced about 11 tonnes of bronze. There were also 175 ingots of glass, in cobalt blue, turquoise and lavender, to be worked into precious objects; 24 logs of ebony from Egypt; ivory in the form of whole or part elephant tusks and hippopotamus teeth, ready to be carved, as well as a few items already carved; tortoise shells, to form the sound-boxes of lyres; ostrich eggshells; 149 jars perhaps from the region of Ugarit, one with glass beads, and some with olives, but most filled with a tonne of terebinth resin, from west of the Dead Sea, probably for burning as incense; and jewellery from the Ugarit region and from Egypt. In short, items originated from all over the Near East, from Cyprus, Egypt, Nubia, Syria and various parts of Mesopotamia. The cargo was probably being shipped at the request of an eastern ruler to the Aegean world. Tantalizingly, there were found two folded wooden writing tablets, of Near Eastern type, but no traces of what was written on the wax that was once inside them. Two Mycenaeans, identified by their swords and other personal items, were on board, probably to escort the cargo to one of the major Mycenaean palatial centres.

The hierarchy of goods in this snapshot of trade between the Levant and the Mycenaean world fits exactly the hierarchy of values in lists of goods exchanged between rulers within the Near East, as known from the Amarna Letters (described above), omitting only the top two goods, gold and silver. But the Mycenaeans were not passive recipients of largesse from their more powerful eastern neighbours. They imported raw materials, to be worked into objects in local style and with local meanings. In return, the Mycenaeans must have been offering other objects in exchange. We do not know for sure what these were, but silver was readily mined in Attica, and Crete was noted for its production of woollen textiles. The Egyptian wall-paintings mentioned above depict the Cretans wearing fine woollen dress, and there is a hint in Linear B tablets that some of the Cretan wool products, and also some of the perfumed oil from Pylos, were produced for export.

The Aegean states also traded to the west, with Sicily, Italy and Sardinia. There were no Minoan or Mycenaean settlements in this area, and trade seems to not to have been directed by the palaces, unlike in the Aegean itself. Instead, independent traders were probably responsible. With the expansion of Mycenaean interests, Mycenaean goods largely replaced Minoan exports in this area, as in the Aegean. But Crete did retain some links with the west. After 1200 BC pottery produced at Khania was traded to Italy and Sardinia and elsewhere, and, to judge from central-Italian-style pottery produced on Crete, some Italians had moved to Crete.

Troy, famous in later memory, lay on the fringes of Mycenaean external connections. The site excavated by Schliemann lies at least 5 kilometres from the modern coast, which makes it hard to think of it as a major maritime power. But studies of the topography of the peninsula where Troy is located have shown that the coastline in the third and second millennia BC was quite different from the present coastline, because the rivers Simois and Scamander have brought down so much silt. In the second millennium BC Troy was perfectly sited to control a large bay, which offered the only deepwater harbour for ships passing through the Dardanelles into the Black Sea. It had emerged by the second millennium as a major regional centre, dominating the north-west of Anatolia and the northern Aegean islands.

Troy's material culture was west Anatolian, to judge from the style of house-building, cults located at gateways, and the one find of writing, a seal inscribed in Luwian, a widespread local language. Troy was, however, on the periphery of both the Aegean and Anatolian worlds. Some Mycenaean pottery of the fifteenth and fourteenth centuries BC was imported to Troy, probably from the eastern Aegean, and imitated locally, but only in very small quantities: around 1–2 per cent of the total amount of contemporary pottery at the site. Troy lay outside immediate Hittite control. King Muttawalli II (1295–1272 BC) had to send a Hittite

Figure 7. Reconstruction of Troy VI: citadel with palatial buildings, and part of the lower city.

expedition to restore order in a place called Wilusa, which seems to have been occupied by a rebel causing trouble to the Hittites and their vassal states. As it is clear that Wilusa lies in north-western Anatolia, and as Troy is the only major archaeological site in the region, Wilusa is probably to be identified with the place we know as Ilion (originally Wilion) or Troy. Wilusa appears also in other Hittite texts of the thirteenth century in connection with further military operations and disturbances. The king of Ahhiyawa seems to have been involved, along with the troublesome Hittite rebel Piyamaradu.

Our understanding of the significance of the site of Troy has changed dramatically since the renewed excavations of the site from 1988 onwards. (It is worth noting that Daimler-Benz, the major sponsors of these excavations, won a UNESCO competition for the importance of their excavations to 'European Cultural Heritage'. Modern excavations, no less than Schliemann's, have their own cultural agenda.) The mound which Schliemann excavated covered only a very small area, less than 2 hectares, which sceptics always argued made it an implausibly small focus for a ten-year Trojan War. More recent archaeological work at the site has shown, by contrast, that Troy was a major site. Schliemann's mound, it is now clear, was only the citadel of a significant settlement on the plain below, covering some 20 hectares (see Figure 7). This settlement was surrounded by a system of fortifications, a huge wooden palisade, with a substantial ditch, 3.5 metres wide and 2 metres deep, to ward off chariot-attacks. These new findings put Troy on the same scale as Pylos in mainland Greece, and the trading state of Ugarit in northern Syria.

Do the excavations of Troy support the idea that there was a Trojan War? Schliemann believed that it was Troy Level II that was sacked by the Achaean forces, but Level II is much too early. It is now clear that Troy Levels VI–VIIa were contemporary with the Mycenaean states. But modern opinions about these levels and their significance have varied greatly, often clouded by wishful thinking concerning the Trojan War. The orthodox view, based on careful analysis of the pottery excavated in 1938, is that VIh and VIIa are two distinct levels. The last level of Troy VI, Level VIh, ended shortly before 1300 BC, and ended as a result of widespread destruction. Troy was then immediately rebuilt, in makeshift fashion, with no sign of a cultural break. This level, known as Troy VIIa, lasted some ninety years, before it was sacked and burnt, shortly before 1200 BC. The orthodox view has been challenged on the basis of the excavations of 1998 and 1999. An alternative view is that Levels VIh and VIIa belong together, that Level VIh was destroyed by enemy action in the middle of the thirteenth century BC, and that the signs of 'destruction' in Level VIIa are in fact the result of ritual activity.

So was either Troy VIh or Troy VIIa the city of Priam, destroyed at the end of the Trojan War? The question is extremely problematic. Many wish to believe that there was a Trojan War, so powerful is the hold of Homer on our imaginations. As a result, people do not always pause sufficiently to ask what sort of work the *Iliad* is, nor what might count as good archaeological evidence for a Trojan War. The *Iliad*, composed five hundred years after the events it purports to describe, is an imaginative creation of a world mostly very different from the contemporary world of the poet. It cannot be treated as a work of history. Archaeology, on the other hand, is good at producing evidence for long-term patterns, but less good in relation to specific events (or alleged events). Making material and textual evidence engage with the same question is normally a mistake, especially so given the imaginative power of the *Iliad*. In the specific question of whether or not Troy was besieged and sacked by invading Achaean forces, the material evidence is almost bound to be ambiguous. According to the orthodox view, the destruction of Level VIh, just before 1300 BC, is contemporary with the peak of Mycenaean power in the Aegean world. Some have assumed that this level was destroyed by enemy action, but others have argued that the scale of the destruction shows that a massive earthquake, and not human hands, was responsible. Was damage to walls the result of earthquake or sack? Were the burned deposits in Level VIIa the product of accident, ritual or enemy action? If enemy action lies behind damage to either Level VIh or VIIa, who was the enemy? The *Iliad* makes the Achaeans responsible, but contemporary evidence also shows considerable Hittite interest in this region.

The Hittite palace archives, admittedly fragmentary, show no aware-ness of a single major Achaean attack on Troy, leading to a destruction of the city. Instead, they suggest that the region of Troy was disputed between Hittites and the Ahhiyawa over a long period of time. Minor attacks were carried out, sometimes by the Ahhiyawa, but sometimes by Anatolian forces under local commanders. It is impossible to imagine a major coalition of Mycenaean forces attacking Troy as late as the time of the 'destruction' of Level VIIa, because at this time the palatial systems on the mainland were collapsing. There might have been a small-scale raid from the mainland at this time, but we must emphasize that there is no archaeological evidence for the identity of the people who sacked Troy VIIa. The most one can say is that conflicts over Troy may have formed the basis for the later legends, as formulated in the *Iliad* (to which we shall return in Chapter 3). But equally, the *Iliad* shows no awareness of the Hittites, makes Miletus not a Mycenaean but a Carian city, ruled by non-Greek-speaking inhabitants of south-western Anatolia, and in its geography of Greece preserves very little knowledge of the Bronze Age situation.

At around the same time as the alleged sack of Troy VIIa, around 1200 BC, the palatial systems on Crete and the Greek mainland came to an end. Three types of explanations have been advanced for these changes: natural disasters, foreign attacks, or internal strife. The problem has been that scholars have tended to be partisans of just one of these explanations: earthquakes are the sole cause of collapse of the palaces, and so on. But monocausal explanations of complex phenomena are usually an oversimplification. Even if earthquakes did cause widespread damage, why did people not simply repair the damage? In fact, all three types of explanations need to be brought into play to account for the collapse of palatial systems that had operated successfully for centuries.

On Crete there has been huge controversy over the date of the 'final destruction' of Knossos, largely because of arguments about the date of the destruction of the palace archives, which is not entirely clear in the records of Evans's original excavation. There is now general agreement that the Linear B administration at Knossos ended by around 1350 BC, and with it the period of Mycenaean involvement in Crete. Crete moved from being dominated by Knossos to having a number of centres. Khania continued to use Linear B through the thirteenth century, but from around 1200 BC onwards there was no further palatial administration anywhere on Crete.

On the mainland, in the early thirteenth century there seems to have been a series of earthquakes, which caused damage to Mycenae, Tiryns and Thebes among other sites. However, the consequence of the earthquakes was not palatial collapse, but the substantial extension of the fortifications of Mycenae and Tiryns, in a new style of masonry, and the construction of workshops and storage facilities on the acropolis at Mycenae. These responses look like the centralization of resources and personnel in the face of perceived external threats.

Late in the thirteenth and early in the twelfth century BC a series of destruction levels are found, for example, at Mycenae and Tiryns, and a single destruction level at Pylos. Earthquake damage is not clearly attested at all mainland sites, and is anyway implausible as the sole explanation of the collapse of the palaces. Attacks from without or within, for which preparations had been made in the previous generation with the extension of fortifications, must have played a major part. Marauders, known as the Sea Peoples, are sometimes claimed to have caused much damage in Egypt, the Levant and Anatolia in this period, but the Aegean islands do not suffer destruction at this point, and there is no sign that the Sea Peoples were responsible for attacks on the mainland; we shall return to them again in another context (below, pp. 57–8). The other old favourite explanation ascribes the destruction of the mainland palaces to an invasion from the north by the Dorians. In later Greek tradition (below, p. 65) this putative 'Dorian invasion' was regarded as one of the great turning points in the early history of Greece, but this account has little more to be said for it than does the story of the Trojan War. The destructions, though widespread, are not simultaneous. It is better to imagine a series of raids and a gradual dispersal of Dorian-Greek speakers across the old Mycenaean world over a period of a century or more. The palatial systems, which may have been suffering in any case from internal economic problems, could not recover from these pressures. The centres collapsed: the palatial megara were not rebuilt; extensive foreign contacts of the sort seen in the Uluburun wreck ceased; administrative systems ended, and with them went the system of writing peculiar to the palaces.

The palaces of Crete and the mainland are often portrayed as the start of European civilization. They were indeed successful and durable institutions, with a high degree of complexity, but they were also very small in comparison to the contemporary Near Eastern states in Egypt, Mesopotamia and Anatolia. It was arguably the superpowers of the Near East in the second millennium that were the real drivers of change. When the palatial systems on Crete and the mainland collapsed, their inheritance to the next generations was meagre. The subsequent period, as we shall see in the next chapter, was a much simpler, and narrower, world. But these palatial cultures loom large for us for two reasons. First, the Cretan and the mainland palaces were run by people who spoke Greek, an early form of the language spoken today by Greeks from Athens to Melbourne. Secondly, memories of this period were crucial to Greeks, Romans and other peoples. For them, the Trojan War and its immediate aftermath formed the upper horizon of their consciousness of the human past, and became the foundation of European identity.

2

The Mediterranean, the Levant and Middle Europe: 1100–800 BC

In the period following the ending of palatial organization on the Greek mainland (around 1200 BC), many existing settlements and religious sites continued in use, but the Aegean world moved into what used to be known as the 'Dark Age' of Greece, characterized by the complete collapse of the palatial systems, loss of external connections and extensive migrations of populations. The term 'Dark Age' is out of fashion, because it is too negative in tone for what we now know of the period. Instead, it is better to talk more neutrally of the transition from the Bronze to the Iron Age. This transition happened at different times in different parts of the Mediterranean world (around 1070 BC in Greece); its earliest phase, on which this chapter will focus, is known as the 'early Iron Age'. The world of the early Iron Age was much less complex in terms of organization and interconnections than what had gone before, but by the end of the period there was an increased level of connections again, especially with the Near East. Here, we shall set in parallel the developments of the Aegean, Italy and Middle Europe in this period, relating them to the changing balance of power in the Near East.

The site of Lefkandi on the island of Euboea offers the best starting point for understanding this period. Named after a modern village (its ancient name is unknown), the site of Lefkandi lies halfway down the west coast of Euboea. There had been a settlement here since at least 2400 BC, but during the palatial period it came under the sway of the palace at Thebes; Amarynthos, about 15 kilometres east of Lefkandi, appears in the Theban Linear B tablets. Around 1200 BC, with the collapse of the organization of the palaces, including that at Thebes, Lefkandi flourished. The site was violently destroyed at least twice during the twelfth century, but was swiftly rebuilt on both occasions. The large and prosperous houses, on a small hill projecting into the sea (the promontory

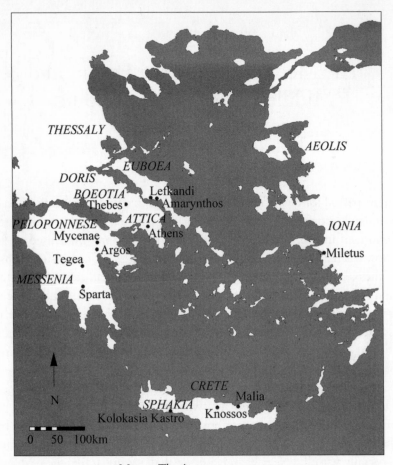

Map 4. The Aegean *c.* 1100 BC.

today known as Xeropolis), extended over about 7 hectares. People continued to live at Lefkandi during the early Iron Age, down to the end of the eighth century. Crucially, there is no break after the collapse of the palaces, between what we call the Bronze and Iron Ages.

The term 'early Iron Age' is particularly well suited to the site at Lefkandi. High-status members of the society had access to the new iron technology, and iron swords and spearheads have been found in warriors' tombs from the site. More dramatically, excavations of the settlement in 2006–2008 discovered a large building: dating to the twelfth century BC, the building measured 12 × 5.5 metres; rebuilt later in the twelfth century, it was then at least 15 × 8 metres. This must have been the residence of one of the major families at Lefkandi. Excavations in 2006–2008 also uncovered part of a major, complex double wall, of early date, eleventh or tenth century; it seems to have been a wall marking the entrance to the settlement, with ritual deposits in front of it.

The cemeteries used by those who lived at Lefkandi are also extremely important. It is relatively unusual for excavations at a single site to uncover both houses and tombs of the same period; at Lefkandi, we can study and compare the spaces of both the living and the dead. The cemeteries lie about 500 metres west of the residential site, on a hillside overlooking the settlement at Xeropolis. There are at least five separate funerary areas, with 193 tombs and 104 cremation pyres, extending over about 5 hectares. The burials here began at the very start of the early Iron Age, and the lack of earlier tombs on this hillside suggests, contrary to the evidence from Xeropolis, that the community at Lefkandi was undergoing radical changes at this time. The richest funerary plot is at Toumba (modern Greek for 'mound'), at the top of the hillside. Around 950 BC the area of the Toumba plot was levelled, and in the middle were dug two shafts, for the burial of a man and a woman (see Figure 8). After the man was cremated on a pyre, his ashes were wrapped in a special cloth and put in a bronze two-handled jar, a treasured object, imported from Cyprus a hundred years previously. The jar was then placed in one of the shafts, along with special iron objects, a sword and spearhead, and a whetstone

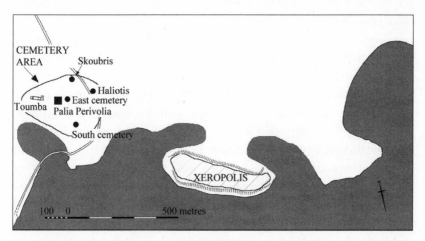

Map 5. Lefkandi. Settlement at Xeropolis in centre; cemetery area, including Toumba, on left; the modern road is also marked. The estimated line of the ancient coast is given; note that Xeropolis was joined to the mainland by only a narrow isthmus, and that the sea was closer to the cemetery area than today.

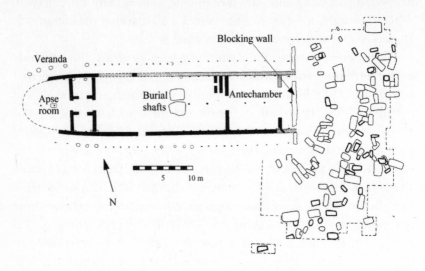

Figure 8. Plan of the 'Heroön' at Lefkandi.

for sharpening them. Next to it was placed the body of a woman, probably his wife, in a wooden coffin, along with lavish gold jewellery; one item, a gold pendant, was another, even older treasure, perhaps imported from Syria, and dating back to around 1700 BC (Plate 7). Next to her head was put an iron knife with an ivory handle. The knife, the fact that both people were probably buried at the same time, and the fact that the woman had not been cremated, suggest strongly that she was killed, or killed herself, in order to be buried with her husband. Four horses were sacrificed, and their bodies thrown in a separate shaft.

These funerary offerings were radically different from those of preceding centuries. In the later Bronze Age, warrior burials do not differ significantly from any other kind of burials: some tombs have weapons in, some do not. By contrast, the early Iron Age warrior graves at Toumba and elsewhere are vastly more lavish than other contemporary graves: the warriors of Lefkandi formed an elite class in early Iron Age society. The killing of the horses and, in many cases, deliberate damage of the weapons in early Iron Age warrior graves act as conspicuous demonstrations of the family's wealth; this family could afford to damage or destroy goods of great value. Also new and striking is the burial of rare and valuable antique objects in the Toumba graves, treasures linking the family to the remote past.

Finally, the different modes of burial for the man and the woman at Toumba were new markers of difference between the genders; the lavishness of the woman's burial is a remarkable indication of the prestige of women within the elite families of the period. Similarly, the earliest of a series of rich graves in central Athens around 850 BC was of a woman. On her pyre were broken dozens of fine pots. Her ashes were placed in a magnificent pottery vessel, along with fine jewellery. Alongside it was placed a clay chest, on whose lid were five model granaries, signs of the basis of the woman's wealth.

The lavishness of the Toumba burials, including the heirloom objects, shows that the man and woman interred here were the leading figures of the community at the time. We can only guess at what their titles might have been, but it is tempting to think of the term *basileus*. In the Mycenaean period (above, p. 26), *basileis* had been local officials, but by the seventh century BC it was used for individual or collective 'nobles'. Those buried at Toumba were certainly distinguished enough to be described in this manner. There are striking parallels between the Toumba burials and the funeral of Patroclus later depicted in Homer's *Iliad* (below, p. 102): common features include the killing of the horses, the cremation of the man, and the wrapping of his ashes in expensive cloth and their deposition in a special metal vessel. These parallels, and the differences from the Bronze Age graves of an earlier epoch, illustrate how much 'heroic' material in Homer was derived not from the age of the palaces, but from the 'Dark Age' centuries immediately preceding his own day.

The status of those buried at Toumba was further emphasized by the construction of an extraordinary building over the two shafts: a huge rectangular structure (50 × 14 metres) with mudbrick walls resting on a rubble stone base about 1.3 metres high. The building had a porch, an antechamber, a central room, with the two shafts, two small rooms on either side of a passageway, and an apsidal room; round it ran a veranda, attested by the surviving holes for the posts which supported the roof. The whole building must have been modelled on houses, but it is much larger than any other contemporary house known in Greece; it is half as long again as the 'hundred-foot' temples of the eighth century BC, and is indeed the largest structure known to have been built in the Greek world for the five hundred years between 1200 and 700 BC. The building, despite its scale, was probably never used, and was largely dismantled not long after it was built. A huge mound of earth was then built on top of it, which happily preserved for the archaeologists the stone base and mud-brick walls of the building to a height of 1.5 metres.

Though this extraordinary building is sometimes known as a 'heroön', or place of hero sacrifices, there is no sign that offerings were made to the deceased, either in the building before it was dismantled, or afterwards on the mound. The mound simply served as a marker of the grand burial. The area to the east of the mound, in front of where the building had been, was used for the next hundred years for a series of exceptionally wealthy graves of both men and women (Plate 8). These later generations buried at Toumba wished to present themselves as the descendants of the couple in the original burial, asserting their claims to be the leading family of Lefkandi.

The extraordinary changes at Lefkandi, and other sites in the Greek world, need to be seen in the context of the wider world of the Near East. There were major disruptions to the Near Eastern political systems established in the mid-second millennium BC, and as a result very few written texts survive from anywhere for this period. Like Linear B, the writing systems and habits of the Near East were tied very closely to

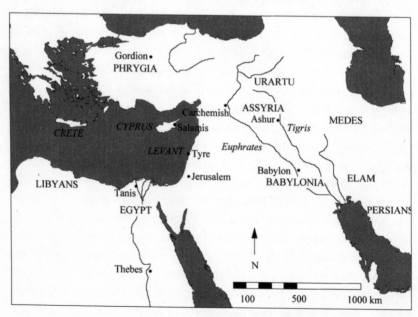

Map 6. The Near East in the early first millennium BC.

particular palatial structures, and when those structures collapsed, the habit of writing went with them.

The relative stability of Egypt's borders might suggest that the country as a whole was also stable in this period. In fact, by the eleventh century BC the country of Egypt was effectively divided between two rulers, a king at Tanis, near the mouth of the Nile, and the high priest at Thebes in central Egypt. Libyans regularly raided from the west; indeed, they successfully claimed the throne of Egypt, forming two of the competing dynasties in this period. The 350 years (1070–712 BC), after the ending of the New Kingdom, known to Egyptologists as the Third Intermediate period, were a highly troubled epoch for the Egyptian state. Egypt lacked stable unitary government, and in the eleventh century the state lost control over its territories in the Levant, although links were re-established with the region in the years between 950 and 850 BC. The period ended with a disastrous series of civil wars in Egypt, and the takeover of the state from the south by Nubians.

Chronic instability also characterized the Hittite kingdom of central Asia Minor. Though it had been one of the major Near Eastern players in the second half of the second millennium BC, the kingdom collapsed completely around 1200 BC. In its place there emerged separate small-scale principalities. In the south-eastern part of the former Hittite kingdom were numerous small states, for example the one based at Carchemish on the river Euphrates. This was a huge walled city, about 110 hectares in size. These new rogue states saw themselves as heirs to the Hittites and are indeed called Neo-Hittite states by modern scholars. Their rulers drew on the names of earlier Hittite kings, and claimed to be the true heirs of the Hittite kingdom, one king styling himself 'Great King', as the Hittites had done. They continued to use Hittite iconography for public sculpture, and their script, though not the language, was a development of Hittite hieroglyphics. These new states, though they did not form a political unity, enjoyed much prosperity, in part thanks to the profitable trade in metals between the kingdom of Urartu (in the region of Armenia) and the Mediterranean states.

The central part of the former Hittite kingdom became the new kingdom of Phrygia, with its capital at Gordion (near modern Ankara). By the eighth century BC Phrygian power extended as far east as the former Hittite capital of Hattusa. The later-eighth-century 'King Mita of Mushki', known from contemporary Assyrian texts, became famous in

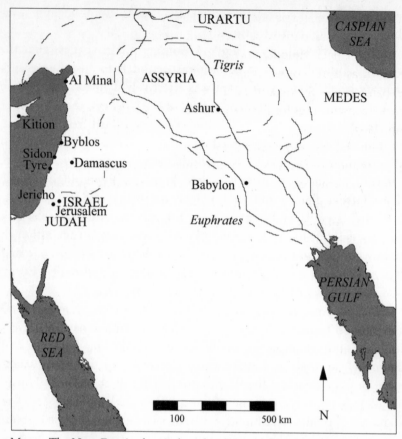

Map 7. The Near East in the ninth and eighth centuries BC. The inner border of Assyria is that of the mid-ninth century BC, and the larger border shows the extent of the state in the late eighth century BC.

later Greek legend as King Midas of the golden touch. Subsequently, the region west of the kingdom of Phrygia emerged as the kingdom of Lydia, centred on Sardis. Lydia seems to have been a fairly minor player in the eighth century BC; its power increased only in the seventh century with the emergence of a dynamic new ruling dynasty, which would eventually claim hegemony over all the Greek states of western Asia Minor. The Lydians also came to claim that they were the ancestors of the Etruscan peoples of Italy (below, p. 73).

In Mesopotamia the great Assyrian state of the second millennium was drastically weakened under repeated invasions from the west, and from Babylonia in the south. For a century after 1050 BC the texts largely dry up, in both Assyria and Babylonia, but from the middle of the tenth century the Assyrians were once again asserting their control over the whole of Upper Mesopotamia (Map 7). This is the beginning of what is known as the Neo-Assyrian empire (883–610 BC). Further Assyrian expansion westwards in the eighth and seventh centuries was to have major consequences for the maritime states of the Levantine coast (below, pp. 86–7).

With the collapse of the old balance of power between Egypt, the Hittites and Assyria, the Levant in the tenth and ninth centuries was left largely to its own devices. The Iron Age cities in modern Lebanon – Tyre, Sidon, Byblos and others – were the direct successors of earlier Bronze Age cities. All these cities lay on the Mediterranean coast, some of them on islands just offshore, and were protected from the upheavals inland by a major chain of mountains (modern Mt. Lebanon, stretching from Hama in the north to the Golan Heights in the south). The inhabitants called themselves Canaanites, which is what they are also called in the Bible, but the Greeks knew them as 'Phoenicians'; this name was probably derived from *phoinix*, the Greek word for 'purple', because of the Phoenicians' pre-eminence in the production of purple dye, an important status symbol in the ancient world. Modern scholars follow the Greeks in using the term 'Phoenicians' for those Canaanites who lived in modern Lebanon and were not dispossessed by the Israelites (although this creates a rather artificial break between Bronze Age 'Canaanites' and Iron Age 'Phoenicians'). In the tenth and ninth centuries, under the leadership of the great naval fortress of Tyre, the Phoenicians became a major power, with trading interests to the south with King Solomon in Israel and as far down as the Red Sea, and in the course of the ninth century their interests also began to extend westwards (below, p. 76).

It was in this same period that the state of Israel first came into being. Although at the time Israel was just one of several small struggling principalities in the Levant, the story of the emergence of Israel has a particular resonance for us, since the lengthy accounts of the process in the Bible constitute a central part of our European heritage.

The biblical narratives are a fine early example of the creation of cultural memory. The first five books of the Bible, the Pentateuch, take the story from the Creation via the sojourn in Egypt to the Exodus from Egypt under Moses and the wanderings of the Israelites for 'forty years' in the desert. These books end with the death of Moses, looking down from the peak of Mt. Nebo (in modern Jordan) over the Promised Land. The story is continued in the books of Joshua, Judges, Samuel and Kings, and it is their narrative that is especially important here. The process of composition of these texts is extremely complex, but it is generally believed that a first version of this history was put together about 620 BC, and a second version during the exile in Babylon about 550 BC. These books of the Bible are not, therefore, objective contemporary accounts of the formation of the state of Israel, but retrospective views, with particular theological, political and social axes to grind.

The conquest of Canaan, the Promised Land, under Joshua (conventionally dated to around 1200 BC) poses particular problems. The first twelve chapters of the Book of Joshua tell of the conquest of the Promised Land from the east, across the river Jordan, in a single military campaign under the leadership of Joshua. The first chapters of the Book of Judges, however, assume that the conquest was the work of a number of separate tribes, not of a united Israel. Nonetheless, both narratives present the coming of the Israelites as a military conquest.

A century of excavations has produced a wealth of material of potential relevance to the evaluation of the biblical narratives, but the interpretation of this material is extremely controversial. The difficulties arise partly because of the religious agendas of individual scholars, but also because (as in the case of the Trojan War), it is intrinsically problematic to try to correlate the evidence of archaeology with historical narratives. Archaeology can give us a very clear picture of long-term cultural processes; it is less good at illuminating the history of specific events.

Though some historians have argued that the archaeological evidence confirms the biblical 'conquest' model, there is some special pleading going on here. The familiar story of the walls of Jericho falling down at the blasts from Joshua's trumpets is an important test case, as Jericho was said to be Joshua's first conquest after crossing the river Jordan. Excavations at Jericho in the 1930s uncovered a great wall, which had collapsed, accompanied by a catastrophic fire; the excavator argued that this was the very wall described in the Bible. Sadly, subsequent excavations in the 1950s showed that the final phase of this wall dated to around 2350 BC, more than a millennium too early. It now seems clear that Jericho around 1200 BC (the time of the Israelite conquest) was a relatively small and undefended site, lacking a major fortification wall. There is a total gap in the archaeological evidence at Jericho between the late fourteenth century BC and the beginnings of renewed settlement in the eleventh and tenth centuries BC – precisely the period in which the Israelite conquest of the region ought to fall. In this case, there is simply no easy way of marrying the biblical narrative with the archaeological evidence.

Similar problems arise with neighbouring towns in Canaan said to have been conquered by Joshua. Take, for example, the town of 'Ai, just north-west of Jericho, whose capture is vividly told in the Book of Joshua. The site of 'Ai, which is well preserved and has been fully excavated, was destroyed in the later third millennium. It was then abandoned until a humble village was established in the ruins of the third-millennium settlement around 1150 BC, only to be abandoned again around 1050 BC. According to the Book of Joshua, 'Joshua burned 'Ai, making it a ruin for evermore, a desolate place even today'. It looks as though this story arose from the desolation of 'Ai visible in the seventh century BC, when the Book of Joshua was written. The flourishing place which Joshua is said to have destroyed had in fact already been abandoned for a millennium by the time the Israelites arrived in Canaan.

Survey archaeology, conducted in this area for many years, suggests a rather different picture. In place of a unified military conquest, it shows a long-term process of peaceful settlement through the twelfth and into the eleventh centuries. The earliest Israelite settlements were located in the less inhabited parts of the hill country, just north of Jerusalem. The area to the south, Judah, was settled only from the tenth century BC onwards. If this evidence is correct, then the seventh-century biblical narratives transformed a slow, peaceful process into a something more dramatic, in order to stress the importance of the obedience of Israel to the will of Yahweh.

The first period of Israelite settlement in the region, known in the Bible as the period of the judges, was followed by the rule of David and Solomon (probably c. 1010–970 BC and 970–930 BC respectively). The biblical narrative gives a strongly idealized picture of their rule. Unfortunately, the archaeological evidence for the tenth century remains very sparse, and we have very little independent control over the biblical account. Though some sceptics have questioned the existence of David and Solomon, there are several strong arguments in favour of a historical kernel to the biblical accounts of these rulers. First, the name of David has appeared on an Aramaic inscription from Tel Dan in northern Galilee dating to *c.* 850 BC, in which a king of Damascus boasted of his victories over a king of the 'House of David' (that is, Judah), and a king of Israel. This inscription provides some support for the idea that David was the founder of a dynasty in Judah, that he was a conquering king, and that there was a second dynasty in Israel to the north of Judah. Secondly, the triple construction of Solomon's temple, as described in the First Book of Kings, corresponds to a type of temple archaeologically well attested in the Levant between 1300 and 800 BC, but not at later periods. Thirdly, just after the death of Solomon, in the reign of Reheboam of Judah, 1 Kings reports an invasion of Judah by Shishak, pharaoh of Egypt. This invasion is independently attested in an inscription of the pharaoh Shoshenq I (= Shishak; 945–924 BC) from the temple complex at Karnak in Egypt, dating to *c.* 925 BC. This Egyptian evidence provides strong confirmation for the biblical account, and suggests that the author of 1 Kings had access to authentic royal annals going back to the tenth century; it would be very surprising for the author suddenly to move from legend to history, when he moved from David and Solomon to the following reign of Reheboam. Finally, 1 Kings refers to a certain 'Hiram, king of Tyre' (969–936 BC) as a contemporary of Solomon. The historicity of this reference is supported by the presence of a King Hiram at exactly this point in a later but apparently accurate king-list for Tyre.

What does all this add up to? It is impossible to be certain, but it seems that, on balance, the overall outline of the biblical narrative for the period from David onwards is likely to be broadly correct. David captured Jerusalem, and made it the capital of a newly organized kingdom. He moved the Ark of the Covenant there, and probably took steps towards building a temple, attempting to centralize the Yahweh cult under royal patronage. His sucessor Solomon then built the great temple and a large royal palace in Jerusalem, on a ridge 200 metres north of the city of David.

Archaeological evidence is very limited, because of later use of the site of the Temple: such evidence as might still exist probably lies buried underneath the Dome of the Rock. As the ridge was quite narrow, Solomon built a massive rectangular platform for his buildings. The size of the platform is known with near certainty, covering no less than 5 hectares, about the same size as the whole of the rest of the settlement at that time. The Temple was similar in design to earlier Canaanite temples, but was much larger and grander in execution, requiring huge amounts of local labour. Solomon collaborated with the Phoenicians, as we noted earlier, in exploiting trade routes to the south. As a result he was able to hire Phoenician craftsmen and buy the finest timber (cedars of Mt. Lebanon) for the temple. Nonetheless, this Temple was quite unlike any which had been built in the region before this point. As Solomon is said to have announced, 'I have built the house for the name of Yahweh, the God of Israel.' Whereas both earlier and later Near Eastern temples normally housed images of the deity, Solomon's Temple was 'for the name of Yahweh'; it contained no graven image.

The biblical stories of David and Solomon cast a retrospectively rosy glow over their reigns. The biblical accounts reached their final form after the kingdom had fallen apart and after Solomon's Temple had been destroyed. We should resist the temptation to assume that all aspects of later Judaism were already securely established in the tenth century BC. Even the biblical accounts themselves make it clear that this was not the case. Major religious reforms are ascribed to the seventh-century King Josiah, who took drastic action against other, competing cults, and ordered the celebration of the Passover. 'No Passover like this one had ever been celebrated since the days when the judges ruled Israel or throughout the entire period of the kings of Israel and the kings of Judah.' This throw-away sentence warns us that the institutions of Judaism were the result of a long process of gradual evolution, not a single moment of reform or revelation even if most of the biblical texts suggest otherwise.

Modern explanations of the age of disorder in the Near East have ranged from the global to the specific. The old global explanation was that the old superpowers buckled under persistent pressure from the mysterious Sea Peoples *c.* 1200 BC, whom we met at the end of the previous chapter as a possible cause of the final destruction of the palaces of Crete and the Greek mainland.

As with most monocausal explanations, this will not do. The Sea Peoples are attested specifically only in Egyptian sources of two royal campaigns, in 1220 and 1186 BC (Plate 5). One of these texts claims, 'No country could stand before their arms: Hatti (the Hittites), Kode (Cilicia in southern Turkey), Carchemish (on the Euphrates), Arzawa (west of the Hittites) and Alashiya (Cyprus).' Though this seems at first sight agreeably clear and specific, the text is so highly coloured that it cannot be taken at face value. The 'Sea Peoples' were probably a unified force only in the eyes of the Egyptian kings who took the credit for beating them. Carchemish shows no signs of destruction by Sea Peoples or anyone else in this period, and the Neo-Hittite state at Carchemish shows absolute continuity in its preservation of earlier Hittite traditions. Admittedly, around 1200 BC Hattusa itself was destroyed, but there is no sign of an invasion by Sea Peoples; an obscure people called the Kaska, from the mountainous area to the north of Hattusa, who had long been sporadically attacking the Hittites, are more likely to have been responsible.

Rather than invoking the shadowy Sea Peoples as the primary cause of the collapse of the old order in the Near East, it is better to think first of socio-political problems inside each individual state. There are various signs of internal problems within the Hittite state, including opposition from within the ruling elite, the diminution of royal authority, and increasing insubordination of vassal rulers. Crucial imports of grain, brought in via a port on the south-east coast of Turkey, had been disrupted; it was probably as a consequence of this disruption that the Hittites sent a naval expedition to restore their authority over Cyprus.

The Near East had long suffered from the activities of various small marauding groups, and these raids certainly increased in this period, thereby exacerbating the internal problems of the Near Eastern superpowers. Small-scale piratical raids along the coasts probably intensified. Other people from southern Asia Minor in the thirteenth and twelfth centuries seem to have hired themselves out as mercenaries for various states, including the Libyans in their wars against the Egyptians. The Egyptians themselves sometimes employed such mercenaries. One such group, the Peleset, were settled by the Egyptians as garrisons in Palestine. With the breakdown of Egyptian power outside Egypt, the Peleset broke off into independent communities; these were the warlike people known to their eastern neighbours and rivals, the Israelites, as the Philistines.

The violent upheavals which engulfed the Near East around the turn of the millennium are important for the Greek world in various ways. To start with, they offer a series of analogies to the changes which were under way in Greece. The breakdown of centralized control is a common theme across the entire Near East, but the forms this took varied in different regions. While Egypt weathered the storm, and Assyria eventually recovered its former empire, the Hittite empire fragmented into a number of smaller states, as local dynasts successfully claimed territory for themselves. The collapse of the Hittite empire may provide a useful analogy for the breakdown of the Mycenaean kingdoms in Crete and mainland Greece.

The disturbances in the Near East also had direct consequences for the Greek world. The prosperous trading networks exemplified in the Uluburun wreck could continue only if there were stable Near Eastern entrepôts. The sack of Ugarit, where the Uluburun ship may have originated, around 1200 BC meant the end of that particular trading network; new trading connections could only be built up once new Near Eastern entrepôts had emerged to take their place.

The collapse of the palatial systems on Crete around 1350 BC and on the Greek mainland around 1200 BC was followed by what some call a 'post-palatial twilight'. But it was a twilight, not complete darkness; in many places, the lights stayed on. On Crete, most settlements did undergo some contraction in size, but some places, for example, Khania and Malia, continued to be prosperous, with new houses being built. In addition, new territorial units were created, with settlements located away from the sea in readily defensible locations. For example, in Sphakia people lived at a new site, Kolokasia Kastro, on a steeply sloping prong, with sheer cliffs to the north and crags on almost all the other sides (Plate 19). At around 600 metres above sea level, the site afforded superb views over the coastal plain to the south, and up a gorge to the north. Kolokasia Kastro overlaps chronologically with the nearby site of Patsianos Kephala, on a gentle saddle between two hills, which replaced it altogether by around 800 BC. The site at Patsianos Kephala is located at a much lower altitude (c. 250 metres), and so was able to exploit more fully the resources of hills, plain and sea.

Though Cretan palatial control over religious life came to an end, people continued to worship at many of the same sites. Some peak sanctuaries and caves continued to be popular throughout this period, and down into the Iron Age. But it is important not to claim too much from such a statement. Continuity in the religious use of a site does not necessarily mean that there was also continuity in religious practices or beliefs. As religion was deeply embedded in social and political structures, it was bound to change radically with the collapse of the palaces. Nonetheless, radical change does not mean that the past was entirely written off. As we saw in Chapter 1 in the context of Pylos, what is important is the uses people make of what they know about past rituals and places.

It is particularly telling that the ruins of the old palaces, strong presences in the Cretan landscape, were reused, not for settlement, but for religious purposes. At Knossos, the early Iron Age settlement was just west of the palace, and the palace itself was the setting for various cults. A cult in the Spring Chamber, which was partly modelled on a Bronze Age cult in the Shrine of the Double Axes, continued to be celebrated down into the ninth century BC. By the eighth century at the latest, a new sanctuary, dedicated to the goddess Demeter, was established just south of the palace. Since this sanctuary too is situated beside a water source, it is possible that it was a direct continuation of the Spring Chamber cult. In the south-west corner of the Central Court of the palace a second new cult was up and running by the eighth century, and the worshippers were certainly aware of the site's palatial past; elsewhere in the palace a Minoan bull fresco was still visible in the eighth century.

Relevant to the early Iron Age sanctuaries at Knossos are the changes in the contemporary cemetery, just north of the palace. This cemetery, in use from the eleventh century onwards, at first had a great variety of tombs. From the end of the ninth century, some people were buried in chamber tombs, probably reused from the Bronze Age. The first burials here were lavish, and were then followed for some centuries by large numbers of more modest burials. The funerary pottery was also inspired by Bronze Age motifs. It looks as though in the ninth century some families won themselves a prominent position in local Knossian society by playing up their connections to the ancient architectural and pottery styles. It is hard to say exactly what these new Iron Age communities made of their Bronze Age predecessors, but it is very striking how eager they were, both through ritual activity on the ancient palace-sites and through their elite burial practices, to relate their new world to the surviving traces of the palatial past.

On the Greek mainland during the twelfth and early eleventh centuries, Bronze Age Mycenaean culture ended not suddenly, but gradually. The sites at Mycenae and Tiryns were not abandoned after the destruction of their palaces. Houses were rebuilt, and there were some new large buildings, but by the early eleventh century the citadels were changing their functions: graves are found on the citadel at Mycenae and on the

Acropolis at Athens, which probably indicates the final abandonment of the old hilltop settlements. It is also a sign of the times that the graves were simple pits, rather than the more elaborate and expensive chamber tombs of previous centuries. The gradual demise of Mycenaean culture was accompanied by an increase in cultural regionalism. On the island of Euboea, four of the five main Bronze Age settlements continued after the collapse of Thebes, which had previously controlled much of the island. Some fourteen settlements are known from the period after about 1050 BC (the early Iron Age). Most of them are small, but they were probably inhabited continuously from the Bronze Age through to the early Iron Age. The site at Lefkandi, which we have met already, was probably typical of the main places on Euboea. At Lefkandi, despite at least two major destructions, there was continuity from the end of the Mycenaean world down into the early first millennium BC.

Nonetheless, the archaeology paints a depressing picture of the Greek world in the centuries after the fall of the Mycenaean palaces. Overall, the number of inhabited places in mainland Greece fell by two-thirds in the twelfth century, and by another two-thirds in the eleventh century. This was the low point, and recovery then began: settlement numbers doubled in the tenth century, and doubled again in the ninth–eighth centuries. Of course, settlement numbers on their own mean nothing: the crucial variable is settlement size. If individual places were larger in the eleventh century than before or later, the drop in the number of settlements would be less significant. But in fact the scale of settlements in the early Iron Age is generally smaller than that in the periods on either side. Some have tried to quantify the extent of the drop in population, but such estimates are premature on the basis of what we know at present.

It seems obvious that population levels fell at the end of the Bronze Age, and increased again in the course of the early Iron Age. Not only did the number of settlements fall, but the places themselves were less complex than what had gone before. Clustered, or 'nucleated', settlements did persist, especially on Crete, where they ranged from 1 to 4 hectares, but on the Greek mainland, 'settlements' often consisted of a few loose groups of dwellings, each with just a handful of houses. There is no sign of centralized organization, no grand stone architecture, and no clearly delimited public spaces.

The later Greeks seem to have preserved the memory of this drastic fall in population numbers. The *Cypria*, an epic of the seventh century BC, which tells the story of the Trojan War roughly down to where Homer's *Iliad* starts, claimed that Zeus brought about the Trojan War and its loss of life in order to relieve the earth of its existing over-population. It is hard not to think that we have here a dim recollection of the catastrophic population decline after the end of the palaces; for the audience of the *Cypria*, the world was a smaller and meaner place than it had been in the days before the Trojan War.

An important element in the recovery of Greece was the re-establishment of its old external contacts. While in the Bronze Age these overseas links had been organized mostly by the palaces, now connections were made by a new class of people. In the eleventh century Lefkandi was in contact with other settlements in the Aegean, and by the tenth century it was part of a Euboean hub with connections to other communities in central mainland Greece, the coast of Thessaly, and some of the Aegean islands. These connections were partly underpinned by the fact that from around 950 BC Euboea was at the forefront of moves to reconnect with the Levant. Contacts with the Levant had dropped off dramatically in the eleventh century, but in the tenth century the Levantine situation was transformed by the emergence of a new centre at the powerful city of Tyre. Between 950 and 900 BC increasing quantities of Euboean pottery, drinking cups and two-handled jars (probably used to transport olive oil) begin to appear at Tyre and other Levantine sites. This pottery may indicate the temporary presence of Euboeans in this region in search of prestigious items; the debate over whether it was Euboeans or Phoenicians who carried the pottery is discussed further in Chapter 3. One important prestige material which travelled from Levant to Euboea was the new metal, iron. The iron for the swords and spearheads found in tombs at Lefkandi probably came from Cyprus, either directly or via Tyrian intermediaries.

Cyprus' major metal resources were of great importance in this period. In the Bronze Age, Cyprus, known as Alashiya, had been an important source of bronze, both to the east and to the west; it was probably Cypriot bronze that was carried on the ship that sank off Uluburun. The collapse of the major contemporary states towards the end of the thirteenth century, and the closing down of overseas markets, led to the abandonment of the existing urban settlements on Cyprus in the twelfth century. But the interruption of urban life on Cyprus was quite short-lived, especially in comparison with the long period of decline in the Aegean. Already in the eleventh and tenth centuries a new pattern of urban settlement was established on Cyprus which would endure for the rest of Classical antiquity.

This new pattern may be connected with the arrival of Greek-speaking settlers from the Aegean. In later periods, stories were told which claimed that the kingdoms of Cyprus had been founded by Trojan War heroes; the city of Salamis on Cyprus had supposedly been founded by Teucer, half-brother of Ajax. In addition, and very unusually, literacy was not lost on Cyprus after the end of the Bronze Age. In the Bronze Age, the Cypriots had used a local script derived from Minoan Linear A. Since this Cypriot script does not seem to have been restricted to the administration of the urban centres, it may (unlike the scripts of the Cretan and mainland Greek palaces) have survived the abandonment of the Cypriot Bronze Age centres. In the Iron Age, what is probably a development of this Cypriot script (the 'Cypriot syllabary') was used to transcribe two different languages, the new Greek language and a local language, so-called 'Eteocypriot'. The Cypriot syllabary continued to be employed on Cyprus for writing Greek even after the invention of the Greek alphabet in the eighth century, and indeed survived as late as the third century BC.

The strength of cultural continuity reflected in the history of the local Cypriot writing-systems hints at the resilience of the local societies of Iron Age Cyprus. The early creation of a new, stable settlement system was partly due also to the ability of the islanders to move from bronze to iron production. The Cypriot principalities were the first states in the Mediterranean to organize industrial production of iron, and their prosperity was bound up with this new technology. It was primarily the island's rich mineral resources which drew the Phoenicians to found their first overseas colony here, on the south coast of the island at Kition (modern Larnaka) (below, p. 87).

According to later Greek tradition, the period after the Trojan War was characterized by mass movements of Greek-speaking peoples around the Aegean basin. There were said to have been four major migrations in the Aegean: the Aeolians eastwards across the Aegean; the Boeotians south into what became called Boeotia; the Dorians south to the Peloponnese; and the Ionians east to Asia Minor. In the fifth century BC it was calculated

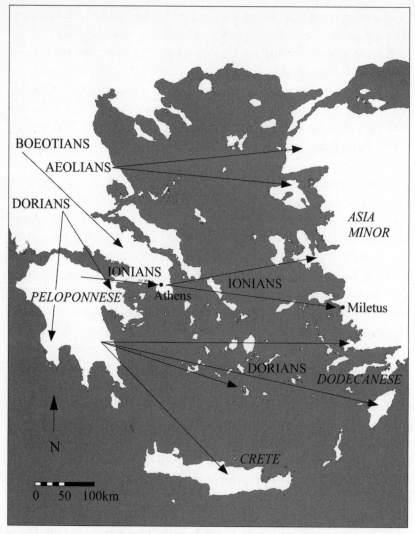

Map 8. Migrations according to Greek tradition.

that the Aeolians migrated first, and were succeeded by the Boeotians, sixty years after the fall of Troy, then the Dorians, eighty years after the fall of Troy, followed shortly by the Ionians.

These great migrations formed an important part of the historical consciousness of later Greeks, and a rich mythological tradition grew up around them. The Boeotians claimed to have been expelled from Thessaly in northern Greece, moving south to the territory around Thebes, what had previously been called the land of Kadmos. Kadmos was understood to have been the founder of Thebes, far back in the early heroic age, and the originator of a dynasty that ruled until after the Trojan War. So far so good. The oddity about Kadmos is that he was also said to have been a Phoenician, sent by his father to search, vainly, for his sister Europa, abducted by Zeus to Crete. The Boeotians claimed to have occupied the territory of the expelled Kadmeians, and their migrant origins were commonly accepted by the fifth century BC.

The Dorian inhabitants of the Peloponnese also saw themselves as post-Trojan War immigrants. The Dorians were said to have originated in north-central Greece, and to have invaded southern Greece in order to restore the sons of Heracles, the Heracleidae, to their ancestral home in the Peloponnese. This story, like the Boeotian migration, was widely accepted by the fifth century BC; we shall examine some of the uses later made of this account of the Dorian invasion of the Peloponnese in the next two chapters. Disturbances following the Dorian invasion were also said to have resulted in the expulsion of the Ionians from their original homelands in the northern Peloponnese. According to the most popular account, the Ionians settled first in Attica, and from there moved on again, under the leadership of the sons of the Athenian king Kodros. As we shall see in Chapter 4, the Athenians of the fifth century BC used this story as the basis of their claim to be the 'mother-city' of the Ionians; however, there was probably a different, and earlier, account of the Ionian migration in which the Ionians went directly east across the Aegean from the Peloponnese, without stopping in Attica at all.

The Ionian migration eastwards was said to have resulted in the conquest of twelve cities along the west coast of Asia Minor. The party under Neileus, one of Kodros' sons, made for Miletus. The Ionian invaders killed all the males they captured, marrying their wives and daughters; these forced marriages were said to be the origin of a Milesian law which forbade women to sit at table with their husbands or to address them by name. In the second century AD the grave of Neileus would be pointed out on the left of the main road, not far from the south gate of the city. The islands south of Ionia (the modern Dodecanese) were also said to have been colonized by mainland Greeks at around the same time, by Dorians, not long after the return of the Heracleidae to the Peloponnese.

The historicity of these migrations is deeply controversial. Although many of the details of the migrations as presented by later Greek writers do not stand up to serious scrutiny, linguistic and archaeological evidence does suggest that these later traditions were not invented out of thin air. Modern linguistic analysis has shown that there were three main Greek dialect groups in the Aegean by the seventh century BC. The so-called West Greek dialects were concentrated in north-western and central Greece, the Peloponnese, Crete and the Dodecanese; the Aeolic dialects were spoken in Thessaly, Boeotia, and north-west Asia Minor; and Attic-Ionic dialects were spoken in Attica, Euboea, the central Aegean islands and along the central part of the Asia Minor coast. The distribution patterns of these three dialect groups overlap quite neatly with the migration stories.

However, it is less clear whether this 'dialect map' really constitutes independent evidence for the migrations. The Greeks were themselves perfectly conscious of the general linguistic map of Greece, and it is quite possible that it is precisely the distribution of the various dialects which lies behind some of the later Greek accounts of the migrations. In addition, we cannot assume that the linguistic distribution pattern is the result of waves of mass migrations. Dialects, and languages, can change as the result of the movement of relatively small numbers of people. And the relative uniformity of dialect in Ionia, for example, could be the result, not of an original wave of migrants to the region speaking the same dialect, but of later harmonization of different local dialects.

Nonetheless, despite these caveats, it is undoubtedly the case that the linguistic map of central and north-western Asia Minor was quite different by the Classical period from what it had been in the Bronze Age. In the late second millennium BC the population in that area had spoken Luwian, a non-Greek language; by the mid-first millennium BC, the inhabitants spoke a dialect of Greek. It seems very likely that some sort of migration ultimately underlay this linguistic change.

Archaeological evidence has also been brought into play. As we have seen, the collapse of the Mycenaean states cannot be attributed to assaults by Dorian migrants. Nor is it easy to claim that the Dorians filtered into the Peloponnese during the 'palatial twilight', taking over an already weakened area. The number and size of sites in the Peloponnese were in decline in this period, and there is nothing to mark out the material culture of the period as having intrusive northern elements. Indeed, the Dorians are archaeologically indistinguishable from 'earlier' peoples in the Peloponnese. This negative point, however, does not argue against the idea of some sort of immigration by Dorians; that the early Israelites are often difficult to distinguish archaeologically from the Canaanites does not show that the biblical stories of the Israelite migration are entirely false.

In Ionia, we are on firmer ground. The collapse of the Mycenaean palaces of Crete and the Greek mainland, combined with the decline of Hittite power in the east, left the Mycenaean settlements in the central and southern part of western Asia Minor very exposed. Milawanda (Miletus) had been ruled by a vassal of the Hittite king Tudhaliya IV, under whom a fortification wall was built. The site was left wide open to foreign assaults after 1200 BC, and was certainly destroyed around 1100 BC. There was then a new beginning. Some eleventh-century pottery, found on top of the ruins of the old fortification wall, shows close connections to contemporary pottery from the western Aegean. By the tenth century, pottery from Miletus continues to imitate west-Aegean styles, but was now being made of local clay; this might suggest that some foreign craftsmen had settled at Miletus. These similarities in pottery styles can hardly be taken as proof of the great migratory expedition of Neileus and his men from Attica to Miletus, but they do suggest that these later traditions may have had some real historical foundation.

The migration stories cannot be used to reconstruct the events of the centuries following the fall of the mainland palaces in any detail. These stories were developed in later generations in support of contemporary imperatives. But it is too sceptical to claim that later Greeks were simply inventing past events, and hence present identities, for their own purposes. The Greeks' sense of the sequence of events that connected the Trojan War and its aftermath to the present day was ultimately based on real, albeit hazy, memories of the real circumstances of the Aegean world in the eleventh and tenth centuries BC.

The changes from the Bronze to the Iron Age took different forms in different regions. In the Aegean, palatial systems collapsed and settlements were abandoned, with new settlements located in different and often less accessible places. The modern name for this new epoch, the 'Iron Age', derives from a major technological change which occurred in this period. Iron had been used in the palatial period, but only exceptionally, for special gifts and for some rituals. In the course of the eleventh and tenth centuries, iron-working techniques spread through the Aegean, probably from Cyprus, and reliable sources of iron ore were located, so that by 900 BC iron had become the practical and bronze the decorative metal. This technological change was driven in part by the emergence of new local elites, whose status was founded on their highly profitable exploitation of the new technology.

In the central and western part of the Mediterranean and in middle Europe the picture is rather different. The new metal technology spread here too, slightly later than in the Mediterranean, but without causing violent dislocations. The period from 1300 to 700 BC was marked by a slow growth in the number and scale of settlements. It is symptomatic of the lack of ruptures in western Europe that the great monument of Stonehenge, erected around 2300 BC, remained in use throughout this period. Local pottery of the late Bronze Age and early Iron Age has been found in holes surrounding the central construction, and around 1100 BC, ditches were dug to extend the approach way to Stonehenge by 2 kilometres towards the river Avon. It does not follow that rituals at Stonehenge remained the same, but this type of activity at Stonehenge shows much more continuity with the Bronze Age past than does (for

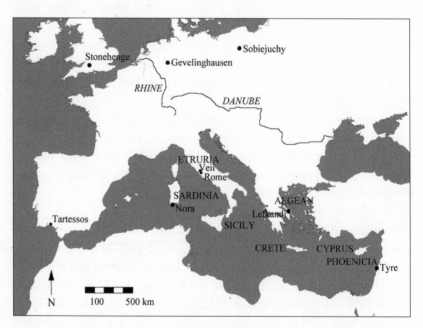

Map 9. The Mediterranean and middle Europe in the tenth and ninth centuries BC.

example) the sporadic and partial Iron Age reuse of the Cretan Bronze Age palaces.

Further to the south, the vast area stretching from Spain to Italy and from France to Poland, can reasonably be taken as a whole ('middle Europe'). Although there are regional variations within this area, there are also striking differences between the middle European zone and the areas to the west (the Atlantic system, namely the west coasts of Iberia and France, and the British Isles and Ireland) and the north (the Nordic system). The first common factor is burial practices. Around 1300 BC there was a general shift in middle Europe from inhumation to cremation. After cremation, the ashes were gathered up, placed in an urn, and buried in special cemetery areas. Cremation did not take over completely, and in some regions did not take over at all, but the practice of urn burials is sufficiently widespread to have given the name 'Urnfield' to the whole period from 1300 to 700 BC.

In a few cases, scattered across middle Europe, the cremated remains were marked out by mounds of earth, or even elaborate stone-vaulted chambers, with rich grave goods. These were presumably the remains of major local figures, whose memories were important to their heirs (as at Lefkandi). Although it is possible that the shift to cremation was associated with changes in beliefs about the dead or the afterlife, the body coming to be seen just as a vehicle for higher things, this idea is mere speculation: when the opposite change (from cremation to inhumation) occurs in the well-documented second and third centuries AD it cannot be linked to any changes in belief. The beginnings of urn burials in middle Europe may be just a matter of fashion.

The second main unifying factor in this region is the social organization of the living. Throughout middle Europe, societies seem to have been under the control of warrior leaders. Their prestige can be seen from the fact that huge numbers of bronze weapons were ceremonially, and very lavishly, disposed of, some in graves, and others in ritual deposits. Fighting was the prestige activity of the age, though of course it does not follow that a great deal of actual fighting went on. So prestigious was it that some of the bronze weapons so carefully placed in ritual deposits seem to have been made for show, perhaps for parades as well as for deposit: a flashy beaten bronze breastplate was less effective as protection against sword blows than a simple and much cheaper leather jerkin. The evidence for weaponry is sufficiently rich that we can build up a clear picture both of what was normal across the area, and also of regional divergences. A typical warrior kit consisted of a bronze helmet, breastplate, greaves, round shield, sword and bronze-tipped spear. Regional variations in this assemblage can be seen in the Danube region, the north-western Alps, western Europe and northern Italy. The differences lie in the precise shape of the helmet, the design of the sword and spearhead, and the decorations on the shield and greaves. The regional differences in armour form part of the evidence for broad regional patterns, though they need not also imply the existence of large regional political powers.

The area was also unified technologically. A neat example of technology transfer within the area comes from glass production. True glass production originated in the Levant, as with the 175 ingots of coloured glass on the Uluburun wreck. Glass of this type found in Europe may have been imported in the form of ingots. Distinct from true glass production is the local production of primitive glass, known as 'faience'. Because it is fired at much lower temperatures than true glass from ingots, faience is much easier to produce. Excavations in northern Italy have found glass beads, crucibles with glass sticking to them, and partially fused glass. Analysis of this Italian glass shows that it was made from local materials, not from supplies imported from the east. It was a highly desirable technology, because it created brightly coloured objects. Because faience was attractive, the technology for making it spread throughout temperate Europe. The technology was small-scale, and used only for making coloured beads, but it was very pervasive.

Bronze-making was the major technology of the period in middle Europe. Alloying copper and tin to make bronze was nothing new in 1300 BC, but the late second millennium BC saw significant technological improvements, and a huge increase in the scale of production. Moulds became more complex, and the lost-wax method of casting was invented. This method, which permits the modelling of much finer details, was later used in the Renaissance by sculptors like Benvenuto Cellini, who left a vivid description of the process in his autobiography. Bronze-workers seem to have moved around a good deal. The hoards of broken bronze objects intended for melting down and reuse must have been carefully buried by migrant bronze-workers, who intended to return and use the metal on another occasion. The movement of these skilled workers also helps to account for the relative homogeneity of style of bronzes over long distances. For example, two bronze burial urns from

Figure 9. Bronze urns, from Gevelinghausen (north-central Germany) on left and from Veii (in central Italy) on right. Actual height: *c.* 38 centimetres.

north-central Germany and from central Italy are of almost the same size, have very similar shapes, and decorations drawn from the same repertoire (see Figure 9). Not only were funerary practices common across middle Europe, but so too were the objects used in the funerals.

The warrior elites, whose bronze weapons we have examined, stood at the top of the local social pyramid. Their wealth and power rested on their ability to control the production of metals and the passage of goods in their area. Living in the largest settlement, they held sway over fairly small territories, of the order of 150–200 kilometres across. Under them were subordinate elites, living in smaller settlements, and under them individual farms and perhaps twenty to sixty small hamlets; these subordinate elites controlled territories maybe 20–25 kilometres across. In other words, Urnfield societies had complex social and political structures, even if each individual 'state' was on quite a modest scale. The settlements of the warrior elites began to be fortified around 1100 BC, which marks a significant growth in ambition on the part of individual Urnfield societies. In south-west Germany, for example, the settlements were evenly distributed, along the sides of river valleys, 10 to 15 kilometres apart. These fortifications were not just for show: most fortified settlements show signs of destruction at some point in their history. It was becoming increasingly necessary to defend one's home against attacks by one's neighbours.

A good example of a modest, fortified settlement is Sobiejuchy in north-central Poland, a well-excavated site, which can serve as a model for other middle European sites of the period. Sobiejuchy was probably first settled in the late Bronze Age, and continued through into the Iron Age. The site, of modest size (6 hectares), was situated on an island in a lake and was defended by a wooden stockade. The settlement was based on an agricultural subsistence economy. There was intensive cultivation of a range of crops: millet, wheat, spelt, emmer, beans, lentils and peas. Pigs, sheep and horses were reared, and wild animals and fish caught for added protein. Sobiejuchy was typical of other middle European communities in its animal husbandry and in the cultivation of a wider range of crops than in earlier periods. The houses had efficient means of storing grain. Pottery loomweights show that clothes were produced locally, and metal objects too were made here. Houses filled the whole of the inside of the stockade; their plans cannot be recovered, but at a nearby site houses were quite large (9 × 8 metres), with an upper storey.

The cemetery for the community at Sobiejuchy, 500 metres away, has also been excavated. From the number of graves, it has been estimated that about 600 people lived at Sobiejuchy. This means that Sobiejuchy was a substantially larger site than had been normal earlier in the Bronze Age, and is part of the evidence for a general increase in population in middle Europe in the Urnfield period. So there was some growth in scale, but Sobiejuchy remained a basically subsistence settlement, with no imported luxury goods, and with domestic pottery quite unlike that of contemporary sites only 15 kilometres away. In this respect, it was typical of most middle European settlements in the Urnfield period. It was rich in terms of local resources, but not in terms of imports of prestige items. The settlement shows no signs of planning, or of craft specialization, which makes it hard to see Sobiejuchy as a primitive town.

In northern and central Italy also, settlements increased in size during this period. The names given to the periods in central Italy, the region later known as Etruria, imply radical change in the early first millennium BC: late and 'final' Bronze Age (1300–900 BC); and early Iron Age, or Villanovan, named after the type site of Villanova near Bologna (900–700 BC). But in fact developments here, as in middle Europe, were continuous between the Bronze and Iron Ages. In the late Bronze Age, settlements consisted of small hamlets, located on naturally defensive sites. The average size of settlements was a modest 4 to 5 hectares. In the ninth and eighth centuries the number of settlements increased, and the size of the largest settlements in southern Etruria grew dramatically.

One of these sites is the hilltop site of Veii (modern Veio), from whose cemetery comes the bronze funerary urn we saw earlier. Archaeological surface surveys show hamlets scattered across most parts of the hilltop site; these hamlets are increasingly large, and indeed soon reach a scale unprecedented in this area. From them grew the major urban centre of Veii, whose fifth-century fortification walls surrounded an area of 190 hectares. The origins of the later pattern of states known in this area in the seventh and sixth centuries BC can thus clearly be traced back to the early Iron Age; the emergence of centralized states in northern Italy seems to have been an independent local development, unaffected by developments in Greek urbanism in mainland Greece or in southern Italy (described in the next chapter).

The post-Villanovan period in central Italy, from 700 BC, is termed Etruscan. This modern terminology, like the distinction between the final Bronze Age and the Villanovan period, implies a radical break, possibly even the arrival of new migrants. The origin of the Etruscans was already a hotly debated question in antiquity. We do not know what stories the Etruscans themselves told about their origins, but in the fifth century BC the Greek historian Herodotus traced the Etruscans back to the Lydians of western Asia Minor. As a result of a period of sustained famine, claims Herodotus, half the population of Lydia had emigrated to the west, under the leadership of a certain Tyrrhenos. They settled in central Italy, changing their name from Lydians to Tyrrhenians, after the name of their leader.

Although Herodotus' story has had its modern advocates, who have argued that migrants from Asia Minor settled in northern Italy and took over Villanovan settlements in the eighth century BC, it is now clear that this explanation does not work. The language of the Etruscans is hard to classify. It was unique in Italy, and its only 'cousin' was the obscure pre-Greek language of the island of Lemnos in the Aegean; whatever its real origins, it certainly did not derive from Lydian. Archaeologically, there is no sign of destructions, or even attacks, at the end of the Villanovan period, and no sign that the inhabitants of Etruria after 700 BC were different from those living there before 700 BC. Contrary to the story of eastern origins for the Etruscans, it now seems certain that the 'Etruscan' period evolved organically from the Villanovan.

Throughout this long period of evolution among the Urnfield societies of Italy and middle Europe, easterners were beginning to have major impacts on coastal areas of the central and western Mediterranean. In the Second Palace period Minoan and Mycenaean traders had expanded their field of operations westwards to Sicily, Italy and Sardinia. An example of material that came back with them is a sword in the Uluburun wreck, which probably originated in Sicily or southern Italy. After the Second Palace period, Aegean-style pottery continued to be used in the central Mediterranean, but scientific analysis of the clays from which it is made has shown that in the thirteenth century it was produced locally in southern Italy. After the collapse of the Cretan and mainland Greek palaces Aegean craftsmen must have moved to south Italy, either permanently or seasonally, and produced pottery there.

Meanwhile Cypriot traders and craftsmen were also operating in the central Mediterranean, though we do not really understand what they were doing there. In the thirteenth and especially twelfth centuries we can trace close Cypriot contacts with the central Mediterranean islands of Sicily and Sardinia, especially in terms of metallurgy. Large numbers of copper ingots from this period have been found on both islands: on Sardinia they occur at no fewer than twenty-six different Bronze Age sites. Scientific analysis of the lead isotopes in the copper has shown that the Sardinian ingots originated from mines in northern Cyprus, even though Sardinia has its own native sources of copper. In addition, a Cypriot origin can also be demonstrated for various metal-working tools, such as sledgehammers, tongs and charcoal shovels, which have been found on Sardinia. Nonetheless, the bronze figurines produced on Sardinia are of purely local design, depicting warriors and other figures of daily life: shepherds offering sacrifices, wrestlers, musicians, and women nursing children.

Around the same time as these technological imports to Sardinia from the east, native Sardinian settlements were undergoing dramatic changes. More than 4,000, perhaps as many as 7,000, stone-built structures (*nuraghi*) are known on the island. The simplest are just towers, up to 18 metres high, of large stone blocks, not all of local material. Some have outer walls round them, and most stand at the centre of larger settlements. In many parts of the island they are found less than 2 kilometres apart, and represent what was probably the most intense land-use in the island's history. Most of the *nuraghi* seem to date to the second half of the second millennium BC, some continuing in use down into the first millennium. The rapid growth of population implied by the *nuraghi*, combined with the import of sophisticated Cypriot metallurgical techniques, suggests an extraordinary level of prosperity on Sardinia in the last centuries of the second millennium BC.

Both on Sardinia and in other parts of the central-western Mediterranean, there is a gap of four centuries between the trading contacts of the Cypriots in the thirteenth–twelfth centuries BC and the creation of settlements here by Phoenicians and Greeks in the eighth century BC (described in the next chapter). These centuries are now gradually coming into focus. To judge from the finds of Cypriot personal brooches in Sicily, Italy, Sardinia and even in Iberia, Cypriots remained active in the west after the twelfth century, and it is clear that Phoenicians were active in the west well before they founded their first settlements there in the eighth century. We have already glanced at the emergence of Phoenician power in the early Iron Age, and the subsequent eastern and southern expansion of their trading interests in association with King Solomon of Israel. This was followed by a concerted westwards expansion of Phoenician trading interests in the tenth and ninth centuries. Phoenicians built a temple to a Phoenician deity at Nora in southern Sardinia in the ninth century, and a Phoenician tomb near Knossos of the ninth/eighth century included both material from a Phoenician jeweller and a pottery vessel from Sardinia.

Some Phoenicians had probably already reached the western limits of the Mediterranean by the tenth century. From Huelva (ancient Tartessos), on the Atlantic coast of south-west Iberia, comes a wonderful hoard of 400 bronze objects dating to the mid-tenth century BC, including 92 spearheads and 62 spear-butts, 78 swords, 29 daggers, 17 arrowheads, fragments of helmets, 14 buttons, 10 rings, 4 complete safety-pin brooches and 5 necklaces. The objects were found in a river mouth, and are probably what is left of a shipwreck; alternatively, they may be a ritual deposit. Most of the armour was made in the Atlantic coastal region; the swords are characteristic of the Atlantic coast as far north as Britain, and there is also an Irish type of spearhead. The hoard thus exemplifies the intense cultural and trading links along the Atlantic seaboard in this period. But there are also some objects from the eastern Mediterranean: a bronze helmet probably originating in Assyria, and safety-pin brooches of two distinctive types from the eastern Mediterranean, Cyprus and the

Levant. The Huelva hoard illustrates the existence of connections between people from the eastern Mediterranean and the Atlantic trade circuit as early as the tenth century BC. Contacts between the Levant and Tartessos were such that 'ships of Tarshish [that is, Tartessos]' is a standard phrase in the Hebrew Bible for major trading vessels. It was 'ships of Tarshish' that Hiram of Tyre and Solomon of Jerusalem used for their regular expeditions down the Red Sea in search of 'gold, silver, ivory, apes and peacocks'.

Looking at the very different worlds of middle Europe, the western Mediterranean, the Aegean and the Levant in the first centuries of the first millennium BC, the clearest distinction is not that between east and west, but between the countries to the north and the south of the Alps in this period. Wherever one looks in the Mediterranean world around 800 BC, whether it be Phoenicia, Cyprus, mainland Greece, Sardinia or northern Italy, the signs of economic and political lift-off are there. All of these very different societies were undergoing mass population growth, rapid technological development, and the beginnings of advanced state-formation. North of the Alps, in middle Europe and beyond, there is no sign of anything of the kind. For whatever reason, the Urnfield societies of temperate Europe did not experience the same kind of lift-off as their neighbours to the south. This claim is not the result of cultural prejudice on the part of two authors trained in Greek and Roman history; it is accepted also by archaeologists specializing in middle Europe. The Mediterranean lift-off is not easy to explain, but must be connected with (among other things) the successful intensification of agriculture, which supported increased populations, the emergence of strong community bonds and successful local leadership, and the existence of entrepreneurs, whose trading activities enhanced developments back home. Whatever the precise reasons, this is the moment when the Mediterranean world decisively pulled ahead of Europe north of the Alps. The age of the Mediterranean city-states was about to begin.

3

Greeks, Phoenicians and the Western Mediterranean: 800–480 BC

At the dawn of the eighth century BC, a new town was founded on the west coast of the island of Euboea. The earliest settlers were probably refugees from the Dark Age town of Lefkandi, which had been abandoned in the early eighth century, for reasons unknown. This little settlement, stretching between a fine natural harbour and a naturally defensible acropolis rock facing the Greek mainland, bore the name of Eretria. Here, around 720 BC, a local prince was buried in extraordinary splendour. The dead man's ashes were set in a bronze cauldron, with a second cauldron to serve as a lid; four swords and six spears were buried alongside him. Over the next forty years fifteen more family members were buried around this original tomb, in rich graves adorned with weapons and gold jewellery. For sheer ostentatious display of wealth, no other site in Greece at this period can match this group of Eretrian tombs. But around 680 BC, the series of burials came to an abrupt end. A huge triangular monument was built over the tombs, transforming an active private burial plot into a public cult site. This elite family had passed out of the present-day world of Eretria and become part of its past. A line had been drawn; the age of the *basileis* was at an end. In the eighth and seventh centuries BC individual communities right across the Greek world were beginning the slow process of turning themselves into *poleis*, 'citizen-states'.

The rise of the Greek *polis* will be the central theme of this chapter. After exploring the evidence for the emergence of *poleis* in mainland Greece in the eighth century BC, we shall move on to see how the culture of the Greek world in this period was transformed under the influence of the civilizations of Egypt and the Near East. We shall see how, in turn, this cultural revolution spread to the central and western Mediterranean with the great colonizing movements (both Greek and Phoenician) of

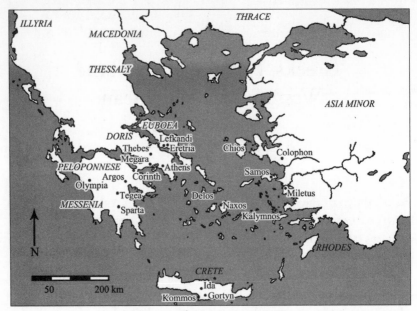

Map 10. The Aegean *c.* 700 BC.

the eighth and seventh centuries BC. We then return to the world of the Greek *polis*, and the Greeks' growing sense of a common 'Hellenic' identity in the sixth century BC. The chapter closes at the turn of the fifth century BC, with the Greek *poleis* facing the rise of a new Great Power in the east, the empire of the Persians.

We begin with the notoriously difficult question of what a *polis* actually was. Essentially the term refers to a 'citizen-state', a clearly defined territory under the authority of a single political community. The key concept is that of the community, the body of *politai* or citizens. The period 800–500 BC is characterized by the ever-increasing participation in the business of politics – literally, '*polis*-affairs' – by the ordinary man. And there were a lot more ordinary men around in 500 BC than in 800 BC: the eighth century BC, in particular, seems to have been a period of explosive population growth throughout the Greek world. Around 600 BC a disgruntled aristocrat, the poet Theognis of Megara, complained that his *polis* was coming to be dominated by 'people who formerly knew neither justice nor laws, but wore tattered goatskins around their sides and lived outside this *polis* like deer'. Needless to say, class distinctions between the goatskin-clad masses and the increasingly grouchy elite did not disappear overnight. The average *polis* in the period 700–500 BC was probably dominated, formally or informally, by a small aristocratic elite of a few wealthy families. But the fledgling citizen-states soon began to develop formal structures of authority which the Dark Age chiefdoms had never possessed. The process of power-sharing between elite families led to the definition of specific political offices and magistracies. The seventh century saw the emergence of the earliest law-codes, most of which are specifically concerned with limiting the powers of individual magistrates. In several states, a single family managed for a period to exclude its rivals from office, in which case the government was called 'tyranny', a term which did not develop its negative connotations until the later fifth century BC. There is some truth in the ancient view that tyranny marked a step towards true democratic government, since tyrants were largely reliant on the consent and support of the wider political community.

Whatever the precise mode of government, the crucial development in this period is the increasing sense of belonging to a political community. By 500 BC, self-identification as a citizen of a *polis* was so central to social relations that it became embedded in Greek naming practices. Henceforth, Greeks were known by a given name, their father's name, and the name of their *polis*: 'Cleomenes, son of Anaxandridas, Lacedaemonian'.

The evidence of archaeology can also help us trace the rise of the *polis* as the dominant form of social organization in the Greek world. Here, we focus on two crucial developments. The first is the eighth- and seventh-century proliferation of rural sanctuaries in marginal districts, whether at the fringe of a plain, in mountainous areas or on the coast. These sanctuaries can be regarded as highly visible ways of delimiting a political territory, of staking out a claim to a boundary between one's own land and that of one's neighbours. The case of Corinth may serve as an example. Corinth lies on a narrow neck of land, the Isthmus, connecting the Peloponnese to mainland Greece proper (see Map 11). In the early Iron Age, the population of the Isthmus region seems to have been small and widely dispersed. Only two sites in the region show any regular and continuous activity: a small communal sanctuary at Isthmia, and a loosely nucleated settlement at Corinth itself. In the early eighth century a new sanctuary dedicated to the goddess Hera was founded at Perachora, in an extremely isolated coastal position on the far north-eastern limits of the Corinthian sphere of control. Despite its unpromising location, on a rugged peninsula with poor water supply and a tiny harbour, Perachora had developed by the early seventh century into one of the richest sanctuaries in the Greek world, attracting lavish dedications of gold, jewellery, scarabs and faience. It was precisely the fact that Perachora was so far from the main centre of settlement which gave it its appeal: it ostentatiously marked the furthest reach of Corinthian power.

The fact that these rich dedications exist at all is important evidence for a change in the attitudes of the aristocratic elite towards their communities, as in the tombs at Eretria. The eighth century sees an abrupt rise in the quantity and quality of votive offerings in sanctuaries, marking a shift from display of elite wealth in exclusively private contexts, particularly burials, to a more public sphere of highly visible dedications. Dedications of bronze tripods and arms and armour start to appear at the old Isthmia sanctuary in the eighth century, in a pattern of increasing expenditure which culminates in the seventh century with the construction of the first monumental temple at Isthmia, a rectangular building measuring 40 × 14 metres, with stone walls and a tiled roof supported by wooden columns. We might add that the sheer human resources and corporate organization required to produce a building of this kind is a

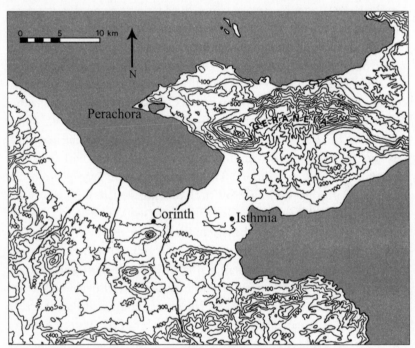

Map 11. Corinth, Perachora and Isthmia.

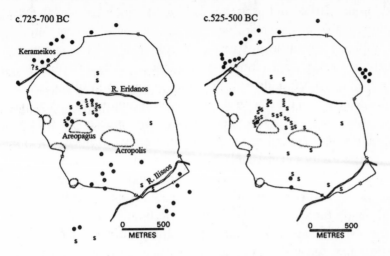

Figure 10. Changing patterns of cemeteries and settlements at Athens, 700–500 BC. Cemeteries are marked with solid circles, and traces of settlement are marked 'S'.

fairly reliable marker of the emergence of a centralized Corinthian state.

A second type of archaeological evidence for *polis*-formation, which begins to appear at a slightly later date, is the emergence of clearly defined urban spaces. In the late eighth century BC Corinth consisted of a cluster of hamlets, separated by broad open spaces and market gardens, loosely concentrated around a looming acropolis rock, the hill of Acrocorinth. Eighth-century Athens presents a very similar picture (see Figure 10). In both cases, eighth-century burials are found scattered across the entire settlement area, with separate burial plots grouped around each individual cluster of habitation. After 700, however, all the cemeteries are very swiftly pushed outwards into a single outer zone, beyond the inhabited area altogether: a sharp distinction is drawn between the spaces reserved for the living and the dead. The inhabitants of the cluster of hamlets had chosen to combine to form a single bounded conurbation. Over the course of the seventh and sixth centuries, open areas within these conurbations gradually started to take on the function of civic and economic centres for the whole community. By the late sixth century, this new public space, the *agora* ('gathering-place'), had been clearly marked off from residential districts and reserved for public functions. Within the urban space, a distinction was drawn between the public and private spheres.

This division of a settlement into different zones, separating residential

81

and burial districts and private and public spaces, is perhaps the most distinctive sign of the emergence of a unified political community. In many cases, probably in most cases, this 'zoning' of different spaces with different functions led ultimately to full-scale urbanization: a sharp increase in population density, the construction of a wall surrounding the settlement, and the emergence of a market economy. By 500 BC most citizen-states were also city-states, with a single densely populated urban centre. But although urbanization was certainly widespread, it was not in fact a necessary and inevitable stage in the rise of the *polis*. Notoriously, the political centre of Sparta in the southern Peloponnese was never more than a loose cluster of five unwalled villages; no one has ever wished to deny Sparta the status of a *polis* on that account. Nonetheless, as early as the seventh century the villages of Sparta had developed the use of a single *agora*, defined in a seventh-century Spartan constitutional document as the space 'between Babyka and Knakion', a river and a bridge respectively. Once again, the most reliable evidence for political unification is the division of private and public space.

We have already seen one major change in the patterns of elite behaviour: the shift from the display of wealth in private contexts, particularly burials, to a more publicly visible investment in sanctuaries and temples. Another marked shift occurs over the same period, in the kinds of objects which aristocrats wished to be associated with. In the course of the eighth and seventh centuries BC the material culture of the Greek elites was transformed under the influence of Near Eastern and Egyptian models. This transformation is visible in almost every aspect of Greek material culture, so much so that these two centuries have become known to archaeologists as the 'Orientalizing' period of Greek history.

Most fine Greek pottery of the eleventh to the early eighth centuries BC had been decorated in the so-called 'geometric' style, characterized by abstract linear designs (meanders, zigzags, compass-drawn circles), although figural representations of animals, humans and even primitive narrative scenes were becoming ever more common. In the course of the eighth and early seventh centuries, the geometric tradition was un-ceremoniously scrapped, to be replaced by an entirely new style. As before, figures are painted in black, but they now possess physiognomical details, incised with a sharp instrument. An entirely new repertoire of naturalistic figures appears out of nowhere: wild beasts, fabulous monsters and exotic plants like lotus flowers, unknown in Greece (see Plate 6). This is not evolution, but an outright revolution. Both the technique and the imagery of these new vase-types derive directly from the pottery and metalwork of the Levant and Near East. The influence of north Syrian bronze-work can be seen on Crete already in the eighth and early seventh century, in an extraordinary collection of bronze shields and cymbals from the cave of Zeus on Mt. Ida. These bronze objects, with animal-head bosses and circular friezes depicting Assyrian-style hunting scenes, may actually have been made by immigrant Syrian artisans. However, there can be no doubt that most oriental-style bronzes in Greece were made by Greek craftsmen imitating eastern styles. In the seventh and sixth centuries, bronze cauldrons with cast griffin and lion heads attached to the upper rim were among the most popular dedications in Greek sanctuaries. The earliest of these were certainly imported from the Levant, but Greeks were soon producing these exotic objects in large numbers: we can infer the existence of specialized Greek workshops producing griffin attachments for the great sanctuaries of Olympia in the Peloponnese and the temple of Hera on the east Greek island of Samos.

Syria was not the only source of inspiration. From the mid-seventh century BC Greek sanctuaries began to fill up with statues of standing male figures, life-size or larger, always naked, facing forward, with one foot slightly advanced. These monumental statue-dedications, known as *kouroi*, have no precedent in Greek art, and scholars agree that the form is directly imitated from contemporary Egyptian stone sculpture. It is possible, though less certain, that the monumental stone temples which appear for the first time in the Greek world in the seventh century BC also owed something to the example of Egyptian temple architecture.

A different part of the Near East, coastal Phoenicia (whose crucial role in the tenth- and ninth-century Levant was described in the last chapter), was the source of one of the most important imports to the Greek world from the east. The Greek alphabet is a light adaptation of the Phoenician alphabetic script, which had been in use since at least the twelfth century BC. The names of the letters of the Greek alphabet carry Phoenician names: *alpha*, *beta*, *gamma*, corresponding to Phoenician *aleph*, *beth*, *gimel*, 'ox', 'house', 'stick'. Originally, we may suppose, this was a mnemonic sequence designed to help Phoenicians learning to read and write; the sequence was preserved for the Greek alphabet, even though the names themselves had no meaning, and hence no mnemonic function, in a Greek context.

The date at which the alphabet was imported to Greece has been deeply controversial, but a consensus has hardened around the early eighth century. We have not a single example of Greek alphabetic writing before 775 BC, yet inscriptions from the latter half of the eighth century BC number in the dozens. This innovative new technology spread fast. Eighth-century Greek inscriptions on pottery have been found at Al Mina in Syria, Cretan Kommos, Rhodes and Kalymnos in the Dodecanese, the Aegean islands of Naxos and Euboea, Athens, and the Euboean colony of Pithecoussae on the bay of Naples. Most of these texts are everyday owners' inscriptions or dedications, 'I am the drinking-cup of Korakos' and suchlike. Perhaps the most remarkable early written texts yet known to us are the hundreds of inscribed potsherds of the seventh and sixth centuries BC from a sanctuary of Zeus on the peak of Mt. Hymettos, just south of Athens. The content of these short texts seems, at first sight, to bear little relation to their function as dedications to Zeus: nonsense-inscriptions, alphabets, even the names of other random Greek deities. The key to understanding the Hymettos dedications is provided by one sherd on which the dedicator's name is followed by the telling words *tade autos egrapse*, 'he wrote this himself'. Alphabetic writing was still a sufficiently rare and prestigious skill that even the smallest scrap of writing, a bare *alpha beta gamma*, could be considered a worthy offering to the god.

Near Eastern influence can be detected not only in pottery and metal-work, sculpture and the alphabet, but also in much early Greek literature and myth. The earliest surviving Greek literary work is probably the *Theogony* of Hesiod (around 700 BC), a narrative poem describing the origins of the world and the genealogies and internecine wars of the gods. Many of the stories of the gods recounted in the *Theogony* have strikingly close parallels with Hittite, Babylonian and other Near Eastern wisdom literature. For example, Hesiod describes how the sky-god Ouranos was castrated by his son Kronos. Kronos goes on to have five children by his wife Rhea, but fearing a prophecy that one of them will eventually depose him, he swallows each one immediately after its birth. The sixth child is the storm-god Zeus, whom Rhea saves by presenting Kronos with a Zeus-shaped stone wrapped in baby's clothes, which he duly swallows. Zeus grows up to conquer his father, and Kronos is forced to vomit up all his earlier children, along with the deceptive stone. The stone is eventually set up as an object of worship at the oracular shrine of Delphi. Almost every element in this story – the castration of the sky-god, his successor devouring his own sons, the false stone which is later set up as a cult object, the eventual victory of the storm-god – can be closely paralleled in a Hittite theological text of the thirteenth century BC, the *Song of Kumarbi*. In the absence of any Greek literary texts before Hesiod, it is impossible to say exactly when and how the transfer of ideas occurred, but the general direction of traffic is unmistakeable.

The fourth-century philosopher Plato wrote that 'whenever Greeks borrow anything from non-Greeks, they take it to a higher state of perfection'. We do not need to subscribe to Plato's (understandable) value-judgement about Greek borrowings – Greek griffins are not obviously more perfect than Assyrian griffins – to agree that the Greeks were not merely passive recipients of oriental culture. The male *kouroi*-statues, while clearly Egyptian in inspiration, are thoroughly non-Egyptian in execution. Egyptian male statues invariably wear at least a kilt; Greek *kouroi*, by contrast, are almost always nude. Male nudity is unparalleled in Egyptian art, and reflects a distinctively Greek cultural preference. We can see here an oriental prototype being modified to accord with Greek social expectations and tastes. Still more striking is the Greek adaptation of the monumental stone statue-type for female figures. The Greeks had long been producing rather rigid wooden statues of female figures, particularly for cult statues of goddesses. In the mid-seventh century, around the time of the earliest *kouroi*, stone statues of women (*korai*) also start to appear in Greek sanctuaries. Unlike the *kouroi*, these female figures are always depicted fully clothed. Probably the earliest of these stone *korai* is a life-size statue from the small island of Delos, dated to around 650 BC. An inscription cut on the statue's dress identifies her commissioner as a woman, Nikandrē: 'Nikandrē dedicated me to the far-shooter of arrows (the goddess Artemis) – the outstanding daughter of Deinodikes of Naxos, sister of Deinomenes, wife of Phraxos.' It is not clear whether the statue is intended as a representation of Artemis, or of Nikandrē herself, who is defined entirely in relation to her male relatives: father, brother and husband. The interesting thing here is how the Greeks creatively adapted the new medium of stone statuary to fit the purely Greek artistic tradition of free-standing draped female figures (see Plates 9–10).

We have seen that the eighth and seventh centuries saw an 'Orientalizing' revolution in Greek culture and society. A more controversial question follows from this. Objects and ideas are not transmitted by osmosis; they are carried by individual people, physically moving between different cultural zones, trading, talking, eating and marrying with other individuals. How exactly did the Greeks come into contact with the cultures of the Near East and Egypt? Who was carrying what to whom, and, perhaps most crucially, where?

Modern archaeologists have emphasized the key intermediary role played by the Phoenicians, inhabitants of the coastline of modern Lebanon. Phoenicia in the early first millennium BC was divided into a number of independent city-kingdoms, the most important of which were Sidon, Byblos and above all Tyre. These cities held a strategic position between the three great cultural zones of the Near East: Anatolia, Mesopotamia and Egypt. Since the mid-second millennium BC the Phoenicians had acted as intermediaries in the transport of goods between the great powers: the grain supply of the Hittites was largely in Phoenician hands, and the timberless Egyptians were always heavily dependent on Phoenician imports of wood. Then, in the early ninth century, the Phoenician cities had come within the orbit of the Neo-Assyrian empire

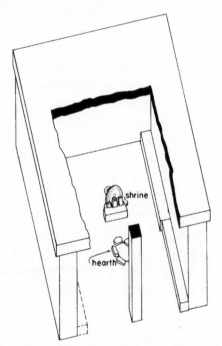

Figure 11. Phoenician tri-pillar shrine at Kommos.

of northern Mesopotamia. The Assyrians demanded a steady flow of Phoenician luxury goods, in particular ivory, metalwork and textiles; Egyptian imports to Assyria were also channelled through Phoenicia. Most importantly, the Phoenicians were the main suppliers of raw materials to the Assyrian kings, of which the most important was iron. The Phoenicians rapidly expanded their sphere of maritime commerce westwards into the Mediterranean to meet this demand. The first port of call was the mineral-rich island of Cyprus; in the late ninth century a Phoenician settlement, complete with monumental temple of the Phoenician goddess Astarte, was founded at Kition on the south coast of the island. From Cyprus, the main shipping route led due west to Crete, and around 800 BC a small Phoenician shrine was built at the harbour site of Kommos on the southern coast of Crete (see Figure 11). Numerous fragments of Phoenician transport jars were also found around the sanctuary. To all appearances, Kommos was not a permanent Phoenician settlement, but rather a watering and trading post, one of a chain of landfalls at which Phoenician ships regularly put in on their way west towards mainland Greece or Libya. By now the Phoenicians must have been in regular contact with Greek maritime traders; the harbour at Kommos is known to have been frequented by sailors from Boeotia in central Greece by the seventh century BC at the latest.

The importance of Crete and Cyprus as points of contact between the Greek world and the Near East is beyond doubt. Whether the Greeks themselves actively penetrated further into the Levantine world is, however, a matter of deep controversy. In the second quarter of the eighth century BC, a new coastal settlement was established at Al Mina in northern Syria, at the mouth of the Orontes river. Virtually all the excavated pottery from the earliest phase of the settlement (c. 775–725 BC) is of Greek, specifically Euboean, origin; during the second phase, which finishes in around 700 BC, around half the pottery is Euboean, with the rest deriving from Cyprus and Syria. Pottery from other parts of the Greek world is almost entirely absent. Who, then, were the inhabitants of eighth-century Al Mina? Sir Leonard Woolley, who excavated the site in the 1930s, argued that Al Mina was a Greek settlement, and until the 1980s most archaeologists subscribed to this view. They emphasized the overwhelming preponderance of Greek Euboean wares in the pottery record from Al Mina, and the fact that no other site on the Levantine coast has produced anything like the quantity of Greek ceramics found at Al Mina. On this view, the Euboean pottery marks the existence of a Euboean *emporion* or 'trading post' at Al Mina.

Over the past thirty years, however, a growing number of archaeologists have vigorously argued that this Greek trading post is a myth. They have emphasized the non-Greek elements in the architecture of the site (mud-brick rather than stone), the absence of Greek-style burials or cults, and the fact that the Euboean pottery consisted almost entirely of drinking vessels, with no sign of the cooking pots and plain day-to-day pottery one would expect at a Greek settlement. On this view, the Greek drinking-cups were brought from Euboea to Al Mina by long-distance Levantine traders, probably Phoenicians, who found Euboean wares particularly desirable. There need never have been any Greeks at Al Mina at all.

The archaeological evidence alone cannot decide the question one way or the other. It is unlikely that there will ever be any objective proof of who brought the Euboean pots to Al Mina and who used them once they had arrived there. That is not to say that the problem cannot be solved. At present the debate hinges on a fundamental disagreement as to whether Greek-style drinking-vessels were attractive and desirable to easterners; a comprehensive study of the types and quantity of Greek ceramics being exported to the Near East in the eighth century might well settle the question once and for all. But the debate over how to interpret the settlement at Al Mina has wider implications, reflecting as it does two opposing and incompatible views of the development of Greek 'Orientalizing' culture in the eighth and seventh centuries. To an older generation of archaeologists, predominantly from Britain and Germany, Euboean Al Mina marks the point at which vigorous and enterprising Greeks gained a foothold on the rim of the orient, from which they could select and assimilate the most valuable skills and technologies of the civilizations of the Near East. To a younger generation of scholars, predominantly from the New World (the United States and Australia), Levantine Al Mina reflects the essential passivity of the Greeks in their encounter with Near Eastern culture. It was, by contrast, the seaborne Phoenicians who made the running in the eighth century, penetrating deep into Aegean waters and flooding Greek harbour-towns with their products, both material and cultural.

The debate is perhaps more about modern ideology than ancient pottery. It is true that the development of the Mediterranean world in the early first millennium BC has traditionally been seen almost entirely from a Greek perspective. As one distinguished archaeologist has put it, there is an inexcusable tendency among historians and archaeologists to portray the non-Greek peoples of the Mediterranean as 'people waiting for something interesting and Greek to happen to them'. It is distressing to contemplate how far the nineteenth- and early twentieth-century characterization of the Phoenicians as 'mere traders' might have reflected, and supported, contemporary stereotypes of Semitic peoples more generally. But there is no less of a danger in overplaying the Phoenician contribution to European history. By a kind of retrospective positive discrimination, the Phoenicians are sometimes given the credit for every significant historical and artistic development of the eighth and seventh centuries, with the Greeks stumbling along in their wake. This is little more than ideologically driven wishful thinking.

Black Athena

The most influential and controversial account in recent times of the relations between the Greek world and its non-Greek neighbours is the mammoth work by Martin Bernal, *Black Athena: The Afroasiatic Roots of Classical Civilisation* (published in three volumes between 1987 and 2006). In this work, Bernal proposed two major theses: first, that the origins of Greek civilization are to be sought in Africa, specifically in Egypt; and second, that since the eighteenth century this fact has been systematically and deliberately concealed by western scholars, whether through Eurocentrism or downright racism.

Reactions to Bernal's work have been passionate, ill-tempered and, at times, breathtakingly arrogant: one critic has suggested that 'Bernal's argument . . . can safely be ignored because Bernal is an expert in Chinese politics, not a trained classicist'. There is certainly much to disagree with in *Black Athena*, not least Bernal's oddly single-minded focus on Egypt as the fountainhead of Greek culture, to the near-total exclusion of the Near East. Nor has Bernal helped his cause by his eager endorsement of such crude and muddled rants as George James's *Stolen Legacy: The Greeks were Not the Authors of Greek Philosophy, But the People of North Africa, Commonly Called the Egyptians* (1954). To be fair, Bernal has never gone so far as to argue, as James and others have done, that Cleopatra or Socrates was black, or that Aristotle stole his philosophical ideas from the Egyptians by ransacking the library at Alexandria (founded several decades after Aristotle's death).

Bernal's own position is better represented by his passing reference, in the first volume of *Black Athena*, to 'Pharoahs whom one can *usefully* call black'. Bernal justifies this criterion of 'usefulness' as follows: 'There is no doubt that the concept of "race" is of overwhelming importance today. Thus, I believe that both my emphasis on the African nature of Egyptian civilisation and the presence of people "whom one can usefully call black" among its rulers are important to contemporary readers. This is to counter the cultural debilitation to peoples of African descent brought about by implicit assumptions or explicit statements that there has never been a great "African" culture which has contributed to world civilisation as a whole and that "Blacks" have always been servile.' That seems to us to be decent, fair-minded, and well argued; whether or not it is the right way to go about writing history, we leave to the reader to decide.

The 'Orientalizing' phenomenon of the eighth and seventh centuries BC sets the scene for another major historical development of the period, the simultaneous Greek and Phoenician penetration of the western Mediterranean. Contacts between the eastern and western halves of the Mediterranean between the eleventh and eighth centuries had been very sporadic indeed. Over the first half of the eighth century, this traffic picked up speed. Successive waves of Greeks and Phoenicians sailed westwards in ever greater numbers, founding hundreds of new settlements on the coasts of the western Mediterranean. One of the earliest western outposts was the settlement of Pithecoussae, on the island of Ischia in the bay of Naples, dating to around 770 BC. The location of Pithecoussae, on a small island just off the coast of the mainland, is characteristic of the earliest Greek and Phoenician settlements in the west: Sulcis, on the island of Sant'Antioco off the coast of Sardinia, is very similarly situated. This offshore location reflects the primary role of the early western settlements as ports of trade, gateway communities through which trade was conducted with the indigenous peoples of the hinterland.

In the earliest phase of colonization in the western Mediterranean, no hard line can be drawn between Greek and Phoenician activity. Pithecoussae, although predominantly a colony of Euboean Greeks, was also

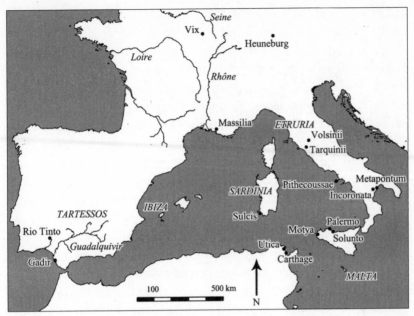

Map 12. The western Mediterranean *c.* 650 BC.

home to substantial groups of Corinthians, Phoenicians and native Italians. It was no doubt due to their multicultural character that places like Pithecoussae were often at the forefront of new developments, such as writing. But Greek and Phoenician colonizing activity in the western Mediterranean soon took sharply divergent paths. The Greek colonies in the west were overwhelmingly concentrated in southern Italy and eastern Sicily, while the Phoenicians directed their attentions towards Spain and North Africa. More interestingly, there are clear differences in the physical form and functions of the new settlements. A few concrete examples will illustrate the point.

The earliest Phoenician contacts with the western Mediterranean seem to date to the tenth and ninth centuries BC, but it was not until the early eighth century that Phoenician traders began to settle permanently in the far west. The emergence of a west-Mediterranean Phoenician diaspora was remarkably rapid. In the late ninth and eighth centuries, the Phoenicians had established settlements in Tunisia (Carthage and Utica), western Sicily (Motya, Palermo, Solunto), Malta, Sardinia, Ibiza, and the Andalusian coast of Spain. Without exception, the Phoenician foundations in the west were situated so as to tap into pre-existing trading-circuits and areas of surplus production. The great colony of Gadir (later known to the Romans as Gades, whence its modern name of Cadiz) is an excellent illustration of what the Phoenicians were seeking from the west. Gadir is situated on an island off the south coast of Andalusia, just outside the straits of Gibraltar. On the Andalusian mainland lay the region known to the Greeks as Tartessos, essentially consisting of the Guadalquivir valley and the Huelva region. Here the Phoenicians encountered a late Bronze Age people whose contacts with the wider Mediterranean world had hitherto been tentative at best. However, the indigenous Tartessians controlled one of the major precious-metal sources of the Mediterranean, the Rio Tinto mines in the Huelva province, with rich seams of copper, silver, gold, lead and iron. Local exploitation of these mines in the tenth and ninth centuries seems to have been on a fairly small-scale, and more or less restricted to copper-extraction. The eighth-century Phoenician settlers at Gadir brought with them new silver-smelting technology, vastly superior to the metallurgical techniques employed by the native Iberians; crucially, they could also provide a ready-made market for bulk precious metals in their eastern Mediterranean homeland. From the mid-eighth century we see a massive acceleration of activity at the mines of the Huelva and Guadalquivir regions, as the Tartessian elites realized the profits to be gained from exporting silver and other metals through their new Phoenician trading partners.

We should lay equal emphasis on what did *not* happen at Gadir. Although the Phoenician settlement undoubtedly prospered, it remained an offshore trading post, never exercising any kind of political dominance in southern Andalusia. We have no indication that the Phoenicians made any attempt to annex Tartessian resources outright, or even to occupy and cultivate their own patch of territory on the mainland. Instead, economic expansion at Gadir took the form of a rash of maritime daughter-colonies, spreading north and south along the Atlantic coastlines of Portugal and Morocco, through which the Phoenicians could tap into another pre-existing commercial system, the east Atlantic tin trade. Phoenician settlement in the western Mediterranean has been neatly described as 'maritime urbanization'. Although the western colonies did eventually become self-sufficient, places like Gadir were fundamentally dependent on the merchant shipping routes, like umbilical cords tying them to their Phoenician mother-cities in the eastern Mediterranean.

The Greek experience in Sicily and southern Italy was different. The colony of Metapontum, on the gulf of Tarentum in the instep of southern Italy, is an extreme but not wholly uncharacteristic example. This part of the south Italian coast was originally inhabited by an indigenous Italic people known to the Greeks as the Oenotrians. By the first half of the seventh century BC, the most important settlement in the region was at a small hill-site called Incoronata, about 8 kilometres inland, inhabited by a mixed population of native Oenotrians and a small group of 'pre-colonial' Greek settlers. Around 630 BC a large group of Achaeans from the north-east Peloponnese settled on the coast at Metapontum. Incoronata was promptly abandoned; when the site was occupied again a generation later, there was no longer any trace of the indigenous Italians. Shortly after the arrival of the Greeks at Metapontum, a new Greek sanctuary was founded at San Biagio, 7 kilometres north-west of the new urban centre, and very close to the recently abandoned site of Incoronata. It is tempting to suppose, on the model of outlying religious centres like Perachora in mainland Greece, that this sanctuary was in part intended to stake out the new settlers' claim to all the territory lying between Metapontum and San Biagio. This territory was soon being parcelled up into rectangular farm-plots; the agricultural productivity of the region increased sharply, with the introduction of crop rotation and new Greek-style farming techniques. It appears that the early history of Metapontum was marked by violent displacement of the native Italic population, and aggressive acquisition and cultivation of large stretches of agricultural land, which were then divided into egalitarian plots for new Greek settlers. These settlers were clearly eager to achieve self-sufficiency right from the outset, and had no particular interest in maintaining good relations with their Italic neighbours. The picture could not be more different from the Phoenician model of settlement in Andalusia.

However, not all Greek settlements in the west were inspired purely by land-hunger. Perhaps the clearest example of a Greek settlement prospering through commerce with its non-Greek neighbours is Massilia, modern Marseilles, founded by Greeks from western Asia Minor around 600 BC on a magnificent natural harbour near the mouth of the Rhône (see Map 13). Southern France was the last area of the western Mediterranean to be opened up to eastern influence. In the seventh century BC the Etruscans had established a handful of trading posts on the Golfe du Lion, through which Etruscan wine was exported to Provence, Languedoc and the Rhône valley, but no Greek or Phoenician

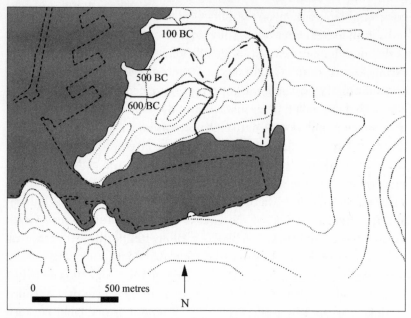

Map 13. Massilia, showing the area of the settlement at three moments, 600, 500 and 100 BC. The settlement was located on the slopes north of the magnificent natural harbour; dashed lines within that harbour and to the west represent the modern coastline.

settlements are known in the region before the founding of Massilia. For the first fifty years or so of its existence the Greek settlers at Massilia seem to have been content to act as middlemen on the existing trading route between Etruria and Provence-Languedoc. Meanwhile, however, the Massiliots were also busy establishing an agricultural enclave on the coastal plain around the settlement, introducing viticulture to the region for the first time. Once local production of wine reached a sufficient level, the Massiliots could effortlessly undercut Etruscan imports. Around 540 BC Etruscan wine-jars abruptly stop being imported to southern France, to be replaced by a near-total monopoly of new-style wine-jars produced at Massilia itself. Massiliot wine was soon pouring northward through the Rhône corridor between the Massif Central and the Alps, into lands which had previously enjoyed minimal contact with the cultures of the Mediterranean (see Map 14).

Thus far we have focused on the differences in the character of the Phoenician and Greek colonization of the west. We turn now to the overall impact of this western colonization on the course of European history. We have already seen how Greek society in the eighth and seventh centuries was transformed under the influence of Egyptian and Near Eastern art and technology. So too the cultures of the native elites of western Europe underwent profound changes through their integration into the Orientalizing culture of the eastern Mediterranean. In the Phoenician sphere of influence, the Tartessian elites of the Huelva region and Guadalquivir valley profited enormously from Phoenician export of their precious metal resources. Predictably enough, these local princes adopted the trappings of Phoenician culture with a vengeance. The huge princely burial mounds in the Guadalquivir valley rapidly start to show strong influence of Phoenician burial practices, and the graves themselves increasingly contain valuable luxury goods (bronzes, ivory and gold jewellery) of Phoenician origin. By the fifth century BC, a highly sophisticated new urban culture had emerged along the Mediterranean coasts of Spain under Phoenician and Greek influence (see Plate 17). We shall return to the changing world of the fifth- and fourth-century Iberians in Chapter 6.

In the 'Greek' sphere of influence in southern France, the opening up of the trade route from Massilia up the Rhône valley had an even more

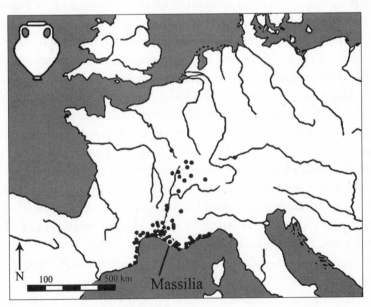

Map 14. Distribution of Massiliot wine-jars, c. 560–500 BC.

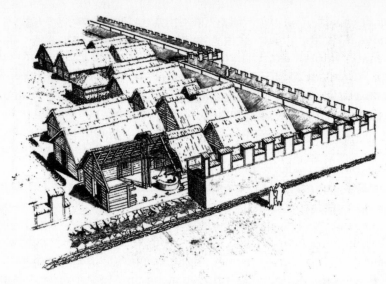

Figure 12. The south-east corner of the Heuneburg, with 'Greek-style' mud-brick fortifications. Note the density of housing within the wall-circuit.

powerful impact. In the late 'Urnfield' period (above, pp. 69–72), the region north of the Alps, from Burgundy in the west to the Czech Republic in the east, was home to a stable, relatively homogeneous Iron Age cultural group collectively referred to by archaeologists as the Hallstatt culture (named after a salt-mining town in Austria). In the sixth century BC, as prestige goods of Mediterranean manufacture began to travel north along the Rhône corridor in increasing quantities, the western half of the Hallstatt zone underwent an extraordinary transformation. A new elite class emerged, residing in Greek-style fortified hilltop towns, marked out from their contemporaries by their conspicuous consumption of Greek luxury goods. The most thoroughly excavated of the Hallstatt princely residences is at the Heuneburg, on the river Danube near the modern town of Ulm. In the early sixth century BC, the Heuneburg was rebuilt with a new, planned layout of houses, encircled by a rectilinear defensive wall built of sun-dried bricks (see Figure 12). The fortification wall is unique in Europe north of the Alps, and seems to have been constructed by a Greek or Etruscan architect.

Appropriately enough, these enthusiastic consumers of Massiliot wine were particularly keen to purchase Greek wine-drinking equipment. The Hallstatt elites adapted Greek drinking practices to fit their own needs; in some cases, Greek drinking-vessels seem to have been used for drinking mead rather than wine. One of the most westerly of the Hallstatt princely residences was located at Vix, near Châtillon-sur-Seine, some 300 kilometres west of the Heuneburg. A Hallstatt queen was buried at Vix around 500 BC in a huge barrow tomb (see Plate 13). The deceased queen was laid out on a wagon in traditional Hallstatt style, wearing a fine golden torc or necklace of local manufacture. The burial is, however, dominated by an enormous bronze *krater* or wine-mixing bowl, probably made in one of the Greek cities of southern Italy, accompanied by several fine Attic drinking-vessels.

The heyday of the Hellenizing West Hallstatt chieftains, distinguished from their fellows by their self-conscious adoption of Greek culture, was cruelly short-lived. No more than two generations after the burial of the Vix queen, a huge square enclosure, 25 metres long on each side, was laid out nearby, to mark the tomb of another royal couple. At the entrance to the tomb stood a pair of stone statues, one of a male warrior, the other of a seated female wearing a torc. Soon after their erection, the two statues were decapitated and the tomb-enclosure was violently destroyed; this was the last of the royal burials at Vix. As we shall see in Chapter 5, the emergence of the West Hallstatt princely states had sparked revolutionary disturbances among the Celtic societies of central and northern Europe, with far-reaching consequences for the history of the Mediterranean world in the fourth and third centuries BC.

The arrival of the Greeks in the western Mediterranean had a similarly profound and far-reaching impact on the native peoples of the Italian peninsula. The ninth and eighth centuries had been marked by a dramatic growth in the size of settlements in central and northern Italy (above, pp. 72–3). The process is particularly clear in southern Etruria, where five huge nucleated centres, Caere, Tarquinii, Veii, Volsinii and Vulci, each between 100 and 200 hectares in size, had developed by the end of the ninth century. It is very striking that no Greek or Phoenician colonies are known anywhere on the west coast of Italy north of the bay of Naples, the longest stretch of coastline anywhere in the western Mediterranean left untouched by Graeco-Phoenician colonization. It is tempting to suppose that the unusually precocious urban development of Etruria left the region out of bounds for Greek and Phoenician settlers.

After the foundation of the earliest Greek colonies on the bay of Naples (Pithecoussae and Cumae) in the mid-eighth century BC, contacts between the Etruscans and the Greek world intensified. Fine Greek pottery appears in ever larger quantities in Etruscan tombs after 750 BC, and by the late eighth century Etruscan potters were producing high-quality local imitations of Corinthian geometric pots. One particularly lavish Etruscan burial from Tarquinii, dating between 700 and 675 BC, also contains a wide range of luxury Egyptian imports, including a fine faience vase carrying the name of the pharaoh Bokenranf (717–712 BC). The Etruscans had clearly wasted no time in tapping into the great trading networks of the eastern Mediterranean. The Etruscans rapidly adopted the new Graeco-Phoenician alphabet for writing their own native language; the earliest Etruscan inscriptions date to around 700 BC, a mere two generations after the first surviving graffiti back in Greece.

Around 600 BC Etruscan society entered a new phase. At Tarquinii, the urban fabric was for the first time cast in stone, with impressive new monuments including an 8-kilometre fortification wall, a large temple, and an ingenious water-distribution system. Simultaneously, the Tarquinians also founded a new harbour-town on the coast, Gravisca, as a trading-post for Greek merchant shipping from the East. The sixth century also saw a new peak in pottery imports from mainland Greece. Between 580 and 475 the Etruscans imported huge numbers of fine Athenian black-figure and red-figure vases, some of them made especially for the Etruscan market, an unusually large proportion of which have survived intact in elite Etruscan tombs. Sixth-century Etruscan tombs are quite unlike anything in mainland Greece at this period, taking the form of monumental stone chambers, often with intricately painted interiors; at Volsinii (modern Orvieto), the necropolis is laid out on a neat grid-pattern, with 'streets' of uniform stone tomb-chambers, each labelled with the occupant's name. This ostentatiously egalitarian form of burial seems to be unique to Etruria.

'Etruscan' vases

Ancient painted pottery began to attract the interest of Italian and British antiquarians and collectors in the early eighteenth century. Most of the vases purchased by the early collectors came from tombs in Etruria and southern Italy, and it was naturally supposed that they were originally produced in Etruria. The most influential British collector was Sir William Hamilton (1730–1803), British envoy to the court of Naples from 1764.

In 1766 Hamilton commissioned a fantastically lavish four-volume cata-logue of his *Collection of Etruscan, Greek and Roman Antiquities*, which he declared to be 'equally proper for the completing of well understood Collections of Prints and Designs, or to furnish in a manner not only agreeable but useful and instructive, the Cabinet of a Man of Taste and letters'. Hamilton's 'Etruscan' collection had an enormous influence on eighteenth-century British taste; in particular, the simple compositions and sedate themes favoured by Hamilton had a formative impact on the early neo-classical movement in Britain. In 1769 Josiah Wedgwood opened a ceramic factory in Staffordshire, which he named 'Etruria', inspired by Hamilton's collection of impeccably tasteful 'Etruscan' vases. The six vases produced on the opening day of the new factory were modelled on a red-figure vase in the Hamilton collection depicting Hercules in the Garden of the Hesperides; each vase carried the bold inscription ARTES ETRURIAE RENASCUNTUR, 'The Arts of Etruria are reborn.'

The belief that 'Etruscan' vases were originally made in Etruria was already being challenged in the eighteenth century – if they were native Etruscan work, why were all the painted vase-inscriptions in Greek? – and it is now thought that most of the vases discovered in Etruria were produced in the Kerameikos potters' district of Athens. But eighteenth-century views on the artistic value of 'Etruscan' vases have had a more lasting influence. Hamilton's lavish catalogue was primarily intended to push up the market value of his collection of vases (which he later sold to the British Museum for an astronomical sum). Consequently, he argued that 'Etruscan' vases were valuable and highly prized objets d'art in antiquity. This assertion is very dubious indeed. The highest price known to have been paid in antiquity for an Athenian painted vase is three drachmas, less than half the price of a second-hand ladder at the same period (eight drachmas), and vases with painted figures were only about a third more expensive than plain black vases. Nonetheless, a high artistic and monetary value is still attributed to sixth- and fifth-century painted pottery by many private collectors. In December 1993, a single sixth-century Etruscan vase was sold at Sotheby's for more than £2 million.

The Etruscan reaction to the coming of the Greeks was very different from the local responses in Iberia and the West Hallstatt zone north of the Alps. Although the Etruscans borrowed many aspects of Greek material culture, the uses they chose to make of that culture were highly creative and innovative. The great phase of Etruscan urban development in the sixth century BC, although made possible by the influx of new wealth and new technologies from the Greek world, was ultimately wholly independent of the Greek *polis*-model. Through becoming part of the wider Mediterranean world, bound together by Greek and Phoenician merchantmen, the Etruscans reaped huge economic and social benefits, without losing their distinctive local urban culture.

Whether looked at from Gravisca or Vix, Incoronata or Tartessos, the period from the eighth to the sixth century BC undoubtedly marks a critical stage in the development of Europe. Local cultures continued to flourish – in some cases, as in Etruria, in spectacular style – but the big story of the period is the ever-increasing connections between those cultures. The Greek and Phoenician diaspora in the west tied the whole Mediterranean into a single macro-economic system, with an increasingly homogeneous material culture stretching from Tyre to Gadir and from Massilia to Euboea, in which Egyptian faience was as prized at Tarquinii and Perachora as it was at Nineveh and Carthage. By 500 BC, we can for the first time talk about the Mediterranean world as a single cultural unit.

The Greeks had begun to use alphabetic writing some time in the early eighth century BC. The very earliest surviving pieces of writing are not hugely informative, but one short vase-inscription of the late eighth century offers us a remarkably evocative glimpse into the ways in which the first western Greeks conceived of their past. The text derives from the earliest Greek settlement in the west, the Euboean trading-centre of Pithecoussae on the bay of Naples. Here, around 730 BC, a boy of about 12 was buried along with a full set of Greek drinking-vessels, including a small drinking-cup of east Greek, possibly Rhodian, origin. This cup carried a three-line verse inscription in the Euboean script (see Figure 13): 'I am the cup of Nestor, good to drink from. / Whoever drinks from this cup, he will immediately / Be seized by the desire of fair-crowned Aphrodite.' This little scrap of verse, nicely evoking the mixture of wine, poetry and sex which characterized the early Greek aristocratic drinking party or *symposion*, is also our earliest indirect evidence for the existence of an oral poetic tradition about the Trojan War. That tradition knew of a hero called Nestor, king of Pylos, who went with the Achaean army to

Figure 13. Greek verse inscription on 'Nestor's Cup' (Pithecoussae, *c.* 730 BC). All three lines are written from right to left.

Troy. He took with him a famous cup, embossed with gold studs, with golden doves at the base of the handles, so large and heavy that an ordinary man could scarcely raise it from the table when full. The tiny clay drinking-vessel from Pithecoussae, claiming to be the mythical cup of Nestor, is in fact a joke. For the joke to be effective, we must assume that civilized drinking circles at Pithecoussae were expected to be au fait with a common tradition of oral epic poetry on the Trojan War – an oral tradition which achieved its final written form a generation later in the poems known as the *Iliad* and the *Odyssey*.

The *Iliad* and *Odyssey* are epic narrative poems of the heroic Bronze Age past (see Chapter 1 above), written down in the new alphabetic Greek script. The *Iliad*, some 16,000 lines long, recounts the events of a few dramatic weeks in the tenth year of the Achaean siege of Troy, culminating with the death and burial of the Trojan hero Hector. The *Odyssey*, 12,000 lines long and partly modelled on the *Iliad*, describes the return of one of the heroes of the Trojan War, Odysseus, to his native island of Ithaca after ten years' wanderings. Although the ostensible focus of both poems is narrow – the first line of the *Iliad* announces its theme as 'the rage of Achilles', and more than a quarter of the poem is dedicated to a single day's fighting – the *Iliad* and *Odyssey* in fact offer us a vast and compelling panorama of the whole heroic age, glimpsed through long similes, flashbacks, and stories told by the heroes themselves.

The world described by the *Iliad* and *Odyssey*, both in terms of social structure and material culture, is an intricate composite of different periods. At times the ostensible Bronze Age setting is accurately evoked; at others, the poems clearly reflect the conditions of the ninth and eighth centuries BC. So the poems often refer to woollen and linen clothing being treated with perfumed oil to make it fragrant and shiny, a practice unknown in Iron Age Greece, but well attested in Mycenaean Linear B texts. In some cases we can see strands from different periods being woven together. In the twenty-third book of the *Iliad*, Achilles, the son of Peleus, holds funeral games for his dead companion Patroclus, at which a series of luxury goods are offered as prizes in the various athletic contests, including a large unworked lump of iron.

> Now the son of Peleus set down a lump of unworked iron,
> Which mighty Eëtion once used as his throwing-weight;
> But swift-footed godlike Achilles had slain him,
> And taken the iron away in his ships with other spoils.
> He stood upright, and spoke his word among the Argives:
> 'Rise up, those of you who wish to try for this prize.
> Even if the victor's rich fields lie far away from any town,
> He shall have the use of it for five full years;
> For neither his shepherd nor his ploughman will need to travel
> To the city for lack of iron, since this will supply their needs.'

At the beginning of this passage, the lump of iron is a prestige object in its own right, with intrinsic value as a precious metal. But by the end, it has been transformed into a practical source of utilitarian goods: the winner is expected to melt the iron down and cast or hammer it into tools. The technology to produce iron tools of this kind only emerged in Greece around 1000 BC (the beginning of the 'Iron Age'). The first four lines of this passage seem to reflect an attitude towards iron characteristic of the late Bronze Age (1600–1070 BC); the last four lines assume the technological innovations of the early Iron Age (1070–900 BC).

Derek Walcott's *Omeros*

In September 1990 the Caribbean Nobel laureate Derek Walcott published *Omeros*, a narrative poem of epic length, set on his home island of St Lucia. No work could more clearly show the continuing vitality of Homer as a source and inspiration. The protagonists, Achille, Hector, Helen and Philoctete, live out Homeric stories among the fishing boats and cafés of the Caribbean. The fisherman Philoctete is confined to shore by a shin-wound, inflicted by a rusty anchor, which refuses to heal. Helen, a beautiful waitress, leaves her lover Achille for his friend Hector, a one-time fisherman who now works driving a minibus-taxi. When Hector dies in a car-crash, Helen, now pregnant by one or other of the two men, goes back to Achille, and Philoctete's wound is eventually healed by a wise woman, Ma Kilman, manager of the No Pain café.

Even while drawing on Homer's poetry for the names, attributes and actions of his characters – often with dazzling ingenuity and grace – Walcott refuses simply to pay homage to his Homeric model:

> Why not see Helen
> as the sun saw her, with no Homeric shadow,
> swinging her plastic sandals on the beach alone,
> as fresh as the sea-wind?

In a key scene, Achille, suffering from sunstroke, imagines himself returning to the Congo, where he meets his father Afolabe and the men of his ancestral village. The episode is, on one level, an imitation of Odysseus' journey to the underworld in Homer's *Odyssey*, where Odysseus meets the ghosts of his mother Anticleia and his dead comrades from the Trojan War. But as he talks with his African ancestors, Achille realizes that he himself is the ghost; his father can neither remember his son's real name, nor understand his 'Homeric' name, Achille.

> The sadness sank into him slowly that he was home –
> that dawn-sadness which ghosts have for their graves,
> because the future reversed itself in him.

The vision ends with a raid on the village, and Achille watches his ancestors being led away in chains, to be transported across the Atlantic to Caribbean slavery. Achille is permanently cut off from his African past, but – Walcott suggests – he can never feel at home in the European cultural tradition represented by Homer. At the end of the poem, the narrator is left watching a sea-swift soaring between 'both sides of this text', his Homeric literary model and the real world of the rootless fishermen of St Lucia:

> Her wing-beat carries these islands to Africa,
> she sewed the Atlantic rift with a needle's line,
> the rift in the soul.

It is the expression of this 'rift in the soul' that makes Walcott's reading of Homer so powerful and unexpected.

This kind of multiple layering implies that the *Iliad* and *Odyssey* as we have them are the product of many centuries of evolution. The poems must stand at the end of a long tradition of oral poetry, stretching back into the second millennium BC. For centuries, we infer, successive generations of oral poets had sung of the Trojan War and the wanderings of Odysseus. The songs which they performed were neither memorized verbatim nor entirely improvised on the spot, but were built up from a large and flexible repertoire of formulaic elements, ranging from single epithets ('flashing-eyed Athena') and lines of verse ('then resourceful Odysseus answered him/her and said . . .') to entire formulaic scenes (feasting, arming, dying). We should imagine a gradual accretion of formulaic elements over time, in which imprints of the material culture and values of earlier societies are preserved, as in the inner rings of a tree-trunk.

At some point between 700 and 650 BC, this flexible and evolving oral tradition attained a fixed and immutable form: it is clear that in the late seventh and sixth centuries BC the Greeks knew just one canonical form of each poem. In short, the poems were written down. An individual, not a committee, must have been responsible for these final versions. The question of how much of the poems' undoubted emotional power and poetic beauty is to be attributed to the final 'redactor', and how much to the anonymous oral tradition on which he drew, goes right to the heart of the nature of artistic inspiration. Could successive generations of oral poets, gradually reworking and expanding the work of their predecessors, be collectively responsible for the magnificent and moving portrayal of Achilles in the *Iliad*? Or must we assume the input of a single mastermind, an original genius who took the formulaic elements of the oral tradition and transformed this mass of bronze and iron into gold?

The question of the authorship of the *Iliad* and *Odyssey* became a matter of intense interest in the late sixth century BC. The strongest claim came from a corporation of rhapsodes or 'singers of stitched verses' from Chios, called the Homeridae. Their name probably originally meant no more than 'assembly-singers' (from the Greek word *homaris*, assembly). However, by the sixth century the Homeridae were claiming to be the descendants of a blind Chiot poet called 'Homer', author of the *Iliad*, the *Odyssey*, and several shorter hymns to Greek deities. Although the poet's Chiot origins were soon being fiercely disputed by a dozen or more cities, the name stuck.

It was in this same period that Homer, as we must now call him, achieved a canonical position in Greek culture. At the end of the sixth century the philosopher Xenophanes of Colophon complained that Homer's false ideas about the gods had become universally accepted, since the *Iliad* and *Odyssey* formed the basis of everyone's education. In about 520 BC recitations of the Homeric poems were made a regular feature of the festival of the Greater Panathenaea at Athens. Unfortunately, the existing poems had embarrassingly little to say about the Athenians, aside from a passing mention in the catalogue of the Greek fleet in the second book of the *Iliad*. This omission was rectified by means of a few judicious additions to Homer's text, describing the cult of Erechtheus on the Athenian Acropolis, praising the Athenian leader Menestheus, and claiming that the force from the island of Salamis fought alongside the Athenian contingent. This last addition is particularly telling. In the eighth and seventh centuries, Salamis had belonged first to the larger island-state of Aegina, and subsequently to the Athenians' neighbours, the Megarians; it was not until the mid-sixth century that Salamis was incorporated into the Athenian state. At a time when the Athenians' claim to Salamis was controversial at best, it was highly desirable to be able to show that the islanders had fought alongside the Athenians in the Trojan War.

The co-option of Homer for nationalist purposes is an important step in the creation of a communal past for themselves by the developing citizen-states of the Greek mainland. At the start of this chapter, we looked at the earliest stages of *polis*-formation in mainland Greece. We saw that one of the signs of the emergence of a new *polis*-identity at Eretria in the early seventh century was the transformation of a lavish private tomb-complex at Eretria into a public cult site: even as the Dark Age kings of Eretria faded into the past, the Eretrians took pains to preserve the memory of those past rulers as part of their common civic identity. A similar process of public 'memorialization' can be seen developing in many other parts of the Greek world at this period. The late eighth century had seen a sharp increase in the number of offerings being made at Mycenaean chamber and tholos tombs, particularly in Attica and the southern and eastern Peloponnese. In several cases we can be confident that it was entire communities, rather than isolated individuals, which chose to honour the resting places of their ancestors. So around 625 BC, when a fairly ordinary group of 'geometric' tombs was uncovered by

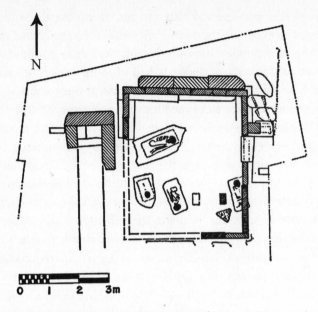

Figure 14. Sacred enclosure ('hero-shrine') around 'geometric' graves in the *agora* of Corinth, *c.* 625 BC

building work in the *agora* of Corinth, the graves were immediately ringed with a sacred enclosure and made the centre of a cult (see Figure 14). The emergence of communal hero-cults of this kind is an early marker of a sense of collective *polis*-identity. These anonymous heroes were understood to be the ancestors not of individual elite families, but of the whole political community.

In a few cases, Bronze Age remains were positively associated with particular figures from the mythical past. The case of Sparta, in the far south of the Peloponnesian peninsula, is particularly interesting. In the late eighth century BC the Mycenaean palace site of Therapne near Sparta, which had been derelict for almost 500 years, began to attract small dedications, initially placed directly on and among the ruins. The mid-seventh century saw the construction at Therapne of a monumental stone hero-shrine to Helen and Menelaus, the husband and wife whose separation had sparked the Trojan War. The Spartans of the eighth and seventh centuries evidently identified the ruins of Mycenaean Therapne with the palace of the hero Menelaus.

At first sight it seems rather paradoxical that the Spartans should have been so keen to assert their connections to Menelaus and Helen.

Menelaus was the grandson of Pelops, the mythical hero who had given his name to the Peloponnese (literally, 'island of Pelops'). The Spartans themselves were generally believed to have been responsible for extinguishing the Pelopid line. According to Sparta's own account of its past, as recorded by the Spartan poet Tyrtaeus in the seventh century BC, the Spartans originated in Erineos, a city far to the north in the central Greek region of Doris. In the generation after the Trojan War, the descendants of Heracles, the Heracleidae, were said to have appealed to the Dorians to help restore them to their rightful place as rulers of the Peloponnese. According to this story, the Dorians had successfully invaded the Peloponnese, killing or expelling the last Pelopid king of Sparta, Tisamenus, son of Orestes, and installing the Heracleidae in his place. The kings of Sparta were understood to be the linear descendants of the Heracleidae, and the rest of the Spartans to be the descendants of their Dorian supporters.

Whether or not this story reflects a historical 'Dorian migration' of the late Bronze Age (above, pp. 63–7), it is clear that the Spartans collectively saw themselves as post-Trojan War immigrants. Nonetheless, the Spartans also vigorously identified with the old, pre-Dorian dynasties of the Peloponnese. In the mid-sixth century BC a Spartan visitor to the central Peloponnesian city of Tegea fortuitously discovered what he believed to be the tomb of Orestes, the son of Agamemnon, upon which the bones were promptly repatriated to Sparta. The bones of Orestes' son Tisamenus were also uncovered by sixth-century Spartan archaeologists, at Helice in the northern Peloponnese. By returning the bones of their mythical precursors to their Spartan homeland, the Spartans were emphatically asserting continuity between the pre-Dorian Pelopid dynasty and their own present-day political community.

The interesting point is that we can see the Spartans defining their communal identity in two alternative ways. In one context, they could choose to emphasize their specifically Spartan identity, as a community rooted in a particular territory in the Peloponnese. As inhabitants of Sparta, they were heirs to the Pelopid kings of the heroic past, and made offerings to local Trojan War heroes like Menelaus and Orestes. In another context, they could emphasize their Dorian identity, as part of a wider ethnic group beyond the bounds of the Peloponnese. Their kinship ties with the Dorians of central Greece had a political reality: in 457 BC the Spartans sent a major expedition to Doris to protect their kinsmen from aggression by their Phocian neighbours. Ethnic and territorial identities were not exclusive.

However, and rather unexpectedly, there is one aspect of collective identity missing from all this: the Spartans' sense of being Spartan and of being Dorian is not accompanied by a sense of being Hellenes, being 'Greek'. Nor is there much sign in the Homeric poems of a positive concept of Greekness. For Homer, the geographical term Hellas refers to a small region in the Spercheios river valley in central Greece, and the Achaeans of the *Iliad* are not sharply ethnically or linguistically distinguished from the Trojans. It was only in the early sixth century that we find the first hints of a wider Hellenic self-consciousness. An anonymous poem of the early sixth century, the *Catalogue of Women*, argued that the various ethnic groups inhabiting Greece – Dorians, Aeolians, Ionians, Achaeans – were all descendants of a mythical king, Hellen. But the clearest evidence of this emerging 'Panhellenic' identity comes from the world of international athletics.

The most important inter-regional sanctuary in the Greek world was the sanctuary of Zeus at Olympia, in the far western Peloponnese. The development of Olympia was slow; since the sanctuary was not under the control of any one *polis*, there was little incentive for anyone to invest in monumental architecture at the site. Since the eighth century BC Olympia had played host to regular athletic contests, the origins of which are marked by a steep increase in the number of bronze tripods dedicated at Olympia (if their interpretation as victory dedications is correct). The participants seem initially to have been local aristocrats, but competitors were soon coming from further afield. Then, in the early sixth century, three major developments occurred at around the same time.

First, three new international athletic festivals were instituted between 582 and 573 BC, the Pythian games at Delphi, the Nemean games at Cleonae, and the Isthmian games at Corinthian Isthmia. A formal four-year festival cycle was set in place: Olympic games in Year One, Pythian games in Year Three, and Isthmian and Nemean games in Years Two and Four. The Olympics, too, were probably reorganized and set on a more official footing at this point. Secondly, the nature of participation at the Olympic games underwent a subtle shift. Whereas previously athletes had competed for individual glory and prestige in the eyes of their aristocratic peers, both at home and in neighbouring cities, from the early sixth century we start to see athletes competing on behalf of their home cities. The entire political community began to have an interest in their *polis*'s fortunes at the Olympic games. By the early fifth century BC, and perhaps earlier, participation in the games was restricted to Greeks. Thirdly, the early sixth century marks the beginnings of monumental architecture at Olympia. The construction of the first stone temple at the site, dedicated to the goddess Hera, was swiftly followed by lavish stone treasuries paid for by the cities of Sybaris, Metapontum, Gela, Sicyon, Epidamnus, Selinous, Cyrene and Megara, built in order to house those cities' various Olympic dedications. The simultaneous decision by several Greek cities to start investing heavily in Olympia reflects the cities' increasing sense of being part of a wider Greek community, stretching from Sicily to the western coast of Asia Minor.

It is hard to say how far this growing sense of 'Greekness' was influenced by the emergence of a new and threatening power on the eastern horizons of the Greek world. In the late seventh and sixth centuries BC the political order in the Near East had undergone revolutionary changes. Between 616 and 608 BC the Assyrian empire was overwhelmed by an alliance between the Babylonians and a semi-nomadic tribal group from north-west Iran, the Medes. Assyrian imperial territory in the fertile crescent was inherited by Babylon, while the Medes established a fragile hegemony in western Iran and eastern Anatolia. Among the west-Iranian tribes within the Median orbit were the Persians, an initially obscure nomadic group inhabiting the modern province of Fars in south-western Iran. In 550 BC the Persian king Cyrus successfully rebelled against Median dominance, capturing the Median capital of Ecbatana in the same year. Persian expansion was astonishingly swift. The year 547 BC saw the conquest of the Anatolian peninsula, including the Greek states of the western Asia Minor coast. In 539 the short-lived Neo-Babylonian kingdom fell, and by the late 530s Persian rule had been extended into eastern Iran and Afghanistan. After Cyrus' death fighting the nomadic tribes of the central Asian steppe, his son Cambyses launched a simultaneous land and sea invasion of Egypt. By 525 BC the Persians had taken possession of an empire stretching from the Nile to the Hindu Kush. Cambyses was eventually succeeded by a usurper from another Persian noble clan, Darius the Achaemenid; the new Achaemenid royal line lasted until the fall of the Persian empire in 330 BC. In the course of his long reign (522–486 BC), Darius extended the eastern and western boundaries of the empire still further, conquering

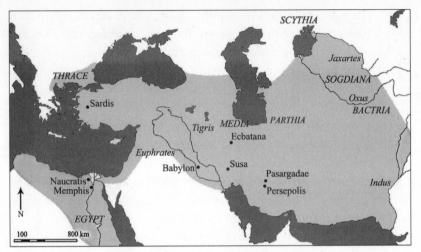

Map 15. The Persian empire *c.* 500 BC

the Indus valley and much of modern Bulgaria (ancient Thrace).

The Great King carried the title 'King of countries of all kinds of people'. The Persians never pretended that their realm was anything other than a dizzying kaleidoscope of different cultural groups. Nor did they make any attempt to impose a uniform culture or system of government on their subjects. The empire was divided into a number of provinces or satrapies, governed by Persian satraps, usually relatives or dependants of the Great King. The routine business of administration and government was delegated to pre-existing local elites, tied to the satrapal court through reciprocal gift exchange. So long as these elites, which in the Ionian Greek cities took the form of tyrant dynasties, could guarantee the regular payment of tribute, the satrap interfered very little in native affairs.

One of the most striking images of the cultural pluralism inherent in the Persian conception of empire comes from Darius' royal palace at Persepolis, near modern Shiraz in south-western Iran. The central building in the Persepolis palace-complex is a vast columned hall known as the Apadana, usually interpreted as an audience chamber in which the King received foreign delegations. The north and east porches of the Apadana are accessed by long shallow staircases, decorated with panels of relief sculpture depicting delegations from each of the twenty-four different subject peoples of the empire. Each delegation wears highly distinctive local dress, and brings a tributary offering characteristic of their native country: so the Parthian ambassadors are shown bringing a two-humped

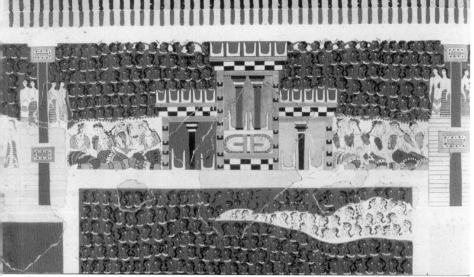

1. Reconstruction of miniature fresco from Knossos (central section), *c*.1600 BC (p.20). Tripartite shrine in the middle, flanked by seated women, and above and below, massed heads of men, both perhaps watching a ceremony such as bull-leaping in the Central Court of the palace.

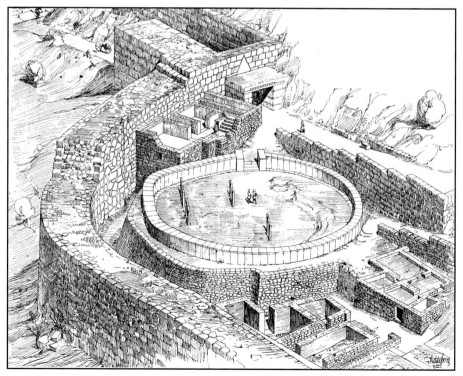

2. Restoration drawing of Grave Circle A at Mycenae, in the thirteenth century BC. The grave circle has upright slabs marking the graves, and two people for scale. The new fortification wall runs to its left, up to the Lion Gate (p. 25).

3. A bard singing of the past, on a fresco from Pylos, shortly before 1200 BC (pp. 24–5).

4. An archaeologist investigates bronze ingots on the wreck of a Bronze Age ship that sank at Uluburun, south–west Turkey, shortly before 1300 BC (p. 38).

5. The Pharaoh Ramesses III, standing on eight captive Sea Peoples, symbolically dominates the victory of his fleet over that of the Sea Peoples (p. 57). Below, captive Sea Peoples are led off to his victory celebrations. This scene was carved on the outside north wall of his mortuary temple at Medinet Habu, opposite Thebes, 1186 BC.

6. Corinthian perfume bottle in 'Orientalizing' style, with the head of a lion, and scenes below of seventeen men fighting and of a horse race and hare hunt, *c.* 640 BC (pp. 82–3).

_____1cm

7. Gold pendant, with skilful granulation, from the woman's grave in the Toumba building, Lefkandi. An heirloom from Syria, dating to *c.* 1700 BC, 750 years old when buried *c.* 950 BC (p. 48).

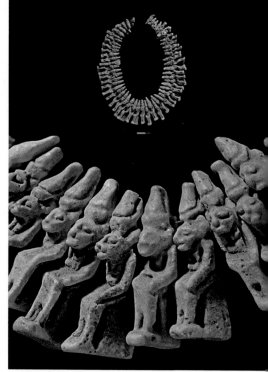

8. Necklace of figurines in faience (a glass-like material) from grave dating to *c.* 900 BC, just east of the Toumba building, Lefkandi (p. 50). Below is a detail of the necklace showing the figurines in the form of a seated lion-headed goddess wearing the double crown of Egypt. This is a Phoenician conflation of two different Egyptian goddesses: Isis and Hathor.

9 and 10. Statue of a young woman, dedicated on the Athenian Acropolis *c.* 530 BC. On the left, the marble statue, with traces of paint; on the right, a restored cast, painted in original colours (p. 85).

11. Reconstruction of life-size bronze statues of Harmodius and Aristogeiton, the slayers of the Athenian tyrant in 514 BC, a commemorated in the Athenian agora in 476 BC (p. 130).

12. A Centaur, already wounded in his back, tries in vain to escape a Lapith, on a panel from the Parthenon, c. 440 BC (p. 116).

13. The contents of the tomb of a Celtic queen from Vix (central France), *c.* 500 BC (p. 97). She was buried in a wagon (reconstructed on the right), with lavish imported objects. The Greek bronze vessel, perhaps for mead, stands 1.64 metres high.

14. Bibracte (Mont Beuvray, in central France) seen from the air (pp. 233–4). In the late second and first centuries BC, the site extended over the now heavily wooded hills in the centre.

15. Celtic bronze shield, *c.* 350-50 BC, found in the river Thames at Battersea Bridge, London. The three bosses each have nine roundels, each with red 'enamel' inlay. The design, with its swinging lines, is characteristically Celtic (p. 164).

16. Statue of a Dying Gaul, marked by a torque round his neck and an un-Greek moustache, lying on a shield, trumpet and sword. Roman copy of a Hellenistic statue, probably set up at Pergamum by an Attalid king in the late third or early second century BC (cf. p. 167).

Bactrian camel (the chief draught animal of the central Asian steppe), while the Indians carry small vessels, probably containing spices or gold dust (see Figure 15). Below each of the four corners of the Apadana were buried silver and gold inscribed plaques, naming the four corners of Darius' empire: from the Scythians of the central Asian steppe to Ethiopia, from India to the Lydians of western Asia Minor. Along with these plaques were placed symbolic deposits of luxury goods from each of the four corners of the world, although only those from the far north-west of the empire survive (a handful of silver and gold coins from Lydia and Ionia).

The Persepolis Apadana presents a vision of a universal Persian Commonwealth of Nations, a world of diverse cultures and customs united around the person of the Great King. Even at the very heart of the empire, in Iran and Mesopotamia, Persian art and architecture consciously and deliberately reflect this diversity. The royal palaces themselves are architectural hybrids, mingling styles and techniques from various subject cultures. A long building-inscription from Susa, in southern Mesopotamia, proudly emphasizes the far-flung origins of the specialist craftsmen who contributed to the construction of Darius' palace at Susa: 'The stone-cutters who worked the stone were Ionians and Lydians; the goldsmiths who worked the gold were Medes and Egyptians; the men who worked the baked bricks were Babylonians.'

Figure 15. Foreign delegations from the Apadana reliefs at Persepolis. Above: Parthians bringing vessels and a two-humped Bactrian camel; below: Indians bringing battleaxes, a mule, and vessels containing spices or gold dust.

Not all of the Great King's subjects appreciated his multicultural aspirations. The Ionian Greek cities of western Asia Minor, far from being economically exploited by an imperial power, were flourishing under Persian rule. Since the seventh century BC the Ionians had enjoyed a profitable trade in luxury goods with the Saïte dynasty of Egypt, thanks to the existence of a communal Ionian trading post at Naucratis in the Nile delta; after 525 BC this trade received a welcome stimulus from the incorporation of Egypt into the Persian empire. Nonetheless, despite these economic benefits, the Persian-backed tyrannical regimes in Ionia were deeply unpopular, particularly since several of the Ionian cities had enjoyed democratic constitutions before the Persian conquest. In 499 BC the Ionian Greeks revolted from Persia with the support of two of the mainland Greek cities, Athens and Eretria. The revolt soon spread to the island of Cyprus, and in the first year of the uprising the Persian satrapal capital in the west, Sardis, was sacked. But once Darius mobilized his Phoenician war-fleet, the Greeks stood little chance. In 494 the Ionian revolt was summarily crushed, and the rebellious cities subjected to horrific reprisals. Miletus, the most populous city of Ionia and the glory of the east Greek world, was wiped off the map: its women and children were enslaved, and the surviving men deported to the Persian gulf.

Next it would be the turn of the Ionians' mainland Greek allies. A punitive seaborne raid in 490 BC succeeded in torching the city of Eretria, although the Athenians successfully repelled a Persian landing on the coastal plain of Marathon. But this minor Greek victory did little more than postpone the inevitable. Over the following few years, along the northern shore of the Aegean, a broad military road was carved out of the landscape, stretching westward from Persian-held Thrace to the borders of mainland Greece. Finally, in 481 BC Darius' successor Xerxes gave the order for a huge Persian army to muster in eastern Asia Minor.

In the mid-sixth century, looking back with satisfaction to the long-vanished empire of the Assyrians, the poet Phocylides of Miletus had written that 'a small and well-governed *polis*, perched on a rock, is greater than senseless Nineveh'. Now, for the first time, that defiant maxim was going to be put to the test.

4

Greece, Europe and Asia:
480–334 BC

Between the Aegean and the Sea of Marmora runs a narrow strait, in places little more than a kilometre wide. This slender strip of water, dividing the Gallipoli peninsula from the main Turkish landmass, was known to the Greeks as the Hellespont. At the narrowest point of the straits, facing one another across the continental divide, lay the Greek cities of Sestos and Abydos. The Greeks said that a young man from Abydos, Leander, had once loved the priestess of Aphrodite at Sestos, Hero. Every night, Leander would swim the straits between the two cities, guided by a lamp burning in Hero's tower. One night, a storm arose, and Hero's lamp was blown out; Leander lost his way in the ocean and was drowned, and Hero is said to have thrown herself from her tower in grief.

Byron at the Hellespont

On 3 May 1810 the 22-year-old Lord Byron swam the Hellespont between Sestos and Abydos in a self-conscious imitation of Leander's nightly journeys. It took him an hour and ten minutes, and the currents were so tiring that he wondered whether 'Leander's conjugal powers must not have been exhausted in his passage to Paradise'. Byron was at this point some seven months into a seventeen-month trip to Greece and Turkey. In *Don Juan*, Byron recalled the impact made on him as a young man by prolonged contemplation of Greece under Ottoman rule:

> The mountains look at Marathon –
> And Marathon looks on the sea;
> And musing there an hour alone,
> I dream'd that Greece might still be free.

Marathon was a well-chosen backdrop for Byron's musings on the freedom of the Greeks. It was at Marathon, in 490 BC, that the Athenians had successfully repelled the first Persian assault on Greece, foreshadowing the greater victories of 480 (Salamis) and 479 (Plataea). John Stuart Mill went so far as to claim that the battle of Marathon, 'even as an event in English history, is more important than the battle of Hastings'. When the Greek War of Independence broke out in 1821, Byron instantly attached himself to the Greek cause, and in January 1824, he travelled in person to Missolonghi, the centre of Greek resistance to the Ottomans in the Adriatic.

At first sight, Byron's contribution to the success of the Greek War of Independence does not look especially impressive. During his three and a half months' stay at Missolonghi in 1824 he never saw action, and the sum total of his military leadership was an abortive attempt to raise a private army to capture the Ottoman fortress of Lepanto in the gulf of Corinth (a plan with romantic associations: it was at Lepanto, in 1571, that a Spanish, Venetian and Genoan fleet had first won a decisive naval victory over the Ottomans). Nonetheless, the talismanic importance of Byron's presence in Greece can hardly be overstated. Byron was at the time the most famous poet in Europe, and his death at Missolonghi of fever in April 1824 focused European attention on the Greek cause more effectively than any Turkish atrocities could have done. Byron is still today a Greek national hero; there are few Greek towns which do not have a street named after him.

On a winter's day late in 479 BC, a Persian was nailed to a cross on the European shore of the Hellespont. The sea below was thick with Greek warships, fresh from the liberation of Sestos, the Persians' main garrison-town in the region. The crucifixion of Artayctes, the unfortunate Persian governor of the town, was an act heavy with symbolism. Two years earlier, the Persian king Xerxes had led a vast army across those same straits, with the aim of annexing the entire Greek peninsula to the Persian empire. To transport his army across the Hellespont, the Great King had lashed the two shores together with a bridge of boats. As Xerxes marched on into Europe, Artayctes had given the local Greeks a memorable lesson in Persian power by plundering the tomb of a local Greek who had dared to attack the Great King's territory. This Greek was the hero Protesilaus, whose tomb stood at Elaeus on the tip of the Gallipoli peninsula. According to Homer, Protesilaus had been the first man to fall in the Trojan War, killed as he leaped ashore onto the coast of the Troad.

Xerxes' invasion of Greece was a humiliating failure. Late in the summer of 480 BC, an Athenian-led fleet of 310 ships crippled the Persian navy – probably twice the size of the Greek fleet – in a huge engagement off the island of Salamis. The following year, Xerxes' land army was decisively beaten by an enormous Greek coalition force (some 40,000 infantrymen) at the battle of Plataea. Even before the defeat of Xerxes' army in Greece, an allied Greek fleet had sailed east to take the war into the King's own territory in western Asia Minor. On the very same day as the battle of Plataea, the subject Greeks of Ionia won their independence with a crushing victory over Persian forces in the foothills of Mt. Mycale, just north of Miletus. After the liberation of Ionia, the Greek fleet sailed north to the Hellespont to destroy Xerxes' bridge of boats, only to find that the bridge had already been broken up. After the capture of Sestos, and the brutal execution of its Persian governor, the chariot of the Great King himself was found lying on its side, abandoned in a field near the straits. No Persian King would ever attempt a campaign in the west on such a scale again.

The execution of Artayctes makes a sombre end to the Persian Wars. His cross, overlooking the straits where the bridge of boats had stood, was a mute reminder of the hubris of the Great King, the man who had attempted to yoke two continents together. Protesilaus was avenged. As the Greeks reflected on their extraordinary victory over the Persians, the first time that so many Greek states had combined against a common enemy, the parallels with the Trojan War began to seem ever more striking. Both wars had seen an allied Greek force unite to fight against non-Greeks; both times, first at Troy and now in the heart of Greece itself, the Greeks had won.

It is perhaps not surprising that the Greeks began to entertain the idea of a primordial division of the world into two opposing halves. In the early fifth century, the first attempt at universal geography, the *Journey Round the World* of Hecataeus of Miletus, was divided into two books, the first on 'Europe', the second on 'Asia'. Hecataeus pictured the inhabited world as a circular disc, encircled by the outer ocean. This disc was

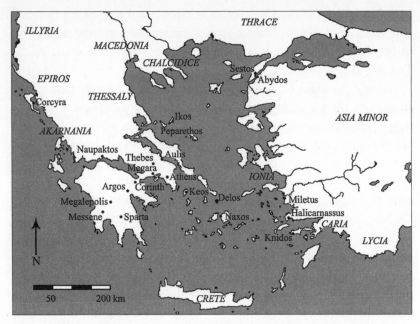

Map 16. The Aegean world in the fifth and fourth centuries BC.

divided into two equal halves, Europe and Asia, separated from one another by a single band of water, the Mediterranean and the Black Sea, linked by the Hellespont. In 449 BC, when the Athenians inflicted another crushing defeat on the Persian naval and land forces at the island of Cyprus, the Athenian victory monument claimed that no greater victory had occurred 'since the ocean divided off Europe from Asia'. Two years later the Athenians began work on a huge new treasury of the goddess Athena on the Acropolis, the building known to us as the Parthenon. The sculpted panels (metopes) on the four sides of the building, fourteen of which are now in the British Museum, pitted Greeks against Amazons, Greeks stood Trojans, the Olympian gods against the giants, and Greek Lapiths against Centaurs (see Plate 12). The message could not be clearer. Greece stood on one side of a vast cultural divide: order against chaos, civilization against savagery, male against female, west against east. An anonymous medical treatise of the late fifth century, *Airs, Waters, Places*, later attributed to the physician Hippocrates, explicitly argued that Europeans and Asiatics were biologically different. Since Asia has a milder climate than Europe, with fewer extremes of temperature, its inhabitants too are softer and gentler by nature than Europeans. The very fact of living in Asia renders them feebler, less courageous and more liable to despotic government. The Greeks began to apply a single term for all those unfortunate enough to live in the inferior, Asiatic half of the world: *barbaroi*, the 'barbarians'.

The most sustained attack on this crude ethnic dualism came, unsurprisingly, from a Greek native of the Asia Minor coast. 'Herodotus of Halicarnassus here presents the results of his enquiry, so that the deeds of men may not be forgotten with the passage of time, and that great and wondrous works, some performed by Greeks, some by barbarians, might not lack renown, and in particular to explain why they fought with one another.' So begins Herodotus' enquiry (the Greek word is *historiē*) into the causes of the Persian Wars. In the mid-fifth century BC Herodotus travelled extensively throughout the Mediterranean world and the western half of the Persian empire. By combining oral accounts of the past with his own observation of surviving monuments, natural phenomena and local customs, he produced a prose narrative of unprecedented length, intellectual depth and explanatory power. Herodotus' *Histories*, which reached its final form in the 420s BC, has a far more ambitious aim than simply describing the progress of hostilities between the Greek world and Persia. It is true that it concludes with a detailed and thrilling account of Xerxes' invasion of Greece. But much of the first half of the work consists of long ethnographical essays on the history and customs of the various 'barbarian' races on the fringes of the Greek world: Lydians, Persians, Babylonians, Egyptians, Scythians and Libyans. To the modern reader, these essays can look like digressions from Herodotus' main theme. In fact, they are central to it. In the course of his long ethnographic description of Egypt, Herodotus casually remarks that the Egyptians use the term 'barbarian' for anyone who does not speak their language. Unlike most of his contemporaries, Herodotus was well aware that 'barbarian' is a relative term. One of his major purposes in conducting his enquiries was precisely to combat the crude Eurocentrism which lumped all the non-Greek races together as generic *barbaroi*. In this respect, Herodotus had no successors. No Greek or Roman author would write of non-European peoples with such sympathy and insight again.

Herodotus and the Iroquois

In 1724, Joseph-François Lafitau, a Jesuit missionary from Bordeaux, published a huge two-volume work on the *Customs of the American Savages, Compared with the Customs of the Earliest Times*. The book was based on observations collected during six years' work as a missionary to the Iroquois at Caughnawaga, near Montreal on the St Lawrence river, between 1712 and 1717. Lafitau was by no means the first to attempt an ethnology of the 'savages' of the New World, but, thanks in large part to the influence of Herodotus, he has some claim to being the father of modern ethnology.

In his account of the customs of the Lycians, on the south coast of Asia Minor, Herodotus remarks that the Lycian way of life resembled that of the inhabitants of Crete, where he supposed the Lycians to have originated. 'However, one custom which is peculiar to them, and like nothing to be found anywhere else in the world, is that they take their names from their mothers rather than from their fathers. Suppose someone asks his neighbour who he is: he will describe himself in terms of his mother's ancestry – that is, he will list all the mothers on his mother's side. Also, if a female citizen and a male slave live together as a couple, her children are considered legitimate, whereas if a male citizen, even one of the highest rank, marries a woman from another country or a concubine, his children have no rights of citizenship.' Lafitau accurately observed that Iroquois society, too, was matrilineal: the order of succession lay in the female line, and women had a strikingly prominent role in Iroquois decision-making processes. Lafitau thus conjectured that the Iroquois, like the Lycians, were descended from a hypothetical original group of pre-Greek inhabitants of the Aegean, whose society, Lafitau argued, in contrast with that of the Classical Greeks, was matriarchal.

It is to arguments of this kind – mistaken though they were – that Lafitau owes his reputation as the founder of comparative ethnology. Earlier ethnographers had simply assumed that the American Indians were the descendants of older and superior European societies. In the customs of the New World savages, they saw nothing more than muddled and degenerate perversions of original Judaeo-Christian religious customs. Lafitau, however, refused to grant automatic priority or cultural superiority to the societies of Christian Europe. Instead, he described the structure of

Iroquois society in its own terms; he then compared Iroquois culture to the earliest European societies known to him, those of the Classical Aegean, in order to make deductions about the customs of what we would now call prehistoric societies. This great leap forward in ethnological method (the idea of 'reciprocal illumination') is unimaginable without the influence of Herodotus' clear-eyed and sympathetic descriptions of the non-Greek peoples of his day.

The choices which each Greek state had made in the face of Xerxes' invasion had a long afterlife. Thebes, in particular, would never live down the stigma of having fought on the Persian side at Plataea, and the Thebans were for ever branded as 'Medizers' (the Greeks seldom bothered to distinguish between Persians and Medes). After the liberation of the Greek cities of Ionia in 479 BC, the Peloponnesians brought forward a proposal for a mass exchange of populations between Greece and Asia. The Ionians would move to the Greek mainland, and occupy the cities of those Greeks who had fought on the wrong side in 480–479. In return, the Medizing Greeks would be shipped to Asia to live under the rule of the Great King. The Athenians, however, strongly opposed the abandonment of the Ionian cities, 'feeling', says Herodotus, 'that the Peloponnesians had no right to decide the fate of Athenian colonists'. As we shall see, this particular claim about the origin of the Ionians was by no means an innocent one.

The war against Persia continued under the auspices of a new naval alliance, the Delian League, under the leadership of the Athenians. The original members of this alliance were those states which had most to fear from Persian reprisals: the Greek cities of western Asia Minor and the Hellespont, and the islanders of the central and eastern Aegean. Allied states were required to make contributions to the war effort in the form of ships, or, if they preferred, in cash. From its very outset, this league had a dual identity. On one level, it had the pragmatic purpose of maintaining Ionian freedom from Persia; contributions in silver were ostensibly in order to fund anti-Persian operations in the east Aegean. But the alliance was also framed in terms of a revival of ancient ties between Athens and the Ionians. The Ionians were believed to have migrated to the eastern Aegean from Attica (above, pp. 64–7), and so the Athenians and Ionians could consider themselves as ancient mythological cousins. Significantly, the League treasury was located on the sacred island of Delos. In earliest times Delos was believed to have been the site of a great festival of all the Ionians, described in the sixth-century *Homeric Hymn to Apollo*; the island was also the birthplace of Apollo, mythological ancestor of all the Ionian peoples. Common Ionian ethnicity was built into the ideology of the league from the outset.

If alliance members had expected the Delian League to be a voluntary association, they were soon disabused of that idea. The first allied state to attempt to leave the league, the island of Naxos, was promptly besieged by an Athenian fleet and, in the words of the Athenian historian Thucydides, 'enslaved'. As the Persians were steadily swept back from the coasts of the Aegean, more and more states were incorporated into the Delian League, including many – Carians, Lycians, Thracians – who were not even Greek, let alone Ionian. By 454 BC at the latest, the League treasury was moved from Delos to Athens. The war with Persia had effectively ceased by 449 BC, when there may have been a formal peace treaty between the Athenians and the Great King. Yet the annual silver contributions continued to be collected just as before; around the same time, the Athenians started referring to the allied states as 'the cities which the Athenians rule'.

Over the seventy-five-year history of the Athenian empire – for so the Delian League had rapidly become – the Athenians developed a sophisticated ideological framework to justify their dominance over large parts of the Greek world. 'We', wrote the Athenian tragedian Euripides in his *Erechtheus*, 'are autochthonous by birth; but other cities, scattered randomly by a throw of the dice, are immigrants from elsewhere.' The Athenians claimed to be the one Greek people who were 'sprung from the soil', always inhabiting the same land since time immemorial. The contrast with the Peloponnesians, recent Dorian immigrants from central Greece, was deliberate and pointed. In earliest times, the Athenians argued, an Athenian mother had borne the mythical figure Ion to the god Apollo. Since Ion was the founding ancestor of the Ionian race, all the cities of Ionia could plausibly be regarded as colonies of Athens.

The Athenians exploited this myth of primordial Athenian colonization to the full. As the universal mother-city of the east Greek world, Athens claimed regular religious offerings from her supposed colonies. Each subject state was required to send a cow and suit of armour to the Greater Panathenaea, the four-yearly 'All-Athenian' festival, as a mark of gratitude.

In the 420s BC the Athenians sent out heralds to all the cities of the Greek world, reminding them that an Athenian, Triptolemus, had been the first to bring the gift of grain to mankind. The tribute-paying states were ordered to send a tithe of their annual grain-harvest to Athens, and the rest of the Greeks were 'invited, though not required' to do likewise. It is unlikely that this invitation went down well in Sparta.

Athenian imperial ideology was based on the understanding that the subject states were all colonies of Athens. Of course, the overwhelming majority were nothing of the sort. As we have seen, several tribute-payers in Thrace and on the south-west coast of Asia Minor were not even Greek. What is interesting about the myth of Athenian colonization is that the Athenians felt the need to justify their empire in terms of the distant past. This way of using the mythological past to assert present-day territorial claims can be seen developing elsewhere in the Greek world during this period. In the early fifth century the Argive plain in the eastern Peloponnese was shared between at least four separate *poleis*: Argos on the western side of the plain, and Mycenae, Tiryns and Midea to the east. The latter three cities worshipped at a common sanctuary of Hera, the Heraion, also on the eastern side of the plain and connected to Mycenae by a Sacred Way. In the early 460s BC an aggressively expansionist Argos destroyed all three of its neighbours, and constructed a new Sacred Way connecting the Heraion directly to Argos, thereby incorporating the whole of the Argive plain into its own territory. In order to justify its activities, Argos promoted a new version of the myth of the return of the sons of Heracles to the Peloponnese (above, p. 107). According to the Argives, once the Heracleidae had reconquered the Peloponnese, the peninsula was divided by lot between the four surviving descendants of Heracles: Kresphontes received Messenia, Sparta went to the two sons of Aristodemos, and Temenos was allotted Argos. In destroying the cities of the eastern Argive plain, the Argives were doing no more than re-establishing the lot of Temenos in its original form. The Heraion was theirs by ancestral right.

By the mid-fifth century the Aegean had essentially become an Athenian lake. This fact cries out for explanation; empires do not happen by accident. Massive Athenian naval dominance is part, though only part, of the answer. Thanks to a furious ship-building programme in the decade before the Persian invasion, the Athenians could draw on a war-fleet of up to 300 triremes, far beyond the resources of any other Greek city. But

Figure 16. The four *poleis* of Keos.

there were also deeper undercurrents favouring Athenian growth. A glance at a map of the Mediterranean is enough to show that the Aegean presents one of the most fragmented landscapes of the European land-mass, characterized by a plethora of tiny islands and rocky peninsulas. This peculiar geography encouraged extreme political fragmentation. It has been calculated that in the year 400 BC the Greek world was home to at least 862 independent city-states or *poleis*, the vast majority of them located in and around the Aegean basin. Most of these individual city-states were extremely small; a *polis* with a population of more than 10,000 was unusual. The island of Keos in the northern Cyclades is fairly typical, with a estimated ancient population of between 4,000 and 6,700, distributed between no fewer than four *poleis* (see Figure 16).

The typical small Aegean island is separated from its immediate neighbours by a few kilometres of sea at most. Contact and exchange between these densely clustered maritime *poleis* was extremely easy; political fragmentation does not mean isolation. The microcellular geography of the Aegean archipelago created ideal conditions for economic specialization within each individual *polis*. So long as it continued to produce enough grain to feed itself, a little island like Keos could concentrate its energies on specializing in acorns or red ochre, secure in the knowledge that olive oil or pumice stone could always be imported from one of its neighbours. The tiny islands of Peparethos and Ikos, in the northern Sporades, produced enough high-quality wine to service a substantial market as far away as the Black Sea. By the fifth century BC these local networks of specialization and exchange were sophisticated enough to support a total Aegean population probably higher than at any other period before the twentieth century. By way of comparison, the highest recorded population for the island of Keos in modern times is a mere 4,900, as recorded in the census of 1896; today, the permanent population is around 2,400.

The fragility of this prosperous network was ruthlessly exploited by Athens. Once a single large state achieved maritime dominance in the Aegean, the extreme fragmentation of the smaller *poleis* became a disastrous liability. No fewer than 248 states are known to have paid tribute to Athens at one time or another during the fifth century. Most of these were tiny communities like the four cities of Keos, which could never have hoped to resist Athenian naval power. The Athenians were thus able to tap into a ready-made system of production and distribution of goods and natural resources. An aggressive Athenian monopoly on Kean red ochre is attested for the revived Athenian empire of the fourth century. Similarly, we can see Athens developing a monopoly in timber imports from the north Aegean littoral; an alliance with the Macedonian king Perdiccas, probably dating to the 430s or 420s BC, stipulated that Macedonian oar-handles were to be exported to Athens only.

In its complexity and sophistication, the fifth-century Athenian empire was unlike any state which had existed in Europe up to this point. There were said to be 700 Athenian officials permanently serving overseas, more than four times as many as would later be sent out to administer the provinces of the entire Roman empire. Multiple copies survive of a decree published in every subject city imposing uniform coins, weights and measures throughout the empire. One aspect of the imperial administration deserves particular emphasis. From 454 BC the Athenians began regularly inscribing their financial records on stone. Every year one-sixtieth of the tribute paid by each allied state was set aside as a tithe for the goddess Athena; annual records of these payments were set up on the Acropolis, on the monumental stone tablets today known (somewhat misleadingly) as the Athenian tribute lists. Simultaneously, the Athenians began recording temple inventories, building accounts, property sales and lists of casualties on stone. Athens was the first state in the Greek world to develop a 'documentary habit' on anything like this scale. The importance of this for the modern historian can hardly be overstated. Thanks to this explosion of documentary evidence, the economic history of Classical Athens can be studied to a level of fine-grained detail unimaginable for any other city-state. Athens' contemporaries, by contrast, can seem almost laughably backward in this respect. The other great power of the Greek world, Sparta, has left us a mere handful of fifth-century inscriptions. One of these shows voluntary allied contributions to the Spartan war-fund being paid in the form of raisins; it seems that Sparta's primitive documentary habits reflected an equally primitive local economy.

By the late 450s, imperial revenues collected from 'the cities which the Athenians rule' were openly being spent on purely Athenian projects. A huge building programme on the Athenian Acropolis was initiated in the 440s BC (see Figure 17). The modern visitor is most likely to be impressed by the Parthenon, a spectacular treasury of the goddess Athena, which effectively served as the central bank of the Athenian imperial state. For the Athenians, the true marvel was the Propylaea, the monumental gatehouse to the Acropolis. Unlike the Parthenon, the Propylaea was a secular building with no particular function. The ability to lavish such expense on a mere gatehouse, albeit one of staggering size and beauty, was itself a stark statement of Athenian wealth and power.

Most important of all, the wealth now pouring into Athens created the conditions for a political revolution within the Athenian state itself. Sixth-century Athens had been a loosely federal commonwealth, with much of the Attic peninsula enjoying virtual independence from the urban centre. Around three-quarters of the population of Attica lived outside the city, in villages and hamlets known as demes. Many of these demes, such as the charcoal-burning town of Acharnae in northern Attica, were large enough that they could have been small city-states in their own right. In the last

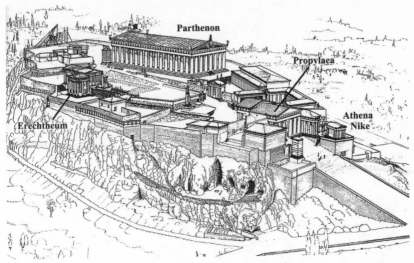

Figure 17. The Athenian Acropolis

decade of the sixth century BC, the Athenian constitution underwent a major overhaul, primarily intended to give the outlying demes a voice in the central *polis*-government. Under the new constitution, drafted by the aristocratic politician Cleisthenes, all major decisions were taken by an assembly open to all adult male Athenian citizens (including inhabitants of the outlying demes). The agenda for the assembly, which met only once or twice a month, was drawn up by a new full-time council of 500, the *boulē*. A fixed quota of elected annual councillors was assigned to each deme in proportion to its population: the largest deme, Acharnae, sent twenty-two councillors each year, while the smallest hamlets took turns to send a councillor every second year.

The Athenian Acropolis

The Athenian Acropolis is today dominated by four great monuments, rising dramatically out of the bare rock: the Parthenon, the Erechtheum, the Propylaea, and the temple of Athena Nikē, all four of them constructed between 447 and 407 BC. It would be all too easy to suppose that the modern Acropolis preserves an unspoiled and changeless image of the Acropolis of the late fifth century BC. But the Acropolis which we see today is essentially a reinvention of the 1830s. In the early nineteenth century the Acropolis was a densely occupied garrison-village, its ancient monuments overlaid with medieval and modern buildings: the shell of the Parthenon housed a small eighteenth-century mosque, built on top of the ruins of a larger mosque of the 1460s, itself a converted Byzantine church. In the early years of Greek independence from Ottoman rule, it was decided to 'restore' the Acropolis to its pristine Classical form, as a symbol of the national identity of the newly revived Greek state. Over the next fifty years, everything more recent than the fifth century BC was methodically scraped off the surface of the Acropolis: the existing hilltop village, the remains of the Parthenon mosque and a fourteenth-century Florentine tower built into the corner of the Propylaea were all demolished. By the 1890s the excavator could claim to have 'delivered the Acropolis back to the civilized world, cleansed of all barbaric additions, a noble monument to the Greek genius'. From a different perspective, the modern Athenian Acropolis could be seen as an extraordinary act of cultural forgetfulness: in attempting to forge a link between the modern Greek state and the Classical Greek past, the nineteenth-century Greeks violently erased the entire intervening two millennia of Macedonian, Roman, Byzantine, Frankish-Florentine and Turkish rule.

All this is in marked contrast with the behaviour of the fifth-century Athenians. At the time they were built, the Acropolis monuments were carefully fitted in around much older buildings. One corner of the Propylaea is cut off so as not to disturb a short stretch of Mycenaean fortification wall at the western end of the Acropolis (see Figure 18): even though this stretch of wall was rendered invisible by the construction of the Propylaea, the fifth-century Athenians could not bear to damage this modest survival from their heroic past. The temple of Athena Nikē stands on top of a monumental bastion, faced on all sides with smooth ashlar marble blocks, constructed in the 440s BC; buried in the heart of this bastion, a sixth-century altar to the same goddess was lovingly preserved in its original location.

The Cleisthenic constitution had set in place for the first time a truly representative framework for Athenian political activity. However, for the first fifty years of the new constitution, the participation of poorer

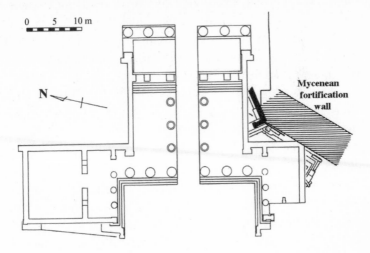

Figure 18. The Propylaea, with the corner of the south-west wing of the gatehouse cut off to accommodate a stretch of Mycenaean fortification wall.

Athenian citizens in politics was limited by the state's inability to pay its officials. Since an entire year's service without pay as a councillor was financially unthinkable for most Athenians, political activity remained, as before, in the hands of a relatively small number of wealthy families. Around the middle of the fifth century the revenues of empire began to be diverted towards daily salaries for councillors, public officials and, eventually, assembly attendees. At the same time, in a stroke of extraordinary boldness, election to public office was abolished, and public officials and councillors began to be appointed by lot from all Athenian citizens. Tenure of office was limited to one year. As a result, probably as many as half of all male Athenians over the age of 30 were required to take their turn on the city's advisory council.

The breadth of political participation under the Athenian radical democracy is unparalleled in world history. Yet in many respects, the Athenian constitution was far more restricted than any modern European democracy. Women had no political role of any kind, though they were recognized as Athenian citizens for the purposes of marriage and childbearing (in order to qualify for citizenship, a boy had to be of Athenian citizen parentage on both sides). In law, women were perpetual minors, unable to own property or represent themselves in court. If a man died without leaving male heirs, the law required that his daughters be promptly married off to their closest male relatives, in order that their father's property should stay within the extended (male) family. Of course, total seclusion was impracticable for most Athenian households: a daughter was an extra pair of hands, and as the fourth-century philosopher Aristotle remarks in his *Politics*, it was impossible to stop the wives of the poor going out of doors. But it is the Athenian ideal which is revealing here. It is clear from Athenian literature and vase-painting that the ideal Athenian woman was silent, obedient, good at sewing, and pasty-faced from permanent seclusion indoors. The assertive heroines of Athenian tragic drama – Medea, Antigone, Clytemnestra – are effective and shocking precisely because they deviate from these norms.

The world of Athenian civic religion is at first sight a partial exception to this rule. The chief deity of Athens, Athena Polias, was female, and as such (in accordance with normal Greek religious practice) was served by a female priestess and attendants. In Athens, as in other Greek cities, there was a major annual religious festival restricted to women only, the Thesmophoria. The festival had its own female officials, and although women were not officially regarded as deme-members, the various Athenian demes were represented at the Thesmophoria by the wives of fellow-demesmen. Women even seem to have gathered and held assembly-meetings at the sanctuary of Demeter in Athens, in a kind of female mirror-image of the male assembly. However, the Thesmophoria is perhaps best regarded as a classic 'role-reversal' festival, like the Saturnalia at Rome, in which slaves played at being masters for the day. Similarly, at the Thesmophoria, women were granted exceptional licence, and got to play out male roles for the three days of the festival; once the festival was over, the normal gender roles were reasserted.

It is a striking fact that women were considerably worse off in Classical Athens than in most other parts of the Greek world. For example, a fifth-century law-code from Gortyn on Crete shows that Gortynian women could own and inherit property, marry and divorce with relative freedom, and even have free children by a male slave. Similarly, Spartan women enjoyed legal rights and a degree of social liberty which horrified Athenian observers; by the late fourth century two-fifths of Spartan land was said to be owned by women.

We are left with the paradox that the most egalitarian state in the Greek world was also one of the most repressive in its treatment of women. The explanation may lie in the unusually high value placed on citizenship under the radical democracy. In most Greek *poleis*, as in sixth-century Athens and most other societies in history, social status was determined by wealth. With the opening up of political activity to every adult Athenian male, the only significant status distinction became that between the citizen and the non-citizen. As the gulf between rich and poor was closed, above all through the practice of allotment to public office, the gulf between citizens and non-citizens widened. Those classes in society, like women, who were excluded from the citizenship, thus found themselves worse off than they would have been in a less democratic society. Similarly, it seems that the slave population of Athens increased dramatically in the fifth century BC, as paid labour on another man's behalf came to be seen as unworthy of a citizen.

All that said, the Athenian democracy still strikes us as a radically new and progressive form of constitutional government. The Athenians would have found this a deeply alarming idea. In pretty much any given context, the Athenians liked to believe that they were acting *kata ta patria*, 'according to ancestral custom'. Reform, to the Athenian way of thinking, was something to be resisted as a matter of principle. It is, paradoxically, a measure of the success of Cleisthenes' reforms that the man himself was instantly erased from popular memory. Once the new Cleisthenic system was successfully in place, the Athenians cheerfully claimed that they were not reforms at all, but long-standing elements of their ancestral constitution. By the mid-fifth century at the latest, the incorporation of the rural demes into the Athenian state was attributed to the hero Theseus, slayer of the Minotaur, whose conquest of Attica was commemorated in a new 'Festival of Unification', the Synoikia.

An even more striking example of this retrojection of the new constitution into the distant past is the case of the ten eponymous heroes. As part of the Cleisthenic reform package, the Athenians had been divided into ten new tribes, each named after a national hero of the distant Athenian past: Cecrops, Acamas, Ajax and others. These tribes were entirely artificial and homogeneous in composition, each consisting of three clusters of villages, one from the coast, one from the inland district, and one from the plain of Athens itself. Nonetheless, the tribes and their tribal heroes rapidly developed a central role in Athenian religious life. Statues of the ten eponymous heroes were set up in the Athenian *agora*, and the ten heroes received regular sacrifices as the mythological founders and ancestors of their respective tribes. The Athenians clearly saw nothing incongruous in treating these thoroughly modern political units as if they were kinship groups of the deepest antiquity. Conversely, any practice which could plausibly be described as 'ancestral' was entirely immune from democratic reform. When new priesthoods were established, such as the priestess of the cult of Athena Nikē in the 440s BC, they were duly appointed on democratic principles (by lot from all Athenian citizens). However, we have not a single case of such principles being imposed on a pre-existing cult. The most important sacred official in Athens, the priestess of Athena Polias – by far the most prominent and authoritative female figure in the Classical Athenian *polis* – continued to be appointed from the members of a single aristocratic clan, the Eteoboutadae, as late as the second century AD.

Perhaps most telling of all, in the Athenian popular mind-set, the establishment of the Cleisthenic democracy in the late sixth century was rapidly elided with the fall of the tyranny of the Peisistratids. Since the mid-sixth century BC political life at Athens had been dominated by the Peisistratid family, who dominated public affairs and ensured that the major annual magistracies were always held by their friends and dependants. In 514 BC, a member of the Peisistratid clan, Hipparchus, brother of the tyrant Hippias, was murdered by two Athenian lovers, Harmodius and Aristogeiton, as a result of a private quarrel. Four years later, in 510 BC, the tyranny of Hippias was at last overthrown, thanks to a Spartan invasion of Attica; it was not until 508 or 507 that the constitutional reforms of Cleisthenes were set in motion. For fifth-century Athenians, the story of the fall of the tyranny and the establishment of representative government was annoyingly unheroic: the tyrants themselves had been expelled by the Spartans, and the new constitution – or rather, in the Athenians' eyes, the restoration of the elusive 'ancestral constitution' – was the work of an unglamorous aristocratic politician. So the lovers Harmodius and Aristogeiton were quickly elevated to the role of revolutionary tyrannicides; it was they, not the Spartans, who had ended tyranny at Athens, thereby re-establishing the traditional Athenian democracy. Hero cult was paid to the two men, and they received the unique honour of a pair of bronze statues in the Athenian *agora*, the only statues of historical Athenians to be set up in the *agora* throughout the entire Classical period (see Plate 11). As the lyrics of a wildly popular fifth-century drinking song have it, 'I shall carry my sword in a branch of myrtle, like Harmodius and Aristogeiton, when they killed the tyrant and made Athens equal before the law.' This popular myth of the Athenian 'tyrannicides' – already debunked by Thucydides in the late fifth century – had a long and potent afterlife (below, pp. 228–9).

Relations between the Athenians and their mainland Greek neighbours grew increasingly tense over the course of the fifth century. Relations with Sparta had been irreparably damaged by a curious diplomatic incident in 462 BC. In the eighth century BC the Spartans had conquered Messenia, the region to the west of Mt. Taygetos in the south-west Peloponnese. The natives of Messenia were reduced to collective slavery, and were known as helots or 'captives'. Spartan prosperity was founded on the ruthless exploitation of the helots, on whom the Spartans ritually declared war every year. In the wake of a devastating earthquake at Sparta in the early 460s BC, the helots rose in revolt, and the Spartans were forced to spend much of the decade engaged in a gritty guerrilla war against their former slaves. In 462 the Spartans called on Athens for help against the rebels. The Athenians sent a large army to Messenia, but on their arrival, the Spartans had a change of heart, and dismissed the Athenian force without explanation, apparently fearing that the Athenians might decide to support the helots after all. As a result of this insult, the Athenians promptly broke off relations with Sparta and struck an alliance with Sparta's main enemy in the Peloponnese, Argos (which we shall return to shortly). When the helot war was eventually brought to an end, the surviving rebels were received by the Athenians, who settled them at Naupaktos, an Athenian dependency on the north shore of the Corinthian gulf. The settlement at Naupaktos was to be a thorn in Sparta's side, and a source of simmering resentment against Athens, for the rest of the century.

Leonidas at Stalingrad

The ethos of Classical Sparta held a particular appeal for the National Socialists of inter-war Germany. Hitler greatly admired the Spartan custom of rejecting and destroying biologically inferior offspring, thereby preserving their pure and essential racial characteristics. As few as 6,000 Spartans, he claimed, had ruled over 350,000 helots (these numbers are, incidentally, wholly fantastic); the German *Volk* was destined to do the same.

In 480 BC, as Xerxes' army swept southwards through central Greece, a force of 300 Spartans under King Leonidas had mounted a heroic and doomed attempt to hold the pass at Thermopylae. On 30 January 1943, with the German Sixth Army encircled at Stalingrad, Goering explicitly compared the defence of Thermopylae with the defence of Stalingrad, in a stirring speech which received wide circulation in Germany. Quoting Simonides' famous epigram on the 300 Spartan war-dead at Thermopylae ('Go tell the Spartans, passerby, / That here, obedient to their laws, we lie'), Goering confidently predicted that the – by now inevitable – German defeat at Stalingrad would in future days be commemorated in similar terms. Simonides' epigram was rewritten for the occasion: 'If you come to Germany, go tell them that you saw us fight at Stalingrad, obedient to the law laid down for the security of the German people.' The response of the German '300' at Stalingrad was sadly disappointing; on 1 February Field-Marshal Paulus, having no desire for a heroic Leonidas-style death, chose instead to surrender himself and the frozen remnants of the Sixth Army to the Russians.

One of the most powerful responses to the Nazi exploitation of Spartan ideology can be found in Heinrich Böll's short story 'Wanderer, kommst du nach Spa . . .', first published in 1950. In the last months of the war, a horrifically wounded young German soldier is brought to an improvised field-hospital near the front line, at Benndorf. The boy gradually realizes that the hospital is his own old school, which he had left only three months previously. As he lies in the operating theatre, he sees hanging on the wall a blackboard carrying the truncated beginning of Simonides' epigram on Thermopylae, 'Stranger, if you come to Spa . . .'. The words are in his own handwriting, chalked on the board during a writing lesson only a few months earlier. A moment later, the dying boy realizes that he has lost his own arms and right leg in the fighting; his own, horribly truncated body now mirrors the cynical Nazi slogan, cut off midway through the word 'Sparta'.

In 431 BC full-scale war broke out between Athens and Sparta. The general view at the time was that the war had been sparked by a trade blockade imposed by the Athenians on their small neighbour, Megara. Nonetheless, the real cause of the war was growing fear of Athenian power at Sparta and, in particular, Corinth. During the 430s BC Athens expanded its sphere of influence into the Adriatic and southern Italy, an area which had traditionally been dominated by Corinth. Athenian alliances with Corcyra (modern Corfu), the Akarnanians (at the mouth of the Corinthian gulf), Rhegium in southern Italy and Sicilian Leontini, posed an unmistakable threat to Corinthian interests in the west. When Athens laid siege to the small city of Potidaea, a Corinthian colony in the north Aegean, it was one provocation too many.

The Peloponnesian War (431–404 BC) was fought on a bewildering number of different fronts, from Sicily to the Hellespont. The turning point in the war was a disastrous Athenian attempt to conquer Sicily (415–413 BC); huge numbers of men and ships were committed to this western adventure, which ended in total defeat for Athens. The Athenians struggled on for almost another decade, but when the Persian satraps of western Asia Minor intervened on the Spartan side, defeat was only a matter of time. Athens was forced to surrender in 404 BC.

The Spartans' stated aim of 'freedom for the Greeks' – which effectively meant the dismantling of the Athenian empire – had brought them widespread goodwill in the early years of the Peloponnesian War. By 404 the hollowness of this slogan was all too apparent. Persian support for Sparta had been on the explicit understanding that the Greek cities of Asia Minor, under Athenian control since the Persian Wars, would return to the Persian fold. However, after the defeat of Athens the Spartans tore up their agreements with Persia and set out to regain their reputation as liberators with a grand campaign in western Asia Minor on behalf of the Ionian cities. Evidently, the ideological appeal of the crusade against the barbarian was as potent as ever. In 396 BC, shortly before crossing to Asia, King Agesilaus of Sparta sacrificed at Aulis, in imitation of the sacrifice performed by Agamemnon as the Achaean fleet mustered for the Trojan War. Nonetheless, after limited successes, Sparta was roundly defeated by a Persian naval force at the sea-battle of Knidos; humiliatingly, the commander of the Persian fleet was an Athenian exile in Persian service, Conon. The failure of Sparta's Asiatic ambitions was formalized by a peace treaty with the Great King in 386 BC, in which the King's suzerainty over the cities of western Asia Minor was explicitly recognized for the first time.

The King's Peace of 386 also guaranteed the autonomy of all the Greek states of the mainland and Aegean. The uneasy peace which ensued in mainland Greece was shattered by an unprovoked Spartan attack on Thebes, the major power in central Greece at this period. Thebes had been a major Mycenaean settlement in the Bronze Age (above, pp. 22–4). In the fourth century BC the remains of the Mycenaean palace were still visible on the acropolis of Thebes; the ruins were understood to be the palace of Kadmos, the alleged Phoenician founder of Thebes, after whom the acropolis was named (the 'Kadmeia'). The main Classical settlement at Thebes lay in the Boeotian plain, below the Kadmeia. The Kadmeia itself, the sacred heart of the city, was largely given over to sanctuaries and civic buildings, many of which were deliberately sited in relation to the remains of Kadmos' palace. In 382 BC, while the Thebans were celebrating the women's festival of the Thesmophoria (during which the Kadmeia was conveniently empty of men), the Spartan general Phoebidas took the opportunity to seize the Kadmeia and install a puppet pro-Spartan government, thus turning Thebes into a Spartan satellite. Phoebidas' actions sent shock waves through the Greek world, and utterly wiped out what little remained of Sparta's moral authority. The Spartan attack on the Kadmeia was more than just the seizure of a convenient fortified citadel, in breach of the truce; it was also an unprovoked violation of a sanctified area. Worse still, Phoebidas must surely have been aware that the Thesmophoria was going on at the time. The religious festival had provided the Spartans with an ideal opportunity to strike, but made their impiety all the more glaring.

Spartan dominance in mainland Greece came to an end when a Spartan army was crushed by the Thebans under the leadership of Epaminondas at the battle of Leuctra in 371. In the wake of the humbling of Sparta at Leuctra, the Thebans took the monumental step of liberating Messenia, the old home of the helots, from Spartan control. With Theban support, a new *polis* of Messene was founded on Mt. Ithome, the centre of the unsuccessful helot revolt of the 460s BC. The new city was ringed with a massive fortification wall, 9 kilometres long, one of the most impressive anywhere in mainland Greece; Sparta was evidently not expected to give up its helots without a fight. Archaeological survey work in Messenian territory shows a significant rise in population at this period, implying that the new state was swelled with immigrants from abroad. Some of these are likely to be the descendants of the helots settled by the Athenians at Naupaktos in the mid-fifth century; others, more controversially, claimed to be the descendants of an original group of diaspora Messenians in Sicily and southern Italy, who had fled the Peloponnese at the time of the original Spartan conquest of Messenia in the eighth century.

The new Messenian *polis* provides us with a fascinating case of ethnogenesis, a community actively creating its own common memory and history. The Theban liberation of 370/369 BC, and the return of the self-proclaimed Messenian diaspora, was framed as a restoration of the pre-conquest Messenian state. However, there is no real reason to think that any such state had ever existed. True, the Spartans had conquered Messenia in the eighth century BC; but there is no sign that the 'Messenians' of the eighth century had been a unified people with a common Messenian identity, let alone an independent *polis*. When the *polis* of Messene was formed in the fourth century BC, the free, pre-Spartan past out of which the city's traditions and legends were shaped was almost entirely imaginary.

The new Messenian state was divided into five tribes, all of them named after heroes descended from Heracles: Hyllos, Kleolaios, Aristomachos, Kresphontes and Daiphontes. This emphasis on the Messenians' descent from the children of Heracles (the Heracleidae) taps into the same mythological tradition as that used by Argos to justify its conquests in the eastern Peloponnese in the early fifth century. Just as the Argives had done a century earlier, the Messenians legitimized their new state by presenting themselves as the heirs to one of the three 'lots' of the Heracleidae in the Peloponnese. Conveniently, the story was confirmed by the re-discovery of the supposed physical remains of that distant past. The mid-fourth century saw an explosion in the quantity of religious offerings at Bronze Age Mycenaean tombs in the Pylos area of western Messenia. Mycenaean tombs were regarded as evidently pre-Spartan; by implication, they could be understood as belonging to the original Messenians. Stories of heroic resistance to Spartan domination began to crystallize around an early guerrilla hero, Aristomenes of Messene, who was even made the subject of an epic poem, the *Messeniaka* of Rhianus.

Naturally, all of this was furiously denied by the Spartans, who consistently refused to recognize the legitimacy of the state of Messene. Messenia was Spartan land, bequeathed to them by their ancestors, now temporarily occupied by a city of slaves. But Sparta was no longer in a position to affect realities on the ground. The loss of Messenia, even more than the defeat at the hands of Epaminondas at Leuctra, marked the end of Sparta as a major power. To make things worse, in the early 360s the

Arcadians, a fractious and backward people in the central Peloponnese, united together to found a new federal capital on the northern borders of Spartan territory, once again with Theban support: Megalepolis, the 'big city'. Sparta was now encircled by hostile powers. The Thebans promoted the liberation of Messene and the foundation of Megalepolis as part of a general programme for the freedom of the Greeks. 'By my councils, Sparta was shorn of her glory and sacred Messene at last receives her children; by Theban arms Megalepolis is ringed with walls, and all Greece is autonomous in freedom' – so claimed the inscription on the base of a statue of Epaminondas at Thebes.

The creation of a new, autonomous Messenian history in the mid-fourth century tells us a great deal about the ways in which the fifth- and fourth-century Greeks thought about their past. The stories which the Messenians chose to tell about their mythical origins were not new. On the contrary, the return of the Heracleidae to the Peloponnese was one of the few fixed points in the universal Greek mental map of the past. The common genealogies and stories about the heroes of what we call the Bronze Age were used by cities like Messene to justify their place in the Greek world and to describe and explain their relations with their neighbours. These stories were flexible enough to accommodate new political circumstances like the creation of the *polis* of Messene. As we have seen, one of the key turning points in the political history of the fifth century BC was the Athenians' decision in 461 to break off their alliance with Sparta and ally themselves with the city of Argos in the eastern Peloponnese. Three years later, in 458 BC, the tragedian Aeschylus presented his *Oresteia* trilogy at the Athenian dramatic festival of the Dionysia. The trilogy recounts the return of the Trojan War hero Agamemnon to his native Argos, his murder by his wife Clytemnestra, and her own death at the hands of her son Orestes – a story familiar to any Greek, except perhaps for the location of Agamemnon's palace at Argos (most people would have placed it at Mycenae). At this point, Aeschylus strikes out on his own. Orestes, he claims, fled to Athens, where he was tried by the Athenian homicide court on the Areopagus hill; on his acquittal, he swore eternal friendship between Athens and his native city of Argos. A new version of an old story is here used to explain and bolster the new political alliance between the two cities.

The development of historical writing from Herodotus onwards should be set in the context of these sorts of uses of the past. Herodotus is aware of a difference between the early prehistory of Greece and the historical past, but struggles to express exactly what the difference actually is. At one point he tells us that Polykrates, tyrant of the island of Samos *c.* 535–522 BC, was 'the first of the Greeks we know of who had the plan of ruling the sea – except for Minos of Knossos and anyone before him who ruled the sea. But of the so-called human race, Polykrates was first.' Herodotus recognizes that Minos somehow does not quite count, but is unable to explain why. Is the difference between Polykrates and Minos just a question of the availability of reliable evidence – one of Herodotus' informants was a Spartan whose grandfather had fought against Polykrates – or is there something else about Minos which makes him different in kind from someone like Polykrates? Herodotus' puzzlement is very revealing. For us, this problem is easily resolved: we call Polykrates a 'historical' figure and Minos a 'mythical' or 'legendary' figure. But this distinction would not have meant anything to a fifth- or fourth-century Greek. Myth and history existed on a continuum; it was hard to establish the facts about Minos, because he lived a long time ago, but no one ever seriously doubted his existence.

Part of the problem was that the Greeks had no easy way of establishing how long ago a given event had happened. Each city-state had its own particular calendar, and there was no universally agreed way of distinguishing one year from another. The Athenians named each year after their main civic official, the archon ('the year of the archonship of so-and-so'), but even the Athenians seldom used archon-years as a way of dating a particular past event – after all, not many Athenians carried the entire archon-list around in their heads. The fifth century BC saw the first attempts to create a universal chronology for the past. In the 420s BC Hellanicus of Lesbos compiled the first universal history laid out in strict chronological order, based on the sequence of priestesses of Hera at Argos. The priestesses of Hera are not the most obvious choice as a chronological backbone for Greek history; like the Athenian archons, the Argive priestesses were of little significance outside Argos. Probably Hellanicus believed that the Argive lists of priestesses stretched back further, and were more reliable, than any other city's list of civic officials. Hellanicus' system was not widely adopted, and his method was fiercely criticized by Thucydides. It was not until the third century BC that a commonly accepted way of expressing the date of past events (by Olympiads) came into use.

Instead, the normal way of dating past events was in relation to some significant occurrence: a generation before the Persian Wars, three generations after the return of the Heracleidae to the Peloponnese. The stories of the Trojan War served a crucial function here, by serving as the earliest universal reference point. Few Greeks would have cared to say exactly how long ago the Trojan War happened; that was not the point. Rather, the Trojan War was a fixed point around which other early events could be pegged. It allowed the Athenians to specify that their alliance with Argos went back to the generation after the fall of Troy; it allowed the Messenians to claim a continuous history back as far as the return of the Heracleidae in the second generation after the fall of Troy. The legendary origins of the city of Messene were not simply, as in modern fairy stories, 'once upon a time'; instead, the city's early history was firmly pegged in relation to the universal date-horizon provided by the Trojan War.

Over the last two chapters, we have traced the development of the Greek *polis* from its eighth-century origins down to the mid-fourth century BC. The culture of the Greek city-states was unlike anything that had existed in Europe before. This was, above all, the first truly urban culture to emerge on the European peninsula. Between 40 per cent and 90 per cent of the total population (*c.* 1,200 people) of the little *polis* of Koressos on Keos lived within the walls of the city itself. The total population of Classical Boeotia can be estimated at 165,000–200,000, of whom around 100,000 (50 per cent or more) lived in urban centres. That is a staggeringly high percentage. In AD 1700 the urban population of Europe as a whole was only around 12 per cent of the total population; in the Netherlands, one of the most urbanized parts of continental Europe, the urban population may have reached 40 per cent. Although the comparison is not a wholly scientific one – historians disagree on how large a settlement has to be before it can be called 'urban' – the basic fact, that the Greeks of the fifth and fourth centuries were city-dwellers, is beyond dispute.

More characteristic of the wider European world in this period were the Greeks' northern neighbours, the Illyrians, Thracians and Macedonians. The Illyrians inhabited a large region of the western Balkans, roughly equivalent to modern Albania, Bosnia and Croatia. The upper Adriatic was little known to the Greeks in the Classical period; it was widely believed, for instance, that a branch of the Danube flowed into it, along which one could sail as far as the Black Sea. Illyria is one of the few areas of Europe in which Greek influence seems actually to have declined over this period. Greek pottery and jewellery is quite common in Illyrian elite tombs from the mid-sixth to the mid-fifth century, but disappears thereafter. Rough hilltop fortresses, probably places of refuge for lowland villages, start to appear in the course of the fifth century, but there are no signs of true urban settlements until the early Hellenistic period (the late fourth and early third centuries BC). The Illyrians seem to have been supremely unaffected by developments only a couple of hundred kilometres to the south.

In Thrace, a huge stretch of the eastern Balkans bordering on the Black Sea, things were different. Southern Thrace, roughly equivalent to modern Bulgaria, was unified in the early fifth century BC under a single royal dynasty, the Odrysians. The Odrysian Thracians co-operated enthusiastically with their Greek neighbours. Greek trading posts, such as the well-excavated site of Pistiros in the upper Maritsa valley (the ancient river Hebros), were established under royal protection in the heart of Thracian territory. In dealing with the Thracians, 'it was', says Thucydides, 'quite impossible to get anything done unless one first produced a present'. From the mid-fifth century BC, Greek prestige goods, particularly precious metalwork, flowed into Thrace in enormous quantities. The Thracians themselves imitated and adapted Greek artistic styles, combining them with Scythian and Persian elements to create a new local culture of startling originality. Nonetheless, it would be quite wrong to say that Thrace was therefore 'Hellenized' during this period. The social structure of Odrysian Thrace seems to have been little affected by the import and creative imitation of Greek luxury goods. As in Illyria, there is little sign of urbanization until the early Hellenistic period. A typical Thracian village of around 400 BC, as described by the Greek historian Xenophon, consisted of a scatter of wooden huts, each surrounded by a fenced enclosure for cattle. The Thracian aristocracies took what they wanted from the Greeks, without being absorbed into the Greek cultural orbit.

To the west of the Thracians, where Greece connects with the Balkan peninsula proper, lay the kingdom of Macedon. The region is divided into two parts: lower Macedonia, a huge coastal plain around the Thermaic gulf in the far north-west Aegean, and upper Macedonia, a sequence of rugged highland plateaux stretching westwards into the Balkan mountains, bordering on Illyrian territory. The culture of the ancient Macedonians was strikingly different from that of their Greek neighbours to the south. The Macedonians did not share the Greeks' passion for monumental temple-building. Aristocratic wealth was instead directed towards extraordinarily lavish burial-practices. Massive tumuli of the fifth and fourth centuries BC dot the Macedonian landscape. The tombs themselves often contain prodigious quantities of precious-metal vessels and jewellery. 'Warrior-burials' of a kind unknown in Greece since the seventh century, with arms and armour buried alongside the deceased, continue well down into the Hellenistic period. All of this is far more reminiscent of the Celtic elite cultures of central and northern Europe (below, pp. 163–4) than of anything going on in Greece at this point.

The controversy over whether or not the Macedonians were ethnically Greek has a long history. As we saw in the previous chapter, participation in the Panhellenic games at Olympia and elsewhere became a crucial marker of Greek identity in the seventh and sixth centuries BC. When King Alexander I of Macedon attempted to enter for the Olympics, sometime shortly before the Persian Wars, his fellow-competitors objected on the grounds that he was not a Greek. In the event, Alexander successfully argued that the royal house of Macedon (though not, interestingly, the Macedonians more generally) was of Argive descent, and was allowed to participate – he came joint first in the 200 metres. But the general drift of the story is clear. The ordinary Greek view was that the Macedonians were, if not quite barbarians, definitely not part of the club. Alexander himself was later given the rather double-edged epithet 'Philhellene', or 'friend to the Greeks'.

Linguistically, it now seems certain the Macedonians spoke a rough northern dialect of the Greek language, barely intelligible to non-Macedonians. The name 'Philip', we are told, was pronounced 'Bilip'. But 'Greekness' in the fifth and fourth centuries BC was not so much based on a common language as on a shared culture. Speaking Greek was less important than behaving Greek. Similarly, even today, the British are in many respects culturally far closer to their immediate European neighbours, the Dutch or the Germans, than they are to the North Americans with whom they share a language. And Macedonian culture was, as we have seen, radically different from that of its Greek neighbours. The Macedonians were ruled by kings; they were organized into *ethnē* or tribes rather than city-states; wealth was displayed in lavish burials rather than grand religious sanctuaries. In the face of such stark cultural differences, it is no surprise that both the Macedonians and the Greeks chose to see themselves as ethnically distinct.

The former Yugoslav Republic of Macedonia

The question of the ethnicity of the ancient Macedonians has become inextricably entangled with modern Balkan politics. Under Ottoman rule (from the fourteenth to the early twentieth century), the territory of ancient Macedonia was inhabited by a bewildering mixture of ethnic groups: Greeks, Turks, Albanians, Slavs, to say nothing of substantial Jewish and Gypsy minorities. In 1913 this territory was partitioned between Greece, Bulgaria and Serbia (later Yugoslavia). Both Bulgaria and Greece rapidly adopted a policy of enforced ethnic and linguistic uniformity. The Greeks denied outright the existence of any separate Macedonian ethnic group, in either antiquity or the present day. Both the ancient and modern Macedonians were Greeks, pure and simple. In Yugoslavia, things were different. In 1944 Tito established a separate People's Republic of Macedonia within the Yugoslav federation, with its own distinct Macedonian language (related to, but distinct from, other Slavic tongues) and Macedonian Church. For the Greeks, this Yugoslav 'Macedonia' was a contradiction in terms, inhabited as it was by Slavs who could not possibly possess any claim to the name 'Macedonian'.

With the break-up of Yugoslavia in 1991, the 'Macedonian question' entered a new and increasingly acrimonious phase. On 17 November 1991 the Republic of Macedonia declared its independence from Yugoslavia. However, the recognition of Macedonia as an independent state by the European Community and the United Nations was immediately derailed by Greek objections over the country's designation. The Greeks successfully argued that the EC should not recognize any of the former Yugoslav republics which used a name 'that implies territorial claims towards a neighbouring Community state'. The situation was not helped by the stated aim of some extreme Macedonian nationalists to 'liberate' those parts of Macedonia 'temporarily occupied' by Greece. In 1993, a compromise was brokered by which the Republic of Macedonia would provisionally be referred to by all parties (including the EC and the UN) as 'the former Yugoslav Republic of Macedonia' (FYROM). Confusingly, it was agreed that this should not be understood as the country's official *name*, but merely as a way of *referring* to the country pending a resolution of the dispute (hence 'former', without a capital letter). Inconveniently, members of the UN General Assembly are seated in the Assembly Hall according to alphabetical order. Greece objected to representatives from the FYROM being seated under 'M', since that would imply that the 'real' name of the country was 'Macedonia'; the Republic of Macedonia similarly objected to its representatives being seated under 'F' or 'Y'. As a consequence, Macedonian delegates to the UN are today seated under 'T' for 'The', between Thailand and Timor.

In 359 BC Philip II succeeded to the throne of lower Macedonia. Not the least of Philip's achievements was the permanent incorporation of the semi-independent principalities of upper Macedonia into his lowland kingdom. Philip's son, Alexander the Great, would later remind these highlanders that they had previously been 'helpless nomads, clothed in animal hides, pasturing a few animals on the mountains'; it was Philip who gave them cloaks to wear instead of skins, brought them down into the plains, and – most tellingly – started the process of turning them into Greek-style city-dwellers. The neighbouring tribes in the central and western Balkans, the Epirots, Illyrians and Paeonians, were swiftly brought into the Macedonian orbit, by means of marriage alliances or military force. Philip then turned his attention eastward, to the vast agricultural and mineral resources of the Greek cities of the Chalcidice peninsula and the Thracian coast. Between 357 and 348, these cities were either incorporated into Philip's kingdom (Amphipolis, Pydna, Potidaea) or annihilated (Olynthus). Simultaneously, Philip was exploiting discord between the Greek states to the south. An exhausting struggle for the mastery of central Greece between Phocis and Thebes (355–346 BC) was brilliantly turned by Philip to his own advantage. A plea from the Thessalians for support against Phocis in 353 had handed Philip effective mastery of Thessaly; by 346, with the break-up of the Phocian state, Philip was left as the dominant player in the central Greek mainland. Finally, in late summer 338 BC Philip shattered the combined forces of Athens and Thebes on the battlefield of Chaeronea. The political independence of the city-states of mainland Greece was at an end; the whole of the southern Balkan peninsula was now effectively subject to Macedonia. Within the space of twenty years, Macedon had grown from a minor state on the northern fringes of the Greek world to the greatest power of the eastern Mediterranean basin.

Political subjection to Macedon had less impact on the Greek cities than one might have expected. Philip, like his ancestor Alexander I, chose to downplay the cultural differences between Greeks and Macedonians (or at least between Greeks and the Macedonian royal house). Significantly, his silver and gold coinages carry images commemorating his victories in the horse race and two-horse chariot race at the Olympic games, in 356 and 348 respectively; for Philip, as for Alexander I, participation in the Olympic games was a way of signalling his cultural affiliations with the Greek world. Rather than imposing direct Macedonian rule on the Greek states, Philip established a Common Peace, to be enforced by a League of Greek states, with regular meetings at Corinth. Naturally, the dominant position in the League of Corinth, the office of *hegemon* or 'leader', was reserved for Philip and his descendants. Only Macedonian leadership would preserve the unity of the Greek world. The Athenian orator Isocrates, in his pamphlet *Philippus* of 346 BC, had already emphasized the European character of Philip's kingdom – Philip was the 'greatest of the kings of Europe' – as a means of identifying Philip's interests with those of the Greeks without actually having to argue that Philip *was* Greek. It is no coincidence that Philip's youngest daughter, born shortly after his victory at Chaeronea, was given the name 'Europa'. (Philip was well aware of the propaganda value of a well-chosen name: in 351, shortly after bringing Thessaly into the Macedonian orbit, he had named another daughter Thessalonike, 'victory in Thessaly'.)

When Philip was murdered in a court intrigue in 336 BC, he was succeeded by his eldest son, Alexander III ('the Great'). Alexander continued his father's policy of cultural Hellenism. When Thebes rebelled against Macedonian rule in 335 BC, Alexander sacked the city and sold the inhabitants into slavery, presenting his actions as belated retribution for Theban Medizing during the Persian Wars. The house of the Panhellenic poet Pindar, who had written a praise-poem of Alexander's ancestor, Alexander I the Philhellene, was ostentatiously spared. Around the same time, Alexander refounded Plataea, the site of the decisive battle against Xerxes' forces in 479, which had been destroyed by Thebes in 373. It was all too clear where the young king's thoughts were tending. Philip had long been contemplating a pan-European campaign against the Persian empire; indeed, at the time of his death, an advance party of

Macedonians and Greek allies was already ravaging Persian territory in western Asia Minor, under the Panhellenic auspices of the League of Corinth.

Early in his history of the Peloponnesian War, Thucydides remarks that the term *barbaros* is nowhere used by Homer, 'because, in my opinion, the Greeks were not yet distinguished from barbarians by means of a single common name'. This is a very acute observation. The *Iliad* shows little interest in ethnic or cultural differences between the Achaeans and the Trojans. Thucydides has grasped the crucial point that the concept of the barbarian is inextricably bound up with the idea of Greekness; only once the Greeks began to see themselves as a single people with shared characteristics – common shrines, common language, common ancestry – did they learn to regard non-Greeks as a single group. Likewise, Homer has no sense of a division of the world into two separate continents. As late as the sixth-century *Homeric Hymn to Apollo*, 'Europe' is simply a convenient term for mainland Greece north of the Isthmus, with none of the broader geographical and political connotations which it would develop in the fifth and fourth centuries. The 150 years between Plataea and Chaeronea had seen the emergence of a common Greek identity, forged by the violent encounter with the Persian barbarian. The boundary between Europe and Asia thus took on immense cultural significance. Finally, with the rise of Macedon as the dominant power in the Greek world, being European necessarily came to signify something more than being Greek. Philip and Alexander, in their attempts to link the Greek and Macedonian cultural spheres, could plausibly be claimed as the first self-conscious Europeans.

In 334 BC Alexander marched east from Macedon. Shortly before crossing the narrow straits of the Hellespont, he turned aside to sacrifice at the tomb of Protesilaus at Elaeus. Like Protesilaus, as his ship beached on the shore of the Troad, Alexander made sure to be the first to leap ashore onto Asian soil. The two continents were about to be brought closer together than ever before.

5

Alexander the Great and the Hellenistic World: 334–146 BC

In the eighteenth chapter of the Qur'an, an account is given of an enigmatic figure called Dhūl Qarnayn, the Two-Horned One. Allah is said to have given Dhūl Qarnayn power over the earth, enabling him to travel to the outer limits of the world, east and west. Most later Islamic scholars agreed that the figure of Dhūl Qarnayn was an allegory of Al-Iskandar, Alexander the Great. The two horns represented Alexander's rule over the two halves of the world, Rūm (Europe) and Persia. The ancient conquests of Al-Iskandar were understood as prefiguring the Arab conquests of the seventh and eighth centuries AD, which created an Islamic empire stretching from the Atlantic to India. At the city of Cadiz, beyond the straits of Gibraltar, where the Mediterranean and Atlantic meet, Al-Iskandar had built a lighthouse, indicating the point beyond which it was unsafe for ships to sail. In the far north, at the fringe of the central Asian steppe, he had constructed a great iron wall to keep out the unclean races of Gog and Magog. It was Alexander who had fixed the limits of the civilized world once and for all.

The geographical extent of Alexander's conquests was indeed astonishing. Between 334 and 330 BC Alexander overran the Asia Minor peninsula, Syria, Egypt, and the Persian heartlands of Mesopotamia and western Iran. The last Achaemenid king, Darius III, was overwhelmed in two great battles, at Issos and Gaugamela; the passing of the Persian world order was ceremoniously marked by the burning of the palaces of Xerxes at Persepolis in the winter of 331/0 BC. It is telling that after the capture of the four Persian royal capitals, Babylon and Susa in southern Mesopotamia and Persepolis and Ecbatana in western Iran, Alexander dismissed the Greek contingents in his army. The campaign of revenge for the Persian invasion of Greece, ostensibly undertaken on behalf of the League

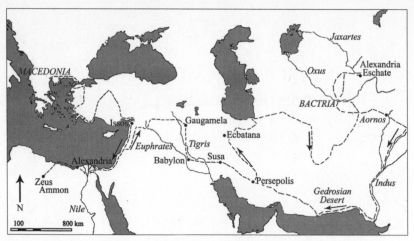

Map 17. The campaigns of Alexander the Great, 334–323 BC.

of Corinth, was at an end. But Alexander himself pressed on eastwards across northern Iran, in pursuit of the fugitive Darius III. After Darius' assassination by his own courtiers, the emergence of a Persian pretender to the throne, Bessus, drew Alexander into a long and gruelling guerrilla campaign in the central Asian satrapies of Bactria and Sogdiana (modern Afghanistan, Uzbekistan and Tajikistan). The deep isolation of the royal court, chasing ghostly Persian rebels across the endless central Asian steppe, fuelled Alexander's growing paranoia and megalomania; shadowy plots against the king's life were followed by summary executions, and for the first time Alexander began to expect divine honours from his court and subjects.

Alexander the Great and the Ottoman conquest

In 1453 the city of Constantinople fell to the Ottoman armies of Mehmed the Conquerer, thus bringing to an end the thousand-year history of Byzantium, the 'New Rome'. As we are told by several Latin authors who witnessed the siege of Constantinople, or who met Mehmed shortly afterwards, the Conqueror had a particular interest in the history of Alexander the Great. 'He wished to be recognized as the master of the earth and all its peoples, that is to say, as a second Alexander; it is for this reason that he used to read the works of Arrian, who compiled a careful account of the deeds of Alexander, on an almost daily basis.'

The idea of a fifteenth-century Turkish sultan reading Arrian's *Anabasis* (the longest surviving Greek history of Alexander, written in the second century AD) might seem rather unlikely at first sight. However, Mehmed's own private copies of Arrian's *Anabasis* and Homer's *Iliad*, commissioned after the fall of Constantinople, are still preserved today in the imperial library of Topkapı Palace in Istanbul. The court historian Kritoboulos of Imbros, a Greek who completed his hagiographical biography of the Conquerer in the mid-1460s, claimed to be recounting for his fellow-Greeks a career which was 'in no way inferior to that of Alexander of Macedon'. No doubt influenced by Mehmed's admiration for Alexander the Great, Kritoboulos presented Mehmed as a new Alexander, who had succeeded (through the conquest of Constantinople) in once again yoking together Europe and Asia. Mehmed himself liked the idea that he was repeating Alexander's campaigns in reverse. Kritoboulos recounts how, in the course of his campaign against the island of Lesbos in 1462, Mehmed passed by the ruins of the site of Troy, just as Alexander had done in the summer of 334 BC. He asked that the tombs of Achilles, Ajax and the other heroes be pointed out to him, and praised them both for their deeds and because they had found so fine a writer as Homer to commemorate them. Shaking his head a little, Mehmed reflected how God had at last, after many generations, allowed him to avenge the sack of Troy and punish the enemies of the Trojans. With the fall of Constantinople, the Greeks had finally paid the penalty for the long centuries of injustices towards 'us people of Asia'.

In spring 327 Alexander turned south, and later that year he led his army over the Hindu Kush into India. In the late sixth century BC Darius I had claimed India as part of the Persian empire, but his conquests were probably short-lived; there is virtually no archaeological evidence for Persian presence in the lands beyond the Khyber Pass. For the first time, Alexander was extending his conquests beyond the boundaries of the Persian empire. But the invasion of India was perhaps not as much of a leap into the unknown as it might appear. Due to an unfortunate geographical misconception – that the Indian Ocean was an inland lake – Alexander had believed that the Indus river was connected to the upper course of the Nile. On reaching the Punjab, he could simply sail back downstream to the Mediterranean. This idea was initially confirmed by the presence of lotus flowers and crocodiles in the Indus. Since the fifth century BC, Greek botanists had believed that certain flora and fauna were unique to particular parts of the world; it was well known that lotuses and crocodiles were to be found only in the Nile. When the true geography of the region finally became clearer, the result was mutiny among Alexander's Macedonian troops, who refused point-blank to continue their march eastwards. The long journey back to the west, down the Indus river and across the Gedrosian desert (modern Baluchistan), was marked by increasingly reckless and gratuitous slaughter of native populations. In summer 323 BC, in the midst of preparations for a naval assault on the Arabian peninsula, after a massive drinking bout with his Macedonian companions, Alexander, king of the world, died at Babylon.

Alexander's premature death makes it hard to judge quite how far he was planning to go. Arrian, the author of the fullest surviving history of the Macedonian conquests, believed that his intended empire had no geographical limits; Alexander would never have been satisfied even if he had added Europe to Asia and the British Isles to Europe. The actual course of Alexander's Far Eastern conquests tells against this view. With the exception of the Indian provinces – which were abandoned within a generation – Alexander made no attempt to extend the limits of the Persian empire. In the north-east, Alexander advanced only as far as the limits of Cyrus' campaigns, the Syr Darya river in what is now Tajikistan. The foundation there of a new city called Alexandria Eschatē, or 'Alexandria the Furthest' (probably the modern city of Khujand) shows that further expansion to the north was explicitly renounced. Indeed, in most respects, the vast empire which Alexander left behind bore a striking resemblance to that which he had set out to conquer. The old Persian provinces ('satrapies') were preserved, though now with Macedonians rather than Persians acting as provincial governors. The Persians had believed that their empire encompassed the entire inhabitable world, stretching southwards and northwards to where heat and cold respectively made it impossible to live, and Alexander seems to have accepted this view of world geography. Alexander's empire was nothing less, but also nothing more than, the *oikoumenē*, the 'inhabited world', as defined by his Persian predecessors.

At no stage did the Macedonians see themselves as striking out into the unknown. Their conquests all took place within the limits of the world mapped out by the travels of Greek heroes of the remote past. In the winter of 332/331 BC, Alexander travelled deep into the Libyan desert to consult the oracle of Zeus Ammon, in emulation of two of his supposed ancestors, Heracles and Perseus, both of whom were said to have visited the oracle. Where existing Greek stories failed to provide precedents for a stretch of Alexander's campaigns, suitable precedents were simply invented. When Alexander stormed the mountain fortress of Aornos, high in the tribal regions of modern Pakistan, considered by the locals to be impregnable even for a god, this was swiftly spun into a legend that Heracles had tried and failed to capture the fortress. The presence of ivy in the mountains north of the Khyber Pass, a plant closely associated with the god Dionysus, encouraged Alexander to think that he was following in Dionysus' footsteps. Since no pre-existing mythological tradition associated Dionysus with India, the Macedonians had to use their imaginations. A new episode was added to the god's career, describing how Dionysus conquered the sub-continent some time in the distant past, bringing civilization and the rule of law to the barbarous Indians. On this interpretation, Alexander was merely restoring Graeco-Macedonian rule to a society which owed its existence in the first place to the conquests of Dionysus. Late in 325 BC, when the Macedonians finally emerged from the crossing of the Gedrosian desert, their own successful reconquest of India was celebrated with a week-long drunken riot in honour of the god, with Alexander himself playing the role of Dionysus. And so it was that the venture into India, the wildest and most remote campaign ever undertaken by an ancient general, was brought firmly back within the familiar realms of Greek and Macedonian mythical geography.

Alexander was succeeded by his mentally deficient half-brother Arrhidaeus and his own unborn baby, the child later known as Alexander IV. Neither was capable of ruling Alexander's empire in his own right, and it was clear from the outset that a regent would be required. Unfortunately, Alexander's tendency to concentrate all power in his own person had left no obvious candidate for the post. The decade immediately following Alexander's death was characterized by violent clashes between self-appointed regents of the kings, none of whom possessed sufficient authority to hold the vast empire together. Arrhidaeus was assassinated in 317 by Alexander's formidable mother Olympias, who seems to have been aiming at the Macedonian throne in her own right, and the young Alexander IV was quietly done away with in 310.

By this stage it had become clear that the real players were the Macedonian governors of the old Persian satrapies. Most of these men were veterans of Alexander's campaigns, and could draw on the formidable financial and military resources accumulated by their Persian predecessors. The most energetic of these satraps was a man of Philip's generation, Antigonus the One-Eyed, governor of Phrygia in central Asia Minor. By the time he declared himself king in 306 BC Antigonus had won for himself a huge realm in Asia Minor and Syria, ringed by four other great powers, Ptolemy in Egypt, Seleucus in Babylon and the Far East, Lysimachus in Thrace, and Cassander in Macedon. Antigonus was killed in battle in 301 BC, and his short-lived empire was carved up between the other dynasts. However, his son Demetrius the City-Besieger managed to rebuild an impressive kingdom, this time in Macedon and mainland Greece. By 281 BC, when Lysimachus' Thracian realm was overrun by the 77–year-old Seleucus, the essential balance of power for the next century had become clear: the Ptolemies in Egypt and the Levant, the Seleucid dynasty in Asia, and the descendants of Antigonus in Macedon.

The dynastic legitimacy of the new kingdoms was shaky to say the least. None of the three families which eventually triumphed in the wars of the Successors bore any blood relationship to Alexander himself. Their claim to a share of the conqueror's throne had to be justified by other means. Ptolemy, conveniently, had been one of Alexander's boyhood friends, and he cheerfully encouraged the rumour that he was really a bastard son of Philip II, and thus half-brother to Alexander himself.

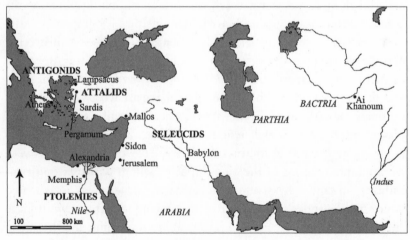

Map 18. The Hellenistic kingdoms in the third century BC.

Ptolemy also possessed the most potent royal relic of all: Alexander's body. The king's funeral cortège had been shamelessly hijacked by Ptolemy's agents while it was being transported back home to Macedon, and the embalmed corpse of Alexander was put on display in a glass coffin in the Ptolemaic capital of Alexandria. Although the other dynasts were unable to claim such intimate links with Alexander, they could at least copy his image. For centuries, royal portraits from all corners of Alexander's former empire depicted the kings as clean-shaven, with an upturned gaze, wild, flowing hair, a quiff, and divine attributes of one kind or another, just like Alexander (see Plate 31a). Alexander provided a model and an ideal of kingship, against which all his Successors would be judged.

To treat the Successor kingdoms as part of the history of Classical Europe might seem to be stretching the definition of 'Europe' a bit. After all, most of Alexander's empire lay deep in Asia; the royal capitals of the Seleucid kingdom were located in modern Syria and Iraq, and its eastern marches bordered on China. The principal reason why the Seleucids and Ptolemies deserve a place in European history is their role in spreading Greek culture among the non-Greek populations of the former Persian empire. Since the late nineteenth century this process of 'Hellenization' has given its name to the entire historical epoch: the three centuries after Alexander's death are today generally known as the Hellenistic age, an age not merely of Greekness but of *becoming* Greek.

The Hellenization of the east had begun well before the fall of the Persian empire. Over the course of the fifth and fourth centuries BC, the non-Greek peoples of western and southern Asia Minor had been profoundly influenced by the culture of their Greek neighbours. The native dynasts of Lycia, for example, certainly employed Greek sculptors for their lavish funerary monuments. The Nereid Monument (*c.* 400–380 BC), now in the British Museum, is a fairly characteristic case. It is probably the tomb of a Lycian dynast by the name of Arbinas, a member of a pro-Persian family controlling a small fiefdom in the Xanthos valley in western Lycia. Despite Arbinas' political sympathies, both the architecture and sculpture of the Nereid Monument are thoroughly Greek in inspiration. When recounting his military exploits in prolix verse inscriptions, Arbinas chose to have the texts written in both the Lycian and Greek languages. Even this pro-Persian dynast wished to present himself to his subjects as culturally Greek.

The progress of Hellenization in Asia sharply accelerated after Alexander's conquests. Between 332 BC, when Alexander founded the great city of Alexandria on the Mediterranean coast of Egypt, and the mid-third century BC, hundreds of new Greek cities were established across the breadth of the *oikoumenē*, from Egypt to Afghanistan. One of the best known is the Greek colony at Ai Khanoum, near Mazar-i Sharif on the modern Afghan–Tajik border, excavated by French archaeologists in the 1960s and 1970s (see Figure 19). Here, in the heart of ancient Bactria, the Hellenistic settlers could exercise in a Greek-style gymnasium, equipped with olive oil imported all the way from the Mediterranean. Papyrus fragments of an unknown philosophical work by Aristotle were excavated here; under a Bactrian sun, tragedies by the Athenian playwright Sophocles were performed in a Greek theatre. At the heart of the city, in the hero-shrine of the city-founder Kineas, Delphic maxims were inscribed for the moral improvement of the Greek colonists: 'as a child, be well-behaved; when a young man, self-controlled; in middle age, be just; as an old man, a good counsellor; at the end of your life, free from sorrow.' Ai Khanoum mimics the outward forms of the Classical Greek polis so effectively that it is an effort to recall that this was not an independent citizen-state like fourth-century Athens or Messene, but a tiny cog in the vast engine of a Macedonian military dictatorship stretching from the Aegean to Kandahar. The countryside around Ai Khanoum was farmed, not by free Greek citizens, but by a subject population of Bactrian serfs with names like Oxyboakes and Atrosokes, whose taxes were collected and processed at a Persian-style palace sprawling across the central zone of the city, before being sent west to Syria and Mesopotamia to fund the colossal Seleucid armies. Whatever else Hellenization may have meant, it certainly did not mean giving Oxyboakes the vote.

Throughout Alexander's former empire, the segregation between the Graeco-Macedonian ruling class and their non-Greek subjects was all but total. At best, a few bilingual Egyptians, Persians and Syrians could aspire to jobs as clerks, accountants and tax-collectors. Of all the thousands of royal officials, courtiers and high-ranking officers in the Ptolemaic and Seleucid kingdoms, less than 3 per cent were anything other than Greek or Macedonian. In the mid-250s BC, a Greek businessman and camel-trader in Egypt, Zeno, received a letter from one of his Egyptian agents, who complained that his immediate superiors had

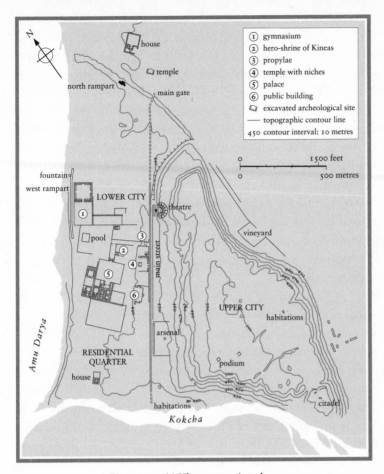

Figure 19. Ai Khanoum, site plan.

maltreated him, starved him and refused to pay him his salary, 'because I do not speak Greek'.

The Hellenization of the non-Greek people of the *oikoumenē* was, then, by no means an article of royal policy. Instead, the transformation of local cultures was driven from below. In a world where Greekness meant power, there were strong incentives to adopt the trappings of Greek culture as best one could. We saw in the previous chapter that the creative manipulation of Greek stories about the remote past played a central role in the formation of the Messenian state. This kind of manipulation now took on a new urgency. Early in his campaign, Alexander had advertised a 'new deal' for the Greek cities of Asia Minor:

both freedom from taxation and (albeit limited) political autonomy. When Alexander arrived at the obscure Cilician town of Mallos, on the south coast of Asia Minor, in late summer 333 BC, the Mallians had their story ready. Culturally speaking, there was nothing Greek about Mallos at all. But one of their local Cilician divinities was, they argued, none other than the mythical hero Amphilochos of Argos, who had founded Mallos some time in the distant past. Therefore the Mallians, however Cilician they might look, were in fact the descendants of Argives. The reason why this was such an ingenious line to take was that the Macedonian kings also claimed to be of Argive descent, tracing their ancestry back to the Argive hero Heracles. Alexander was sufficiently impressed by this appeal to kinship with Macedon that the Mallians were instantly accorded the status of a Greek city and received full tax-exemption. The message was clear enough: Greek ancestry meant favourable treatment.

It is hardly surprising that in the late fourth and third centuries BC hundreds of cities in western Asia, from Lydia to Syria, suddenly discovered Greek gods and heroes at the roots of their family trees. Some cities were fortunate. According to one Greek version of the myth of Europa and the bull, Europa and Kadmos were the children of Agenor, king of the Phoenician city of Sidon. When Europa was abducted by Zeus, Kadmos set out from Phoenicia to search for his sister; he eventually settled in Greece, founding the city of Thebes in Boeotia. Few Phoenicians would even have been aware of this story before the third century BC: Europa, Kadmos and Agenor were purely Greek figures, with no place in native Phoenician mythology. But once it dawned on the Sidonians that they already held a special place in the Greek legendary past, they seized on the story with enthusiasm. From the early second century BC the figures of Europa and the bull start to appear on the coins of Sidon. Around 200 BC a Sidonian athletic victor at the Nemean games – a highly significant event in itself, since only Greeks were allowed to participate at the Panhellenic games – described Sidon as the 'house of the sons of Agenor', and spoke of the delight felt by the Thebans, 'the sacred city of Kadmos', at the success of their Phoenician mother-city at the games. The Sidonians were learning fast: the monument on which the victory was recorded, written in impeccable Greek elegiac couplets, is the earliest Greek inscription known from Sidon. Other non-Greek states had to work much harder at reshaping their past. The inhabitants of the little town of Harpagion in north-west Asia Minor, named after a Persian general called Harpagus, furiously denied they had anything to do with the Persians at all. Instead, their town was named after the seizing (*harpagē*) of Ganymede by Zeus, which had, they claimed, happened right there at Harpagion.

Hellenism in Asia Minor

In the nineteenth century there were around 1 million Greeks living under Ottoman rule in Asia Minor, making up some 8 per cent of the total population. Most of the Greek population was concentrated in the far west of the peninsula, with smaller communities living in Cappadocia and on the Black Sea coast. In the early nineteenth century the Greeks of Asia Minor had lived in small *koinotites* ('communities'), relatively cut off from one another and with very little sense of a collective identity. Once an independent Greek state had emerged on the far side of the Aegean in the 1830s this began to change very rapidly. Increasing numbers of Greek schools and literary societies were established in the provincial towns of Asia Minor, offering an educational system modelled on that of the fledgling Greek state. In Sinasos, deep in the heart of rural Cappadocia, the school curriculum included Greek history, Church history, Xenophon, Isocrates, Demosthenes and Plato; Ottoman studies are conspicuous by their absence. The emphasis on ancient Greek culture was crucial in fostering a new sense of Greek national identity among the Asia Minor Greeks.

There was also a growing interest in the local history of the ancient Greek cities of Asia Minor. The *Mouseion* and *Nea Smyrnē*, learned journals produced at Smyrna in the 1870s and 1880s, published hundreds of ancient Greek inscriptions discovered and copied by doctors and schoolmasters in the small towns of western Asia Minor. Most of these local Greek antiquarians – Dr N. Limnaios of Artaki, G. Sarantidis of Alaşehir – are little more than names to us. However, the gravestone set up by Sarantidis for his 1-year-old daughter Efthalia can still be seen in the ruins of the church of St John at Alaşehir. The inscription concludes with the words 'born on 24 May 1878, died on 18 June 1879, in Philadelpheia'. Virtually all that we know of Mr Sarantidis, apart from the inscriptions which he copied, is the fact that he chose to identify his home town of Alaşehir by its ancient Greek name of Philadelpheia, a name which had not been in use for four hundred years.

The re-emergence of a Greek national identity in Asia Minor ultimately had tragic consequences. As the Ottoman empire imploded at the end of the First World War, the Greek army (with the encouragement of the British Prime Minister, David Lloyd George) occupied first the area around Smyrna, and ultimately much of the western half of the Asia Minor peninsula. The Greek aim – the so-called *megalē idea*, or 'Grand Ambition' – was the establishment of a greater Greek state encompassing all the 'historically Greek' territories around the Aegean sea. After two years of bloody warfare (1920–22) the Greeks were driven out of the peninsula. In 1923 Greece and Turkey agreed a general exchange of populations; more than a million Greek Orthodox inhabitants of the Ottoman empire, most of them from western Asia Minor, were relocated to Greece, ending a Greek presence that had lasted some three and a half thousand years.

This 'rediscovery' of a Greek past by the non-Greek city-states of Phoenicia and western Asia Minor was accompanied by an enthusiastic adoption of the trappings of Greek civic life. Characteristic Greek institutions and public buildings – theatres and council-houses, the use of silver and bronze coinage, athletics and the culture of the gymnasium – were widely taken up across the Near East. A few enterprising local historians, like Berossos in Babylon and Manetho in Egypt, wrote histories of their native countries in the Greek language; the surviving fragments of Manetho's work include elements from various Egyptian historical traditions (king-lists, prophecies and priestly autobiographies), woven with remarkable success into a Greek-style narrative history. One of Manetho's main aims was to correct the hit-and-miss account of Egyptian history in the *Histories* of the Greek historian Herodotus. Others responded to Herodotus' work in more self-interested ways. In the mid-220s BC the city of Sardis, former capital of the Achaemenid province of Lydia, sent an embassy to Delphi to seek recognition of their status as a Greek *polis*. The Sardians appealed to the ancestral goodwill shown by Delphi towards their city; it seems that they were relying here on the first book of Herodotus' *Histories*, which gives a long account of the warm relations between the sixth-century Lydian king Croesus and the Delphic oracle. The Sardians' route into the privileged Greek club was evidently smoothed by their prominent position in Herodotus' work.

Not all the inhabitants of the Near East found it so straightforward to assimilate their local cultures to that favoured by the ruling power. In the late 170s BC a group of cultural Hellenizers at Jerusalem petitioned the Seleucid monarch Antiochus IV Epiphanes for permission to reorganize Jerusalem as a Greek *polis*, and establish a gymnasium in the heart of the city. There is no real evidence that this group had any intention of reforming or 'Hellenizing' the Jewish religion itself. However, a few years later, in 167 BC, Antiochus IV decided to suppress the Jewish religion by force. The observation of Jewish religious practices was forbidden by law, circumcision was punishable by death, and a pagan altar to Zeus Olympios was built on top of the great altar of burnt-offering in the Temple at Jerusalem. Why Antiochus should have tried to impose this policy of enforced Hellenization remains very unclear; as we have seen, most of the Hellenistic monarchs were quite happy for their non-Greek subjects to stay non-Greek. Indeed, subsequent events in Judaea made it all too clear why Antiochus' predecessors had refrained from imposing European cultural norms on their subjects. Jewish resistance was widespread, violent and ultimately decisive: the Temple cult was restored within three years, and by the 140s Judaea had won effective independence from Seleucid rule.

The apocryphal Book of Daniel, composed in the earliest years of the Jewish resistance in the mid-160s, gives us some sense of the ways in which the Jews tried to legitimize their struggle against Antiochus in relation to the Jewish past. The Book of Daniel purports to be a prophetic text of the sixth century BC, recording the visions of the prophet Daniel in the last days of Jewish captivity at Babylon and the earliest years of the Persian empire. In one of Daniel's visions, a ram (the king of Media and Persia, Darius III) is defeated by a goat from the west (the king of Greece, Alexander the Great), whose horn is broken and replaced by four horns (the four Hellenistic kingdoms, the Seleucids, Ptolemies, Antigonids and – presumably – the Attalids of Pergamum). From one of these horns shall come a little horn (Antiochus IV), who will destroy the Temple, suppress daily sacrifice, and impose the 'abomination of desolation' (the pagan altar at Jerusalem). The reign of this king, predicts Daniel, will come to an end with the Day of Judgement and the dawning of the Kingdom of God – a fairly good indication that the author of the Book of Daniel was writing before the end of Antiochus' reign. It is fascinating to see the Jews of the second century BC trying to weave the history of the Hellenistic kingdoms and the persecution under Antiochus IV into the fabric of the wider Jewish past. The religious crisis of the 160s BC is given meaning and significance through the 'discovery' that it had all been predicted by a sixth-century Jewish prophet in exile at Babylon.

Similar writings were certainly circulating in Egypt at the same period. One particularly remarkable text of the late second century BC, the *Oracle of the Potter*, claims to record a prophecy once made by an Egyptian potter to Pharaoh Amenhotep, one of four pharaohs of that name who reigned in the second millennium BC. The Oracle predicts that the patron deity of Alexandria will abandon that city and come to Memphis, the old native capital of Lower Egypt, 'and the city of foreigners which was founded will be deserted'. The abandonment of Alexandria will mark the end of 'the period of evils, when a crowd of foreigners like fallen leaves descended on Egypt'. The Potter was overly optimistic: the Greeks were not expelled from Egypt, and Alexandria is still going strong today. Nonetheless, the *Oracle of the Potter* continued to circulate in Egypt as late as the third century AD, representing a deep undercurrent of local cultural resistance to Macedonian, and later Roman, rule.

It is a striking fact that, throughout the Hellenistic world, it was the culture and institutions of the Greek *polis*, rather than those of Alexander's Macedonian tribal state, which triumphed. Even the Macedonian dialect of the Greek language, like most of the other regional Greek dialects, died out in the Hellenistic period, to be replaced by a universal form of Standard Greek, the so-called *koinē* or 'common tongue', based on the old local dialect of Athens and Ionia. Although the political centres of the world now lay in Mesopotamia, Egypt and Macedon, the old city-states of mainland Greece evidently lost none of their cultural significance in the Hellenistic age. The Aegean basin was always the main theatre of conflict between the Hellenistic superpowers, and hence it is perhaps unsurprising that all three of the major dynasties took particular pains to present themselves as cultural philhellenes.

None of the Hellenistic dynasties flaunted their philhellenism more openly than the Ptolemaic kings of Egypt. In the winter of 279/8 BC, the Ptolemaic capital of Alexandria saw the first celebration of a four-yearly festival, the Ptolemaieia, in memory of the founder of the Ptolemaic dynasty, Ptolemy I Soter (reigned 305–282 BC). Quite by chance, a long description survives of an extraordinary procession laid on during one of the first celebrations of the Ptolemaieia. The main part of the procession was a reconstruction of Dionysus' return from India, in which a 6–metre-high statue of Dionysus lounging on an elephant was followed by an exotic menagerie of oriental animals: elephants, camels, leopards, cheetahs, ostriches and so forth. Ethiopian tribute-bearers – presumably genuine Indians were not available – carried 600 elephant tusks and 2,000 logs of ebony. A total of 57,000 cavalry and 23,000 infantry were said to have marched alongside. At the very end of the procession came a golden statue of Alexander himself, on a chariot pulled by a team of four elephants.

This stupendously tasteless procession gives us some sense not only of the spectacular wealth of the Ptolemaic house, but also of the way in which it wished to be seen by its subjects. Native Egyptian culture was conspicuous by its absence. Among the floats was one bearing statues of Alexander the Great and Ptolemy. Alexander was accompanied by a personification of the city of Corinth, and beside Ptolemy stood a personification of Virtue (*aretē*). Behind them came a cart filled with women, wearing lavish jewellery and robes, representing the Greek cities of Ionia and the islands which Alexander had liberated from the Persians. The symbolism here comes as something of a surprise. The figure of Corinth is clearly intended to recall the League of Corinth, the alliance of mainland Greek states in whose name Alexander had led the invasion of Asia in 334 BC. This League had been a dead letter by Alexander's death in 323, if not before; by the 270s BC it was ancient history. Nonetheless, by setting a statue of Ptolemy alongside personifications of Alexander's United States of Greece and the free Greek cities of Asia Minor, the Ptolemies were proclaiming continuity with Alexander's policy of freedom and autonomy for the Greeks. That fits very well with the wider political aspirations of the Ptolemaic dynasty in the early third century BC. The Ptolemies took great pains to be seen as the defenders of Greek liberty. In 287 BC the city of Athens had successfully revolted from Antigonid Macedon with Ptolemaic help; for twenty-five years the Ptolemies actively supported an independent democratic regime at Athens.

A particularly original and influential aspect of the Hellenizing pretensions of the Ptolemaic dynasty was the establishment of a great library and scholarly community at Alexandria dedicated to the service of the Muses, the *Mouseion* or Museum. The most important of the first generation of scholars at the Museum, Callimachus of Cyrene (in modern Libya), produced a critical inventory of all surviving Greek literature in 120 volumes, which also served as a kind of vast library-catalogue. Works were catalogued according to literary genre, many of which were now clearly defined for the first time. Later in the third century, another Museum scholar, Eratosthenes, produced the first critical chronology of Greek history, based on lists of victors in the Olympic games. The earliest Olympic victor known to Eratosthenes was a certain Koroibos of Elis, whom he dated to 776 BC. The influence of Eratosthenes' work can be gauged by the fact that as recently as 2007, the earliest period of Greek history available for study at Oxford University was deemed to begin in 776 BC. For pre-Olympic history, Eratosthenes used a list of Spartan kings, which allowed him to place the return of the Heracleidae to the Peloponnese in 1104/3 BC, and the fall of Troy eighty years earlier, in 1184/3 BC. Some modern scholars have been impressed by the apparent 'fit' between Eratosthenes' date and the apparent destruction of Troy VIIa c. 1200 BC. But this 'fit', if such it is, cannot be anything more than a coincidence, since Eratosthenes had not a scrap of evidence for his date of 1184/3: the evidence which would have allowed him to carry his chronology back beyond the first Olympiad never existed.

Many of Eratosthenes' dates were clearly little more than guesswork – he placed Homer in the eleventh century BC. But the importance and originality of his work lay in its method. This was the first attempt to produce a respectable chronological framework for early Greek history based on exclusively documentary sources: lists of kings, Olympic victors, priests and civic magistrates. The compilation of works of this kind, dictionaries, handbooks and encyclopaedias, reflects a new way of thinking about the past. The scholars of the Museum were for the first time attempting to classify and organize their cultural heritage. A by-product of this fever of scholarly activity was the drawing up of a fixed canon of Greek poets and orators, whose work was judged especially worthy of study and imitation. The first hints of the emergence of this canon came during the reign of Alexander the Great, when the Athenian statesman Lycurgus deposited authorized copies of the tragedies of Aeschylus, Sophocles and Euripides in the city archives at Athens, and imposed a legal obligation on actors to stick to the official texts. In the early second century BC the scholar Aristophanes of Byzantium, head of the royal library at Alexandria, drew up select lists of first-class authors: three tragic poets, nine lyric poets, ten orators and so forth. Aristophanes' lists of canonical authors were tremendously influential, playing a major role in determining which Greek authors continued to be copied and so survived down to our own day. Just as Eratosthenes had chosen not to carry his chronological work beyond the death of Alexander, so Aristophanes' lists included not a single Hellenistic poet, orator or historian. Even the most successful poets of the Hellenistic age, Philitas, Theocritus, Aratus, were never accorded 'canonical' status. The Romans habitually referred to the authors selected by Aristophanes as *classici* or 'of the first class'. It is ultimately to the scholars of Ptolemaic Alexandria that we owe our concept of the 'classical'.

Of equal, if not greater historical significance was the work of the Museum in the fields of science and mathematics. Here the achievements of Alexandrian scholars were, quite simply, breathtaking. The *Elements* of Euclid, composed in Alexandria around 300 BC, was still in use as a school textbook in Britain in the late nineteenth century. Archimedes of Syracuse, one of the outstanding geniuses of antiquity, is probably best known today for his method of measuring the density of solid objects through water displacement ('I found it!', the original '*eureka* moment'). However, Archimedes' most important and original work lay in the field of geometry: his proof that the value of *pi* lies between $3^1/_7$ and $3^{10}/_{71}$ would alone suffice to establish him as mathematician of the first order. Mathematical methods were applied to questions of geography by, once again, the polymath Eratosthenes. In his book *On the Measurement of the Earth*, he used a method of remarkable elegance and simplicity to estimate the earth's circumference as 39,689 kilometres, astonishingly close to the true figure of 40,011 kilometres.

Greek mathematics and science in Baghdad

In the mid-eighth century AD, after the rise to power of the 'Abbāsid caliphate in the Near East, the caliph Al-Mansūr (AD 754–75) initiated a great translation movement of Greek mathematical and scientific works. This movement, subsidized at public expense and conducted with remarkable scholarly rigour, continued throughout the ninth and tenth centuries. Among the earliest works to be translated were Euclid's *Elements* and the vast work on mathematical astronomy by Claudius Ptolemaeus, which we still know by its Arabic name, the *Almagest*. The greatest of the Arabic translators, Hunayn ibn-Ishāq (AD 808–73), who is said to have been able to recite Homer by heart, describes the pains he took to locate good Greek manuscripts: 'no one has yet come across a complete Greek manuscript of Galen's *de Demonstratione* . . . I travelled in search of it in northern Mesopotamia, all of Syria, Palestine and Egypt until I reached Alexandria. I found nothing except about half of it, in disorder and incomplete, in Damascus.'

The scholars of ʿAbbāsid Baghdad used and developed Greek mathematics for the practical needs of the Islamic state. Around half a century after the translation of Euclid's *Elements* into Arabic, the ninth-century mathematician Al-Hwārizmī tells us that the caliph Al-Maʾmūn 'encouraged me to compose a compendious work on algebra, confining it to the fine and important parts of its calculations, such as people constantly require in cases of inheritance, legacies, partition, law-suits and trade'. The precise measurement of the circumference of the earth was a matter of particular interest, since the *qibla*, or direction of prayer, could be determined only by knowing the distance and orientation of Mecca from any point on the earth's surface. In this field, Eratosthenes' work was not superseded until the early eleventh century, when a superior method was finally devised by the great Persian scientist Al-Birūni.

The legacy of the Arabic translators is incalculable. The great flowering of Arabic philosophy in central Asia (Avicenna) and Andalusia (Averroes) during the eleventh and twelfth centuries is unimaginable without the impetus provided by the translation of the philosophical works of Aristotle. In the twelfth century it was largely through Latin translations of Arabic works that Greek philosophical and scientific thought was reintroduced to western Europe. Still today, several important Greek mathematical and medical works, including Hero of Alexandria's *Mechanics*, parts of Apollonius of Perge's *Conic Sections* and Galen's *Anatomical Procedures*, survive only in their Arabic translations.

The vast new world opened up by Alexander's conquests was ripe for exploration. Geography, botany and ethnography flourished. Megasthenes, a Seleucid ambassador to the court of the Indian king Chandragupta, wrote a comprehensive history and geography of India, including the first known description of the Indian caste system. The Red Sea and the Persian gulf were opened up, and the elephant-hunters of the Ptolemies penetrated deep into Ethiopia and the Sudan. Perhaps the most spectacular of these journeys of exploration was that of Pytheas of Massilia, undertaken around 320 BC. Sailing out through the straits of Gibraltar, Pytheas travelled north from Cadiz along the Atlantic coast. From Land's End in Cornwall, he circumnavigated Britain in a clockwise direction; finally he reached a land called Thule, 'where the night is extremely short, two or three hours, so that only a short interval passes between sunset and sunrise'. The exact location of Thule is still disputed, but most probably Pytheas had made landfall on either the Shetlands or Iceland. On his return journey across the North Sea, Pytheas may have sailed east as far as Denmark. It is telling that Pytheas' discoveries in the far north were treated with scepticism and contempt by the historian Polybius (*c.* 200–118 BC). Pytheas had few successors; it was not until the Roman conquests of the first century BC that Europe north of the Alps finally lost its status as *terra incognita*.

As Pytheas skirted its northern shores, temperate Europe was passing through a period of violent social upheaval. As we saw earlier (pp. 95–7), the Iron Age Hallstatt culture of middle Europe, stretching from the Rhône valley to the modern Czech Republic, had been profoundly transformed in the late sixth century BC by its contact with the Greek trading cities of the Mediterranean coast. In the mid-fifth century BC, there was a dramatic collapse in the main centres of the West Hallstatt chiefdoms. Some, like the great princely residence at the Heuneburg, were violently destroyed; at those settlements which survived, there is a sharp decline in the number of royal burials and imported prestige goods from the Mediterranean world. An entire way of life had vanished in a single generation.

The West Hallstatt elites had stood at the head of a wealthy agricultural society, grouped around royal centres and manufacturing towns, mostly lying on the trade routes to the south. But the material prosperity of West Hallstatt culture was based on a highly unstable relationship with their northern neighbours. The raw materials with which these elites had purchased their Mediterranean luxuries – slaves, furs, amber and metals – were largely procured from the warlike Celtic peoples living beyond the Hallstatt zone to the north. Around the middle of the fifth century, this procurement system broke down altogether. The Celtic warriors of the Marne valley, the Moselle and Bohemia overran the old West Hallstatt chiefdoms, and took over the system of trade with the Greeks and Etruscans for themselves.

These northern warriors are today generally known as the La Tène Celts, taking their name from the site of La Tène at the eastern end of Lake Neuchâtel in Switzerland. In the central La Tène regions in north-west Europe, large fortified residences are almost unknown, and the burials of La Tène aristocrats reflect the society's overwhelmingly military ideology: war-chariots and weapons, rather than drinking-vessels, were the norm. Chieftains proved and reaffirmed their status through successful raiding, at increasingly greater distances from the La Tène northern homelands. The relations of these Celtic societies with the Mediterranean world were very different from those enjoyed by the princes of the Heuneburg or Vix. Luxury imports from the south (particularly Etruscan Italy) continued, but now we find them being adapted and modified by their new owners: bronze jugs from Italy were often reshaped by local metal-smiths and recarved with Celtic-style decoration. By the fourth century Mediterranean imports had become distinctly rare. Instead, the Celts had developed their own distinctive repertoire of locally made prestige goods, decorated with floral motifs, especially palmettes, and stylized, swirling representations of humans and animals (see Plate 15).

Over the course of the fourth century BC burial goods decorated in the unique La Tène style start to appear in clusters of burials spread ever more widely across central and southern Europe. This dramatic expansion of La Tène material culture, southwards into northern Italy and eastwards into the Balkans, can be interpreted in several different ways. The trad-itional view holds that the spread of La Tène culture is the mark of an entire people on the move: a great phase of mass Celtic migration and conquest, beginning around 400 BC, and culminating with the settlement of perhaps as many as 300,000 men, women and children in new homes on the fringes of the Mediterranean world. However, some archaeologists have recently argued that these mass migrations are a phantom. Instead, the widespread diffusion of Celtic art and burial customs in the fourth and third centuries BC perhaps reflected an enthusiastic adoption of La Tène culture by non-Celtic communities, who had become familiar with the goods and lifestyles of their northern European neighbours through trade.

Superficially, the modern debate over the Celtic migrations appears similar to the problem of Al Mina (see above, pp. 87–9). We saw there that the predominance of Euboean Greek pottery at Al Mina, interpreted

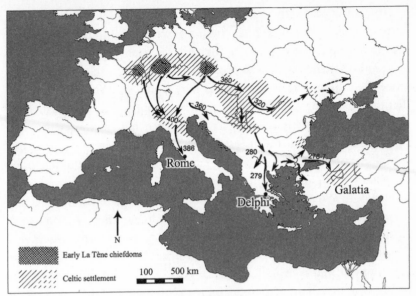

Map 19. The Celtic migrations.

by an earlier generation of archaeologists as showing the existence of a Euboean settlement at Al Mina, might reflect only the desirability of Euboean pottery to native Syrians. Strictly speaking, no Euboean need ever have visited Al Mina at all. Archaeological evidence alone can never give definitive answers to questions about the physical movements of ethnic groups. But the case of the 'phantom' Celtic migrations is in fact quite different from that of the phantom Euboeans at Al Mina. The crucial point is that the Celtic migrations, unlike the settlement at Al Mina, are directly attested by a mass of Greek and Roman historical records, both documentary and literary. And in this case, the written evidence (describing mass Celtic invasions of Italy in the early fourth century, and of Greece in the early third century) and the archaeological evidence (showing a steady expansion of Celtic material culture into northern Italy and the central Balkans over the same period) are in perfect alignment with one another.

The story told by Greek and Roman historians, then, is very likely to be substantially correct. In the first decade of the fourth century, a large group of Celts crossed the Alps and settled in the Po valley, in northern Italy. Raiding bands swept across Etruria and central Italy; Rome itself was sacked in around 386 BC. Simultaneously, another group was spreading devastation eastwards along the Danube, and by the mid-fourth century, the Celts were firmly installed in Hungary and Transylvania. In 335 BC, the year before his crossing into Asia, the young Alexander the Great was met by an embassy from the Danubian Celts, seeking an alliance with Macedon. When the king asked the Celts to name their greatest fear, hoping that they would say 'You', they replied that the only thing they feared was the sky falling on their heads. There is something strangely thrilling about this fleeting encounter between Celtic migrants from the forests of northern Europe and the future conqueror of India, as if two great currents of history had touched for an instant, and parted again.

Finally, in 279 BC the Celts of the lower Danube region launched a mass invasion of the Greek peninsula. The Macedonian and Thracian lowlands were pillaged, and despite heroic efforts by a hastily assembled Greek coalition force, one band of Celts succeeded in forcing the pass of Thermopylae and pouring into central Greece. This vast Celtic army was finally shattered in a great battle, fought in the midst of a snowstorm, at the very gates of the oracular sanctuary of Delphi; it was said that not a single Celt escaped alive. The following year, a second group of Celts crossed the Hellespont into Asia Minor. The cities of western Asia Minor endured a horrific decade of indiscriminate raiding by roaming Celtic warbands, until at last, in the early 260s BC, the Celts settled deep in inland Turkey, on the northern fringe of the Anatolian plateau around modern Ankara. These Anatolian Celts, known to the Greeks as the Galatians, retained many of the traditions and much of the social structure of their north European homeland. The geographer Strabo, writing in the early first century AD, tells us that the Galatians, living in the heart of the scorching and treeless Anatolian steppe, still used the term *drunemetos* for their assemblies, literally a sacred grove of oak trees, as though they were still gathering in the dark forests of Bohemia and the Rhine. The Celtic tongue could still be heard in the wilds of inner Anatolia as late as the sixth century AD.

The Celtic invasions hit the Greek world like a thunderbolt. Nothing of the kind had been seen in Greece since Xerxes' invasion two centuries earlier. The parallels between the two invasions were soon being exploited for political purposes. The prime movers in the defence of mainland Greece in 279 were the Aetolians, a populous but somewhat backward Greek tribe from west-central Greece with a reputation for piracy. After the victory over the Celts, the Aetolians promptly set up the shields of the defeated barbarians in the metopes of the west and south friezes of the temple of Apollo at Delphi, mirroring the Persian shields which had been placed on the north and east sides by the Athenians after the victory at Marathon in 490 BC. A new festival was established at Delphi under Aetolian patronage, the Soteria or 'Festival of Salvation', ultimately to become one of the major events in the Greek festival calendar. The Aetolian League, previously a relatively minor federal state, swiftly grew into one of the major powers of the Hellenistic world, enveloping many of its smaller central Greek neighbours.

Something very similar happened in Asia Minor. In the later third and second centuries BC the brunt of the seemingly endless struggle against the Galatians was borne by the rulers of a small independent principality in north-western Asia Minor, the Attalids of Pergamum. The great phase of Attalid expansion, which would end with the entire western half of the peninsula coming under their control, began when Attalus I of Pergamum (reigned c. 240–197) defeated the Galatians at a great battle at the sources of the Caicus river, around 240 BC. The Attalids consistently presented their victories over the Galatians as the latest in a grand succession of wars between Greeks and barbarians, mythical and historical. Around 200 BC Attalus set up a dramatic victory dedication on the Athenian Acropolis (see Figure 20). Four pedestals, each around 30 metres long, were erected south of the Parthenon, with free-standing statue groups of gods fighting giants (Gigantomachy), Athenians fighting Ama-

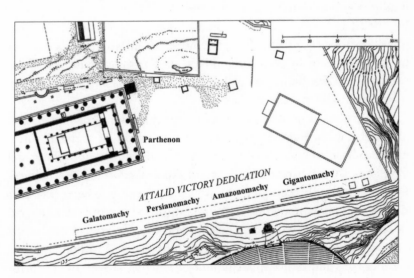

Figure 20. Attalid victory monument on the Athenian Acropolis, c. 200 BC.

zons (Amazonomachy), Greeks fighting Persians (Persianomachy) and, inevitably, Attalid soldiers defeating the Galatians (Galatomachy). The monument itself is lost, but Roman copies of several of the statues survive. The imagery of this monument, reinforced by its location at the foot of the Parthenon, deliberately recalls the sculptural programme of fifth-century Athens, and in particular the metopes of the Parthenon, on which gods, Lapiths and Greeks calmly mastered the various barbarian enemies of Greek civilization. Attalus claimed to be the latest hero of the ongoing defence of Greece against the barbarian, successor to the victorious Athenians of Marathon and Salamis.

His choice of Athens as the site for the monuments to his victory over the Celts is telling. In the second century BC, the cultural prestige of Athens was probably greater than it had ever been in the Classical period. In the 420s BC, at the height of the Athenian empire, the Athenians had requested a tithe of the grain-harvest from the entire Greek world, in recognition of Athens' self-appointed status as mother-city of the Ionians and the cradle of Greek civilization. Three hundred years later, the rest of the Greeks finally caught up. In 125 BC the Delphic amphictiony (an international body responsible for the affairs of the sanctuary at Delphi) voted lavish honours for the Athenians, 'since', we are told, 'it was the Athenian people, being the fount and origin of all things beneficial for humanity, who raised mankind from a bestial existence to a state of civilization'. A contemporary inscription from Maronea in Thrace describes Athens as the 'ornament of Europe'. The Hellenistic monarchs outdid one another in conspicuous generosity towards Athens. The city-centre filled up with huge new public buildings paid for by philhellenic kings: the Attalids themselves funded two lavish market-buildings or stoas, one in the Athenian *agora*, the other on the south slope of the Acropolis.

The resurgence of Athens in the second century BC reminds us that although the Hellenistic *oikoumenē* was a world of regional super-powers, it also remained a world of wealthy, self-governing, autonomous Greek cities, with specific local concerns and distinctive regional cultures. In this respect, the conquests of Alexander the Great were less of a watershed than is sometimes supposed. The cities continued to engage in regular warfare with their neighbours, to compete for prestige at an ever-growing circuit of Panhellenic festivals, and to build massive fortifications and lavish public buildings, whether at their own expense or that of the kings. Under the Hellenistic monarchies, the *polis* did not merely survive; it flourished. To judge from the mass of surviving documentary evidence, inter-state diplomacy achieved new heights of complexity and sophistication. In the late third century BC, as part of a sustained effort to protect their coastlines from the ravages of Cretan pirates, the Athenians struck a treaty with the west Cretan city of Kydonia (modern Khania). The basis of the treaty was the mythological kinship between the two peoples: as the Athenians could claim to be the descendants of Ion, son of Apollo, so the Kydonians claimed to be descended from Kydon, another of Apollo's many sons. The Greek mythological tradition was sufficiently flexible that, if one tried hard enough, any given *polis* could plausibly be connected to almost any other. Several cities employed professional historians among their diplomatic corps, men who were capable of explaining exactly why the people of Xanthos in Lycia (for instance) ought to help pay for the new city wall of far-off Kytenion in central Greece.

These convoluted kinship ties can appear faintly ridiculous. But the Greek cities took them perfectly seriously. In 196 BC the Greek city of Lampsacus in the Troad (the far north-west of the Asia Minor peninsula) appears to have been suffering from raids at the hands of one of the Galatian tribes of central Asia Minor. In response to this, the Lampsacenes sent an embassy to the city of Massilia in southern Gaul to ask for a letter of introduction to the Galatians. This embassy is deeply bizarre. It is extremely unlikely that the Anatolian Celts, living deep in inland Asia Minor at the opposite end of the Mediterranean from Massilia, had ever even heard of the Massiliots. Certainly, Massilia had long enjoyed close trading relations with the Celts of the Rhône valley; but the idea that this might carry any weight with the Galatians, who had cut off all ties with their central European homelands more than 200 years previously, is frankly absurd. The really interesting thing here is the Lampsacenes' expectation that the Galatians would be susceptible to the kinds of arguments used in ordinary Greek kinship diplomacy. 'The western Celts have an ancestral alliance with Massilia; therefore you, as Celts, have a special connection with Massilia. We, the Lampsacenes, are kinsmen of the Massiliots [both Lampsacus and Massilia were originally colonies of the Ionian city of Phocaea]; therefore you, as "allies" of the Massiliots, ought also to be allied with us (or at least stop raiding us).' Who can say what the Galatians made of all this.

*

The same Lampsacene embassy which visited Massilia went on to pay a visit to the most important non-Greek city in the western Mediterranean. Rome was at this point just beginning to emerge as the dominant power in mainland Greek affairs. Since the 280s BC the Romans had been steadily expanding their influence along both shores of the Adriatic. In 214 BC, while Hannibal was ravaging Italy, an energetic young king of Macedon, Philip V (reigned 221–179 BC), seized the opportunity to try to re-establish Macedonian control over the eastern Adriatic. After several years of shadow-boxing between the two powers, in 211 BC the Romans allied themselves with the Aetolian League against Philip. The war was an unusually vicious and bloody one; the Aetolians and Romans collaborated in selling entire cities into slavery. Not without reason, the Aetolians were accused of consorting with barbarians for the enslavement of Greece. Eventually, in 197 BC, the Macedonian army was defeated at the battle of Cynoscephalae in Thessaly and Philip was effectively expelled from mainland Greece. The Lampsacenes were understandably eager to get off on a good footing with this new superpower of the Hellenistic world. Once again, they rolled out a complex argument based on mythological kinship. The Romans were descendants of the Trojans, who had moved to Italy after the fall of Troy at the end of the heroic age. As inhabitants of the Troad, the ancient homeland of the Trojans, the Lampsacenes were thus kinsmen to the Roman people.

The Romans, unlike the Galatians, were entirely receptive to this way of thinking. Since the early years of the war against Philip, the Romans had learned the importance of presenting themselves not as foreign barbarians but as kinsmen and benefactors to the Greeks. The Roman general Titus Flamininus, the victor of Cynoscephalae, set up lavish dedications at the sanctuary of Delphi on which he was tactfully described as a descendant of Aeneas, the Trojan hero responsible for the foundation of Rome. Finally, at the Isthmia festival of summer 196 BC, Flamininus proclaimed the freedom of the entire Greek world; all Roman troops were withdrawn from Greece two years later. The symbolism was well chosen. Flamininus' choice of the Isthmian games at Corinth for his proclamation recalled the earlier role of Corinth as the meeting-place of the Greek alliance against Persia in 480 BC, and as the seat of Philip II's League of Corinth in the late fourth century. The freedom of the Greeks had been regularly declared by the Hellenistic monarchs, but none had taken such concrete steps to ensure it as the Romans had now done. Flamininus himself was hailed in terms appropriate to a Hellenistic monarch: he issued a gold coinage in his own name, carrying a heroic Alexander-style portrait of himself on one side, and on the other, his name being crowned by a winged Victory (see Plate 31b). The poet Alcaeus of Messene celebrated the Roman victory with a resonant comparison: 'Xerxes led a Persian host to the land of Greece, and Titus led another from broad Italy; but one came to lay the yoke of slavery on Europe's neck, the other to free Greece from slavery.' The wheel of Macedonian fortune had at last turned full circle: the new barbarian despot was none other than Philip V of Macedon, and it was Rome which had emerged as the true champion of the freedom of the Greeks.

Once the Romans had shown themselves willing to intervene in Greek affairs, their Greek allies could seldom resist the temptation to call in Roman firepower in support of their own interests. In the late 190s BC the Attalid kingdom of Pergamum was under fierce attack from their neighbours to the east, the Seleucid dynasty of Syria; the most vigorous of all the Seleucid monarchs, Antiochus III (reigned 223–187 BC), was trying to re-establish Seleucid rule over the whole of the Asia Minor peninsula. Although the Attalids had been allies of Rome since the early days of the war against Philip V, this was not Rome's war. For all that the new Attalid king, Eumenes II, bombarded the Roman Senate with hair-raising tales of Seleucid ambitions in continental Europe, it is clear that Antiochus, unlike Philip, posed no direct threat to Roman interests. Nonetheless, Eumenes got his army. In 190 BC the Roman general Scipio Africanus crossed the Hellespont in support of Pergamum; Antiochus was expelled from Asia Minor, and most of the western half of the peninsula was handed over to Eumenes. The Romans were evidently quite happy to play the role of police officers of Europe; equally happy, for the time being, to leave the actual running of east Mediterranean affairs to their Greek allies.

Since the reign of Alexander, the Greek states had regularly worshipped the Successor monarchs as gods. With the emergence of Rome as the dominant power in the Greek world, similar divine honours began to be offered to Roman generals and magistrates (including Flamininus). More striking is the establishment in several Greek cities, during the 190s BC, of the cult of a new goddess, Roma, the personified power of Rome itself. The worship of Roma was not an import from Rome, but a Greek innovation, expressed in purely Greek religious terms. A few states did go a little further in trying to understand their new 'benefactors'. Around the time of the Roman victory over Antiochus, the inhabitants of Chios, an island-state lying just off the Asia Minor coast, established a new festival in honour of the goddess Roma. But the island's loyalty to Rome was also marked by the dedication of a visual image (it is not clear whether it was a statue, relief or painting) depicting the birth of Romulus, the founder of Rome, and his brother Remus. The Chiots were eager to please; they had made some effort to inform themselves about the Romans' own traditions about their city's foundation. But even here the Roman-style depiction of Romulus and Remus is associated with a thoroughly Greek-style religious festival to Roma.

In the late 170s BC, the eastern Mediterranean world must have looked superficially much as it had done a century earlier. A strong king still ruled in Macedon: Perseus (reigned 179–168 BC), who had succeeded his father Philip V in 179 BC, had restored much of the territory and prestige lost by Philip at Cynoscephalae. Mainland Greece retained a precarious freedom; indeed, for the first time in its history, the entire Peloponnese was united under the umbrella of a single strong federal state, the Achaean League. Despite the loss of Asia Minor to Eumenes II of Pergamum, the Seleucid kingdom under Antiochus IV (reigned 175–164 BC), with its capital at Antioch on the Orontes (modern Antakya, in southern Turkey), was still the dominant power in Asia. But all that was about to change. The Romans, the 'common benefactors' of the Greek world, had scrupulously withdrawn their troops from the east after every intervention; in return, they expected their dispositions in Greece to be observed. Perseus, in his efforts to rebuild Macedonian power in the central Balkans, and in particular through his eagerness to win the goodwill of the mainland Greek states, was felt to have breached the spirit of those arrangements. Perseus could hardly have challenged Rome directly, but he certainly threatened the balance of power in the southern Balkan peninsula. In 171 BC, in response, yet again, to an appeal by the unscrupulous Eumenes, the Romans fabricated a quarrel with Perseus and once more declared war on Macedon. After a crushing Roman victory at Pydna in 168 BC, Perseus' kingdom was dissolved; the king himself was paraded as a captive through the streets of Rome.

Meanwhile, the Seleucid king Antiochus IV had taken advantage of Rome's entanglement in Macedonian affairs to launch a dramatic and ambitious invasion of Ptolemaic Egypt. In summer 168, while Antiochus was besieging Alexandria, he was met by Roman ambassadors, who curtly ordered him to leave Egypt immediately. When Antiochus replied that he needed time to consult his advisers, the leader of the Roman embassy, Gaius Popillius Laenas, drew a circle in the sand around the king's feet, and told him that they required a reply before he stepped out of it. Mindful of the fate of Macedon, Antiochus bowed to the inevitable; the Seleucid armies were instructed to withdraw.

Roman interventions in Greek affairs, which had so far been fairly benevolent, had begun to take on a hard and unpleasant edge. By the end of 167 BC one of the four superpowers (the Antigonids of Macedon) had simply ceased to exist; another (the Seleucids) had been summarily humiliated; the remaining two royal houses (the Attalids and the Ptolemies) owed their kingdoms to Roman support. The fact of Roman dominance was soon rendered all too clear. Macedon had been left free after the fall of Perseus, but in 148 BC, after an abortive attempt to restore the Antigonid monarchy, the region was reduced to the status of a tribute-paying province under a Roman governor: this was the first Roman province east of the Adriatic. Two years later, in 146 BC, when Roman envoys attempted to intervene in an internal dispute in the Achaean League, the ambassadors were jeered and pilloried by an assembly at Corinth. The Roman response was swift and ruthless. Later that same year, the forces of the Achaean League were annihilated by Roman legions, and the city of Corinth, cradle of Greek liberty in the Persian Wars, where only fifty years earlier Flamininus had declared the universal freedom of the Greeks, was wiped off the face of the earth.

Polybius begins his history of the rise of Rome with the assertion that the conquests of Alexander marked no real turning point in history. The Macedonian empire (or rather, empires) of the Hellenistic age was simply the third in a sequence of transient hegemonies: the Persians, the Spartans and the Macedonians. This is a slightly surprising claim from our perspective – not least in privileging the Spartan empire over the Athenian – but it contains more than a grain of truth. For Polybius, the crucial point was that the Hellenistic monarchs had not concerned themselves with anything west of the Greek mainland; Italy, Sicily, Libya and Sardinia were untouched by the Macedonians, and the barbarian peoples of mainland Europe were simply unknown to them. Hence world history down to the second century BC was, in his view, 'scattered', held together by no unity. It was left to the Romans to unite world affairs into a single organic whole.

Early in 86 BC, when King Mithradates VI persuaded much of mainland Greece to revolt one final time from Roman rule, the Roman general Cornelius Sulla appeared before the walls of Athens. An Athenian embassy came and urged Sulla to spare the city, recounting the exploits of Theseus and the heroism of the Athenians during the Persian Wars. Sulla replied simply that he had come to teach Athens a lesson, not to learn ancient history. Nothing could express more clearly the divergent paths which the histories of the western and eastern Mediterranean had taken since the fifth century BC. It is time to turn our attention to events in the Italian peninsula.

6

Rome, Carthage and the West:
500–146 BC

'Where the strong current divides Europe and Libya.' This quotation from the Roman poet Ennius, writing his *Annals* in the 180s and 170s BC, encapsulates the theme of this chapter. The *Annals* described the conflict between the Romans and the Carthaginians in Spain, and in particular a sea battle in the straits of Gibraltar and the subsequent surrender of Gades to the Romans in 206 BC. We have already observed how the opposition between Asia and Europe was represented as the driving force of the eastern Mediterranean. Around 200 BC Philip V of Macedon had proclaimed himself 'master of Europe'. Shortly afterwards, Philip and Macedon were made subject to the Romans, and in this quotation Ennius might be implying a new take on the old dichotomy: the struggle now was between Europe and Libya (modern North Africa).

We have already seen the changes in the Greek world, following the Persian Wars of 480 BC: the emergence of the new power of Athens, its struggles with Sparta, the warring Greek states, the rise of Macedon, the conquests of Alexander the Great and his Successor kingdoms. Into that world, Rome entered from the end of the third century BC. Here we explore the Roman story, from its beginnings right through the period covered by the previous two chapters. The story begins with Aeneas' flight from the sack of Troy to Italy, and Romulus' founding of Rome (traditionally in 753, or 751 or 748 BC) and its line of kings. The last king was expelled and Rome became a Republic in 507 BC. Internally, power now rested with the two consuls, the Senate and the popular assemblies. There were struggles for power within Rome between two groups, known as patricians and plebeians, but externally Rome's power spread first over the Latin states in its immediate vicinity, and then over much of the rest of the Italian peninsula by the third century BC. The other major player in this region was Carthage, founded in the late ninth

Map 20. The Italian peninsula in the third and second centuries BC.

century by Phoenicians from Tyre. As it became by far the greatest Phoenician city, the Romans normally referred to its inhabitants as 'Poeni', the Latin for Phoenician; the related adjective 'Punicus' has been taken over into the English word 'Punic'. From the late sixth century BC Rome had diplomatic relations with Carthage, and this had peacefully defined their respective spheres of influence, but the growing power of both states brought them into conflict in the third century BC. The three Punic Wars (264–241 BC, 218–202 BC and 149–146 BC) left Rome victorious, with control over central North Africa and parts of Iberia (modern Spain and Portugal). In the meantime, Rome had also been drawn into the Greek world. The destruction in 146 BC of both Carthage and Corinth marks a turning point in the history of the Mediterranean.

This outline of Roman history was what was normally accepted in Rome by the first century BC. Our problem is that we lack full contemporary sources for most of the period down to 146 BC, or even later. For

Roman expansion from 220 to 167 BC, we have the Greek historian Polybius, contemporary only with the end of his narrative, and his work too does not survive complete. Our principal narratives are those by Livy, writing at the end of the first century BC, and Dionysius of Halicarnassus, writing shortly afterwards. One difficulty is that Livy's work, which covered events up to his own time, is complete only to 295 BC; Dionysius' history narrated events only to the outbreak of the First Punic War, but is fragmentary from 447 BC onwards. More seriously, as we shall see, much of the received outline of Roman history which they present is extremely problematic, as later generations made use of the past for their present political ends. But, put more positively, those uses of the past are what make Roman history interesting. Instead of dismissing stories of Aeneas and Romulus, on the grounds that they tell us little about very early Rome, this chapter explores the telling of such stories in the course of the Republic.

A key context within the Italian peninsula for the re-creations of the past was a great diversity of cultures and languages. Greeks had been in contact with the region in the Bronze Age, and had been trading with, and settling in, the Italian peninsula since the eighth century BC. In the fifth and fourth centuries BC there were twenty-three Greek *poleis* in the southern part of the peninsula. The most northerly of these *poleis* were Neapolis (modern Naples) and adjacent Kymē (Latin: Cumae); the rest were in the toe, instep and heel of Italy, with another forty-seven in Sicily. The settlers were mainly from the Greek mainland and Greek was the dominant language of the settlements, in the case of Neapolis as late as the Roman empire. The mainland Greeks had been trading with the Etruscans since the eighth century BC, and Etruria formed a special export market for Greek pottery and other goods. These imports were used by local elites for their own purposes, and played a major role in the transformation of Etruscan society in the sixth century BC. Rome, lying between the Greek communities of southern Italy and the Etruscans to the north, also had contacts with the Greek world from an early date. Rome and the settlements immediately around it did not import Greek goods on the scale that the Etruscan cities did, but some of the contacts were more than merely transient. In the sixth century BC an Athenian pot was deposited as an offering in the sanctuary of the god Vulcan in the area of the Roman Forum. The striking thing is that the pot was decorated with a scene of the Greek god Hephaestus ascending to heaven on a donkey, a common Greek story. The association between Hephaestus and Vulcan, which was later absolutely standard, must have been in the mind of the dedicator of this pot at this early date. But the gods of Rome, though they may sometimes have been imagined on Greek lines, were thought of as Roman and not Greek.

The linguistic map of the Italian peninsula was very complex. In the eighth century the Etruscans had taken over from Greeks their alphabet, which they employed to write down their own language (above, p. 98). This was the first time that writing had been employed in the Italian peninsula. By the sixth century at the latest, nearly twenty languages, and associated dialects, of Italy also had alphabets, mostly derived from the Etruscan alphabet. Within the diversity of languages in the Italian peninsula, there were three major language groups: Greek in the southern

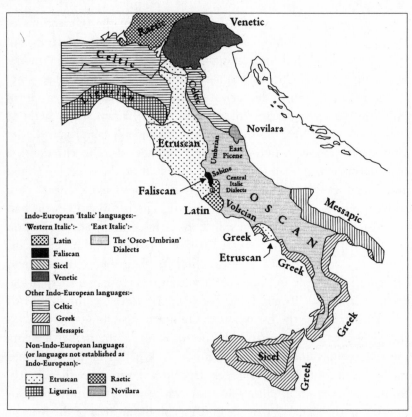

Map 21. Languages of the Italian peninsula, c. 400 BC.

coastal areas; Etruscan in the north-west; and Oscan-Umbrian (also known today as Sabellian) in the centre and south. Etruscan and three other minor languages were not Indo-European in origin; this is partly why Etruscan remains rather opaque to us today. Oscan-Umbrian was the most important member of a group of 'Italic' languages, as the linguists classify them. Other members are Venetic, in the region of modern Venice, if indeed it is correctly classified as an 'Italic' language, and Latin. Around 400 BC Latin was a minor member of this group. Even within Latium, Latin varied: around 200 BC Praeneste had a reputation in Rome for linguistic differences from Rome.

Dante and the languages of Italy

The linguistic diversity of Republican Italy reminds us that we need to avoid talking of 'Italy' in this period, which is why we have used instead the geographic circumlocution 'Italian peninsula'. There was no natural unity to the peninsula. Its unification was something achieved by the Romans in the course of the centuries to come, with its culmination in the first century BC. The linguistic unification achieved by Rome in the same period did not last for ever. Around AD 1300, in a wide-ranging treatise *De vulgari eloquentia* ('On eloquence in the vernacular'), the poet Dante surveyed the fourteen or more Italian vernaculars of the peninsula in his own day, which were regional, but which also varied within each region. Modern scholars note that these vernaculars had developed in parallel out of spoken Latin, and that there were in addition small outposts of Greek and Albanian in the south. Dante was seeking justification for the use of an Italian vernacular in which he could write high literature, in opposition to what he saw as the artificial language of Latin, in which paradoxically he had written this treatise, and the contemporary vernaculars of Provençal and French. He argued in favour of a supra-regional illustrious vernacular, which already existed, he claimed, in poetry. This vernacular was in reality related to his own vernacular of Tuscan. Dante used a less elevated and more wide-ranging version of the supra-regional vernacular a few years later in *The Divine Comedy*, but it was the literary Tuscan used by the fourteenth-century authors Petrarch and Boccaccio, as canonized in the Renaissance, which eventually formed the basis of modern Italian.

Stories about the earliest years of Rome were in circulation by at least the middle years of the Roman Republic. They had points of reference in ancient monuments and rituals in and around the city, which reinforced their significance. Evander was an important early figure and would feature prominently in Virgil's *Aeneid* as Aeneas' guide round the site of the future Rome and as the father of Pallas. He was said to have come to the area from Arcadia in the Peloponnese sixty years before the Trojan War, and to have founded the first settlement in Rome on the Palatine hill, allegedly named after the town of Pallantion in Arcadia. He was held responsible for founding a major cult of Hercules. The story was that Hercules was passing through Italy on his way back to Greece, having captured the cattle of Geryon, one of the canonical twelve Labours of Hercules. The cattle were seized by a local monster, Cacus, but Hercules defeated him. In turn, Evander established a cult of Hercules at the Ara Maxima ('Greatest Altar'). The altar itself, as rebuilt in the second century BC, was probably on a monumental base, covering 22 × 32 metres and 4 metres high; the rites were celebrated through the Republican and imperial periods; the 'steps of Cacus' were displayed on the slopes of the Palatine Hill.

The story of Hercules and the cattle of Geryon seems to have been widespread by a very early date. In the fifth century BC the Greek historian Hellanicus of Lesbos tells how a calf which had escaped from the herd wandered all down the peninsula and swam the straits to Sicily. Heracles, pursuing the calf, asked all the inhabitants if they had seen the calf (*damalis* in Greek). They replied in their own tongue, referring to the *vitulus*, the Italic word for calf, and so Heracles named the whole land Vitulia, after the calf. This nice 'Just So' story, which implies that Hellanicus knew a little Italic, is perhaps the best early evidence for a widespread local sense of Italy as an entity. The calf, or bull, as the symbol of Italy will recur in the political and military struggles of the first century BC.

Aeneas, in his flight from the sack of Troy, eventually arrived in Italy, where he met the elderly Evander. The king of the neighbouring peoples, Latinus, initially fought Aeneas, but then made peace with him, a peace which was cemented by marriage between Aeneas and his daughter Lavinia. In her honour, Aeneas named his first settlement in Italy Lavinium. Aeneas' son Ascanius (also known as Iulus) founded another settlement nearby, at Alba Longa, which his descendants ruled for many generations. As we shall see, the local association of Aeneas and his family with Lavinium and Alba Longa was firmly established by the fourth century BC.

When was Rome itself founded? The oldest versions, told by Greek authors, placed the foundation in the immediate aftermath of the Trojan War. Hellanicus of Lesbos, for example, in a meticulous work of chronological scholarship, had Aeneas coming to Italy, with Odysseus, and founding the city, which he named after Romē, a Trojan woman. We do not know whether these Greek authors picked up and developed stories circulating in Italy already at this date, but this early chronology, associating the foundation of Rome with the fall of Troy, was normal until the end of the third century BC. An alternative chronology placed the founding of Rome much later than the Trojan War. Given Eratosthenes' dating for the sack of Troy, 1184 BC, some writers by the end of the third century BC were placing the foundation of Rome around the middle of the eighth century BC. This sort of date eventually became canonical: everyone in British schools used to be taught that Rome was founded in 753 BC. The gap between the sack of Troy and the eighth century BC was filled by a sequence of rather anonymous kings of Alba Longa.

The last king of Alba Longa, a usurper who had killed his elder brother, had a daughter, Rhea Silvia. She became a Vestal Virgin, and was thus sworn to chastity, but was seduced by the god Mars. She was imprisoned, and her twin boys were exposed in a basket. The basket was carried away by the river, ending up caught by a fig tree. A she-wolf suckled them in a nearby cave, a shepherd and his wife reared them, and the boys, Romulus and Remus, grew up to depose their usurping father and to found a new settlement where they had been reared. This story of the foundation of Rome has early roots. On the Palatine hill, the she-wolf's cave, the Lupercal, was the focus of an ancient annual ritual; and an ancient reed hut, said to be the shepherd's hut, was dutifully preserved and restored as necessary, probably until as late as the fourth century AD. Other monuments accrued: in 296 BC a statue of the she-wolf suckling the boys was erected at the site of the famous fig tree, and was then featured on the first silver coins to be minted at Rome, in the 260s BC. This statue, which does not survive, is different from the famous Capitoline Wolf, as featured in the imagery for the 1960 Rome Olympics and the AS Roma football club: that statue might be even older (sixth century BC), though scientific tests have suggested that it is a product of the thirteenth century AD; this huge difference in date is due to the lack of good comparanda for the statue. Imagery of the she-wolf and twins was used by the Greek city of Chios in the early second century BC (above, p. 172).

One story about Romulus was that he established an asylum in his new city, and that the mixture of those who sought refuge here, political refugees and slaves, was a significant feature of Rome. The presence of slaves among the refugees corresponded to an important aspect of later Roman practice: slaves who were formally freed by their masters received Roman citizenship. According to Philip V of Macedon in 214 BC, instructing a city in Thessaly (northern Greece) to admit resident Thessalians and other Greeks to its citizenship, grants of citizenship to ex-slaves were responsible for the expansion of Rome and the creation of its numerous colonies. No Greek city-state regularly treated its ex-slaves in this way. The Roman practice was underpinned by a story that Servius Tullius, the sixth king, was himself the son of a slave, and that he founded a cult of Fortune, whose mutability made the cult popular with slaves. Rome saw itself as growing from very mixed origins, in contrast to the Athenians, who prided themselves as being indigenous to Attica. But two very different lines were taken as to the nature, and desirability, of the mixture, depending on the political circumstances. Opponents of political populism in the first century BC talked of the Roman populace as the 'dregs of Romulus', the scrapings of the barrel that made up Rome. On the other hand, for those in the first century AD in favour of welcoming non-Italians into the Senate Romulus' asylum was an important precedent (see below, p. 257).

Rome has what might seem an excessive number of founding figures, in comparison with the one founder that most states claimed. So one might think that originally Rome had only one founder (Romulus), and that associations with Aeneas are quite late. But Aeneas, Latinus and Romulus have in common that they were worshipped after their deaths (unique at Rome in the Republican period), but under another name: Aeneas as Pater Indiges, Latinus as Jupiter Latiaris and Romulus as Quirinus. These cults are ancient, and their associations with the three founding figures go back well into the Republican period. It might also seem odd to associate Rome, even indirectly, with Aeneas, a Trojan and therefore enemy to the Greeks. Was this a story developed at a time when the Romans saw themselves as anti-Greek? In fact, the Trojans were almost never seen as anti-Greek, let alone as 'barbarians'. The war between the mainland Greeks and the Trojans was the first major war of Greek history, and many communities sought to link themselves to the Greek world by claiming descent from Trojan refugees. The final example of this strategy is the story told by the twelfth-century historian Geoffrey of Monmouth, in his *History of the Kings of Britain*, following one of the traditions reported in a ninth-century historical compilation. This claimed that Brutus, grandson of Aeneas, was exiled for killing his parents, and after many wanderings reached an island, now named Britain after him, where he defeated and killed the giant descendants of Albion, and founded the British monarchy. Though some people at the time were very critical of Geoffrey's work, his attempt to create a framework for early British history, and to relate a remote island to the springs of civilization, was still accepted by some British antiquarians as late as the eighteenth century.

Rome was ruled by seven kings, from Romulus to Tarquinius Superbus. Later tradition was clear about the sequence of kings, and about their varied contributions to the development of Rome: Romulus created the Roman Senate, and the organization of Roman tribes; Tarquinius Priscus, the fifth king, expanded Rome's power to the north and celebrated the first triumph; Servius Tullius, the sixth king, reformed the Roman army and the structures of the city of Rome. In fact, this narrative breaks down at the first hurdle: it is impossible to imagine only seven kings ruling Rome over a period of 250 years, with average reigns of about forty years.

Modern archaeologists have tried to outline the growth of the city in this period. Some have been seduced by the desire to find archaeological confirmation of the canonical stories, hailing an eighth-century BC wall on the Palatine as the work of Romulus. Others, rightly, have argued that it is wrong to use the historical tradition to suggest that the institutions of the later Roman state predate the physical growth of the city; instead, they argue that inferences should be drawn directly from the archaeological data, without contamination from the later historical tradition. It is clear that in the eighth and seventh centuries BC there was increased activity in the area of Rome. By the end of the seventh century Rome had become quite urbanized: the Forum area had been reorganized; cult sites had developed in several places, including the Capitol; stone houses had replaced huts on the Palatine. Rome was moving in the same directions as contemporary settlements in Etruria, like Veii, which we examined in Chapter 2, and indeed in Greece. In the sixth century BC a massive wall was built round the city, securely dated at nearly two dozen spots. Eleven kilometres long, and running round all seven hills of Rome, the wall enclosed an area of about 425 hectares. It made Rome more than twice the size of any Etruscan city, and put it on a par with the major states in southern Italy and Sicily. The construction of the wall implies a unified state by this time, with its own army. In later tradition, the wall was ascribed to Servius Tullius, but it is a mistake to use the archaeological evidence to support details of the historical tradition about the kings.

Tidy Roman historical traditions about the seven kings also run foul of Etruscan traditions. An intriguing piece of evidence about Servius Tullius is a tomb painting from Vulci in Etruria, dating to the second half of the fourth century BC, which is much earlier than any surviving Roman source. With the people all carefully labelled, the painting depicts on opposite walls a scene from the *Iliad* of the sacrifice of Trojan prisoners at the funeral of Patroclus, and a scene from the history of Vulci also involving an attack on defenceless opponents. The *Iliad* scene, which also includes elements of Etruscan imagery, is a good example of how the Etruscans borrowed and adapted from Greek culture, and must be intended to be parallel in some way to the scene of local history. The local scene depicts events of the sixth century BC, 200 years previously (see Figure 21). The brothers Avle and Caile Vipinas (Aulus and Caeles Vibenna in Latin) and others from Vulci were fighting a grouping of men from Volsinii, Sovana and Rome. Among the Vulcians was one Mastarna, who freed Caile Vipinas from his bonds; another man is shown killing Cneve Tarchunies Rumach, that is, Gnaeus Tarquinius of Rome. The Vibenna brothers of Vulci were important historical figures of the sixth century. The Gnaeus Tarquinius may be related to the Tarquinii known as kings, who both seem to be called Lucius. The episode preserved at Vulci is therefore of fighting between aristocratic warrior bands. The episode also hints at a future event featuring Mastarna, the loyal supporter of the Vibenna brothers, who is shown freeing one of them. Etruscan written traditions survived into at least the first century AD, when they were studied by the future emperor Claudius, a real scholar. Claudius reported that Etruscan sources claimed that Servius Tullius was once the most faithful companion of Caelius Vivenna and took part in all his adventures. Subsequently, driven out by a change of fortune, he left Etruria with all the remnants of Caelius' army and occupied the Caelian Hill, naming it thus after his former leader. Servius changed his name (for in Etruscan his name was Mastarna), and was called by the name I have used, and he obtained the throne to the greatest advantage of the state.

This story conflicts, as Claudius notes, with the Roman tradition that Servius was 'the son of Ocresia, a prisoner of war'. It conflicts even more with another Roman tradition, which we have already met, that Servius was the son of a slave impregnated by a divine phallus. This complex set of stories illustrates the richness of local traditions in Etruria, depicted in the Vulci tomb at a time when the area was coming under severe pressure from Rome, and preserved long after Roman conquest. It also shows the fragility of Roman traditions about their kings, who may have been more like leaders of the aristocratic warrior bands seen in the Vulci tomb than formal kings, and emphasizes the extent to which the Romans came to write the Etruscans out of their own history. This Roman perspective in its turn has until recently led modern scholars too to separate Roman and Etruscan developments in this early period.

Stories about Numa, Rome's second king, reveal further complexities within Roman traditions about the regal period. According to Ennius, Numa founded the basic religious institutions of Rome, and ordered the perpetuation of what he had established after his death. This is an admirable and straightforward story, if perhaps slightly dull. But, also according to Ennius, Numa had consorted with the water nymph Egeria,

Figure 21. Painting from tomb at Vulci (known as the François Tomb, after its discoverer). From left: Caele Vipinas is freed by Mastarna; Larth Ulthes stabs Laris Papathnas Velznach (= of Volsinii); Pesna Arcmsnas Sveamach (= of Sovana) is killed by Rusce; Venthical[. . .]plsachs (of somewhere not now identifiable) is killed by Avle Vipinas; Marce Camitlinas is about to kill Cneve Tarchunies Rumach.

and it was from her that his religious inspiration came. Later Roman sources were embarrassed by the Egeria story, and sought to rationalize it away, but it is a genuinely early tradition about Numa. Some even thought that Numa could coerce Jupiter to come down to earth, and make him provide information by trickery. Numa's successor, Tullus Hostilius, found his instructions about how to coerce Jupiter, and tried them out at a time of crisis, but he and his sons were killed by a thunderbolt. These stories show that relations with the gods were in origin not simply a matter of rational human ordinance, but that the founding king had power that had not been passed on to his successors. Religion was not an attempt to seek out divine truths, let alone to coerce divine powers, but a more limited system of relating to the gods in a manner appropriate for mortals. This conception of religion seems to have been prevalent in 181 BC, when Numa's coffin was discovered by chance. The coffin contained a number of papyrus rolls, perfectly preserved. Some claimed that these rolls contained philosophy inspired by the Greek philosopher Pythagoras. This claim cannot be literally true, as Numa predated Pythagoras by 150 years, but it may be that the 'discovery' of the books was part of an attempt by members of the elite to impose new religious practices on Rome in the guise of tradition. Whatever the truth of this idea, the Roman authorities decided to destroy the books. They were too dangerous, and there could be no going back to the days of Numa himself.

The Roman calendar

The fundamentals of the Roman calendar went back to the regal period. The Romans believed that originally, under Romulus, the year had ten months, beginning in March. The first four months, March to June, were named after gods (for example, Mars or Juno), or so it was often claimed. But the fifth to tenth months, July to December, were originally named after the numbers five to ten; months five and six, Quintilis and Sextilis, were subsequently renamed after *Julius* Caesar and *Augustus*. But as Romulus' calendar was poorly devised, Numa, it was believed, undertook major reforms: he created two additional months (January and February); he regularized the length of months; and he made 1 January the start of the year. Making any calendar fit the annual period of the earth's rotation around the sun (365 days, 5 hours and about 49 minutes) is difficult, and during the Republic ad hoc adjustments to Numa's calendar were ineffective, so that by the mid-first century BC the calendar was 67 days ahead. The reform by Julius Caesar in 46 BC added two temporary months to deal with the 67 days, and decreed a regular extra day every fourth year. This Julian calendar remained in force in the west for the next millennium and a half, but its relation to the solar year was inexact, so that by AD 1582 the calendar was ahead by ten days. In that year Pope Gregory XIII decreed the omission of the extra ten days, and slightly modified the system of leap years, which were suspended in years ending in oo, unless they were exactly divisible by 400. Because the reform was decreed by the Pope, it was much resisted, even in Catholic countries, with riots in Augsburg. In Protestant Britain the Gregorian calendar came into effect only in 1752. The Orthodox Church in Russia and some other countries still uses the Julian calendar for fixed religious festivals, so that their Christmas falls on 7 January. The modern western calendar, whether Julian or Gregorian, is thus a direct continuation of the Roman calendar.

Stories about the early and middle Republic were, like those about the regal period, much affected by later events. Individual families had much to gain from enhancing the roles of their ancestors. A tomb perhaps of the Fabii, one of the major families of Rome, includes a third-century BC fresco with military scenes. They depict otherwise unknown occurrences in Rome's wars with the Samnites of central Italy, perhaps those carried out by a Fabius who was consul five times between 322 and 295 BC. It was clearly in the interests of the family to preserve, or enlarge, the deeds of its members.

Another tomb in Rome, of the Scipios, a key family in the third and second centuries BC, is especially important. Started in the third century BC, the tomb was modelled on earlier Etruscan family tombs: though cremation was the norm by this time, family members were inhumed in sarcophagi, which were arranged in order of importance round the tomb of the founder Barbatus (consul 298 BC) and labelled with elaborate verse inscriptions. The tomb was extensively modernized in the middle of the second century BC, as part of a move to give it more public prominence (see Figure 22). It was given a grand frontage in the latest style, in which were prominently displayed portrait statues of members of the family,

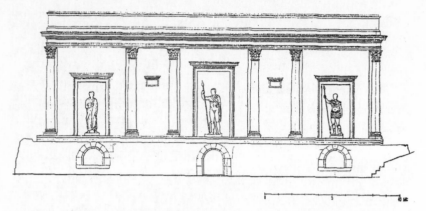

Figure 22. Tomb of the Scipios, reconstruction of frontage.

and of the poet Ennius. The inscription on the sarcophagus of Barbatus merits quotation: 'Cornelius Lucius Scipio Barbatus, born with Gaius as his father, a brave and wise man whose appearance was equal to his virtue, who was your consul, *censor* and aedile, captured Taurasia and Cisauna from Samnium (?), subdued all Lucania and took away hostages from it.' Two lines which precede this text were subsequently erased, perhaps because they included a claim that Barbatus was the founder of the family, a claim best suppressed when later generations came to claim even earlier founders. What was left is a vivid statement by a leading family of Rome of the importance of the male line in a family, physical appearance, holding of public office and achievements in warfare. It also presupposes the importance of the people of Rome: the reference to Barbatus as 'your consul' presumably echoes what had been said in the formal public speech at the grand funeral that was typical for members of the Roman elite. The pressure of competition between members of the elite for success no doubt had consequences for the stories that were told. What is said in the inscription about Barbatus' campaigns is incompatible with the narrative that Livy gave of the same years.

For aristocratic families like the Scipios women had considerable importance. In religion, elite women at Rome had fewer roles than in the Greek world, in that (male) senators held the main priesthoods of Rome, but the wives of senators acted as a body at special moments to supplicate the gods, and were prominent at particular religious festivals; the daughters of senators, too, might be selected to be Vestal Virgins, a prestigious office modelled on that once held by the daughters of the kings of Rome. In death, to judge from the one surviving Scipionic example, women were buried in the family tomb in their own sarcophagi, duly labelled with their names, but with no eulogy of their achievements.

Achievements of male ancestors were of key importance to the next generations. This is very clear in the inscription on the sarcophagus of Barbatus' son (consul 259 BC): 'Almost all agree that this man, Lucius Scipio, was the best of the good men at Rome. He was Barbatus' son, your consul, *censor* and aedile. He took Corsica and the city of Aleria, and gave a temple to the storm-gods in recompense for their help.' Lucius' stress on his ancestry is striking ('He was Barbatus' son'), especially following the implicit recognition that Lucius' claim to be 'the best of the good men at Rome' was contentious. Appeal to the achievements of Barbatus was key to the success of Lucius, which illustrates an important point about Roman political life. Well over half of all men who were consuls between 179 and 49 BC had fathers or grandfathers who had been consuls, and this figure rises to about 80 per cent if more remote ancestors are included. These figures are not evidence of predestination at birth; rather, they show the success of candidates in appealing to their family's past when they stood for election to public office. This type of appeal was entirely typical of the way that the Roman elite operated, but was alien to the contemporary Greek world, whose political values were much more meritocratic.

The political structures of the Roman Republic familiar in the world of Cicero in the first century BC consisted of the Senate, the people and the magistrates. This tripartite structure was perhaps first articulated by Greek observers of Rome, long used to the system of council, assembly and magistrates in Greek city-states. Polybius, writing in the later second century BC, offered a classic statement of the case, arguing that Rome's phenomenal strength in his day was derived from the balance between the three elements. Such views, flattering as they were to Rome, were internalized by the Romans, and came to form part of the ways that they thought about their own state. But it would be a mistake to project, as the Romans did, a tripartite analysis of Rome back into the early Republic, let alone the regal period. There are good grounds for thinking that earlier structures were very different.

An early form of tension was not the balance of power between Senate, people and magistrates, but the polarity between priest and king or magistrate. A story, recounted by Livy and other writers of the late Republic, told of a conflict between the king Tarquinius Priscus, who wanted to make institutional changes without consulting the will of the gods by taking auguries, and the leading contemporary *augur*, or official diviner, Attus Navius. Tarquinius, seeking to belittle the art of augury, asked Navius to divine whether he could do what the king was currently thinking of. Navius took the auguries and said that he could. Tarquinius replied, as he thought triumphantly, that he had been thinking of Navius cutting a whetstone in half. But Navius promptly, and miraculously, did cut the whetstone with a razor. The deed was commemorated at the actual spot, in the Forum, with a bronze statue of Navius, beside which rested the evidence of the whetstone itself. The moral drawn from this tale was that from then on no political or military decision could be taken in Rome without first consulting the will of the gods through augury. In the Republican period we rarely hear of such prominent individual Roman priests as Navius. Conflict between priests acting collectively and the magistrates did still occur, but the conflict involved no miraculous elements. Priestly office at Rome became a monopoly of senators (and in the case of the Vestal Virgins, their daughters), unlike in Greece, where priests were not drawn only from the political elite, and where women commonly held priestly office. By contrast, Navius came from a poor family, and was not a member of the senatorial group of *augures* established by Romulus, but he was also the archetypal *augur* in the Republican period. He even managed miraculously to move the fig tree which had rescued Romulus and Remus, from the banks of the Tiber to the Roman Forum. Stories about the early tension between priest and political authority had continued resonance during the Republic, when priests had supreme authority on matters of religious law, but could act only when called upon to do so by the Senate.

A second possible difference from the later tripartition between Senate, people and magistrates concerns the Senate itself. Later tradition is clear that the Senate was founded by Romulus, and Livy's narrative ascribes a major role to the Senate in the early Republic. It is possible that Livy is guilty of anachronism, in relation not only to the time of Romulus but also to the fifth and fourth centuries BC. Originally, the Senate was probably only an advisory body for the kings and then the two consuls, who took over the king's political powers. The new consuls each year would select such men as they chose to serve on their advisory council.

No doubt some men served repeatedly, but there was no presupposition of continuity in membership. Only with the passing of the Ovinian Law in the 330s BC did failure to be selected for membership of the Senate mean disgrace, and only gradually did the Senate become what it was in the late Republic: a body consisting of all who had held specific magistracies, with lifelong membership, unless the *censor*, a senior magistrate, struck them off for disgraceful behaviour; and hence a body with major political power.

By the second century BC an ambitious Roman man might hope to proceed through a sequence of magistracies, from quaestor up to consul. Each post had specific duties, whether civil or military, and defined powers. The magistrates, numbering thirty-two in the second century BC, were in the position to take initiatives, and so might seem to constitute a sort of government. In fact, they were merely a collection of competitive individuals, each holding office for only one year. Their powers were defined in two ways: the possession of *auspicium*, the power to consult the gods on behalf of the state, and of *imperium*, the power to command men at Rome or in the field. Both *auspicium* and *imperium* were seen as being continuations of the powers held by the kings of Rome. Romulus, in seeking to found the city, sought, and received, favourable signs from heaven. If both consuls died in office, the *auspicia* reverted to the Senate, which appointed as a temporary measure an *interrex*, who would hold elections for new consuls, and ensure the continuity of the *auspicia*. The name of the official, *interrex* ('interim king'), enshrined a belief that the office went back to the regal period. *Imperium*, so the Romans believed, was the power by which the kings had ruled at Rome, and had led their armies out to war. The two consuls inherited this power. Their collegiality acted as a brake on excessive influence in the hands of one man, and they took it in turns to possess the symbols of *imperium*. By the second century BC lower magistrates also possessed *imperium*, lesser than that of the consuls, and carefully defined as appropriate for each post.

The people of Rome had important political roles. When summoned by a magistrate with *imperium*, the people could make informal responses to speeches. When meeting in primary assemblies (*comitia*), the people were responsible for electing the magistrates, for passing legislation and for approving some decisions for action. The *comitia* involved no discussion or debate, just decisions taken by formal vote. Two types of *comitia* were believed to go back to the regal period. Important though the *comitia* were, the Roman elite of the second century BC was clear that Rome was not a democracy in the sense that Athens had been in the fifth and fourth centuries BC; the votes of one type of *comitia* were explicitly weighted in favour of the wealthy classes. The good running of the state depended on a proper balance between the Senate, the people and the magistrates. This balance was possible in part because Rome's 'Republican' institutions were rooted in the period of the kings.

The revolutionary United States and Rome

James Madison and Alexander Hamilton, authors of the *Federalist Papers*, advocating ratification of the new US Constitution, signed themselves jointly as 'Publius', recalling Publius Valerius Poplicola, first consul of the Roman Republic. Despite this type of rhetoric, some modern scholars argue that Rome played a merely decorative role for the Founding Fathers, and that the decisive arguments were those of Italian and English republicans of the previous two centuries. In fact, engagement with the Roman past helped to shape the arguments of the American revolutionaries. Colleges for men placed enormous emphasis on reading Latin and Greek authors, and at least some of the pupils were inspired by what they read. Thomas Jefferson recorded many classical authors in his commonplace book for 1758–73, some 40 per cent of the total, and his later huge library included many Latin texts in which he loved to lose himself. Women read classical books at home, in translation, drawing from them inspiration for their roles in life. Abigail Adams wrote regular letters to her husband, John Adams (Jefferson's great rival), signing herself as Portia, wife of Brutus, even wondering about what rights and duties women should have in the new state.

The Declaration of Independence in 1776, drafted by Jefferson, meant that the former British colonies were now republics, and dialogue with the history of antiquity helped to separate the new republics, the bastions of liberty, from the old feudal and monarchic regimes of Europe. The dangers of tyranny were exemplified in Alexander of Macedon, Julius Caesar and the subsequent emperors; Jefferson considered Tacitus, the great critic of the imperial system, 'the first writer in the world without a single exception'. Positive inspiration was drawn from other ancient examples. The Lycian League, which brought together twenty-three Greek city-states, was held up as a model of an excellent confederate republic. For John Adams, in his *Defence of the Constitutions of the United States of America* (1787), the Roman constitution, as presented by Cicero, was exemplary in showing how to protect freedom and justice through a system of checks and balances. Adams was also impressed by Polybius' analysis of Rome; he included a translation and summary of it in his collection of republican sources, published for use by the delegates at the United States Constitutional Convention. As Jefferson said in 1795, in reference to America's 'experiment' of being governed 'on principals of honesty, not mere force', 'we have seen no instance of this since the days of the Roman republic'.

*

The expansion of Rome's power within the Italian peninsula under the Republic began the process of the transformation of Rome from a state on the fringes of the major players, Greeks, Phoenicians and Etruscans, to a state with the largest ever European empire. Growth within Italy laid the foundations for Rome's expansion overseas, and its conflicts with the Carthaginians, to which we shall return. The initial phase, in the fifth and fourth centuries BC, was the consolidation of power in Latium, the immediate hinterland of Rome. In 507 BC, when Rome made a treaty with Carthage, the state behaved as the principal player in Latium, but shortly afterwards Rome was forced to create a more formalized relationship with the other towns in Latium, in what is known as the Latin League.

This League was held together not only by military force and self-interest, but also by a common sense of the past. Lavinium, 30 kilometres south of Rome, was noted as Aeneas' first settlement in Italy. To the south of the actual settlement were two important sanctuaries. A seventh-century BC burial mound, unusual in this region, received offerings from the sixth century, and in the fourth century BC was rebuilt as a shrine. It may be the monument identified later as the tomb of Aeneas himself. Not far away is a sanctuary with a line of substantial altars, increasing in number from three to twelve between the sixth and fourth centuries BC. They may commemorate the Penates, the powers which Aeneas had rescued from Troy, and to which he sacrificed on landing here. This important cult centre may have been used for sacrifices by the members of the Latin League. The second major location for the Latin League was the Alban Hill, a prominent hill 25 kilometres south-east of Rome. By

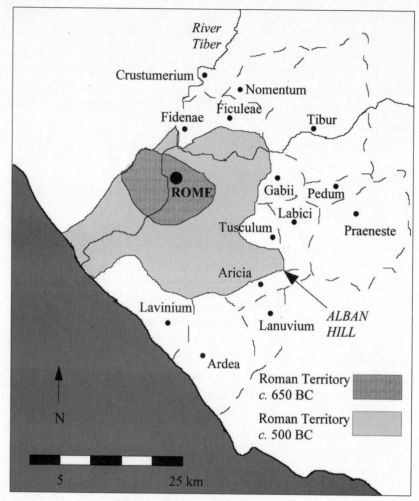

Map 22. Rome and Latium *c.* 500 BC.

tradition, Aeneas' son Ascanius founded Alba Longa. The settlement disappeared, allegedly sacked by Tullus Hostilius, but the nearby sanctuary on the Alban Hill was the location for the major annual festival of the Latin League in honour of Jupiter Latiaris, the deified version of Latinus.

In the course of the fifth century Rome's local power came under pressure, and in the fourth century the Latin allies of Rome revolted. After a series of wars, in 338 BC the old Latin League lost its military and political functions, though its festivals survived. From now on, the male inhabitants of Italy under Roman control fell into four categories: full Roman citizens, Roman citizens without the right to vote, Latins and allies. All communities had two things in common: first, they had relations with Rome, not with one another; secondly, their obligations to Rome were defined in terms of military contributions, not taxes or tribute. As a result, Rome was dominant as far south as the bay of Naples, at the head of a vast army.

The size of Rome's territory in the early fifth century BC was about 900 square kilometres, dwarfing the other individual city-states in Latium. The overall extent of the territory of the Latin city-states at the same period was about 2,350 square kilometres. By comparison, at the same period the territory of Corinth was also 900 square kilometres, the same as Rome, and Athens about 2,400 square kilometres, the equivalent of the territory of all the Latin city-states. But by 338 BC the territory belonging to the Romans (*ager Romanus*) had jumped to about 5,500 square kilometres, and the territory of the new Roman alliances as a whole about 8,500 square kilometres. As a result, Rome could now draw on a huge territory, with vast resources of manpower for its army. The territory was larger than that of any contemporary city-state in mainland Greece, but about half the size of the area of the alliance headed by contemporary Syracuse.

Roman expansion outside Latium started in the fourth century, first to the north into Etruria, and then to the south. The emblematic event in the conquest of Etruria was the attack on Veii, Rome's nearest neighbour to the north, just 17 kilometres away. Veii by the fifth century BC had large fortification walls surrounding a substantial settlement. There had been two major wars over the previous century. The story of the final conflict, as told by Livy, is full and very detailed: a ten-year siege, ending in 396 BC thanks to the Roman response to a prophecy; a Roman stratagem, namely, a tunnel dug to emerge inside the Veiian citadel; the sack of the city by Camillus; and the removal of the statue of Juno, the city's principal deity, to Rome. Livy was right that Veii was captured by Rome, probably in 396, but no details in his description can be relied on. The whole story is an epic elaboration of what happened, with deliberate parallels to the story of the sack of Troy: the ten-year siege, intervention by the gods, the stratagem, and the removal of Juno, which recalls Aeneas' removal of the Penates.

Lays of Ancient Rome

Modern scepticism about the details of the story of the capture of Veii goes back to the founder of modern critical scholarship on Roman history. B. G. Niebuhr's *History of Rome*, first published in German in 1811–12, became an instant success, being translated into English in 1828, and often reissued. Niebuhr has the distinction of being the first modern scholar to try and remove the legendary aspects from Livy's story, in favour of an account derived from the annals written in the Republic. As he says, the annals' 'account of the capture of the city has been entirely supplanted by a poetical story, belonging to the lay or legend, whichever one may choose to call it, of Camillus; an epic narrative, the features of which are irreconcilable with history . . .'.

Niebuhr's reference to a 'lay' alludes to an important element in his theory of the transmission of stories outside the annalistic tradition. Following some earlier scholars, he suggested that lays or ballads, performed at banquets, elaborated stories about early Rome. This idea had a long life in the nineteenth century, and beyond. The most famous exponent of it was Thomas Babington Macaulay. While serving the Raj in India, he composed a set of four *Lays of Ancient Rome*, as examples of Niebuhr's lost lays. First published in 1842, the *Lays* had immense popularity, being required reading in British schools for about a hundred years. Even now many people can recite at least the opening of the first lay, about Horatius at the bridge: 'Lars Porsena of Clusium / By the Nine Gods he swore / That the great house of Tarquin / Should suffer wrong no more.' The irony of the popularity of Macaulay's *Lays* is that their Romantic emphasis on the legendary completely cast into the shadows Niebuhr's critical rejection of the truth of such stories.

In 386 BC Camillus, the conqueror of Veii, was also central to Rome's response to an attack by the Gauls. In middle Europe around 450 BC there emerged what we know as the La Tène culture, based on a strong warrior ideology. Pushed on by population pressure in their homelands, members of three of the newly established tribes crossed the Alps in search of new territory and riches in the Italian peninsula, following routes long known to them through earlier contacts via traders and mercenaries. They took over former Etruscan settlements in the fertile

Po valley, and pressed on down the east coast of Italy as far as Ancona. Some continued south, defeated the Romans and sacked Rome itself. This event left the Romans with an enduring fear of the Gauls, but, as with the capture of Veii, almost nothing that Livy tells us about the 'sack' of Rome is believable. Camillus, the hero of the hour, is compared to Romulus, as second founder of Rome, but the comparison is probably an invention of the first century BC, when, as we shall see in Chapter 7, comparisons with Romulus were topical. Shortly after the sack, using stone from quarries near the recently conquered Veii, the ancient wall round the city was rebuilt, so great was the dread of a repetition of the attack.

After Rome had recovered from the Gallic attack, Roman expansion north continued, and by the early third century BC Rome was clearly dominant in Etruria. By the middle of the third century, its conquests had also extended east and south, across much of central Italy. Roman territory again increased dramatically in scale, a fivefold increase from the 5,500 square kilometres in 338 BC to 26,000 square kilometres in 264 BC (Map 23). This territory extended south as far as the bay of Naples and east all the way across the peninsula. It was a vast area, some 20 per cent of the area of the Italian peninsula, easily outstripping the territory of any Greek city-state and now rivalling the size of the Greek kingdoms to the east. In addition to land owned by the Roman state, Rome had founded 29 Latin colonies (*coloniae*), whose rights were modelled on those formalized in 338 BC for the old members of the Latin League, and which had territories totalling 11,000 square kilometres. Rome also had another 125 or more allies, with territories totalling another 72,000 square kilometres. The whole area controlled by Rome and its allies was thus a massive 108,000 square kilometres. Rome had created alliances, not necessarily formalized in treaties, with its allies, relationships that entailed the supply of military aid to Rome and so enshrined Rome's supremacy. For the next 160 years, with the exception of the Second Punic War, Rome faced almost no challenges to its rule in Italy.

In the following century, between 264 and 146 BC, Rome continued to expand in Italy, both south and north. After the Second Punic War it took severe measures against major communities that had fought on the wrong side. Capua lost its ruling class, all its autonomy including citizenship, and its entire territory. Tarentum was sacked and lost some of its territory. Stiffening of existing treaties and confiscation of parts of

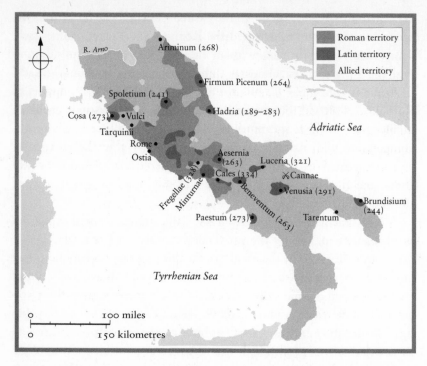

Map 23. Roman domination of Italy in 241 BC. Roman territory stretched south into Campania and across the peninsula to the Adriatic. A network of Latin colonies and Roman allies controlled the rest of Italy south of the river Arno.

civic territory were the main penalties imposed on those who had aided the Carthaginians. As a result, the amount of Roman territory grew, especially in the south of the peninsula. Another twelve Latin colonies were founded between 268 and 181 BC, but the next wave of colonies founded, from 184 BC onwards, were all Roman colonies, where all the citizens had full rights of Roman citizenship. By means of these colonies, Rome began to make its mark on the region between the Apennines and the Po valley, which Rome conquered from the Celts first in 218 BC and again during relentless fighting in the 190s and 180s BC.

Italy as a whole featured in the Roman imagination by the middle of the third century BC. In 268 BC a Roman triumph was celebrated to mark a further increase in territory, on the north-east coast of Italy. As this region marked the completion of the conquest of Italy south of the river Arno, the triumphant general dedicated a temple to Tellus (significantly, 'Earth'), and there set up a map or representation of *Italia*, the whole of the Italian peninsula. The scale of the implied political expectations for Rome was huge. A hundred years later the Elder Cato, a major politician, wrote a work, *Origins*, which placed the origins of Rome in the context of all the major Italian communities, from the deep south of the peninsula to the recently conquered area north of the Apennines. The Veneti in the north-east were of Trojan descent, being founded by the Trojan hero Antenor, and Ameria in Umbria, 70 kilometres north of Rome, was founded 963 years before the outbreak of the recent war with Perseus (171 BC), which comes out as 1134 BC in our calendar. Italy in the middle of the second century was a mosaic of communities, proud of their own past, but also content to follow the leadership of Rome.

Rome in the second century also had the means to control Italy. In 186 BC a major religious scandal involving the cult of Bacchus erupted in Rome. The Roman Senate became extremely alarmed that the sexual improprieties alleged in the cult of Bacchus, the Greek Dionysus, also had wider ramifications. It feared that groups of those initiated into the cult existed throughout Italy, and that they formed an underground network which was politically subversive. Such fears were probably unfounded, though interesting as an insight into the nature of Roman paranoia; Italy did not seem as safe to them as it does to us in retrospect. But the state took decisive action: all Roman colonies and towns in Italy were obliged to follow the Roman decisions, and communities of lesser status were subjected to direct jurisdiction by the Roman consuls. In general, crimes committed in Italy affecting the security of the Roman state – treason, conspiracy and the like – fell under the direct jurisdiction of the Roman Senate. In addition, private individuals and communities in Italy seeking arbitration, damages or protection could, and did, appeal to the Senate.

Latin and Roman colonies, founded throughout the Italian peninsula, also played an important part in the extension of Roman control and Roman values. The traditional view saw these colonies as very uniform, and argued that Cosa, a Latin colony founded on the coast of Etruria in 273 BC, was *the* exemplary site, but in fact there was no single blueprint for these colonies. It is important not to project back to this period practices of a later epoch, and equally important not to impose an allegedly uniform model onto the archaeological evidence from Cosa. Nonetheless, Cosa does illustrate what an evolving Latin colony could be like. After the defeat in 280 BC of Vulci, one of the major Etruscan towns, a third of its territory, 550 square kilometres, was confiscated, and allocated to the new town of Cosa. The territory was centuriated, that is, divided up into rectilinear plots of farmland for the new colonists, some 2,500 men (see also Plate 20); in 197 BC a thousand more colonists were assigned to Cosa, and it was perhaps only then that some of the more distant plots of land were settled by colonists. The town, covering 13 hectares, was laid out on a coastal hilltop, previously uninhabited; the nearby Etruscan settlement was completely sidelined. The settlement of Cosa was protected by magnificent walls and towers – a reminder that the new dispensation had been achieved by force of arms. Within the town, the plan was also laid out in rectilinear style, and the public buildings were perhaps modelled on those of Rome: the buildings for

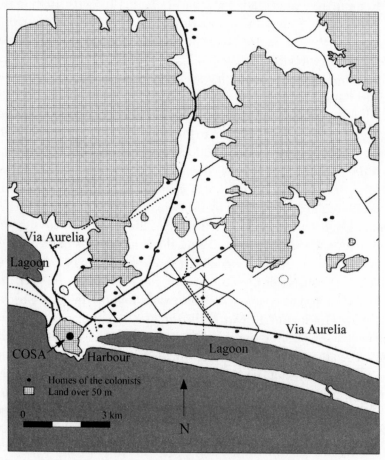

Map 24. Cosa and its territory. The centuriation is shown by the rectilinear grid north-east of the town.

the local senate and assembly may have evoked the design of those in the Roman Forum. The town had an important harbour, and was also connected by land: the Aurelian Road, probably built in 241 BC, ran from Rome up the west coast of Italy past Cosa as far as Pisa, the next major port up the coast. The road, bypassing Vulci and other old Etruscan towns, enabled Roman troops rapidly to reach northern Italy, but also had long-term civilian consequences. The new road network for Italy created the basis for a new human geography of the peninsula.

An important linguistic consequence of the creation of colonies was the spread of Latin. For Cosa, Latin was the native language of the colonists drawn from Rome and Latium, but, equally important, Latin was the official language of all colonies, just as institutions were modelled on those of Rome. Latin was therefore exported to regions of Italy that had previously spoken other Italic dialects, or other languages (Etruscan, Greek, Celtic). In turn, Latin acquired some regional variations as a result of language-learning by people brought up in other dialects or languages, but at Rome there was considerable snobbery about use of rustic Latin and words in Latin borrowed from other Italic dialects or from Etruscan. By the second century BC Latin was the prestige language of the peninsula, and the pressures to adopt it quite widely were considerable. In 180 BC the Greek town of Kymē, which had fallen to Oscan speakers in the fifth century BC, but had received Roman citizenship in 338 BC, asked the Senate for permission to conduct some forms of public business in Latin; the request was granted, but the town could in fact have made the switch without asking the Senate. The local elite must already have been familiar with Latin, but Kymē also remained proud of its Greek past: the prophetic Sibyl was responsible for the oracle of Apollo here, and had been the source for Rome's Sibylline Books in the regal period.

Some local languages died out, or at least were no longer written down, in the third century BC, but others remained important throughout the second century, disappearing in written form only at the end of the first century BC. In the late second or early first century BC, the town of Bantia (just above the instep of Italy) inscribed its own constitution in Oscan. The type of Oscan employed and some of the civic institutions described were heavily influenced by Latin and by Rome, but the use of Oscan at all in this public context shows a desire to make a statement about Bantian distinctiveness in the face of Roman dominance.

Other expressions of local identities remained important after the Roman conquest. Etruscans continued to maintain their own sense of the past until at least the first century AD. Following defeat in a civil war in 80 BC, some losing Etruscans fled to North Africa, to a remote spot some 50 kilometres south-west of Carthage. The leader of the group, who probably came from Clusium (modern Chiusi), founded a new settlement there, which had boundary stones inscribed in a late north Etruscan script. The startling fact is that the inhabitants were called Dardanii, after Dardanus, the founder of Troy. The settlement was intended to be another Troy; sadly, it vanished almost completely. Some Etruscans, like the Veneti and of course the Romans, were proud of their Trojan origins. In Etruria itself, historical memories were also preserved, despite the dying out of most of the leading families in the first century BC. At Tarquinii, in the first century AD an extensive record was inscribed of the role of Tarquinii in the fifth and perhaps fourth centuries BC. Details were given of the military interventions of leaders of Tarquinii in Sicily, and in other Etruscan states (Caere and Arretium), as well as in a war against the Latins. This inscription was in Latin, but must have been derived from local records, in Etruscan. Displayed near the grand old temple in the centre of Tarquinii, the text illustrates the continuing local pride in the prowess of Tarquinii before the coming of the Romans.

In Roman eyes, the Etruscans were the masters of the art of divining the significance of prodigies, the birth of two-headed calves, lightning strikes and the like. Etruscan *haruspices* were regularly consulted by the Senate, which then had to decide what action should be taken as a result of the prodigy. The hereditary skills of the *haruspices* were highly valued by the Roman state, uniquely so for priests who were not Roman. And so highly were these Etruscan skills valued that the Senate passed decrees in the middle of the second century BC and again in the first century AD to encourage the maintenance of the art of the *haruspices* in the leading Etruscan families; the second time was on the proposal of the emperor Claudius. Rome's proper relations with the gods depended in part on the skills of a people whose foreignness was constantly emphasized.

The Roman conquest of the Italian peninsula and then of lands overseas also had consequences for the city of Rome. A victorious general who celebrated a triumph was entitled to build a monument in Rome. The most common type of victory monument was a temple, like that to Tellus. Indeed, most Republican temples were founded by triumphant

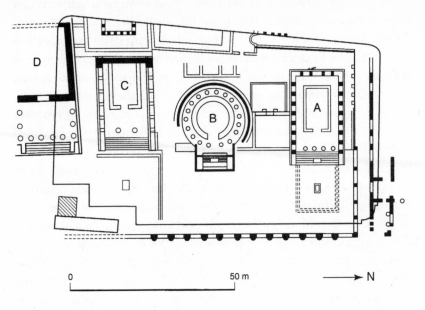

Figure 23. The four temples of the Area Sacra di Largo Argentina. Temple A, perhaps dedicated 241 BC; Temple B, to 'Fortune of this Day', in 101 BC; Temple C, built early third century BC; Temple D, built second century BC.

generals. They were probably built along the route taken by the triumphal procession, and the periods in which they were built (especially 300–250 and 200–160 BC) coincided exactly with the periods of greatest Roman military expansion. A neat example of the density of this temple building is given by the four temples built in the southern part of the Campus Martius, the Field of Mars (the so-called Area Sacra di Largo Argentina; see Figure 23). The four temples, built side by side, overlooked the route of the triumphal processions. They were built between the early third and late second centuries BC. Their dedications are uncertain, but Temple A was perhaps vowed by one Lutatius Catulus, in 241 BC, and Temple B beside it to 'Fortune of This Day' by his descendant, another Lutatius Catulus, in 101 BC. This is a nice example of a senator making the most of the achievements of a distant ancestor.

Rome remained rather undeveloped as a city in the early second century BC, but this was to change in the course of this century. According to a story in Livy, in 182 BC the Macedonian prince Demetrius, who was pro-Roman, was taunted by his anti-Roman enemies at court; among other things, they mocked the appearance of Rome, which had not yet been beautified in either its public or its private spaces. At this point Rome was a backwater in comparison with contemporary Greek cities, with little sign of rational planning and with its new victory temples isolated in the urban landscape. Even in comparison with the Latin towns round Rome, Rome scored badly. In the later second century BC, at Praeneste (modern Palestrina), 40 kilometres east of Rome, a vast new sanctuary was built, making maximum use of a dramatic hill-site. The sanctuary, financed by the profits of the local elite from Rome's eastern conquests, rivalled the largest sanctuaries in the Aegean. Rome could boast no sanctuary like this until the middle of the first century BC. But in the course of the second century BC Rome did become more monumentalized. Aristocratic tombs became more prominent: for example, the tomb of the Scipios, probably located near the temple of storm-gods built by a member of the family, was enhanced with a new façade in the mid-second century BC. The civic centre of Rome also became grander in this period, but not as a result of actions by triumphant generals. Splendid basilicas replaced private houses on the north and south sides of the Roman Forum in 179 and 169 BC; they were paid for by public funds, but still bore the family names of the civil magistrates, the *censores*, responsible for commissioning the buildings. Thus by the 160s BC the Forum looked more like a contemporary Greek *agora*, with a central public space set off by colonnaded public buildings. However, the senatorial elite was suspicious of buildings which might give too much of an opportunity to the people of Rome. The people watched plays and spectacles in temporary wooden theatres. One or perhaps two stone theatres were started in the second century BC, but were pulled down, and only in 61 BC was the first permanent stone theatre started in Rome, a century after stone theatres were built elsewhere in Italy and three or four centuries after they were built in Sicily and other parts of the Greek world.

By the middle of the third century BC, Rome had become one of the major states in the Mediterranean world. Domestic conflicts within Rome had been resolved. The Roman elite provided strong leadership, and Rome's political institutions functioned in a stable fashion. Rome had come to dominate the Italian peninsula south of the Arno, and could draw on its manpower for its armies. This expansion came to draw it into conflict with the adjacent power to the south.

*

Carthage has so far made only cameo appearances in the story. It is time to redress the balance, and to start analysis of the relations between Carthage and Rome with some consideration of how Carthaginians saw themselves. We need to try to escape from the viewpoint of the Roman victors, which inevitably depicted the Carthaginians negatively. Carthage, founded from Tyre in Phoenicia probably in the late ninth century BC, was situated on a spit of land jutting out into the sea. Like other Phoenician colonies of the period, it was well positioned to make the most of trade routes. The archaic settlement covered 25 hectares, or even 45–60 hectares on some estimates, which would place Carthage among the larger Mediterranean towns of the sixth century BC. Its walls are said to have been 37 kilometres long, more than three times the length of Rome's walls at this time. Its harbour was important from the outset, and Carthage had important trading interests in the central and western Mediterranean. From the fifth century BC onwards Carthage made military interventions in Sicily, and from the fourth century BC controlled the coast of North Africa from Cyrene in the east to the Atlantic in the west. The settlements along the coast were probably tied to Carthage by individual alliances, somewhat like relations between the Latins and Rome.

Carthage saw itself as a city with a Phoenician past and a Phoenician present. According to stories recounted by Greek and Roman writers, but possibly based on Phoenician sources, as a result of struggles for power within Tyre a losing faction fled first to Cyprus and then to the site of Carthage. Here their leader, the princess Elissa, was allowed by the king of the local Libyans to found a new settlement (Carthage, *Qart hadasht*, means 'New City' in Phoenician). As the widow of Acherbas, priest of Melqart in Tyre, Elissa had brought with her objects sacred to Melqart, and founded a cult of Melqart at Carthage (Melqart, *milk qart*, means 'King of the City'). Because the Libyan king demanded that she marry him, Elissa, faithful to her late husband, killed herself by throwing herself on a pyre. The story of a foundation from Tyre was mirrored in ritual. Each year the Carthaginians sent tribute to the temple of Melqart at Tyre. In 332 BC, when Alexander the Great was besieging Tyre, he happened to capture the Carthaginian envoys who had brought the annual tribute to Melqart, and he dedicated their sacred ship to the deity whom he called Heracles. Tyre's subsequent loss of political freedom did not break the ties with Carthage, and the annual tribute continued until the destruction of Carthage in the second century BC.

In addition, rituals of Phoenician origin were performed at Carthage. Overlooking one of the city's harbours, Carthage had an open-air sanctuary, in which were buried vessels with the cremated remains of newborn babies and young children, or sometimes animals. The sanctuary is called a 'tophet' today, but this term, borrowed from the Hebrew Bible, was probably not that used by the Carthaginians. Another confusion is that the site is called today 'Salammbô', but this is simply the romantic name given to it by the French excavators of 1922, after the heroine of Flaubert's novel (see below). The sanctuary goes back to the earliest days of the settlement, and continued until the Roman conquest. In an area covering 6,000 square metres, more than 20,000 cremation urns and 10,000 dedicatory stones have been discovered. The latter have imagery alluding to Phoenicia, especially at times of conflict with Rome, and many have texts in Phoenician that refer to two Phoenician deities Ba'al Hammon and Tinnit 'face of Ba'al'. At least a dozen other Phoenician settlements in the west have similar but not identical sanctuaries. Ennius, as part of his general account of Carthaginian customs, mentioned that 'the Carthaginians are accustomed to sacrifice their little boys'. The pathetic reference to little boys can hardly be a neutral ethnographic observation. One might try to rescue the Carthaginians from the negative perspective of the Romans and deny that the cremated remains of children represent child sacrifice, but the ritual was as odd, and to our eyes as repugnant, as it seems: in other cemeteries children were inhumed, not cremated; and inscriptions in the 'Salammbô' sanctuary state that the ashes of the children or animals were an offering vowed to the god. Somehow, this major civic sanctuary was bound up with the self-identity of Carthage, in relation both to its Tyrian past and to the growing threat of Rome.

While maintaining and enhancing their Phoenician identity, the Carthaginians also borrowed from the Greek world. Between the fifth and second centuries BC the religious buildings of Carthage employed Greek styles of decoration, and the private houses are luxurious forms of houses known elsewhere in the Greek world. In 396 BC, as a result of their impiety during military action at Syracuse, the Carthaginians suffered military setbacks and a severe outbreak of plague; they therefore began to worship Demeter and Persephone in Carthage, according to the Greek rites, even involving prominent Greeks resident in the city. This level of Carthaginian interest in the Greek world helps to explain why

Aristotle includes Carthage as the only non-Greek state in his *Politics*, and even treats Carthage, alongside Sparta and Crete, as a *polis* approximating to his ideal.

Carthage also had close relations with the Italian peninsula from the sixth century BC onwards. Three inscribed gold plaques, two in Etruscan and one in Phoenician, from a sanctuary at Pyrgi, a port of the Etruscan city of Caere, and dating to about 500 BC, are especially illuminating. They record donations to the sanctuary by one Thefarie: probably a gift of a statue and also of a temple. In the two Etruscan texts, Thefarie is identified as the ruler of Caere. He made the donations as a thank-offering to the Etruscan goddess Uni, the main deity of the sanctuary (whom the Romans called Juno), who had helped him to rule for three years. So far, this fits comfortably into the picture of Etruscan cities sketched earlier. Indeed, Thefarie may be the immediate predecessor of one of the people mentioned in one of the texts from Tarquinii. It is startling that the third gold plaque is written in Phoenician, perhaps Cypriot Phoenician, and is a parallel version of one of the two Etruscan texts. This must be because Thefarie wished to express his gratitude to the deity of Pyrgi in both his own and the deity's language. The Phoenician version refers to the goddess as Astarte, the Phoenician deity, and places the donation 'on the day of the burying of the god', namely the Phoenician deity Adonis, the consort of Astarte. Even in the parallel Etruscan text, the goddess Uni is referred to as Uni-Astra, the Etruscan form of Astarte. Phoenician impact on Etruria ran deep. Uni-Astra owed her Phoenician origins to the importance of Phoenician Cypriot and especially Carthaginian traders with Caere, for whom the sanctuary at Pyrgi served as a neutral meeting ground. Aristotle mentions in his *Politics* a trading agreement between the Carthaginians and the Etruscans, in which the two sides unusually treated each other like citizens of one city. A luxury ivory 'calling card', dating to 530–500 BC, has been excavated in Carthage, on which a merchant introduced himself in Etruscan simply as 'Puinel of Carthage'. We can imagine the Carthaginian merchant, whose spoken Etruscan was not fluent, showing his 'calling card' on first meeting an Etruscan fellow-merchant.

These close links between Carthage and Etruria are the context for the first formal connection between Carthage and Rome. In the first year of the Republic (507 BC), Carthage struck a treaty with Rome, and perhaps also with other, Etruscan states: the two sides agreed to be friends and not to act against each other's interests. The Carthaginians promised not to meddle with Rome's Latin allies, not to build a fort in Latium, nor to overnight an army there. The Romans promised only not to sail past 'the Fair Promontory' (just north-west of Carthage), and to follow certain conditions when trading with Carthage or Sardinia, specified because of its Phoenician settlements; Rome, however, was free to trade in the Carthaginian zone of western Sicily on the same terms as anyone else. Rome, the junior partner to this treaty, with no overseas military ambitions, was excluded from trading with Carthaginian colonies along the North African coast to the west of Carthage, and had specific restrictions imposed on its trading activities in core Carthaginian areas. In 348 BC a new treaty was struck between the two states. Rome was still treated as primarily a power in Latium, but Carthage sought now both to prevent, not merely to control, Roman trade with Sardinia and North Africa, and also to rule out Roman colonization there. This is the first hint of Rome's ambitions of overseas expansion, which would bring Rome and Carthage into conflict, and which would lead to Rome's expansion into the Greek world.

Explanations of the extraordinary growth of Roman power have been sought ever since antiquity. Polybius, a Greek patriot who came to know Rome from the inside, wrote a history of Rome's rise to power. His primary interest was in how Rome came to conquer the Greek world, in only fifty-three years, from 220 BC to the ending of the Macedonian monarchy in 167 BC. This conquest was not done 'in a fit of absence of mind', as was once said of British imperialism; even if Rome did not herself trigger particular wars, and indeed took pains not to initiate 'unjust wars', Rome's military actions were not simply defensive. Over time it developed the aim of universal dominion, which was underpinned by the peculiar strengths of its constitution. To this Polybian view of Roman expansion, we might want to add various causes which operated at a less conscious level: the need for individual senators to gain military glory in order to advance their careers, as with the Scipios; the financial incentives for both the elite and people of Rome to engage in warfare; and the need for Rome to levy and to employ its allies' manpower in the field each year, or else in effect remit taxation for that year, and in the long run risk losing the medium which held together Rome and its allies. These causes, operating at a deep level of the structures of the Roman state, resulted in a constant pressure towards regular warfare.

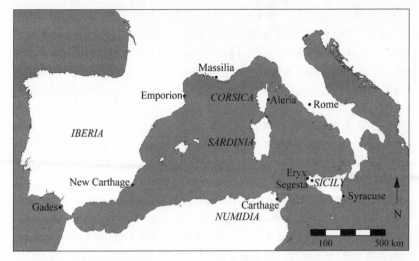

Map 25. The western Mediterranean in the third and second centuries BC.

From a conscious Roman point of view, the explanation of Roman growth was much simpler. Romans held that their extraordinary success and prosperity were due to their uniquely close relations with the gods. In a telling letter of 193 BC, the Roman authorities replied to a request by the people of Teos (a Greek city on the west coast of Asia Minor) that they accept that the city and its territory be declared 'holy' and that the honours for the chief deity of Teos, Dionysus, be enhanced. The Romans gave a key reason for their decision: 'the fact that we have, absolutely and consistently, placed reverence towards the gods as of the first importance is proved by the favour which we have received from them on this account.' This fact the Romans believed to be well known to everybody. They saw themselves as fighting only 'just wars', and their victories as being due to the ongoing piety of the Romans towards the gods. People at the time and subsequently argued that there was more than this to Roman expansion, but this self-estimation of the Romans needs to be added to our explanations of what came to pass.

Major conflict between Rome and Carthage, the First Punic War, broke out in 264 BC. The trigger was trivial, but the struggle soon escalated to become one whose prize was control over all of Sicily, where the Carthaginians had long had their zone. In an early phase of the war, Segesta, a town in the Carthaginian zone of western Sicily, decided to massacre its Carthaginian garrison and go over to the Romans. The Segestans were influenced in this dangerous decision by their kinship with the Romans: they too were descended from Aeneas. A Segestan claim that their city had been founded by refugees from Troy is found as early as the fifth century BC. Here it has particular force because they knew it would dovetail with the Romans' own claim about themselves, and it was to be repeated by Segesta on two coin issues in the first century BC.

Roman victory over Carthage and its ally Syracuse in 241 BC led to a humiliating peace for Carthage, and Roman expropriation of Sicily as its first overseas province. It is easy for us to see the First Punic War as a struggle between the two great western powers, driven by their own immediate imperatives. One of the combatants on the Roman side saw things rather differently. Naevius, in the first Latin epic on a Roman topic, a historical poem on the First Punic War, set the war in a much wider perspective. The poem began with the Romans fighting in Sicily, but then moved back in time, perhaps triggered by the Roman commander seeing representations of myths on a temple in Sicily. About a third of the poem was then set in the remote past, before returning to the present war: Aeneas fleeing Troy; Aeneas in Carthage, and there meeting the Carthaginian queen; and Aeneas reaching Italy, a story which Virgil would develop in his *Aeneid*. The narrative of the war was thus set against a background of history in which Rome had a mission to succeed, but where conflict between Rome and Carthage was not inevitable.

Flaubert's *Salammbô*

When Flaubert's *Salammbô* appeared, in 1862, readers were eagerly awaiting a successor to his wildly popular *Madame Bovary*. They were somewhat frustrated by a historical novel set in ancient Carthage. In 1857, Flaubert, who had long been fascinated by 'the orient', started obsessively reading an incredible range of ancient authors and modern scholarship, more than 100 books in total, including a 400–page treatise on a particular type of cypress for use in his description of the temple courtyard. He took reams of notes, but got bogged down and in 1858 made a trip to Carthage and other places in Tunisia and Algeria, which made him entirely rethink the novel. After publication, Flaubert vigorously defended himself against charges of inaccuracy, while admitting that he took a few minor liberties. In fact, *Salammbô*, though based on a story in Polybius, abandoned

Polybius' sympathy for the Carthaginians in favour of a highly complex representation of an alien, and very violent, society. Flaubert set his story not in the grand narrative of conflict with Rome, but in the aftermath of the First Punic War, when Carthage's mercenaries revolted. The narrative was driven by a love affair between the leader of the mercenaries and a Carthaginian priestess, Salammbô. The novel might look as though it is a straightforward example of western 'Orientalism', in which representatives of western colonizing powers represented the 'orient' as exotically 'other', in such a way as to make it knowable and controllable. In fact, Flaubert avoided any easy hooks for the reader, such as noble representatives of Rome, or wise Greek philosophers, and instead set out to depict a remote society, using unfamiliar vocabulary, and almost no direct speech. The vast learning paraded before the reader did not help, and the French language proved to be a poor tool for mastering the alien nature of Carthage.

The problems of how to represent Carthage have not disappeared. Some modern scholars scarcely seek to escape from the perspective of the Roman victors, who stereotyped the Carthaginians as notorious for their perfidy. Others, who wish to be sympathetic, ignore the evidence of the 'tophets'. Yet others are led, by the fact that Punic is a Semitic language, into racist claims, comparing Carthaginian literature unfavourably with that of another Semitic people, the Jews. Until the last few decades, the struggle between Rome and Carthage was often seen as a racist struggle between Indo-Europeans and Semites for control of the western Mediterranean. Flaubert's novel, though unpopular at the time and little read today, avoids those obvious traps, and poses for us a real challenge.

After the First Punic War Carthage attempted to secure its position in North Africa and to create one in Iberia. A leading Carthaginian family established itself in Iberia, founding New Carthage (modern Cartagena), which had the best harbour on the Mediterranean coast of Iberia. In the seventh and sixth centuries BC Phoenician colonies had lined the southern coast of Iberia, but they had faded in the fifth century. In their place developed an indigenous, urban civilization, in close contact with the Greeks. A document inscribed in Greek on a lead tablet of the later fifth century BC recorded the purchase of a ship by a Greek merchant at the Greek town of Emporion in the north-east of Iberia; the transaction was witnessed by three men with Iberian names. The same lead tablet had previously been used to record in Etruscan a transaction by two Etruscan merchants at 'Matalia', that is Massilia, which illustrates neatly the complexity of economic life in this period. Through such means, the local Iberian elites imported huge amounts of Greek pottery and other artefacts. Like the Etruscans, the Iberians made use of the Greek imports for their own purposes; they created a local style of sculpture, based on Greek models (Plate 17); and an Iberian script, inspired by Ionic Greek. It was this region which the Carthaginians attempted to take over, and which formed the basis for the next conflict with Rome.

The Second Punic War broke out in 218 BC, when Hannibal, starting from New Carthage, launched a surprise attack on Italy, marching over the Alps with his elephants. In three successive years he defeated Roman armies three times; much of southern Italy and Syracuse, the largest city in Sicily, defected to the Carthaginians. But central and northern Italy remained loyal to Rome, and in the end the Romans broke back. The Carthaginians were defeated in Italy, and again in North Africa in 202 BC. As a result, the Carthaginians were confined to central North Africa, and over the next two hundred years Rome went on to fight for control of all of Iberia. The Carthaginians had posed the greatest threat to Rome's seemingly inexorable rise to domination of the Mediterranean world. That is why Polybius chose this point to describe the balance between the three elements of the Roman constitution as the source of the strength that carried them through to final victory.

Rome's ally Massilia was caught up in this war. Its prosperity had been hit in the fourth and third centuries BC, because its trading routes to the north had been disrupted by the emergence of La Tène Celts, but its traders remained active elsewhere. An Egyptian papyrus records a maritime loan of 200–150 BC relating to a voyage to the 'Scent-Producing Land' of the Somali coast: the partners were Greek Egyptians and a trader from Massilia; the guarantors of the loan included another man from Massilia, as well as a Carthaginian and someone from Italy. The international interconnections were here even greater than those seen in the earlier lead tablet. During the Second Punic War Massilia won a naval victory with the Romans over the Carthaginians, which the city commemorated in true Greek style by dedicating a statue of Apollo in the sanctuary at Delphi.

During this war Rome probably continued to present itself as a Trojan foundation, in the face of a foreign foe. In 217 BC, after the second of Hannibal's crushing defeats of the Romans, the Senate tried to appease the gods by building two new temples on the Capitol, one to Mens ('Mind'), the other to Venus Erycina ('Venus of Eryx'). Introducing a deity from Eryx, on the north-west corner of Sicily, needs explanation, especially as the cult there included the un-Roman practice of temple prostitution. Certainly later and probably at the time, the cult had Trojan associations: founded by Eryx, a son of Aphrodite (Latin: Venus), it had been visited by Aeneas, another son of Aphrodite, and the Trojan foundation of Segesta was nearby. The Romans probably wished to make the most of these associations by building a temple to Venus Erycina in the heart of Rome.

Roman historians in the late third and early second centuries BC certainly set the recent past in a long historical context. Fabius Pictor, a leading senator, who composed a history of Rome in the late third century BC, began with the stories of Hercules and Evander, and of Aeneas and the founding of Alba Longa, and continued with the much later events of Romulus, Remus and the founding of Rome in 748 BC. That is, he sought to reconcile the early date established by Eratosthenes for the Trojan War with a much later date for the foundation of Rome; this became the canonical solution, but not immediately. The work passed quite rapidly through the regal period and the early Republic, but ended with a detailed history from the First to the Second Punic War. Pictor is sometimes described as the first Roman historian, which is somewhat unfair to Naevius, and obscures the fact that Pictor wrote in Greek. Pictor, like other upper-class Romans, was bilingual in Latin and Greek, but wrote in Greek, not for a Greek audience, but for a Roman audience which would appreciate his borrowings from the sophisticated tradition of Greek historical writing.

Ennius was a rather different figure. Coming from southern Italy, he claimed descent from Messapus, the founder of the local Messapian people, and boasted that he had 'three hearts', because he spoke Oscan, Greek and Latin (in which he wrote). Though he was an outsider to Rome, leading Romans acted as his patrons, with the Scipios including a statue of him outside their family tomb. The first section of his verse history, the *Annals* (written in the 180s and 170s BC), covered, predictably enough, Aeneas, Romulus and the other kings of Rome, but Romulus, as also in Naevius, is here the grandson of Aeneas, thus eliminating the long years of the kings of Alba Longa who filled the gap between the Trojan War and the date for the founding of Rome. The second section covered the Republican period down to the early third century BC. The remaining two-thirds of the work covered the century down to his own day, omitting the First Punic War, which had already been described by Naevius. It ended with the defeat of Macedon in 197 BC, victory over the Aetolians in north-west Greece in 187 BC, and subsequent wars down into the early 170s BC.

Carthage had prospered after the Second Punic War, being described by the contemporary Polybius as 'the richest city in the world', despite its geographical and political constraints (Plate 18). But Carthage's attack on its western neighbour Massinissa of Numidia, an ally of Rome, meant that Rome now had the opportunity for declaring a just war on Carthage in 149 BC, namely the Third Punic War. The Roman politician Cato had made great play of alleged Carthaginian atrocities, and also wrote of Elissa founding Carthage; like Naevius, he saw the conflict in a long perspective. In 146 BC Carthage was defeated, and the leader's wife immolated herself, showing the enduring power of the memory of Elissa within Carthage itself. The deities of the great city were summoned to Rome, and Carthage was 'devoted' to the gods of the underworld. This infernal dedication of the city had remote precedent in the treatment of some towns in Italy, including Veii, but it had no precedent outside Italy. The city walls were dismantled, roofs removed, making the buildings unusable, and the population sold into slavery. Spoil that the Carthaginians had removed from Akragas in Sicily in 405 BC was restored to its rightful owners. There is a widespread modern story that in addition salt was ploughed into Carthage's soil to make it infertile, but that story was simply invented by a historian writing in 1930. By 125 BC Rome had started to assign the territory of Carthage to its own citizens and in 122 BC Roman settlers were sent to Carthage, but the centre of the city was left vacant for a century after its destruction.

Meanwhile, in the east, the mainland Greeks revolted against Rome in 147 BC, but this was in vain. In reprisal, in 146 BC the Romans sacked the ancient city of Corinth and subjected many cities of mainland Greece to Roman rule. Corinth suffered the same fate of dedication to the gods of the underworld as Carthage; its statues and paintings were removed for display in Rome, in the victorious cities of Italy, in the Panhellenic sanctuaries of Greece, and even in some individual Greek cities, thereby incorporating memory into new contexts.

*

The long-standing conflict between Carthage and Rome had consequences for the way the world was conceptualized. Since at least the fifth century BC the world had been divided into three continents: Europe, Asia and Libya. Herodotus had disparaged the size and importance of Libya in comparison with Europe, on geographical grounds, and there was a long-standing political polarity between Europe and Asia. The wars between Rome and Carthage in the third and second centuries BC weakened the old polarity. Libya took on a fresh importance, and also acquired a new name. In 146 BC the Romans called the conquered Carthaginian territory 'Africa', probably adopting a local name, while avoiding reference to the Poeni. 'Africa' became the usual Latin word not only for the new province but also for the whole third continent.

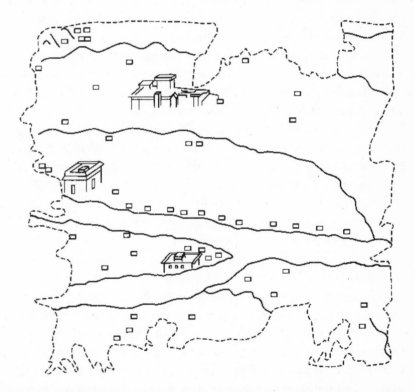

Figure 24. Drawing of part of the map of Iberia in the Artemidorus papyrus. Running across the centre is a wide river, indicated by two parallel lines, joined by a second river. At the junction is a walled town; there are two other walled towns above it. The single lines, probably roads rather than rivers, are flanked by small settlements, indicated by rectangular boxes.

Knowledge of Europe also changed. The Greeks had had little interest in the inhabitants of the inland areas of Iberia and middle Europe, despite long-standing patterns of trade with coastal areas. Massilia, for example, had not served as a channel for the communication of knowledge about the Celts to other Greeks. Pytheas' writings about his far-flung travels to Britain and further north did not include anything about the inland Celts. Roman conquests, in the aftermath of the Second Punic War, began to change this, much as the conquests of Alexander the Great had opened up new stretches of Asia to Greek enquiry. Polybius travelled twice to Iberia and to the sea beyond with his Roman patron, at least as far as southern France, and was given ships by his patron to explore the coast of North Africa. As a result, he was able to describe these regions in a way that no previous author had done, making geography an intrinsic part of history. Such exploration was made possible by Roman expansion, but knowledge thereby acquired also served to consolidate Roman power. Around 100 BC, a Greek scholar, Artemidorus of Ephesus (in western Asia Minor), wrote extensively on the coast, including the Atlantic coast, of Iberia as part of his geography of the world. A hundred or so years later the section on Iberia was illustrated with a very detailed map of at least part of Iberia, including considerable detail on the inland settlements (see Figure 24). In this map, Artemidorus' knowledge, derived as a result of Roman conquest, was complemented with further details of the new Roman world: large towns, roads and smaller settlements. Iberia was now in Roman hands. As we shall see in the next chapter, Roman expansion in middle Europe in the first century BC had similar consequences for the growth of knowledge.

The grand narrative of the period from 500 to 146 BC is clear: Rome's expansion within Italy south of the Arno by 264 BC; its wars with Carthage; and its conquest of most of the Greek world in Polybius' famous fifty-three years between 220 and 167 BC. The two story-lines of Rome's external expansion converge with the destructions of both Carthage and Corinth in 146 BC, events which serve as a neat sign of the supremacy of Rome in the Mediterranean world. Thereafter no state west of the Euphrates had the resources to offer sustained resistance to further Roman expansion. This grand narrative has to be seen in the context of the perspectives on the past held by Romans, Italians and Carthaginians. Beliefs and debates about early histories and traditions helped to shape how individual states developed and interacted.

7

Rome, Italy and Empire:
146 BC–AD 14

Most Gauls, even down to the present day, sleep on the ground, and eat
their meals seated on beds of straw. Their food is very abundant, and includes
milk and flesh of all sorts, but particularly the flesh of hogs, both fresh and
salted. Their hogs actually live outdoors, and they are of exceptional height,
strength and speed; it is certainly dangerous for a person unfamiliar with
them to approach them, and likewise even for a wolf. As for the Gauls'
houses, which are large and dome-shaped, they make them of planks and
wattle, covering them with a thatched roof.

That is how the Greek geographer Strabo, writing early in the first century
AD, describes the people of central Gaul. It is a striking picture of a
primitive people, living an un-Mediterranean life in curiously shaped and
constructed houses, their economy dominated by savage hogs, capable
of killing even wolves. Strabo says explicitly that his account of the Gauls
is drawn mainly from the time before they were conquered by Julius
Caesar. At first sight, his account makes the Gauls seem like the inhabitants of Sobiejuchy in north-central Poland a millennium earlier. In fact,
Strabo is very well aware of the changed world in which the Gauls are
living. They supplied specially woven cloth from their flocks of sheep
and salt meat from the hogs not only to Rome, but also to other parts
of Italy. Unlike the inhabitants of Sobiejuchy, who had no long-distance
connections at all, the Gauls were tied into a long-distance trading
system.

This chapter moves from the mid-second century BC, when the Gauls
were independent of Rome, to the organization of the Roman provinces
towards the end of the first century BC. The area under Roman rule grew
hugely over this period, both in the west and in the east. The growth of
Roman territory had major consequences for how that territory was
administered and conceptualized. But we begin by picking up the issue

GALLIA CISALPINA

RIVER PO

Ariminum •

Firmum
Picenum

ETRURIA
Cosa •
Tarquinii
Rome • • Corfinium-Italica

Arpinum •

Capua •
• Aeclanum
Neapolis • • Pompeii
CAMPANIA
Grumentum
Tarentum

SARDINIA

SICILY
Regium
N
Syracuse •

Carthage •
10 50   100 km

Map 26. The Italian peninsula in the second and first centuries BC.

of the impact of Roman rule on the Italian peninsula from what has gone before, and then move on to political changes within Rome. The period starts with the senatorial elite riding high, profiting from the expansion of the empire. It closes with the transformation of that elite, with the emergence of individual leaders, the civil wars, ending with Augustus' defeat of the forces of Antony and Cleopatra at the battle of Actium in 31 BC, and the creation of an emperor, Augustus, who claimed to be just an ordinary citizen. The death of Augustus in AD 14 offers a convenient end to this story. It is usual to talk of these political changes in terms of a change from 'Republic' to 'empire', but Rome already had an empire in the 'Republic'. As Augustus, like other politicians, represented himself in traditional terms, he would have been horrified to find us making the battle of Actium a break between two historical periods.

The extension of Roman power in the Italian peninsula began to pose major problems for Rome. We have already seen the number of colonies created by Rome in the third and second centuries; Roman ability to intervene in the affairs of allied and other states; and the emergence of Latin as the prestige language of the peninsula. As part of this process the state acquired more territory in Italy. Those cities in the south of the peninsula which had made the mistake of siding with the Carthaginians in the Second Punic War were savagely punished, with the confiscation of some or all of their territory. This newly acquired land became *ager publicus*, 'public land', owned by the state, and leased out to individual Roman citizens. There was notionally a limit, 125 hectares, on how much land any one person could lease, and a rent was payable to the state, but both the limit and the rents were often ignored. The conventional modern analysis is that many upper-class Romans acquired huge landholdings, which they farmed using slave labour, with a shift in some areas from arable to pastoral farming. The upper class thereby dispossessed the local free peasantry, and created vast fortunes for themselves. This analysis depends in part on evidence tainted by the arguments mounted by those who sought to reform the situation. It also needs to be modified because of the great variation in landownership and agricultural practices within the Italian peninsula, and because population increase could have been partly responsible for the growth of the landless poor. The jury is still out as to whether the evidence of archaeological field surveys, which have been undertaken in many different parts of Italy, supports the conventional view. But whatever the causes, there was a strong case that land reform was needed.

The issues came to a head in Rome with the election of Tiberius Gracchus to the junior office of tribune of the people for 133 BC. Tiberius Gracchus came from a distinguished family, with many successful ancestors: he was the grandson of Scipio Africanus the Elder, who had won the Second Punic War, and brother-in-law of Scipio Africanus the Younger, who had sacked Carthage in 146 BC. He might therefore have been expected to compete for the highest senatorial offices and distinctions, as outlined in the texts inscribed in the Tomb of the Scipios. Instead, Tiberius chose to make maximum use of the office of tribune, an office, according to Polybius, which focused on the wishes of the people. This was a novel way of exploiting the Roman political system, with major consequences. He got the people to pass legislation, contrary to the wishes of the Senate, to establish a land commission to sort out abuses of the *ager publicus*: those who had usurped *ager publicus* were to be allowed to keep the amount of land previously stipulated, with additions for up to two sons, and the rest of the land was to be assigned by the commissioners to the landless poor. His legislation was strongly supported by the people, but deeply resented by the upper class, which stood to lose massively from the legislation, but which also had reasonable objections to his political tactics.

Despite the killing of Tiberius Gracchus, to which we shall return, the commission set to work. Of the boundary stones put up in Italy by the commission, fourteen survive, mostly in the area to the south of Capua. They demonstrate an impressive level of detail in the recording of plots of land. A few miles from one of the areas surveyed by the commission, another prominent Roman, whose name does not survive, undertook a major road-building programme through this region, from Regium to Capua. He also claimed to be the first to ensure that shepherds gave way to arable farmers on *ager publicus*; he also built a forum and public buildings here, presumably for the newly settled farmers, in accordance with the aim of Tiberius' reforms to favour the landless poor.

In 123 BC Tiberius' brother, Gaius Gracchus, in his turn became tribune of the people. Tiberius had perhaps sought to make life better for landless Roman citizens in the first instance, but Gaius Gracchus took action that benefited non-Roman Italians, and hence also benefited Rome by securing a steady supply of men for the Roman army. He modified his brother's land reforms, so that an important type of *ager publicus* would not be distributed to Roman citizens but be available for renting by non-Romans. In addition, he subsequently proposed changes to the status of Latin allies, offering them full Roman citizenship, and offering some sort of rights also to other Italians, but the proposal failed. In 121 BC he led an insurrection in support of his legislation, but this too failed and he and many of his supporters were killed.

The extension of Roman citizenship to new categories of people was an issue that did not die with Gaius Gracchus. Italian allies were obliged by their separate alliances to supply troops each year to Rome, but they became increasingly unhappy about their treatment by Rome. Gaius Gracchus had already protested at the outrageous behaviour of a young Roman ambassador towards a humble citizen of a Latin colony and of a Roman consul towards the magistrate of an allied city-state. The disparity of treatment of the Italian allies was especially marked in comparison with the Roman colonies dispersed throughout the Italian peninsula, whose inhabitants, all Roman citizens, were not obliged to serve in the Roman army, and were in principle protected from the abuse of power by Roman magistrates. In addition, the Italian allies desired to share in political and legal decision-making at Rome, including decision-making about the running of empire. Italian allies, therefore, sought to end their unequal relationship with Rome, and to possess Roman citizenship. But their aspirations were frustrated. The final straw was the assassination of a Roman politician, Livius Drusus, who had unsuccessfully proposed the extension of the franchise to the Italians. In 91 BC war broke out between Rome and its Italian allies (Latin: *socii*, hence the modern name 'Social War'). Allies throughout central and southern Italy, from Firmum in the north to Grumentum in the south, took up arms against Rome. According to the historian Velleius Paterculus, whose ancestor had fought in the war, some 300,000 young men died during the three years of fighting. The figure may be an exaggeration, but the conflict was certainly momentous.

By the time the war broke out, the aspirations of the allies had moved on from a desire for Roman citizenship to something quite different: their own state. The allies established a senate of 500 men and their own magistrates, based at Corfinium, which they renamed Italica. Lead slingshot for use against the Romans was labelled with the names of their magistrates and the word 'Itali', Italians, suggesting that the troops saw themselves as fighting as a single force. The silver coinage issued by the rebels reveals especially clearly the rebels' view of themselves. This was a large coinage, comparable in scale to Rome's coinage only ten or twenty years before. It was based on Roman standards, and sometimes copied Roman imagery, but it was strikingly separatist. The writing on the coins was in both Latin and Oscan, the Italic language that was common throughout central Italy. The use of Oscan here is a first sign of a desire to stand apart from Rome. The actual words are more explicit, in that the minting authority was clearly labelled in Latin as 'Italia' and in its

Oscan equivalent 'víteliú' or 'vítelliú' (Plate 31c). In other words, the rebels saw themselves as forming a new state of Italy, for the first and last time until the modern Italian state was formed under King Victor Emmanuel II in 1861. The imagery on the coins proclaimed a specifically Italian identity. Heads of Italia appear, but especially interesting is the close connection between the legends 'Italia' or 'víteliú' and representations of a bull. It looks as though the rebels were drawing on the ancient association between Italic word for calf (Latin: *vitulus*) and the name of the peninsula (p. 180). Especially dramatic are the coins depicting a bull goring a wolf with one of its horns. According to Velleius Paterculus, an Italian commander at the head of a force of 40,000 men outside Rome, exhorted his troops to battle: 'These wolves that have so ravaged Italian freedom will never disappear until we have cut down the forest that shelters them.' The coins show the Italian bull taking retribution on the predatory Roman wolf.

Rome won the military conflict, offering Roman citizenship first to those men who had not revolted, and then in 88 and 87 BC to men in all communities south of the Po. By 70 BC Rome could issue a coin depicting Roma and Italia shaking hands, and the separatist aims of the allies came to be suppressed. Both sides concurred that the aims of the rebels had been simply Roman citizenship, which had now been magnanimously granted by Rome. Emblematic of the consequences of the Social War (and of views of it) is the family of Velleius Paterculus (c. 20 BC–after AD 31). Velleius, writing 120 years after the war's end, presents his ancestors as uniformly pro-Roman. He claimed to be descended from Decius Magius, the leader of those few Capuans who had remained loyal to Rome at the time of the Second Punic War. Velleius' great-great-great-grandfather, Minatus Magius of Aeclanum (east of Capua), raised forces to fight on behalf of Rome during the Social War, helping Sulla in his siege of Pompeii. He received a personal grant of Roman citizenship, and his two sons became Roman senators, though the distinction of this branch of the family seems to have petered out at this point. Velleius' grandfather was a leading soldier, serving Pompey the Great, but in the civil war Velleius' uncle and father were on the winning side of Julius Caesar. Velleius himself served in the Roman army, and then joined the Senate, rising to be praetor in AD 14. His history of Rome, published in AD 30, embodies a loyalist Italian view of the past, presenting the aim of the Social War as simply to obtain Roman citizenship, and also illustrates the new opportunities for members of local civic elites in the service of Rome.

The increased geographic spread of Roman citizenship as a result of the Social War, first to loyalists like Velleius' ancestor, and then even to rebels, resulted in a huge increase in the number of Roman citizens in Italy. Censuses of the mid-second century BC had recorded a number of adult male citizens that ranged between 313,000 and 337,000, numbers which should probably be increased by 20 per cent to allow for citizens serving overseas and under-registration. The most reliable census figure for soon after the Social War is 910,000, which should probably also be increased by 20 per cent. In other words, the enfranchisement of the Italian allies trebled the number of Roman citizens, to a number never previously reached by any ancient state. Not that this increase was unproblematic. After 70 BC, the *censores*, magistrates responsible for conducting censuses, repeatedly failed to complete their work, probably because of the controversial nature of the extension of citizenship.

The spread of domiciles of Roman citizens also affected membership of the Roman Senate. Up to the Social War, senators had been drawn mainly from Rome and Latium, but afterwards senators came from a much wider area. Some, like Velleius' ancestors, did not rise to the consulship, but others did. The most famous case is none other than Marcus Tullius Cicero, of Arpinum, whose inhabitants had possessed full Roman citizenship for the previous hundred years. Cicero, like Velleius' ancestor, had fought as a young man for Sulla in the Social War. On the basis of a loyalist background and proven distinction in legal oratory, he was elected quaestor in 75 BC, thereby joining the Senate. Such people faced considerable opposition from the old guard in Rome. Cicero was disparaged as being merely an 'immigrant citizen of the city of Rome', but he became consul in 63 BC. Cicero turned to his advantage the fact that he was a *novus homo*, a 'new man' with no previous senatorial ancestry. As a *novus homo*, he was not tainted by the corruption that had infected the old guard. Cicero's rhetoric, and fame for other reasons, should not blind us to the fact that the Senate had always taken on new members. What was new after the Social War was the gradual emergence of a Senate with a higher proportion of members drawn from all over Italy. Not that the change was easy, but they did gradually enter the Senate. A certain Quintus Varius Geminus, who entered the Senate under Augustus (becoming praetor), proudly boasted that 'he was the first of all the Paeligni to be made a senator'. As Corfinium in the territory of the Paeligni had been the rebels' capital, Varius' achievement was indeed notable.

After the Social War and the ensuing civil war, the victorious commander Sulla settled huge numbers of ex-soldiers in colonies, especially in Etruria and Campania. One of these colonies was Pompeii, where Sulla settled at least a couple of thousand ex-soldiers. Pompeii was an old town, with city walls dating back to the sixth century BC. Some even claimed that its name was derived from the *pompa*, triumphal procession, of Hercules, pursuing his missing calf down through the Italian peninsula. Pompeii had fought on the side of the Samnites against Rome, but became a Roman ally by the early third century BC, though remaining mainly Oscan-speaking. Its troops helped in the Roman sack of Corinth in 146 BC, and in turn the town received a present of a statue or of luxury metalwork from Mummius, the Roman commander, one of numerous such gifts. This donation is a token of the huge wealth flowing into the town from eastern conquests. Around the middle of the second century BC the temple of Apollo in the forum was restructured, with the Mummius gift being built into the colonnade, marked by an inscription in Oscan; a basilica was constructed for public administration, and the façades of houses along the main streets were rebuilt in stone, presumably at public expense. One local family gained extraordinary wealth from serving Rome in the east. The 'House of the Faun', as it is known today, was rebuilt in the second half of the second century BC to cover an entire city block. The house was, as can still be seen, extraordinarily lavish, including a wonderful mosaic depicting Alexander the Great's defeat of the Persian King Darius. This family sought to elevate itself above the rest of the population, much as the Roman nobility was doing in Rome at the same time, with a house that rivalled a Hellenistic palace, and imagery that presented contemporary eastern conquests in the same mould as those of Alexander the Great.

Despite the communal and individual wealth that flowed into Pompeii, the city sided with the rebels during the Social War, and was besieged by Sulla in 89 BC. Numerous lead bullets and stone balls fired from ballistas into the town survive; we can even read the mustering instructions for the defenders, painted on walls, in Oscan. A decade afterwards, in 80 BC, with Sulla's settlement of ex-soldiers, Pompeii became a Roman *colonia*, with a new name and a new constitution (like Cosa and other colonies discussed in the previous chapter). However, the old municipal constitution operated in parallel to the constitution of the *colonia* for the next generation. Relations between the existing inhabitants and the newcomers were tense for some time; we hear of disputes between the two groups over rights of access to public space, and over electoral procedures, until by the 50s BC members of the original elite were able to join the town council of the *colonia*. Latin became the official language of the community, with Oscan going into decline. The incoming ex-soldiers may have lived mainly on farms outside the town, though the very richest of the newcomers built lavish houses on top of the old city walls, which were no longer needed for defence. In the east of the town, houses were demolished to build an amphitheatre, the earliest known stone amphitheatre, which was dedicated 'to the colonists'.

The linguistic and cultural changes seen at Pompeii are emblematic of changes throughout Italy. For central and southern Italy, the Social War was a turning point. In the northern part of the Italian peninsula, the province of Gallia Cisalpina, 'Gaul this side of the Alps', was granted Roman citizenship by Julius Caesar in 49 BC, and was subsequently known as Italia Transpadana, 'Italy across the Po'. Roman Italy was now the whole peninsula south of the Alps, though unlike modern Italy it did not include Sicily or Sardinia. The Latin language and Roman institutions became increasingly common throughout the peninsula.

There was no official policy to stamp out local languages, or local cultural diversity, in Italy. Latin language and Roman institutions had been dominant since the second century BC, but both were compatible with a bilingualism that could be both linguistic and cultural. At Pompeii, Oscan continued to be used for two generations after the creation of the Roman colony. In Etruria, Latin began to make headway against Etruscan only after the Social War. By the middle of the first century BC, bilingual Etruscan-Latin inscriptions were common, and by the end of the first century BC, Etruscan became increasingly rare. Greek remained the public language of the ancient cities of the south, especially Neapolis and Tarentum, but none of the other languages of Italy had a public use much past the first century BC, though some may have continued to be spoken privately. Within Italy, Latin carried the day. Though there was no state policy to promote Latin, the growing dominance of Latin was in part a consequence of state practices. The ethnic units of the Roman army, which had helped to preserve local languages, disappeared soon after the

Social War, and Latin became the sole official language of the army. The municipal charters of the newly enfranchised communities of Italy, with their rules for local magistrates and local finances, were also all in Latin: this was true even of the Greek-speaking town of Tarentum. The changes also need to be set against the background of severe dislocation in Italy: the violent conflict of the Social War, and the settlement overseas of Italian veterans in colonies outside the peninsula.

There was also a move on the part of the Roman elite to define, and hence preserve, a pure form of Latin, untainted by the polluted language of the flood of immigrants to Rome. From the early first century BC exponents of Latin grammar sought to define proper usage, based not on current practice, which was in flux, but on logical consistency. This concern was not the preserve of educational theorists. Julius Caesar himself wrote a treatise, of which Cicero approved, arguing in support of definitions based on logical consistency, with clear rules about how to decline nouns and which words to preface with an 'h'. It is striking that Caesar found the time to write the treatise while on campaign in Gaul. The newly formulated language became, in the hands of the professional grammarians, the backbone of an educational system throughout Italy and the west.

Some local and regional identities within Italy remained strong. The people of Etruscan Tarquinii in the first century AD were proud of the achievements of their ancestors before the growth of Roman power (p. 202). Not that being Etruscan at this period was straightforward. Maecenas, a powerful cultural figure in Rome under Augustus, was notorious for his luxurious lifestyle, which was attributed to his Etruscan roots. On the other hand, the Sabine area north-east of Rome was seen as the residual home of austere virtues now lost in the corrupt metropolis of Rome itself. The Elder Cato had perhaps associated these Sabine virtues with the origins that local traditions ascribed to the Sabines, namely the famously austere Spartans. The poet Horace, writing under Augustus, set great store by his Sabine farm, which served for him as an image of rustic purity.

The Roman political system in the second century BC could be seen as having three key elements: the Senate, people and magistrates. In Polybius' analysis (p. 189 above), those three elements were kept successfully in balance down to his time. But the values and institutions that prevented individuals from gaining too much power broke down. Aspiring politicians used all the tools available to them to enhance their positions, including appeals to the past. Senators had claimed Trojan descent since at least the fourth century BC, but this type of claim became especially important in the first century BC. Julius Caesar at an early stage of his career, in 69 BC, gave the public funeral eulogy for his aunt Julia: on her mother's side, the Marcii Reges, she was descended from one of the kings, Ancus Marcius, and on her father's side, the Julii, she was descended from the gods. This was because the Julii claimed descent from Aeneas, son of Venus, via his son Iulus. 'Our family therefore has both the sanctity of kings, whose power is supreme among mortal men, and also the claim to reverence which attaches to the gods, who hold sway over kings themselves.' Caesar's rhetorical appeal to the past was typical of the period: claims to Trojan origin were so common that two scholars each wrote a book 'On the Trojan Families'. The fact that Julia had a public funeral itself marks a new level of elite competition. The competition between members of the elite for power and status had become so intense that the female members of their families were now co-opted into the struggles. Whereas the women of the Scipios in the third and second centuries BC had had no individual public prominence (pp. 188–9), women of senatorial families in the first century BC could be deemed to add lustre to their families. The young Julius Caesar was, of course, hoping to gain politically by drawing public attention to the extraordinary ancestry of his aunt.

By the end of the first century BC, Rome was ruled by one family, that of Augustus. It is easy to see the shift in terms of increasingly successful individual leaders, Pompey, Caesar, Antony and Augustus, who in turn broke away from the pack, and it is easy also to analyse their success in terms of naked power politics: ambition, greed, factions and so on. Thinking like this, though it may seem to be hard-nosed and hence reliable, fails to take account of other issues. Focusing on the individual leaders ignores the extent to which they were dependent on the support of their soldiers. At the end of their years of service, these men, mostly drawn from the Italian countryside, demanded land for themselves, forcing their leaders to satisfy their demands. And seemingly hard-nosed analysis does not take account of how individual politicians justified their own actions, or the terms in which they were supported or opposed. Debates about political leadership were moulded in part in terms of the past. The outcome of such debates was that nothing was abolished, and the old forms remained decisively important for the successful leaders.

The importance of the past is especially clear in connection with Tiberius Gracchus. He was elected in 133 BC to a relatively minor magistracy, tribune of the people, but used the latent powers of this office to get the people to pass radical measures concerning the allocation of land in Italy, contrary to the wishes of the Senate. Various historical analogies to his behaviour were drawn at the time, both by Tiberius Gracchus himself and by his opponents. Parallels were drawn with two Spartan kings of a hundred years previously, Agis IV and Cleomenes III. They too had undertaken major reforms of land tenure, and were seen either as noble restorers of the ancestral system, or as populist tyrants. There was the same polarity of views concerning Tiberius Gracchus. His enemies alleged that he had received a royal purple robe and diadem from the Attalid kingdom of Pergamum in western Asia Minor, and was seeking to become king at Rome. It had been legitimate to depose the last king of Rome, Tarquinius Superbus, and a tribune who had misbehaved had lost the authority of the office that notionally protected his person. So people argued that Tiberius Gracchus too could be deposed.

The telling argument was that Tiberius was aiming to become a tyrant; the key evidence was his unprecedented deposition of a fellow tribune, who had been opposing his legislation. Tyranny was a term for sole power wielded unconstitutionally, as against monarchy or supreme magistracies, which had constitutional bases; it was always a term used by the opponents of the individual concerned: no ruler ever termed himself a tyrant. Tyranny was a phenomenon, or an allegation, which recurred throughout Greek history, and was a potent allegation at Rome in the late Republic. Stories were told about three populist leaders in the first century or so of the Republic, Spurius Cassius, Spurius Maelius and Marcus Manlius, who had allegedly aspired to tyranny, and who had been executed. Tiberius' opponents agreed that it was desirable to kill the tyrannical Tiberius, but hesitated to do so. Matters came to a head when Scipio Nasica, the *pontifex maximus*, head of one of the major priestly colleges of Rome, appeared on the steps of the temple of Jupiter Optimus Maximus on the Capitol behind Tiberius Gracchus, who was trying to hold a meeting of the people. What happened next is obscure, but it may be that Nasica, believing that the Senate had already condemned Tiberius, exploited an ancient formula, and consecrated Tiberius to Jupiter, on the grounds that he was about to seize power as a tyrant. Tiberius, thus stripped of the sacrosanctity of the office of tribune, was struck down by one of the other tribunes. His body and those of many of his supporters were thrown into the river Tiber. Not everyone accepted Nasica's defence of the killing of a tribune. He was forced to leave Rome, as ambassador to Pergamum, despite the fact that the *pontifex maximus* was not supposed to depart from Italy. But the deadly power of arguments based on the past was clear. The killing of Tiberius Gracchus, the first act of political bloodshed at Rome for three hundred and fifty years, itself established a precedent.

Machiavelli and Rome

Niccolò Machiavelli (1469–1527) drew deeply on Roman history and political thought to develop his own, original theories. His two principal works seem at first sight to espouse contradictory positions. *The Prince*, written in 1513, focuses on the rule of one man: the prince needs *virtù* in order to overcome the power of Fortune; he should not behave morally, if necessity counsels otherwise, but he should pretend to do so, so as to appear virtuous. This deliberately shocking doctrine (which made his name notorious) was developed in a dialogue with ancient Rome: Hannibal, having conceded victory to Scipio, spoke of the power of Fortune in human affairs; Cicero was wrong to say that fear was a poor basis for lasting power; the emperor Septimius Severus possessed great *virtù*, having the qualities of 'a very fierce lion and a very cunning fox'. The long *Discourses on the First Ten Books of Livy*, perhaps written in the late 1510s, initially seem completely different. Here Machiavelli focused on the early years of the Roman Republic, making use of the copy of Livy which his father had bought forty years previously. He was primarily interested in explaining why Rome rose to such a dominant position, with an eye to lessons for his own day. Like Polybius, he thought that the mixed constitution was crucial, though not for its harmony, but because the tensions within it constrained otherwise violent factions. The two works in fact share common positions. The tough-minded view of human nature underlying *The Prince* is basic also to the *Discourses*. And in the *Discourses*, Machiavelli rejects Cicero's criticism of Romulus' killing of Remus: no sensible person should ever 'censure anyone for any unlawful action used in organizing a kingdom or setting up a republic'. Roman history offered models both for republicanism and for autocracy. Machiavelli explored both, which were extremely pertinent to the fluctuations between principates and republics in contemporary Italy, as happened notably in his native Florence. Machiavelli regarded autocracy as necessary in his time, because of corruption, but republicanism as the ideal. The lessons to be drawn from history were rooted in Roman debates about how the state should be organized and run. Machiavelli stated explicitly that those lessons in political organization had been neglected in his day, and that he wanted to spell them out, just as others had expounded lessons from antiquity for other branches of knowledge. He therefore set out rules that in principle had general validity, leading to the idea of his being the first political scientist.

*

The allegation that Tiberius Gracchus had accepted an Attalid royal robe and crown was made when the Attalid kingdom was bequeathed to Rome

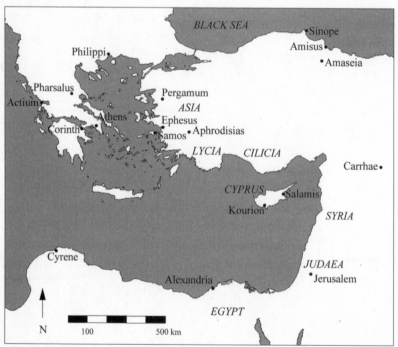

Map 27. The eastern Mediterranean in the second and first centuries BC.

on the death of its last king in 133 BC, and became the province of Asia. This new acquisition was followed by further expansion of Rome's eastern dominion in the later second and first centuries BC. Roman interests extended out from the core formed by the new province of Asia: by 101 BC action started to be taken against 'pirates' based in Cilicia on the south coast of Asia Minor, who were allegedly impeding the passage of Roman goods in the eastern Mediterranean; and in 90 BC expansionist moves by Mithradates Eupator to the north-east of the province of Asia were curbed.

Mithradates' own kingdom was based on the north coast of Asia Minor, with capitals at Sinope (modern Sinop) and Amisus (modern Samsun). Coming to the throne in 120 BC aged only 12, he gradually built up a power base that formed a major threat to Roman dominance in the east. Mithradates, like the contemporary Italian rebels, had an especially negative take on the Roman past, and present. He is supposed to have said that the Romans boasted that their founders were brought up on the milk of a she-wolf; as a result, the entire race had the spirits of wolves, insatiably greedy for blood, power and wealth. In 89 BC he overran the province of Asia, and in 88 he ordered his governors and overseers of individual cities to kill all resident Romans and Italians, men, women, children and even Italian freedmen. Eighty thousand, or maybe even more, were massacred on a single day. Subsequently he wrote to one of his governors to track down a leading refugee from the massacre, who was still in communication with the Romans, 'the common enemies', which was a neat reversal of the common Greek eulogy of the Romans as 'common benefactors' of the human race (above, p. 172).

Mithradates presented himself not simply as the foe of the Roman wolf, but as a ruler with local pasts. In part, he drew on a Persian heritage: on his father's side, he was sixteenth in line from Darius, the last Persian King, and proclaimed himself in Persian style as 'King of Kings'. He also saw himself in relation to a Greek past: on his mother's side, he was related to Alexander the Great and the first of the Seleucid kings. The Greek image became dominant when he decided to invade Asia: he was an old-fashioned liberator, fighting for the freedom of the Greeks of Asia, a slogan that went back to the fourth century BC. Until that point, the back of his coins featured Pegasus, the winged horse of Perseus, the ancestor of the Persian royal line. Thereafter the backs featured a stag, an image which would make Greeks think of the sacred animal of Artemis of Ephesus, the leading sanctuary in the province of Asia. The portraits of Mithradates, even on the Pegasus issues, were already strongly Hellenic, wearing the diadem as the symbol of kingship; on the stag issues the portrait became more idealized and impassioned (Plate 31d). On the coinages of some cities that supported him, his portrait even became merged with that of Alexander the Great, a tactic not employed by any other Hellenistic king. It is striking how potent the image of Alexander was in the east, 230 years after his death, and forty years after the creation of the Roman province of Asia.

Rome fought successfully against Mithradates and against the pirates. The Roman general Gnaeus Pompeius, known as Pompey, went on to annex what remained of the Hellenistic kingdom of the Seleucids, which became the province of Syria, and the state of Judaea. The victorious generals were thanked by the Greeks in familiar terms. Pompey was honoured by a city in Cilicia as being god-like, just as Hellenistic kings had been honoured by other Greek cities, and Sulla, who had captured Athens from a pro-Mithradatic faction, was, it seems, honoured in Rome by the Athenians. A copy was made of a famous statue group in the Athenian *agora*, of Harmodius and Aristogeiton who had killed the alleged tyrant of Athens in the sixth century BC (Plate 11). The copy was dedicated in Rome on the slopes of the Capitol, near the sanctuary of Fides Publica, the cult of the reliability of the Roman state. Rome could be thanked for the overthrow of the tyranny of Mithradates with reference to a historic moment in Athenian history.

Simultaneously, Roman power was expanding hugely in middle Europe. In 125 BC Rome responded to a request for military assistance from loyal Massilia, and within a decade much of southern France (the areas of Provence and the Languedoc) was conquered and converted into a Roman province (Gallia Narbonensis). The building of a Roman road secured the land route between Italy and Iberia, itself in process of being conquered; the Roman name for the road, Via Domitia, is commemorated in signs along the modern motorway that follows the same route.

The Celts in what became the new province lived in a series of nucleated hilltop settlements, modest in size (up to 15–20 hectares), and protected by stone ramparts. The settlements included roads laid out in grid patterns, and monumental stone temples. The inhabitants seem to have learned much about urban life from the Greek town of Massilia and its

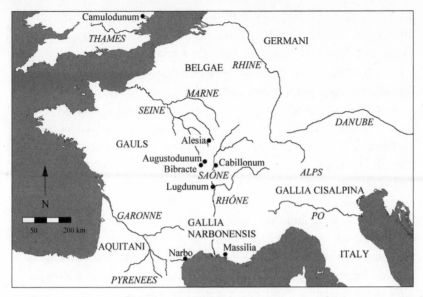

Map 28. Middle Europe *c*. 60 BC.

subsidiary settlements. This relatively urbanized region adapted readily to the new Roman order. A Roman colony was created at Narbo (modern Narbonne) in 118 BC, and the existing nucleated settlements mostly continued through into the period of Roman rule.

The Celts to the north of Gallia Narbonensis lived very differently (above, p. 217). From the third century BC the La Tène Celts had open settlements on level ground, with scattered houses and some industrial activity. From the second century BC onwards, the open settlements were abandoned in favour of hilltop settlements. Some 150 sites of this type are known, from central Gaul to Slovakia. They were large sites, up to 380 hectares, or even 600 hectares east of the Rhine. The modern name for this type of site, *oppidum*, the Latin for 'town' (plural: *oppida*), points to their urban nature. Bibracte (modern Mont Beuvray) in central France is a good example of an *oppidum* (Plate 14). Founded around 120 BC on a hill rising 250–300 metres above the plain, the site was defended by two fortification walls, of local design; the shorter, later wall enclosed some 135 hectares (see Figure 27). Within the walls, there were distinct areas for religious activity, housing, industrial production and a market, but these developed without the aid of a grid pattern of roads. The houses, with their wattle-and-daub walls and thatched roofs, remind us of the un-Mediterranean houses described by Strabo. Bibracte was the central place of the territory of the Aedui, one of sixty Celtic tribes in Gaul at this time. Its territory was huge, covering some 20,000 square kilometres, far larger than that of any normal Greek city-state, and not far short of the extent of Roman territory in 264 BC.

Bibracte, like the other *oppida* in middle Europe, developed for various reasons. Agriculture had become more intensive, and industrial production had increased, both preconditions for further development. The growth of Roman power in the Mediterranean in the third century BC had ended the possibilities for major raids and for mercenary service by the Celts. The mercenaries returned home, and deployed their new-found wealth to build up huge personal retinues, and engaged in rivalry with each other. Extra wealth came from the intensification of local production, and in trade with Rome. A good index of economic complexity is the development of local Celtic coinages. Initially, the coinages were in high denominations (gold and silver), imitating Macedonian coinage. From the mid-second century, with increased contact with Rome, silver coinages started to imitate Roman types, and by the end of the second century small change, in bronze, was being minted, which suggests increased levels of economic activity. In contrast to the spread of urbanization in middle Europe and in Iberia, in the rest of northern Europe there were very few urban sites in this period. In Britain, there were hardly any, and in the north-east European plain, the region of the earlier site of Sobiejuchy, there were none. Here there was no agricultural and technological progress of the sort seen in the regions where *oppida* later developed, and no input from returning mercenaries.

Trade between the *oppidum* regions and the Mediterranean was an important reason for the success of the *oppida*. Such trade was of course not new. Back in the sixth century BC local chieftains could import luxury goods from the Greek world, as in the case of Vix (above, p. 97). The extent of these imports was limited, in that they did not penetrate below the level of chieftains. But from around 130 or 120 BC, when the province of Gallia Narbonensis was created, imports north into central Gaul increased enormously, and for a time there was a symbiotic economic relationship between central Gaul and the Mediterranean. Bibracte had a major river-port 60 kilometres away at Cabillonum (modern Châlon-sur-Saône). Cabillonum could be reached easily from the Mediterranean via the Rhône and the Saône. Hundreds of thousands of wine-jars were imported to Bibracte during the century or so from 130/120 BC, and their contents played an important part in ceremonial feasting.

The wine imported to central Gaul in this period all came from the western side of the Italian peninsula as far down as Campania. One particularly successful wine-exporter was the Sestius family, whose estate was in the territory of the Roman colony of Cosa (above, pp. 199–201). Horace, in a poem on the return of spring, warned Lucius Sestius, appointed consul in 23 BC, about the shortness of human life; once dead, he would not be able to be president of the drinking party, 'lord of the wine', an elegant hint at the basis of the family's wealth. Wine-jars with stamps such as 'SEST' are found along the coast west of Cosa as far as Iberia. They were also imported inland up the Rhône and Saône to sites in central Gaul, including Bibracte, and also inland across the Gallic isthmus as far as Toulouse (Map 29). The importance of the trade is seen very vividly in a shipwreck found near Massilia, which dates to the early first century BC (see also Plate 21). The ship, known as Grand-Congloué 2, contained

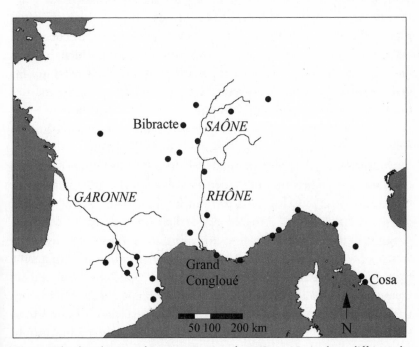

Map 29. The distribution of Sestius wine-jars from Cosa. Notice how different the pattern is from that we saw for the sixth century BC (Map 14).

1,200–1,500 wine-jars, mostly from the Sestius family estate. Ships carrying such cargoes in this period were far larger than any previous ships, but typical of what was required by the new scale of Roman trade.

The Aedui from Bibracte were conscious of Rome not just because of wine imports, but also because the northern frontier of the new province was only 50 kilometres or so from the southern border of Aeduan territory. At an early date they realized that the growth of Roman power offered them an opportunity to consolidate their position in relation to other Gallic tribes, much as Massilia did in the same period. In the second century BC the Aedui claimed kinship with the Romans, and had this claim accepted on many occasions by the Senate. Though we do not know the details, this kinship must have rested on a claim that the Aedui, like the Romans, were of Trojan origin, a type of claim to which we shall return (below, pp. 276–7).

The world changed for the Gauls with the arrival of Julius Caesar. Caesar, who had claimed regal and divine descent at the funeral of his aunt, went on to be consul in 59 BC, and managed to engineer the grant of a five-year overseas command (57–52 BC), covering both Illyricum (part of the modern Balkans) and Gaul. During this period he conquered all of Gaul north of the existing province as far as the Rhine; he even twice invaded Britain. Though Caesar did not make Britain tributary, his Gallic campaigns were phenomenally successful. The incorporation of Gaul, the first Roman provinces remote from the Mediterranean or Black Sea, marked a fundamental shift northwards in the balance of the Roman empire, a shift which would be continued under Augustus.

Understanding the geography and societies of middle Europe developed rapidly in the first century BC. Whereas earlier Greek authors had failed to engage with the Celts, the growth of Roman power provided a new incentive. Polybius and Artemidorus of Ephesus had made significant progress in the second century BC in writing about the geography of the western Mediterranean lands. Posidonius, a Greek intellectual originally from Syria, continued their work. His *Histories*, which began in 146 BC, where Polybius had ended, took the story of Roman expansion down to the conflicts with Mithradates of Pontus. Sadly, the work is known to us only at second hand, but it is clear that he included ethnographic sections on people with whom the Romans came into contact. In order to write the work, Posidonius travelled extensively in the first half of the first century BC, from Iberia in the west, to North Africa and to the Levant. In Gaul he went not only to the province of Gallia Narbonensis, but also into the Gallic lands to the north.

On the basis of this personal investigation, Posidonius wrote an extensive ethnography of the Gauls. He noted the un-Mediterranean houses of the Gauls (the account quoted at the start of this chapter was probably derived from his work). Posidonius was initially shocked by the widespread custom of nailing the heads of defeated enemies to their houses, but noted rather honestly that he gradually became accustomed to it. He also described how their feasting practices expressed their highly hierarchical society: the guest most distinguished in war, birth or wealth sat in the middle of a circle; next to him was the host, and on either side the rest according to their distinction; shield-bearers stood behind them; and spear-bearers sat opposite in another circle, like their masters. The drink was carried round in vessels like spouted cups, made of pottery or silver; the platters for the food might also be of the same materials, or of bronze, wood or wicker. The drink among the wealthy was wine, imported from Italy and Massilia (as already noted), usually consumed unmixed, unlike in Greece, where wine was always heavily diluted with water. For the poor there was an alcoholic drink made from wheat, with honey added, called 'korma', what we call mead.

Posidonius' ethnography was extended and developed, in rather different circumstances, by Julius Caesar. Caesar's *Gallic War*, probably published in 52 or 51 BC, was based on annual reports to the Senate about his progress. Though written in a seemingly artless style, whose alleged simplicity once made it a favourite teaching tool for English schoolchildren, the *Gallic War* was an artful presentation of his achievements. Embedded in the text was a series of claims about the natives whom Caesar encountered. The famous opening ('Gaul as a whole is divided into three parts') set up both the subject of the campaigns ('Gaul') and the major divisions facing Caesar: the Belgae in the north, the Aquitani in the west, and the Gauls in the centre (see Map 28). The three parts were divided from each other by major rivers: the Gauls from the Aquitani by the Garonne, and from the Belgae by the Marne and the Seine. The Rhine formed the boundary with the Germans, and the Ocean with what lay beyond. Each part was made up of many tribes, with different languages, institutions and laws. But despite the differences, Gaul as a whole was depicted, in standard imperialist terms, as an area clearly defined by major rivers, and as an area worth conquering, with stable populations and clearly defined social hierarchies.

A notable peculiarity of the Gauls was the Druids. Caesar depicted them as one of the two leading orders of Gallic society, the other being the knights. The institution apparently originated in Britain, but was now firmly established in Gaul. The Druids were in charge of all religious matters and arbitrated private disputes, and were headed by one supreme Druid. They learned by heart secret religious verses, espoused doctrines on the transmigration of souls, and instructed the young in astronomy and the nature and greatness of the gods. Caesar's picture of the Druids stressed the differences from Roman norms: at Rome most priesthoods were monopolized by the senatorial order, and lacked an overall head at this period. But his depiction is at the same time quite sympathetic to the Druids.

It is hard to decide how much truth there is in Caesar's portrait of the Druids. Gallic archaeology does not help us, but a British cemetery at Stanway outside Camulodunum (modern Colchester) includes an intriguing burial, dated to around AD 40–50. The cremated remains, probably of a man, were accompanied by fine pottery, a set of medical tools, a jet bead, a copper-alloy pan and strainer, a gaming board and eight metal rings with eight metal rods. The final publication labelled the burial simply as 'The Doctor': the medical tools were of local craftsmanship, but with parallels from earlier Celtic Europe; in the strainer was a lump of artemisia (mugwort or wormwood), sweetened with honey, which has known medicinal properties. But there is more to the burial than the 'Doctor' label would suggest. The style of burial and the range of grave goods show that this was a person of considerable importance: the gaming board, of indigenous type, is known from later Celtic traditions as a marker of high status. He was not a warrior, unlike the other major contemporary burial in this cemetery, a man buried with shield and spear, but he was not simply a doctor: the metal rings and rods and the jet bead were probably used for divination. The medical aspects of the burial are remote from the picture of Druids given by Caesar, but the sharp disjunction between 'The Warrior' and our burial conforms to Caesar's picture of a bipartite elite. Given the absence of other control evidence, it is not possible to say if he was actually a Druid, but it is clear that he belonged to the high status group that included Druids, diviners and healers.

Caesar established a sharp distinction between the Gauls and the Germans, across the northern boundary of Gaul, the Rhine. He was proud of his exploits in crossing the Rhine, being the first Roman commander to do so, but made clear that the Germans were not suitable for Roman conquest: their populations were too mobile, their political customs too remote from those of Mediterranean peoples. Even the landscape was too unfamiliar: Caesar described at considerable length the Hercynian forest, indefinable and vast, stretching for sixty days' journey east of the Rhine, populated with bizarre animals: as the elks could not bend their legs, they slept leaning against trees; hunters would secretly weaken the trees in advance, wait for the resting elk to push over the tree, and then capture the fallen animal. Caesar defined Britain as the third part of the north, after the Gauls and Germans. He offered abstract measurements of the whole island, also noting on the basis of a water-clock that the nights were shorter than those in Gaul. Pytheas had already offered measurements of the circumference of the island, and had made a similar measurement of British nights, but Caesar also included an ethnography of the island. Rather like Gaul, Britain was barbarous in some respects: the inland peoples did not practise agriculture, but lived off milk and meat, and wore skins, and all the men dyed themselves with woad. But Britain was also rich in natural resources and suitable for Roman conquest, an implication that would be followed up a hundred years later by the emperor Claudius.

Caesar's political prestige was so enhanced by his conquest of Gaul that his enemies feared for the balance of power at Rome. In early 49 BC Caesar led his army across the Rubicon, a river just north of Ariminum (modern Rimini) that marked the boundary between the province of Gallia Cisalpina and Italy proper. This was not a surprise move, but a deliberate raising of the stakes. 'Let the die be cast', he is supposed to have said, quoting a Greek comedy by Menander, and with good reason: no general could legitimately command troops in Italy proper. Pompey, with the prestige of eastern conquests behind him, claimed the high moral ground of supporting the Senate against the illegal actions of Caesar. Caesar then waged a civil war against Pompey and others, with victory for Caesar at Pharsalus in northern Greece in August 48 BC. From there Caesar went to the eastern Aegean, where in the autumn he bolstered his position by forming agreements with various Greek communities. The league of Lycian communities, friendly to Rome for over a hundred years, had struck a formal treaty with Rome under Sulla, and had made a dedication in Rome on the slopes of the Capitol, near the statues of the Athenian tyrant-slayers put up at the same time. In 48 BC the Lycians managed to negotiate another favourable agreement with Caesar. When the agreement was formalized as a treaty, in 46 BC, before Caesar had returned to Rome, it was described as being between the Roman people and the Lycian league, but the wording made clear that the initial decision was that of Caesar alone, in accordance with a Roman law granting him treaty-making powers. Such supreme power was unprecedented at Rome, but Caesar was canny enough to make use of subsequent ratification by senatorial decree, and to present his search for personal support in the east as a benefit for the Roman people.

In 46 BC Caesar finally returned to Rome, where he no longer had any obvious rivals. The old principles of the balance of power between Senate and people, and of the rotation of office within the senatorial order, had vanished, as a result of increased profits from empire and increased competition within the elite. The problem for all sides was how Caesar's position was to be conceptualized. After the civil war, in 46 BC, Caesar was appointed as *dictator* for ten years, and just before 15 February 44 BC he accepted the office of *dictator* for life (though this turned out to be just one more month). The office of *dictator* conferred on the holder powers greater than those of any other magistrate at Rome. Before the time of Sulla (82–81 BC), the office had last been used in 202 BC, during the crisis of the Second Punic War, and only for six months at a time. In one sense, Caesar's inflation of the office was realistic, but in another it insisted on the fact of his dominance. Was Caesar to be king of Rome? If he was, did memories of the regal period at Rome mean that a Caesarian kingship would be construed positively or negatively?

These issues came to the fore in a piece of public theatre during the festival of the Lupercalia on 15 February 44 BC. We hear of a thrice-repeated offering of a crown by Mark Antony to Caesar, and much puzzlement as to what was going on. The festival itself was one of Rome's most ancient. It originated with a race between Romulus and Remus and their respective supporters, a race won paradoxically by Remus, the slower twin, who did not found Rome. In the late Republic, two teams began the race at the Lupercal, the cave on the Palatine hill where the she-wolf had suckled the twins. They ran naked through the streets of Rome, whipping spectators, especially young women, with strips of goatskin, in a carnivalesque celebration of fertility and communal identity. The innovation of 44 BC was that a third team, the Juliani, headed by Mark Antony, had been created in honour of Julius Caesar, implicitly comparing him to Romulus and Remus. This was one of a series of completely extraordinary honours voted for Caesar in early 44 BC. On this occasion, Caesar was near the terminus of the race, on the speakers' platform in the Forum, seated on a golden chair. Antony, winning the race for the new team, then handed Caesar the crown. As the whole event had been so carefully stage-managed, its controversial culmination must also have been planned by Caesar and Antony. Caesar was to decline the offer of a crown, the symbol of monarchy, in an attempt to make clear that while he had accepted supreme powers for life and honours that compared him to Romulus and Remus, he was not to be seen as a king of Rome. This attempt to make things clear did not work. Contemporaries were baffled as to what had actually happened with the crown: did Caesar send it to the Capitol, saying that the only king was Jupiter? Did he throw it into the crowd, with Antony then ordering that it be placed on the statue of Caesar? Did he place it on a throne, thus implicitly accepting it, with perhaps an implication of divine monarchy? But the whole episode illustrates very clearly how attempts to define political power were bound up with rituals and ideas about Rome's remote past.

The past also hung heavily over the Ides of March 44 BC, the assassination of Caesar just a month after the Lupercalia. The consensus of the various philosophical schools was that it was legitimate to kill a tyrant. This is a chilling consensus, given that tyranny lies in the eye of the beholder, but one with major consequences for Rome. Both Brutus and Cassius, heroes of Shakespeare's play, and fellow-conspirators against Caesar, were seriously committed to philosophy, Brutus to a politicized version of Platonism, and Cassius to Epicureanism. Brutus was clear that it was legitimate to kill an 'unlawful monarch' or tyrant; Cassius, who had converted to Epicureanism in 48 BC at the time of his withdrawal from the political struggle against Caesar, now accepted the argument that circumstances overrode the Epicurean principle of seeking tranquillity. Caesar had to go. The death of Caesar was, however, as controversial as his life. At the time, there was also controversy about the death of Romulus. Some held that Romulus had died peacefully, a revered king of Rome, had ascended to heaven, and was worshipped as a god under the name Quirinus. Others claimed that he became such a cruel and despotic tyrant that the senators killed him, tearing his body limb from limb; this and not apotheosis was why his body disappeared. This polarized view of Rome's past paralleled exactly the views about Caesar: Was he a fine ruler of Rome, worthy of the divine honours voted for him in early 44 BC? Or was he an arbitrary tyrant, who could be stopped only by assassination? The latter was the view taken by Cicero, who was very clear that Caesar had been justly killed as a tyrant. The civil war following Caesar's death ended in 42 BC with the victory of Antony and Caesar's heir, the young Octavius, later known as Augustus, at Philippi. Even before Philippi, Caesar's divine honours had been formalized by a decree of the Senate: he was now 'the deified Julius' (*divus Julius*), with a temple in the Forum, and a special priest. These divine honours became the standard package for emperors on the death of Augustus in AD 14.

Shakespeare's Roman plays

Shakespeare was reproved by Ben Jonson for his 'small Latine, and lesse Greeke', but this snooty put-down of a person who did not go to university ignores Shakespeare's extraordinary ability to absorb ideas, including those from a wide range of works both ancient and modern. A few years after writing *Julius Caesar* (1599), Shakespeare returned to the first century BC with his *Antony and Cleopatra* (1606–1607). These two plays handled topics that were obvious in the later part of the Elizabethan age. Three other works had deeply eccentric settings: the earlier play *Titus Andronicus* (1589–92; set in various periods) and the later plays *Coriolanus* (1608; set in the early Republic) and *Cymbeline* (1610; set in Roman Britain). Some themes recur in the five plays: the tragedy of heroic individuals; tensions between private ties and public responsibilities; the unstable distinctions between rebel and tyrant. What holds the five plays together, perhaps even *Cymbeline*, is the city of Rome, which provides a common context for the plays' political, social and moral themes.

Rome had the advantage for Shakespeare of being acceptably classical, permitting republican ideas to be explored under the radar of the Elizabethan censor. Rome also was not the fixed symbol of any particular virtue or vice, which gave Shakespeare further freedom in relation to political issues. As Lucy Bailey, director of *Julius Caesar* for the Royal Shakespeare Company in 2009, says: 'The questions the play poses are clearly ones that obsessed Elizabethan society: at what point does monarchy become tyranny? Is it possible to rule without resorting to violence and suppression? Is assassination ever justified and does it produce change for the better?'

Shakespeare depicts Cassius urging on Brutus to act against Julius Caesar in emulation of his ancestor Junius Brutus, who had driven the last king out of Rome. Rome is equated with the Republic, the touchstone of liberty, and incompatible with the rule of one man, but this Republican political ideology, defined in very masculine terms, is undermined throughout the play. Political virtue depends upon intense rivalry, and so can become un-virtuous. Brutus is challenged by his wife Portia, who claims constancy equal to that of a man. The people, despised by the conspirators, become political players, as when Antony offers Caesar the crown. And just before Caesar is killed, he makes a fine Republican speech about his constancy in the face of mere personal appeals. His sense of superiority to other Romans is both intrinsically Roman and also what leads to his assassination. Shakespeare well understood the political contradictions of the late Republic.

The alliance between Antony and Augustus turned into a fresh civil war, which threw Augustus, based in Rome, and his western forces, against Antony and his eastern forces. Cleopatra, the Ptolemaic queen of Egypt, had offered her support, and more, to Caesar, who went from the eastern Aegean to Alexandria in 48 BC. She repeated the move in relation to Antony in 41 BC. The 1963 Hollywood film *Cleopatra* (starring Elizabeth Taylor and Richard Burton) neatly and correctly presents her as the descendant of Macedonian kings, living in an Alexandria whose public architecture was Greek, and ruling over a country that was mainly Egyptian. Sadly for Cleopatra, at the decisive naval battle of Actium in 31 BC her forces and those of Antony were defeated. Augustus was now without competitors, the most powerful person in the Roman world.

This civil war left Augustus with blood on his hands, notably the blood of those citizens who were 'proscribed', that is put to death for their money. How were historians in the ensuing time of peace to handle the immediate past? Asinius Pollio retired from public life after celebrating a triumph in 39 BC and devoted himself to literature. He then wrote a famous history of Rome from 60 BC onwards, but ended it with the death of Republican hopes at the battle of Philippi in 42 BC. Even so, Pollio was said by a contemporary poet, Horace, to be courting disaster with his history. Livy, rather remarkably, did not stop in 42 BC, but continued his history of Rome down to 9 BC and the death of one of Augustus' heirs, though he might have intended to take it to a more obvious stopping point. He favoured the Republican Pompey against Caesar, which did not upset Augustus, but it seems that his narrative of the civil wars and the Augustan period cannily concentrated on wars against foreign foes, omitting most of the internal political history of Rome. In addition, he held back the publication of the books that dealt with Augustus' rise to power and sole rule until after the emperor's death. There was too much that could not be said under Augustus.

Augustus himself did not abolish anything. All the political and religious institutions that had existed from the foundation of the Republic continued to operate, if in modified fashions. Augustus avoided Caesar's disastrous experimentation with the office of *dictator*, and instead chose a more modest combination of consulship, or later consular power, and tribunician power to define his position. Augustus also combined, for the first time, the holding of all the major priesthoods of Rome. The cumulation of priestly office came to be seen as the basis for imperial control of the religious life of Rome. But Augustus avoided being given the name 'Romulus', with all its ambiguous connotations, and instead played the role of being just a citizen. Playing this role, with a full awareness that it was just a role, granted both the senatorial order and the Roman people a sense of dignity. It accounts for the forty-five-year duration of Augustus' reign, and established the model of the 'good emperor' from which his successors deviated at their peril (Plate 23).

Like other leading senators, Augustus presented himself as the leading member of a family. In normal senatorial fashion, he used adoption to add new male heirs to the family. His relatives, especially his wife Livia, came to possess great public prominence. In 35 BC she received the right to administer her own affairs without a legal guardian, sacrosanctity equivalent to that possessed by tribunes of the people, and the erection of statues of her in Rome. In the 20s BC Livia was the first woman to have her own official portrait type for statues, which were erected throughout the empire; eschewing showy jewellery and opulent clothing, she was shown as the ideal of Roman womanhood. Livia also built on the religious role of women, who were traditionally involved with festivals associated female virtues of chastity and domestic harmony, by being the

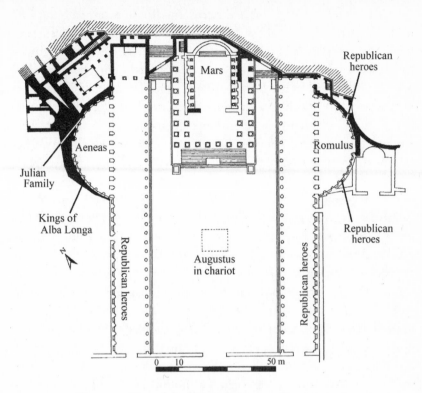

Figure 25. Plan of the Forum Augustum, Rome (2 BC).

first individual woman to build or restore shrines to those cults. Politically, she was always at her husband's side, which has led to much speculation about her nefarious actions on behalf of her blood relatives, as epitomized in Robert Graves's novel *I, Claudius*. Sometimes, Augustus even acknowledged her influence publicly. When turning down the request by the people of Samos for a particular privileged status, Augustus admitted that he was personally well disposed to the Samians, and that he regretted turning them down as he would have liked to have done a favour to his wife, who had been active on their behalf.

Augustus engaged in extensive public building activity in Rome, in his own name and in that of members of his family. As only those who celebrated triumphs were entitled to build in Rome, and as in effect only emperors and members of the imperial family were qualified to celebrate triumphs, other senators lost their entitlement to build, and instead began to monumentalize their home towns in Italy and elsewhere. The Forum

Augustum, built by Augustus in the centre of Rome, nicely embodies the emperor's sense of the past (see Figure 25). The temple in the centre of the Forum was dedicated to Mars the Avenger, with reference to Augustus' 'vengeance' on the Parthian kingdom, east of the Euphrates, which had defeated Rome at Carrhae in 53 BC (Plate 31e), and also on the murderers of Caesar. Mars also had a second level of Augustan reference: he and Venus, who were represented together on the temple pediment, were parents respectively of Romulus and of Aeneas. The colonnades on either side of the temple took these points further. In each colonnade was a series of statues of Republican heroes, each with an inscribed summary of his achievements. In the inset semicircle on the left were statues of the Julian family, focused on Aeneas, and on the right further Republican heroes, focused on Romulus. As not only Aeneas but also Romulus were presented as being ancestors of Augustus, the whole monumental complex presented Augustus as the culmination of Roman history.

There was a strong move to stress the political unity of all of Italy, and to downplay the Social War of two generations previously. Augustus himself, building on the rhetoric of Cicero, claimed that in the civil war 'the whole of Italy (*tota Italia*) swore allegiance to me of its own accord, and demanded me as its leader in the war which I won at Actium'. This was a useful point to make, given that both consuls and a third of the Senate had gone over to Antony's side. Shortly after Actium, Virgil published his *Georgics*, notionally a didactic poem on farming. It included a section known later as the 'praise of Italy', a recognized category of writing at the time: Italy surpassed all other regions of the world in its fertility, and charm; its noble cities, perched on precipitous rocks or with rivers gliding beneath ancient walls; the variety of its major peoples. Virgil's appreciation of Italy was rooted in recent history: the northern limits are given as lakes Como and Garda, in the former province of Gallia Cisalpina, which had been converted into a region of Italy by Julius Caesar only in 49 BC. And Virgil boldly ended the section with reference to himself, as singing didactic poetry from Greece 'through Roman towns', implicitly uniting the city of Rome and the towns of Italy.

Over the next decade Virgil worked on an epic poem, the *Aeneid*. This poem too was rooted in the present: the battle of Actium is described not as part of the civil war, but as a clash between west and east, the ancient gods not just of Rome but of Italy versus the bizarre animal-headed gods of Egypt. This view of Egypt was part of the current political orthodoxy, but the *Aeneid* is not a eulogy of Augustus, the descendant of Aeneas. Drawing on earlier Roman epics, including Naevius, Virgil set the first part of the epic at Carthage, including the great love affair between Aeneas and Dido. Aeneas has to break off the affair in order to fulfil his historic destiny of proceeding to Italy, and he does not emerge well from the Dido episode (Plate 28). When Aeneas reaches Italy, he is told the story of Hercules and Cacus by the humble King Evander (above, p. 180), and given a guided tour by him, seeing for example the Lupercal cave and the Capitol, already numinous with divine power. This is a wonderfully knowing account, as Evander, the 'founder of the Roman citadel', and Aeneas, who we know will found the Roman race, look at the present modest site, but intuit the future city of Rome.

The *Aeneid* was instantly recognized as a classic. A contemporary poet, Propertius, hailed the epic, even in advance of publication, as greater than Homer's *Iliad*, and the poem was immediately adopted as part of the school curriculum, displacing Naevius and Ennius. Virgil came to be taught throughout the Latin-speaking parts of the empire. Thirty-six graffiti in Pompeii are quotations from the *Aeneid*: as the educational system focused on the teaching of writing and grammar, twenty-six of the graffiti are quotations of the first lines of Books 1 and 2. Even in remote Britain, Virgil was known. At Vindolanda, a Roman military base near Hadrian's Wall, two writing tablets include lines from the *Aeneid*, suggesting that the commanding officer employed a tutor to teach the poem to his children. Elsewhere, in Egypt and Judaea, soldiers in the army practised their Latin language skills by writing out parts of the *Georgics* and *Aeneid*. But knowledge of Virgil was not limited to the army, and was not always merely mechanical: very strikingly, in a cave in south-east Iberia someone painted a number of verse texts which are free adaptations of various parts of the *Aeneid*.

After antiquity, Virgil remained on the curriculum, and his works were copied out in extraordinary numbers (below, pp. 317–18). He and Homer were regarded as the greatest poets of antiquity; Virgil became of particular interest for passages which seemed to presage Christianity. Dante, whom we met in the context of the choice of language for his *Divine Comedy*, was perhaps the most original reader of Virgil in the Middle Ages. He had long seen Virgil as someone who expounded Italian consciousness, '*our* greatest poet', as he calls him. In the *Divine Comedy*,

Virgil serves as his initial guide to hell, a sombre figure, weighed down by his inability to have been a Christian because he had lived 'in the time of the false and lying gods'. In the popular tradition in Italy, Virgil became a very different figure. Virgil had been buried just outside Naples, but by the twelfth century it was believed that Virgil had been governor of Naples, and had been responsible for a number of talismanic objects which protected the city from capture, would not allow even flies to enter the city, or prevented the eruption of Vesuvius. Such stories spread rapidly to other parts of Europe, and generated further tales. In France, Virgil was presented by some troubadours as a magician, who possessed a garden in which it never rained, and who created a bell-tower, which moved in time to the bells. After the sixteenth century, these Virgil legends dropped out of popular consciousness, but to this day tourists are shown the 'Tomb of Virgil', in reality an entirely anonymous memorial.

The city of Rome under Augustus took on much of the future greatness intimated by King Evander. Virgil depicted Aeneas, newly arrived at Carthage, gazing in wonder at the energetic building of walls, citadel and theatre, replacing the primitive huts (*magalia*, a Punic word): 'O happy ones, whose walls already rise.' Carthage here reminds Aeneas of the city which he is destined, ultimately, to found, and which Augustus would enhance. According to Augustus' biographer, Suetonius, writing with more than 100 years of hindsight, Augustus was right to boast that he had found the city built of brick and left it in marble. The contrast is exaggerated. The relative modesty of its public buildings in the early second century BC had come to be unacceptable by the end of that century. Leaders earlier in the first century BC, especially Pompey and Caesar, continued to monumentalize the centre of Rome, but Augustus did take things further, as with the Forum Augustum. Suetonius' statement of Augustus' reasoning is especially interesting: he beautified the city 'because it was not adorned as befitted the dignity of the empire...'. Suetonius here picks up a point already made by the great architect Vitruvius, writing under Augustus. Vitruvius began with praise of Augustus for bringing peace after the civil war, for augmenting the state with new provinces and for strongly underpinning the majesty of empire with public buildings. In the course of the first century BC and first century AD, Rome ceased to be the centre of an empire of conquest and became the capital of a different sort of empire, an empire of incorporation, in which the provinces stopped being areas simply to be exploited by members of the Roman elite, and became instead beneficiaries of Roman rule. In turn, Rome saw itself, not as the backdrop for unbridled competition between individual politicians, but as the capital city, whose design and monuments needed to be worthy of the empire.

Mussolini and Rome

Romanità, an idealization of Roman values, was popular with the new Italian state in the second half of the nineteenth century, and was taken up enthusiastically by the Italian Fascists. The nature of the appeal to the Roman past changed over time. From 1922 to 1925, *romanità* served as an ideal for revolutionary action. Mussolini, who came from a village near the Rubicon, modelled himself on Julius Caesar, the saviour of Rome from corruption, though, while Mussolini's men marched on Rome, he himself came down by night sleeper. From 1925 to 1936, Rome offered justifications for territorial expansionism. As Mussolini said to the 1925 Fascist Congress, held in the Mausoleum of Augustus, then a public meeting hall, 'The only city on the shores of the Mediterranean, fateful and fated, that has created an empire is Rome.' Augustus, as the creator of a stable imperial system, became the new model. Then from 1936 onwards, *romanità* was used as one of the justifications for racism, with only pure Italians being the true descendants of the Romans. The lavish 1937 film *Scipio l'Africano* depicted the final conflict between Rome and Carthage as that between order and authority against chaos and democracy, with the Carthaginians seen as uncivilized and Semitic.

Bimillenaries of the births of Virgil (1930) and Augustus (1937) were major events. Some poets drew parallels between Virgil's 'praise of Italy' in the *Georgics* and contemporary celebration of honest peasantry against despicable bourgeoisie. In 1934 Mussolini personally inaugurated a project to clear the shoddy houses clustering round the Mausoleum of Augustus, and to remove the meeting hall from it. The piazza round the Mausoleum was lined with new buildings, decorated with reliefs embodying Fascist ideals; at one side a restoration of Augustus' Altar of Peace, originally located elsewhere in Rome, was erected. The project, one of several at Rome, was finished on schedule, in time for Augustus' bimillennium. Augustus' birth was also celebrated with a huge exhibition, 'The Augustan Exhibition of *romanità*', which received over a million visitors. The exhibition was scholarly, accompanied by a catalogue which is still useful, but also deeply political. The message was spelled out in a quotation from Mussolini himself in the entrance hall: 'Italians, ensure that the glories of the past are surpassed by the glories of the future.' *Romanità* and modernity went hand in hand, justifying a dynamic Fascist empire.

Rome was in the time of Augustus a massive city. According to a treatise on electioneering ascribed to Cicero's brother Quintus, Rome was 'a state formed from the concourse of the peoples of the world', which recalls Romulus' asylum (above, p. 182). Modern estimates of the population of Rome in the early empire often approach one million people. In 5 BC Roman citizens with a legal domicile at Rome received a cash handout from Augustus; they numbered no fewer than 320,000. To figures such as this have to be added citizens' wives and children, resident slaves and freedmen, and visitors to Rome, both citizen and non-citizen, from all over the empire. Rome was a vast city, characterized and supported by much mobility between empire and city. Precise estimates of the area of Rome in this period are difficult. Unfortunately, we do not know the precise geographical limits of Roman legal domicile. By the AD 270s, when Rome had again to be fortified, the new walls enclosed no less than 1,373 hectares, and beyond them were extensive suburbs, extending perhaps 15 kilometres from Rome. But even if we cannot quite quantify numbers or inhabited area, Rome in the early empire was by far the largest city in the Roman empire, twice the size of Alexandria in Egypt, the next largest city. And it was comparable to the capitals of other pre-industrial states. Depending on whether some or all of the urban sprawl round Rome is included, then imperial Rome was as large as or larger than Ch'ang-an in China, the eighth–ninth century AD capital of the T'ang dynasty, or Edo, the capital of Japan in the seventeenth–nineteenth centuries AD.

Freud and Rome

Sigmund Freud (1856–1939), one of the founders of modern attitudes to the self, was a keen student of Latin and Greek at school in Vienna; aged 58, he wrote that there he had seen 'my first glimpses of an extinct civilization (which in my case was to bring me as much consolation as anything else in the struggles of life)'.

When first developing his ideas of the unconscious, he had a curious relation to the city of Rome. Between 1895 and 1898, while on holiday in Italy, he tried to visit Rome five times, but was prevented by a strong inhibition. In *The Interpretation of Dreams* (1900), Freud interpreted this strange phenomenon in terms of his Jewishness, and the endemic anti-Semitism of the day: as a schoolboy he had identified with the Semitic Hannibal, and as an adult he saw the conflict between Hannibal and Rome as parallel to that between the tenacity of Jewry and the organization of the Catholic Church; like Hannibal he was fated not to enter Rome. In fact, after the publication of *The Interpretation of Dreams*, Freud managed to break the inhibition, and became a regular intellectual pilgrim to Rome.

When developing his ideas of the unconscious, Freud returned repeatedly to the excavation of antiquity for analogies. He amassed a collection of some 3,000 antiquities, for which he had a great passion. The collection, displayed not in his private quarters, but in his consulting room and study, was an important part of his professional persona. Athena was a significant symbol of wisdom and rationality for him: in 1938 Freud selected a figurine of Athena as the sole piece to be smuggled out of Austria to England, in case the Nazi authorities confiscated the rest of the collection. Aged 75, he wrote to an admirer that 'despite my much vaunted frugality I have sacrificed a great deal for my collection of Greek, Roman, and Egyptian antiquities, [and] have actually read more archaeology than psychology'. In *Civilization and its Discontents* (1930), Freud, in arguing that memories are never lost but can be brought back to light, outlined the ancient history of the Eternal City, drawing on a 1928 volume of *The Cambridge Ancient History*: a properly informed visitor is, in principle, able to find traces of each period, even if the ruins are in part later restorations, and are dove-tailed into the jumble of the modern metropolis. The archaeology of Rome was an analogy for Freud's project of excavating layers of the human mind.

The relations between Rome and its provinces changed between the late Republic and early empire. In the Republic, Roman governors engaged in arbitration between subject peoples, which sometimes brought increased stability to a region. Honesty was expected from governors and their staff, and sometimes even met with, but when in 60 BC Cicero wrote to his brother, who was governor of the province of Asia, he thought it incredible that his brother should spend three years in Asia without being tempted by offers of material goods, of sexual services or of financial reward to deviate from the path of strict integrity and sobriety of conduct. Human nature being what it is, and with the added need of politicians to recoup election expenses in Rome, governors often failed to regulate their own behaviour. In addition, they abused their positions. Cyprus, annexed in 58 BC and added to the province of Cilicia (southern Asia Minor), found itself at the mercy of Roman officials. The noble Brutus, later famed for his part in the conspiracy against Caesar, lent money to the city of Salamis on Cyprus at an extortionate rate of 48 per cent per annum; Brutus then obtained a supportive senatorial decree; in order to recover the money, one of his operatives borrowed cavalry from the provincial governor, and besieged the town councillors in their council house, where five of them starved to death. Such exploitative behaviour on the part of the Roman elite was outrageous. The pressures of the civil wars sometimes made things worse. In 49 BC Massilia was besieged by Julius Caesar, because the city had earlier taken the side of Pompey, and in punishment was stripped of much of its territory. In 43 BC Lycia, encouraged by one of the envoys who had just formalized the Caesarian treaty at Rome, offered military resistance to Brutus and Cassius, who were collecting troops there for a final campaign against Antony and Augustus. But from Augustus onwards, the provinces were generally at peace, and emperors helped to ensure reasonably effective safeguards in Rome against excesses by Roman officials in the provinces.

Roman rule also affected the internal political structures of ancient cities. At Kourion on Cyprus, members of the town council, once elected annually, came to be elected for life. This change was typical of what happened in cities throughout the Greek east under Roman rule. Councils were transformed so that they became more like the Roman Senate. In turn, Greek cities responded to Rome in terms that helped to negotiate between the Greek and Roman worlds. In AD 14, on the death of Augustus, Cyprus took an oath of loyalty to the new emperor, Tiberius; this oath was part of a new pattern of oaths, which extended to the provinces the oath taken by *tota Italia* in 32 BC. The Cypriots swore by a long series of 'our' gods, Aphrodite, born on Cyprus, Korē, Apollo and so on, 'all the ancestral gods and goddesses of our island'. To this list of deities they added two more: 'the descendant of Aphrodite', Augustus God Caesar, and Eternal Rome; Augustus' claim to descent from Aphrodite, the Greek Venus, was especially telling on this island. By these gods, the Cypriots swore allegiance and worship to Tiberius and his family, correctly understanding that the empire was a family show, and also promised to establish new cults to Roma, Tiberius and the sons of his blood. The phrase 'sons of his blood' is striking. The Cypriots knew that Augustus had claimed descent from Aphrodite, but they did not realize that adoption was the normal way at Rome of guaranteeing male heirs, and that therefore limiting cult to 'the sons of his blood' was politically unacceptable.

By the time that Augustus died, the growing collection of Roman provinces had become a single empire. He was able to leave behind him a summary statement, alas lost to us, about the whole empire: the number and locations of soldiers under arms, the financial balances of the treasuries and the indirect taxes in arrears. Under the Republic, detailed military and financial information did exist in Rome, but individual senators did not normally seek to master it, even if Cicero had regarded such mastery as ideal. No individual in Rome before Augustus had such a grip on military and financial affairs.

Augustus' knowledge was enhanced by improved procedures for censuses, both of citizens and of provincials. In 28 BC, at the start of his reign, he carried out a census, which registered no fewer than 4,063,000 Roman citizens. The census system had failed to cope with the consequences of the enfranchisement of the Italians, and this was the first census for no less than forty-two years. He performed two other general censuses, in 8 BC and AD 14, which returned increasing numbers: 4,233,000 and 4,937,000 citizens. These huge numbers include the perhaps 300,000 adult males of the former province of Gallia Cisalpina, who were given Roman citizenship in 49 BC when this area was converted into a region of Italy, and also the Roman citizens resident in overseas colonies and elsewhere, but the figures are so huge, four times as large as the likely citizen population of Italy in 70 BC, that the Augustan figures probably included at least some women and children. In addition, Augustus instituted a new practice of provincial censuses, which counted both Roman citizens and the rest of the population, and also recorded their property. In Egypt, the censuses were held every fourteen years, in other provinces perhaps not as regularly, but the expectation of repetition

Figure 26. A view through the grand gateway up the monumental approach to the Sebasteion at Aphrodisias. The porticoes on either side displayed a total of 190 sculpted panels, on the Roman empire, the Greek world and the imperial family. The right-hand (south) portico had on its middle storey figures from the remote Greek past (such as Leda and the Swan, Pegasus and Bellerophon, Dionysus and Heracles), and on its upper storey imperial victories, the divine emperors and the gods.

was clear. So was the fact that the censuses were held throughout the empire. This helps to explain the statement of the evangelist Luke: 'It came to pass in those days that an edict went out from Caesar Augustus that all the world should be registered. This was the first registration, when Quirinius was governor of Syria.' There was certainly no simultaneous registration of the whole world, but Luke, writing two or three generations later, understandably conflated the universal practice of provincial censuses with the particular census of Syria and its newly added region of Judaea conducted by Quirinius in AD 6 (see further p. 265); Luke also believed that this census was held when Herod was king of Judaea (37–4 BC), and that it included Galilee, but in both these beliefs he is certainly mistaken. The new institution of provincial censuses meant that the Roman state for the first time had detailed information about the numbers and wealth of its entire population.

The extent of the Roman empire under Augustus was vast, stretching from Iberia in the west to Syria in the east, and from Africa in the south to the English Channel in the north (see Maps 30 and 31). Its extent was made manageable, not only through administration, censuses and the like, but also through images. Augustus' right-hand man, Agrippa, collected material for a great map, which was displayed publicly in a portico at Rome after his death in 12 BC. The map showed to Rome the whole world, and the dominant position of the Roman empire within it. Unlike the old round maps of the Ionians, Agrippa's map was rectangular, going from Iberia in the west to India in the east; it was accompanied by a brief text giving statistics on the dimensions of regions, seas and perhaps rivers; a similar map was to be found in Gaul around AD 300. In addition, at Rome under Augustus another portico displayed selected images of peoples added to the empire by him. Starting under Tiberius, the people of the city of Aphrodisias (in western Asia Minor) drew upon the Roman portico in designing a monumental approach way leading up to a grand temple dedicated to Augustus, known as the Sebasteion, Sebastos being the Greek version of Augustus (see Figure 26; Plate 25). The portico forming the north side of the approach way featured in its middle storey fifty high-relief images of peoples and places added to the empire, or recovered for the empire, by Augustus, from Arabia and Egypt to peoples bordering the Danube and on to north-west Iberia. There were many ways of physically representing the scope of the Roman empire, but they all helped to make the immensity of the empire intelligible.

The empire was also made intelligible in words. Strabo, writing his *Geography* late in the reign of Augustus and under Tiberius, had a view of the world centred on Rome. Strabo himself came from Amaseia (modern Amasya in Turkey), and stood in the tradition of Greek geographical writing represented by Polybius, Artemidorus and Posidonius. His work was structured in traditional fashion, starting in Iberia, moving via Gaul and Britain, to Italy, Greece and Asia Minor, continuing east to Persia and India, and ending the circuit with Egypt and Libya. But his vision of the world was novel. In describing Rome, he emphasizes how the sight of the great monuments of Rome might make one forget instantly everything elsewhere, and he ends his work on 'our inhabited world' with a summary account of how the Romans came to conquer and organize the finest and best-known parts of the world. Though concerned primarily with geography and peoples, Strabo took note of the changes brought about by the Romans. For example, in Gaul he talks about the creation in 43 BC of the Roman colony at Lugdunum (modern Lyons), sited where the rivers Rhône and Sâone join and in the centre of the country. It was from here, he says, that Agrippa planned, in the 30s BC, the system of Roman roads that fanned out to unite the whole of Gaul in a single network. For Strabo, the old division of the world into Europe and Asia, or into Europe, Africa and Asia, was superseded by a vision of the Roman empire, centred on Rome.

8

The Roman Empire, AD 14–284

In AD 48 a small delegation arrived at Rome from the distant plains of northern Gaul. The leading nobles of the north Gallic provinces were seeking the right to hold office in Rome itself, in particular the right to apply for membership of the Senate. The Senate was, unsurprisingly, not especially keen on the idea. The issue was decided by a lengthy speech of the emperor Claudius to the Senate in support of the Gauls' petition.

> Do not shudder at the thought of some dangerous novelty being introduced. Reflect, instead, on how many innovations our state has seen; think how many different changes our constitution has undergone, starting right from the very foundation of our city itself. Once, the city was ruled by kings; yet they failed to pass it on to native heirs. Instead, it was other men, foreigners, who took their place. Romulus was succeeded by Numa, a native of the Sabine country – a neighbour, for sure, but a foreigner nonetheless . . . it was a wholly novel policy, too, when my great-uncle the deified Augustus and my uncle Tiberius Caesar wished to bring into this Senate house the flower of the colonies and municipalities, wherever it was to be found, so long as they were sound and wealthy men.

As we saw in the last two chapters, the question of the incorporation of non-Romans into the Roman state had a long history. Nonetheless, in this speech to the Senate, Claudius was deliberately overturning centuries of received wisdom. The deep conservatism of Roman political thought has been emphasized again and again in the last two chapters. But Claudius now argued that the history of Rome had been characterized by political innovation right from the outset. The main lesson that the past had to offer was the value of political change and novelty. Not only had new men always been freely absorbed into the Roman body politic, but the constitution itself had always been in flux. The Roman historian Tacitus, who included a paraphrase of Claudius' speech to the Senate in his *Annals*, finished the speech with his own telling flourish: 'This proposal, too, will grow old, and that which we defend today with precedents, shall one day be counted as a precedent itself.'

Tacitus, looking back to the reign of Claudius (AD 41–54) seventy years after the event, must have appreciated the irony. By the time Tacitus was composing the *Annals*, late in the reign of the emperor Trajan (98–117), the Republic was gone for good. The *Annals* begin with the words 'The city of Rome from the beginning was held by kings'. Not 'in the beginning', but '*from* the beginning': in Tacitus' eyes, the principate, rule by a single 'first man' or *princeps*, was monarchy in all but name. The revolutionary politics of Augustus had indeed become hallowed precedent.

The *Annals* recount the history of Rome under the Julio-Claudian dynasty (Tiberius–Nero, AD 14–68). In the early years of the Julio-Claudians, unlike in Tacitus' own day, elite resistance to the principate had still been possible. Early in the *Annals*, Tacitus describes how, in AD 25, the historian Cremutius Cordus was prosecuted for high treason. His crime was to have used his work to praise Brutus and Cassius, the assassins of Julius Caesar, and specifically to have quoted Brutus' description of Cassius as 'the last of the Romans'. Defending himself before the Senate and the emperor Tiberius (AD 14–37), Cremutius argued that he had done nothing unusual or seditious. Many earlier historians – Livy, Asinius Pollio, Messalla Corvinus – had praised Brutus and Cassius in fulsome terms. Surely the assassins had now been dead long enough for there to be no danger in giving them their due honour? As Cremutius himself must surely have expected, this argument cut no ice at all with Tiberius. The historian was compelled to commit suicide, and his books were burned. In AD 25, when the last days of the Republic were still within living memory, Caesar's assassination could not simply be dismissed as ancient history. The figures of the 'tyrannicides' carried a particular political and emotional charge. Junia, the sister of Brutus and wife of Cassius, had died only three years earlier, in AD 22; images of her brother and husband were, says Tacitus, 'conspicuous by their absence' in the funeral procession. The contested memory of Brutus and Cassius would remain a raw spot on the Roman imperial psyche for at least another generation; as late as AD 65 a lawyer could be sent into exile for keeping an image of Cassius among the portraits of his ancestors.

In AD 41, after the assassination of the unpopular emperor Caligula (AD 37–41), there was a brief moment when the restoration of senatorial government may have seemed a real possibility. The Jewish historian Josephus, our main source for the last days of Caligula, depicts Caligula's killers as Republican idealists trying to re-establish liberty and the ancestral constitution in the face of tyranny. At any rate, it rapidly became clear that there was no popular support for a return to the Republican system, and the praetorian guard, the emperor's personal bodyguard, acted quickly to have another member of the imperial family, Claudius, acclaimed as emperor. Tyrant-slaying had had its day.

The new ideology of the principate is at its clearest in a chilling essay by the Stoic philosopher Seneca. In AD 55, only fourteen years after Caligula's death, Seneca published a short treatise *On Clemency*, addressed to the new emperor Nero (AD 54–68), Seneca's own former pupil and protégé. It is, says Seneca, right and necessary that the emperor's power should be absolute. The emperor is the animate soul of the body politic; without him, the state would swiftly descend into chaos. Although Seneca stops just short of calling Nero a 'king' (*rex*), he is quite clear that Brutus' fears of autocracy, which led him to assassinate Caesar, were misplaced: the perfect state is, on the contrary, that which is well governed by a just king. The main purpose of the treatise is to urge the new emperor to exercise his limitless power with mildness and restraint, just as Augustus had done. This was the best for which a member of the Roman elite could now hope.

People like Seneca and Tacitus responded to the new world order with realism and caution. Tacitus' first historical work, the *Agricola*, published in AD 98, is a biography of his father-in-law, Julius Agricola. Agricola had been one of Rome's foremost generals under the Flavian dynasty of emperors (Vespasian, AD 69–79; Titus, 79–81; Domitian, 81–96). After a notably successful governorship of the remote province of Britain (AD 78–84), Agricola returned to Rome, only to be hustled into a humiliating premature retirement. There were limits to the glory that a general was allowed to win for himself; no one, however talented, could be allowed to outshine the emperor himself. 'A great reputation', says Tacitus, 'was as dangerous as a bad one.' By accepting his removal from public life, Agricola showed not only good sense, but even a kind of heroism. 'Let those whose habit it is to admire forbidden ideals know that there can be great men even under bad emperors; that duty and discretion, if combined with industry and energy, will bring a man to the same heights of honour as others have achieved through perilous courses and ostentatious deaths, with no advantage to the state.'

Much of the *Agricola* is taken up with an account of Roman rule in Britain, from the initial conquest of the southern part of the island under Claudius (AD 43) to the campaigns of Agricola in northern England and Scotland. Britain was the last major part of western Europe to be incorporated into the Roman empire, and the conquest was drawn-out and bloody. In AD 60 a fierce rebellion broke out in the south-east under the native queen Boudica. The rebels succeeded in sacking the Roman colony at Camulodunum (modern Colchester), along with the towns of Londinium and Verulamium (modern St Albans). The revolt ended in a bloodbath, somewhere in the west Midlands, at which 80,000 Britons were said to have been killed. The defiant speech which Tacitus later puts in the mouth of a – probably fictional – Scottish chieftain, Calgacus, has some truth to it: 'to plunder, butchery, and rapine, they give the lying name of "government"; they create a desolation and call it peace.'

From Boudica to Boadicea

The figure of Boadicea (as she has usually been called) has been put to various different uses by the British over the centuries. During the war with Spain in the late sixteenth century, Elizabeth I was often compared to the original British warrior queen; it is even possible that Elizabeth imitated one of Boadicea's speeches (as reported by Tacitus) in her own speech to the English army at Tilbury in 1588, shortly before the battle of the Armada. In William Cowper's *Boadicea: An Ode* (1782), Boadicea's heroic defeat at the hands of the Romans was set up as an icon and precursor of British imperialism.

Probably the best-known modern image of Boadicea is Thomas Thorny-croft's great bronze statue of *Boadicea and her Daughters* (started in 1856, but not set up until 1902) which today stands in front of the House of Commons in London, next to Westminster Bridge (see Plate 24). Prince Albert took an active interest in the statue's design, urging Thornycroft to render the queen and her chariot in as regal and poetic a manner as possible (a 'throne upon wheels'). Boadicea is depicted as a dignified warrior, wielding a spear and standing poised on her chariot behind a rearing pair of horses. The inscription on the front of the pedestal claims Boadicea as a British patriot and national hero: 'Boadicea, Boudicca, Queen of the Iceni, Who died AD 61, After leading her people against the Roman invader'. On the east side of the pedestal there appears a quotation from Cowper's *Boadicea*: 'Regions Caesar never knew, / Thy posterity shall sway'. Thornycroft's statue quietly encourages the viewer to see Boadicea as the ultimate ancestor of Queen Victoria, Empress of India.

However, not all British images of Boadicea have been so positive. In Tennyson's *Boädicéa* (1859), she is presented as a bloodthirsty fanatic:

Mad and maddening all that heard her in her fierce volubility,
Girt by half the tribes of Britain, near the colony Cámulodúne,
Yell'd and shriek'd between her daughters o'er a wild confederacy.

Tennyson's picture of a crazed barbarian, ruthlessly butchering the defenceless Roman colonists at Camulodunum, is surely intended to recall the atrocities unleashed on the British colonial settlers in India during the Indian Mutiny of 1857.

The site of Boadicea's tomb is unknown; the modern urban myth that she lies buried beneath Platform 10 of King's Cross railway station is no less plausible than any other theory.

Some truth, but not the whole truth. It is of course true that this huge empire was founded on overwhelming military dominance. The western provinces had been created by invasion, looting and, at times, killing on an awful scale. But Roman expansion had more or less come to a halt by the reign of Hadrian (117–38). The Roman empire of the second century AD stretched from the hills of Cumbria to the Nile valley, from the Portuguese coast to the desert plains of Jordan. Military superiority alone is no guarantee of a stable peace; yet that was precisely what Rome achieved. From the late first to the fourth century, with a few notable exceptions, the Roman provinces saw remarkably few internal revolts. Tacitus was right to complain of the difficulty of writing history under the principate; to all appearances, the history of Europe had indeed come to a full stop. The extraordinary success and stability of the Roman empire over the first three centuries AD is a historical problem which cries out for explanation. Much of this chapter will be dedicated to exploring the reasons for that stability.

*

We begin by considering how Roman rule outside Italy actually worked. The Roman empire was not, on the whole, governed by Romans. In any given year, the central government sent out a total of around 160 officials for a subject population of 50 million or more – fewer overseas officials than were sent out from Athens to administer its Aegean empire in the fifth century BC. The most important of these officials were the forty-odd provincial governors, appointed by the Senate or the emperor, each of whom held office for a period of between one and five years. The duties of a governor were not burdensome, being largely confined to provincial jurisdiction and local dispute-resolution. Governors' day-to-day activity seems to have been, for the most part, crushingly mundane: around AD 200, we hear of a governor of Asia (western Turkey) stepping in to deal with a bakers' strike at Ephesus, and in 254 a governor of the same province was expected to fix the day of the month on which a local farmers' market could be held. Instead, most of the real administration of the empire was undertaken by the local communities themselves.

The Roman empire was a world of cities. More than three hundred cities are known in the province of Asia alone; across the whole empire, they certainly numbered in the thousands. The cities – or, more precisely, the local civic elites – were responsible for the assessment and collection of taxes, urban and rural police duties, road-building and maintenance and their own food- and water-supply. One of the most significant changes in provincial administration between the late Republican and early imperial periods was the gradual phasing out of the firms of private tax-collectors (*publicani*), whose activities had caused so much rancour among provincials in the first century BC. By placing the burden of tax-collection in the hands of local bigwigs, Rome neatly delegated a major source of provincial resentment. Cities in the Roman empire, then, were not merely urban conglomerations; they were the indispensable cogs by which the whole imperial machinery turned.

In the eastern half of the Roman empire – particularly in Greece, Asia Minor and the Levant – there was a long tradition of city life, and for the most part, Rome simply preserved the pre-existing urban network. In the west, where far fewer towns had existed at the time of the Roman conquest, the necessary urban centres had to be created from scratch. In the early empire, Roman settlers, usually army veterans, were often parachuted into new model towns (*coloniae*), either founded on virgin territory or, more usually, replacing small native settlements. Elsewhere, pre-existing communities were encouraged to reorganize themselves on an urban model. The experience of the Aedui, a large Celtic tribe in modern Burgundy, was characteristic. In the immediate aftermath of Caesar's conquest of Gaul in the 50s BC, furious building work started at the Aeduan hilltop *oppidum* of Bibracte, on Mont Beuvray. Thatched roofs were replaced by tiles, the streets were laid with paving-stones, space was cleared for a central marketplace and large new Italian-style courtyard houses started to appear. But the basic layout of the town, its meandering streets and dense clusters of tiny dwellings, remained stubbornly un-Roman. Around 15 BC, a full generation after the conquest, the Aedui finally decided that this simply would not do. Taking a deep breath, the inhabitants of Bibracte emigrated en masse to a greenfield site some 20 kilometres away at Augustodunum (modern Autun; see Figure 27). Working from a blank slate, the Aedui planned their new capital so as to look as much as possible like the orderly towns of Roman Italy: laid out on a regular grid plan, orientated around two main streets forming a cross, with a theatre and amphitheatre, massive stone city walls, forum and temples. The scale of the project was immense. Augustodunum was planned from the outset to cover around 200 hectares, with a 6-kilometre circuit wall; it may have taken another two generations before the place ceased to look like a permanent building-site. The really

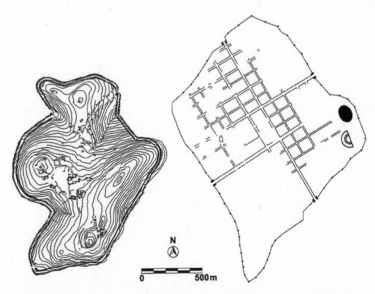

Figure 27. Bibracte (Mont Beuvray) and Augustodunum (Autun)

extraordinary thing is that no Roman governor had ordered any of this. It was the Aedui themselves who decided that they wanted a proper Roman city of their own, to the extent that they were prepared to give up on their first attempt altogether and plan an entire new city from the ground up.

The planned cities of Wren and Hawksmoor

Within a week of the Great Fire of London in September 1666, Christopher Wren presented to Charles II a plan for rebuilding the destroyed parts of the city (see Figure 28). Wren's planned city was profoundly influenced by what he knew of the urban layout of Roman cities under the empire. The whole area around Fleet Street was to be reorganized on the model of the Roman architect Vitruvius' description of the ideal city; the City and Stock Exchange were laid out on the model of the Roman Forum (as rather fancifully reconstructed by Palladio in the mid-sixteenth century), and Greek-style stoas overlooked the river Thames at Billingsgate. Major civic buildings (including, of course, Wren's new St Paul's Cathedral) were situated prominently at the end of long axial roads. Wren's plans for 'Romanizing' London had strong political overtones. In his first *Tract on Architecture*, Wren had written that 'Architecture has its political Use; public Buildings being the Ornament of a Country; it establishes a Nation, draws People and Commerce; makes the people love their native Country, which Passion is the Original of all great Actions in a Common-wealth'. The architects of Augustodunum would surely have agreed.

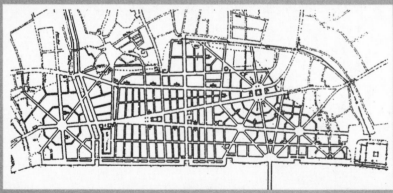

Figure 28. Christopher Wren's plans for the redesign of central London, 1666.

Wren's new 'Roman' London was never built, but architects continued to toy with the idea of remodelling England's great cities on a Roman pattern. In around 1712 Wren's pupil Nicholas Hawksmoor (1661–1736) drew up a grand plan for the redesign of central Oxford on the model of a Roman city. Hawksmoor was an unusually ambitious and eclectic architect (the door-lintels on many of his London churches were influenced by the architecture of the old Persian capital of Persepolis), but his plans for Oxford are still breathtaking. The new city would be entered from the east through a grand processional gate (at the end of modern Longwall Street); the centre of Oxford would be laid out around a civic forum (*forum civitatis*) and a University forum (*forum universitatis*). He even sketched out a rough design for a new University Church, just off the University forum, in the form of a huge peristyle temple, based on the Roman temple of Bacchus at Baalbek in Lebanon. As with Wren's designs for London, and as at Augustodunum, Hawksmoor's vision for Oxford was designed to serve a specific political function: to bridge the traditional gulf between town and university through the creation of grand new public spaces, both civic and academic. The only element of Hawksmoor's design ever to be completed was his fine Clarendon Building, on Oxford's Broad Street.

The size of the provincial cities varied widely. In AD 6 the census of Quirinius had come up with a total of 117,000 citizen men, women and children for the population of the city and territory of Apamea in northern Syria – one of the bigger cities of the empire, with an urban area of around 250 hectares. Alexandria, the largest city of the eastern provinces, had more than half a million inhabitants, and the population of Rome itself may have topped a million in the early imperial period. But these are exceptional cases. The population of the average Roman city should certainly be counted in the tens, not the hundreds, of thousands. Pompeii, on the bay of Naples, had an urban population of around 12,000, with maybe twice that number living in the surrounding countryside. Many were smaller still; indeed, physically there was little to distinguish a large village from a small city. The inhabitants of the Italian city of Rudiae, the birthplace of the poet Ennius, numbered between 2,000 and 2,500. By contrast, the village of Umm el-Jimal in north-west Jordan – its ancient name is unknown – had well over 2,500 inhabitants throughout much of its history, without ever receiving city-status. The crucial difference between Rudiae and Umm el-Jimal was not their physical size, but their administrative function. Similarly, in the modern United Kingdom, St David's in Pembrokeshire (population 1,797, plus cathedral) is a chartered city; the town of Reading (population 230,000, with no cathedral) is not.

The status of these small communities could change over time. In the mid-second century AD, the village of Pallantion in the central Peloponnese successfully appealed to the emperor Antoninus Pius (138–61) to be

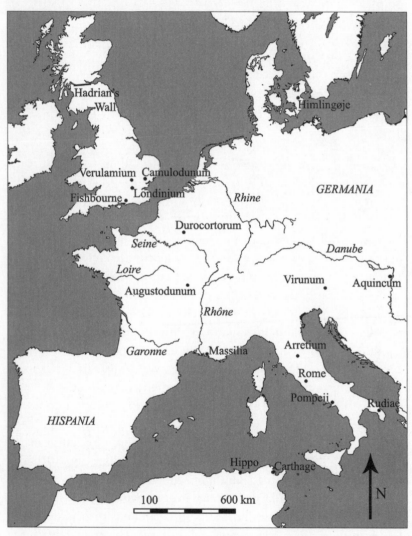

Map 30. The western Roman empire in the second century AD.

elevated to city-status, on the grounds – so they argued – that the legendary Arcadian hero Evander had named the Palatine hill in Rome after his native town of Pallantion. For Pallantion, being a bona fide city was clearly a matter of local pride. The financial benefits may also have been considerable; the emperor was also persuaded to grant them blanket immunity from taxation.

As we saw at the end of Chapter 5, the historian Polybius understood the history of the Mediterranean and Near East in terms of a succession of empires: Persian, Spartan, Macedonian and at last Roman. But the Roman empire differed in several significant ways from the imperial states that had preceded it in the eastern Mediterranean and Near East. For better or worse, two centuries of Persian rule left almost no impact on the culture of the millions of subject peoples in central and western Asia. When Alexander the Great entered Babylon in October 331 BC, he found a city which in terms of administration, material culture, language and religion, was more or less as it had been when the city fell to Cyrus in 539 BC. The Roman empire of the late Republican period, like the Persian empire, was an incoherent mosaic of different cultures, unified by little more than the common experience of Roman political domination. Yet in the course of little more than a century every piece of that mosaic was transformed by the experience of Roman rule. The process of transformation took very different forms in the western and eastern provinces. We shall look first at the western provinces (North Africa, Iberia, Europe north of the Alps), before turning to the eastern or 'Greek' provinces of the Balkan peninsula, Asia Minor, the Levant and Egypt.

By the end of the first century AD, the material world of the western provinces, their architecture, clothing, food and bric-a-brac, had undergone revolutionary changes. We have already seen how the urban landscape of communities like the Aedui was reshaped beyond recognition under Roman rule. Throughout the western half of the Roman empire, similar changes occurred in almost every sphere of life, from language to religious practice, from drinking habits to personal names. The process is generally known as Romanization, 'becoming Roman'.

The concept of 'Romanization' in the western provinces needs to be used with great care. Some modern scholars wish to jettison the term altogether; this is unnecessary, so long as we are clear about exactly who is doing the 'Romanizing'. In what is probably the most frequently quoted passage in all of Tacitus' work, we are told that during his governorship of Britain, Agricola

> gave private encouragement and official assistance to the building of temples, forums and villas . . . he educated the sons of the native leaders in the liberal arts, so that those who had a short time ago spurned the Latin language altogether now strove to speak it with eloquence. Our national dress, the toga, became prestigious and fashionable; and little by little the Britons were led towards the amenities that make vice agreeable, arcades, baths and sumptuous banquets. Among the unsuspecting Britons these things were given the name of civilization, when in fact they merely added to their enslavement . . .

– a characteristically sharp Tacitean coda. This idea of a deliberate 'civilizing mission', whether undertaken from honest or cynical motives, has had a long and unfortunate influence on modern studies of the process by which the provinces 'became Roman'. It is undeniably the case that temples, forums and villas started to be built in ever-increasing numbers in Britain, that Latin was spoken ever more widely, and that the sons of the native elite were educated in Roman ways: by the reign of Tiberius at the latest, the pastiche Roman town of Augustodunum in central Gaul was equipped with a school, where, says Tacitus, the elite youth of the Gallic provinces could receive a decent liberal – that is to say, Greek and Latin – education.

Agricola and India

Tacitus' description in the *Agricola* of the 'civilizing' influence of Rome on the native British elite had a profound impact on nineteenth-century British conceptions of empire. The 1830s saw a major debate over the best mode of education for Britain's Indian subjects, and in particular, whether it was appropriate for Indians to continue to be educated in their native languages, or whether all higher education should be conducted in English. Thomas Babington Macaulay, the later author of the *Lays of Ancient Rome* and the *History of England*, argued strongly in favour of an English-language educational system, for reasons that Agricola would have found very familiar. 'We must do our best to form a class who may be interpreters between us and the millions whom we govern; a class of persons, Indian in blood and colour, but English in taste, in opinions, in morals, and in intellect.' Macaulay is here directly transposing the Tacitean idea of cultural Romanization into an Indian context. In 1838 Charles Trevelyan optimistically predicted that Indians educated in the English style would 'become more English than Hindus, just as the Roman provincials became more Romans than Gauls or Italians . . . The Indians will, I hope, soon stand in the same position towards us in which we once stood towards the Romans.'

By the late Victorian and Edwardian period, that optimism was starting to give way. The assimilation of the peoples of India into the British empire had proved harder than expected. Moreover, archaeologists of Roman Britain had now abandoned the idea of a small, highly Romanized native ruling class acting as local 'partners in empire'. Instead, Francis Haverfield (1860–1919), the pre-eminent Romano-British archaeologist of the Edwardian era, argued that the Romanization of the native peoples of Britain was deep and far-reaching: throughout the province, 'the material civilisation [and] the external fabric of its life was Roman, and the native element almost wholly succumbed to the foreign conquering influence'. By those standards, the 'Anglicization' of India had been an utter failure.

Lord Dufferin, Viceroy of India 1884–8, took a more pragmatic view of the relevance of the ancient world to modern imperial government. The Greeks and Romans were 'people who didn't talk our tongue and who were very strong on sacrifice and ritual, particularly at meals, whose gods were different from ours and who had strict views on the disposal of the dead. Well, you know, all that is worth knowing if you ever have to govern India.'

However, most historians now believe that Agricola – if he did indeed have a policy of active 'Romanization' – was wholly exceptional. For the most part, the conquerors displayed no missionary zeal to convert their uncouth western subjects to the joys of Roman culture. On the contrary, Tacitus in his *Germania*, an ethnographic study of the German peoples (composed shortly after the *Agricola*), showed himself to be an admirer of many aspects of native German society. As we have seen, the new Roman town at Augustodunum was the result of the Gauls' own enthusiasm for the trappings of civilized city life, rather than any top-down initiative by the central government. Put simply, the political dominance

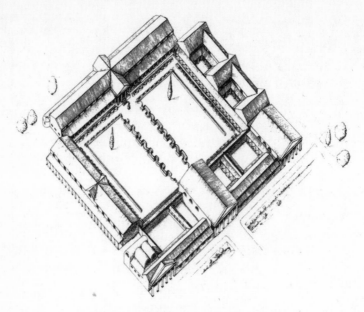

Figure 29. Fishbourne Roman palace.

of Rome made Roman things fashionable. People aspired to be and look Roman, since Roman-ness was associated with power. (We need only compare the overwhelming influence exerted by the material culture – denim, Coca-Cola, basketball – of the only modern superpower, the United States, on the dress, diet and behaviour of the rest of the world.) Moreover, the Roman state was always willing to assimilate people who looked, spoke and behaved like good Romans. Hence there were strong incentives favouring the 'self-Romanization' of the western provincial elites.

The speed with which native elites adopted elements of Roman culture is startling. In the late 70s AD, within a generation of the Roman conquest of Britain, a huge palatial villa was constructed at Fishbourne, near Chichester on the Sussex coast (see Figure 29). This monumental complex, built of stone masonry, consists of four wings surrounding a large formal garden; the rooms were decorated with gaudy wall-paintings, stucco mouldings and fine floor-mosaics. The Fishbourne palace is entirely Mediterranean in layout and decoration; indeed, the labour force may well have been brought over from Italy. Yet the owner of the palace was almost certainly a Romanized Briton, Togidubnus. This man was a member of the pre-conquest aristocracy who had ruled southern Britain as a Roman client king in the years immediately following the conquest.

In an inscription from Chichester, his full name and title are given: 'Tiberius Claudius Togidubnus, great king of the Britons'. The interesting thing here is the presence of the Roman *praenomen* and *nomen* (first and family name), '*Tiberius Claudius* Togidubnus'. Evidently this local chieftain had been granted Roman citizenship as a reward for his compliance at the time of the original conquest. Togidubnus needed no support or encouragement from Agricola to build an Italian-style villa on the Sussex coast: it was all too clear to men like Togidubnus that in order to retain their elite status in the post-conquest world, they needed to become as Roman as possible, as quickly and visibly as possible.

Similar patterns can be seen in more modest contexts. No type of object was more ubiquitous in ancient Europe than pottery, clay vessels used for the storage, preparation and consumption of food and drink. Pottery is thus an unusually good index of cultural change. In some cases, changes in pottery types can be used to map changes in consumption. For example, in the late first century BC and first century AD an Italian type of shallow baking dish made of a rather coarse red pottery ('Pompeian Red Ware') spread rapidly throughout the western provinces, from Spain to Britain. The widespread adoption of these new baking dishes reflected a far-reaching change in western European cookery. The main source of carbohydrates in pre-Roman north-west Europe was porridge, washed down with the main local beverage, beer. However, no self-respecting Roman would dream of boiling grain for porridge; the civilized person ate bread baked in an oven, not porridge boiled in a pot. Hence the sudden appearance of new Pompeian-style baking dishes across the north-west probably marked a mass switch from porridge to bread as the main source of carbohydrates for the aspiring elites of Spain, Gaul and Britain. Drinking habits, too, changed. In the sixth and fifth centuries BC the elites of the West Hallstatt zone north of the Alps had paraded their elite credentials through the consumption of Mediterranean wine; in the early first century BC, the Greek historian Posidonius had noted that the richer European Celts drank wine imported from Italy or Massalia, while the poorer classes drank either wheat beer mixed with honey, or plain barley beer. Over the course of the first and second centuries AD, beer-consumption declined sharply across western Europe; by the end of the first century AD, more than half of the wine being drunk in the Besançon region was produced in Gallic vineyards.

New foods required new dining-sets. Since the mid-first century BC, the standard Roman mass-produced tableware had been a fine glossy red pottery with elaborate rococo relief decoration, mould-cast rather than thrown, known as Arretine ware, after its main centre of production at Arretium (modern Arezzo, in Tuscany). This style of pottery was wildly popular throughout both the Mediterranean world and north-western Europe. Around the turn of the millennium, the market for Arretine ware in Gaul had reached such proportions that independent workshops were set up in southern Gaul to produce imitation 'Arretine-style' pottery to serve local demand. The best known of these local workshops was located at La Graufesenque, near Millau in southern France. The scale of production at La Graufesenque in the latter half of the first century AD is simply staggering: tablewares produced at this single workshop are found not only throughout the Gallic provinces, but as far afield as southern Britain and North Africa. For a generation or more, one of the marks of a civilized Gallo-Roman household was a dinner service of cheap Roman-style Arretine ware from La Graufesenque.

We know a great deal about the mechanics of pottery production at La Graufesenque. When a batch of pots was ready to be fired, a list of the craftsmen responsible for the pots in each batch was scratched onto a plate, which was then fired along with the finished objects and stored away in the factory archives. More than 160 of these lists survive, written in a baffling mixture of Latin and the native Celtic language, showing that the workmen at La Graufesenque were used to switching backwards and forwards between the two languages. Some of the craftsmen on the batch-lists still possessed traditional Celtic names (Cintusmos, Petrecos, Matugenos), though others had already adopted good Roman names (Cornutus, Secundus, Albinus). Each individual finished pot, too, was stamped with the name of the particular potter who had made it – but here something curious starts to happen. Not one of the Celtic names from the batch-lists reappears among the makers' stamps on the pots themselves. Instead, the makers' stamps all offer Latin equivalents for the potters' Celtic names: Cintusmos reappears as Primus, Petrecos as Quartus and Matugenos as Felix. When a consumer bought his dining-set from La Graufesenque, all he would find on his pots was the respectable Latin name 'Felix'; he would have no way of telling that 'Felix' was in fact a bilingual Celt whose real name was Matugenos. The potters at La Graufesenque were, in fact, pretending to be more Romanized than they actually were.

The case of the mock-Roman potters of La Graufesenque is a chastening lesson in the difficulty of judging how far the various local languages of the empire, both east and west, survived the Roman conquest. Officially, the business of the Roman empire was conducted in two languages only: Latin in the western provinces and North Africa (except Egypt), Greek in Egypt and the east. Even in the east, documents of critical importance for the Roman administration – birth certificates, which provided evidence of Roman citizenship, and wills – had to be in Latin, at least until the early third century AD. At first sight, the vast mass of documentary evidence surviving from the period of the Roman empire (inscriptions on stone, papyri, writing tablets, pottery stamps), supports this picture of a linguistically Romanized empire, operating exclusively in Latin and Greek. From the Asia Minor peninsula alone, we have tens of thousands of inscriptions on stone dating to the first three centuries AD. The overwhelming majority are written in Greek, with a much smaller, but still substantial number in Latin. Most of the various native languages of Asia Minor – Lycian, Lydian, Galatian, Carian – are entirely absent. Only in the deep countryside does the Phrygian language appear, on a few dozen bilingual tombstones of the third century AD; we also have a tiny handful of Pisidian texts. To judge from the documentary evidence alone, we would certainly have concluded that the local languages of Asia Minor had died with the Roman conquest, if not before. It is something of a shock, then, to read in the New Testament Acts of the Apostles that when, in the mid-first century AD, the apostles Paul and Barnabas arrived at the small Roman colony of Lystra, the local people hailed them as gods 'in the Lycaonian language'. Not one single word of the Lycaonian tongue has come down to us. Evidently, at both La Graufesenque and Lystra, there was a sharp divide between the languages of administration and public affairs (Latin and Greek respectively) and the languages that people actually spoke in their daily life (Celtic and Lycaonian).

The Latin language

More people speak the Latin language today than ever before. Latin is the native language of some 700 million people, including almost all the inhabitants of South America and western Europe. It is true that most people now give their local dialect of the Latin language a different name ('Italiano', 'Español', 'Français', 'Português', 'Occitan'); in English, we generally call this family of languages the 'Romance' language-group. None of this should blind us to the fact that Spanish, Italian and the rest are simply modern dialects of Latin. It would be quite reasonable to call Latin 'Ancient Spanish'.

Here, once again, is what Tacitus has to say about the Romanization of Britain: 'Our national dress, the toga, became prestigious and fashionable; and little by little the Britons were led towards the amenities that make vice agreeable, arcades, baths and sumptuous banquets. Among the unsuspecting Britons these things were given the name of civilization, when in fact they merely added to their enslavement.'

Here is the same passage in Latin:

> *inde etiam habitus nostri honor et frequens toga; paulatimque discessum ad delenimenta vitiorum, porticus et balineas et conviviorum elegantiam. idque apud imperitos humanitas vocabatur, cum pars servitutis esset.*

And here is the same passage again, in a modern Mexican Spanish translation:

> *Desde entonces, también nuestros hábitos fueron un honor, e frecuente la toga; y paulatinamente se cayó en la seducción de los vicios: los pórticos y los balnearios y la elegancia de los banquetes; y eso era llamado humanidad entre los imperitos, cuando era parte de servidumbre.*

habitus nostri, nuestros hábitos ('our (national) dress/habit'); *paulatim*, paulatinamente ('little by little'); *pars servitutis*, parte de servidumbre ('part of their servitude'). The spelling and grammar have undergone a few changes over the past 2,000 years, but the language is recognizably the same.

Perhaps the most striking case of cultural forgetfulness in the western provinces of the Roman empire is that of the Punic societies of coastal Iberia and North Africa. Unlike the decentralized, pre-literate societies of Iron Age Europe, the Phoenician colonial world of the southern and western Mediterranean was a highly complex city-state culture, with its own flourishing historical and literary traditions. At the time of the destruction of Carthage in 146 BC, entire libraries of Punic literature were broken up and handed over to the petty princes of North Africa; a Punic-language treatise on agriculture in 28 books, written by a certain

Mago, was brought to Italy to be translated into Latin. The Punic language was in fact remarkably resilient under the Roman empire: long inscriptions in Punic are found down to the end of the first century AD, and shorter texts continue to appear well into the third century. Punic was still widely spoken in the late fourth and early fifth centuries AD, not only in the North African countryside, but even among St Augustine's urban congregation at the town of Hippo. Nonetheless, memories of the pre-Roman past were obliterated just as effectively in Punic Africa as they had been in Gaul. We cannot write a history of the Phoenicians in the west before 146 BC; no one considered the history of the Punic world before the coming of Rome to be worth remembering.

Indeed, some of the inhabitants of the old west-Phoenician world positively celebrated the end of Punic history. A century after the Romans had razed Carthage to the ground, Julius Caesar established a new colony of Roman citizens on the site of the old Punic city, calling this too 'Carthage', which eventually developed into one of the largest and most prosperous cities of the western empire. In the second or third century AD, an imperial official by the name of Classicius Secundinus claimed to have found an ancient inscription at Carthage carrying the original victory dedication of Scipio Aemilianus, the Roman general who had destroyed Carthage in 146 BC. Secundinus had the dedication reinscribed and set up once again in its original form. In the third century AD the citizens of Roman Carthage could still muse on the words of Aemilianus, as he gloated over the ruins of Punic Carthage and the bodies of those who had dared to stand against Roman power. This was the only 'version' of Carthaginian history available to the inhabitants of Carthage under the Roman empire.

The impact of Roman rule on the religious life of the western provinces is particularly difficult to judge. Before the Roman conquest, the Celtic tribes of northern Gaul seem each to have worshipped their own, highly local gods: the god Mullo, for instance, was worshipped only in a triangle north of the river Loire, between Rennes, Nantes and Le Mans. Most of these local gods survived the Roman conquest through being identified with one of a very limited range of Roman deities (particularly Mars and Mercury). For example, the principal god of the tribal group of the Remi, in the Champagne region of north-east France, was a figure called Camulus. By the first century AD Camulus was being interpreted as the local manifestation of the Roman god Mars. In his new guise as 'Mars

Camulus', the god continued to be the main patron deity of the Remi and their new urban centre at Reims (Durocortorum).

It is at first sight tempting to regard the survival of native deities like Camulus as a sign of deep-seated resistance to the process of Romanization: although the Remi were now obediently shaving their beards, baking bread, drinking wine and learning Latin, they remained Camulus-worshipping Celts at heart. The trouble with this view is that it fails to take into account the profound degree to which the Remi identified their interests with those of the ruling power. One of the four great triumphal arches leading to the monumental city centre at Reims, the Mars Gate, survives in relatively good shape. The central arcade of this arch carries an image of Mars Camulus; the east arcade has a depiction of the she-wolf suckling the twins Romulus and Remus (see Figure 30); and the west arcade shows Leda and the swan. The imagery is at first sight rather puzzling. Both of the side arcades seem to be depicting episodes

Figure 30. Sculptural decoration on the ceiling of the east arcade of the Mars Gate at Reims: Romulus and Remus being suckled by a she-wolf, surrounded by a frieze of shields, helmets, armour and weapons.

from the foundation myths, not of the Celtic Remi, but of the city of Rome – since the offspring of Leda and the swan was Helen, who was responsible for the Trojan War and thus, indirectly, Aeneas' foundation of Rome. What interest did the Remi have in the myths of the founding of Rome? It has been plausibly suggested that these 'Roman' images on the Mars Gate at Reims represent a claim by the Remi to be the ultimate descendants of Romulus' brother Remus. This would of course make the Remi privileged kinsmen, even 'brothers', of the Roman people, a game which we have seen played repeatedly in the course of this book. This is a strikingly creative response to the fact of Roman rule: while preserving the key elements of their traditional religious practices (the cult of Camulus), the Remi also developed a version of their own mythical origins which linked them to the broader power of the Roman empire.

Clearly, the mere survival of elements of indigenous, pre-Roman culture cannot automatically be taken as evidence for positive cultural resistance to Rome. What, for instance, are we to make of the following Latin inscription, discovered at Southwark in south London in 2002?

Num(inibus) Aug(ustorum)	To the divine will of the emperors
Deo Marti Ca-	And to the god Mars Camulus:
mulo Tiberini-	Tiberinius
us Celerianus	Celerianus
c(ivis) Bell(ouacus)	citizen of Beauvais
moritix	seafarer
Londiniensi-	of the Londoners.
um.	

The inscription, which dates to the late second century AD, takes the form of a dedication to the 'divine will of the emperors' and the god Mars Camulus. The dedication was set up by a man carrying a good Roman name: Tiberinius Celerianus, a native of Beauvais (ancient Caesaromagus Bellovacorum) in northern Gaul. Celerianus describes himself as 'seafarer of the Londoners' (*moritix Londiniensium*), and we should probably understand him to be the agent of a shipping company which transported goods between London and northern Gaul. It is very striking that Celerianus chose to define himself with the curious term *moritix*. *Moritix* is not a Latin word at all, but an ancient Celtic term meaning 'seafarer'. There is, of course, a perfectly good Latin word meaning exactly the

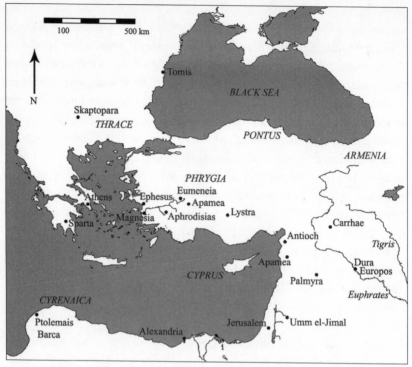

Map 31. The eastern Roman empire in the second century AD.

same thing (*nauta*). Why did Celerianus chose to use the old Celtic word? Was he trying, consciously or unconsciously, to emphasize his local Celtic identity? The real cultural affiliations of a man like Celerianus are desperately difficult to recover: a native of northern Gaul, with a Roman name; worshipper of a superficially Romanized Celtic deity of his native region, but also of the reigning Roman emperors; capable of setting up a dedicatory inscription in impeccable Latin, but opting for a local Celtic term to describe his profession of seafarer.

In the western provinces, as we have seen, there was virtually no institutional memory of the pre-Roman past. The history of native societies before the conquest was largely forgotten, to be replaced by a new, more acceptably 'Roman' past; the local mythology of the Remi in north-east Gaul seems to have been imported wholesale from Rome on the basis of a chance similarity between the names 'Remi' and 'Remus'. Local languages went into a precipitous decline; even local drinking and dining practices were obliterated by the spread of 'Romanizing' pottery and crops, above all the vine. When we turn to the eastern half of the Roman empire, however, the picture looks very different indeed. The spread of Roman cultural artefacts (villas, foodstuffs, Roman personal names, the Latin language) was comparatively restricted. Not only did the Greek language survive, but Greek memories of the pre-Roman past remained as vivid and culturally potent as ever. 'Romanization' is clearly not an appropriate way of thinking about the development of the eastern provinces in the first three centuries AD. Nonetheless, the impact of Roman rule on the Greek-speaking half of the empire ought not to be underestimated, for all that it is less immediately visible than in the western provinces.

By the first century AD, the Greek language had evolved a long way from the language spoken and written in the Classical Greek world. Several cases and moods, notably the optative mood, had all but disappeared. The pronunciation of Greek, too, had changed radically. The letter *beta* was now pronounced as *v* rather than *b*, and the word *kai* ('and') was normally pronounced as *ke* (as in modern Greek). However, over the course of the first and second centuries AD Greek writers and intellectuals increasingly came to reject this 'common' Greek language (*koinē*) of their own day as vulgar and unsuited for literary production. Instead, they reverted to the 'pure' Athenian dialect of the fifth and fourth centuries BC. Huge dictionaries, grammars and handbooks of the Classical Athenian language were compiled to help writers and orators to avoid inappropriate modernisms. The medical writer Galen (129–216) complained at the 'pestilential pseudo-erudition' of writers who use the obsolete Athenian word *rhaphanos* for cabbage, 'as though we were in conversation with Athenians of 600 years ago'. An older contemporary of Galen, Lucius Flavius Arrian of Nicomedia, composed a seven-book history of Alexander the Great entirely in the style of Xenophon, an author more remote from Arrian's own day than Shakespeare is from ours. In one case, a speech attributed in our medieval manuscripts to the second-century AD writer Herodes Atticus, the imitation of classical Athenian prose is so uncannily accurate that some modern scholars have argued that the speech is a genuine Athenian product of the fifth century BC – the ultimate compliment to Herodes' skill.

This culture of 'classicism' eventually came to infect all areas of Greek cultural life. Members of the Greek civic elite – even, and perhaps especially, those who had been granted the privilege of Roman citizenship – named their children after famous Athenians of the Classical period: the emperor Trajan's court doctor, Titus Statilius Crito, carried the name of a friend of the fifth-century BC philosopher Socrates, and his grandson, Titus Statilius Solon, was named after an Athenian lawgiver of the early sixth century BC. Sparta, by now a quiet olive-growing country town, attracted ever-increasing crowds of cultural tourists. The main draw was the opportunity to observe at first hand the legendary Spartan educational system, the *agogē*, supposedly established by Lycurgus in the ninth or eighth century BC. In the late second century AD we hear of a Spartan civic official with the unique title of 'expounder of the Lycurgan customs'; according to one plausible explanation, his job was to act as a professional, full-time tourist guide. Greek and Roman tourists came to watch teenage Spartans practising military drills, wrestling and boxing, playing a rough ball-game called *sphairistikē* (apparently similar to rugby), and participating in a bloody annual 'contest of endurance' at the festival of Artemis Orthia, in which ephebes (older teenagers) had to try to reach an altar protected by whip-bearers – fatalities were apparently not uncommon. In fact, many of these violent games were inventions of the later first century AD, developed to satisfy non-Spartan expectations of what the Lycurgan education *ought* to have been like.

Just as with the survival of native deities in Roman Gaul, it is a delicate question whether this obsessive Greek focus on the distant past reflects a deep-seated cultural resistance to Rome. It is certainly the case that the cities of the Greek world preserved a far stronger sense of their own local identity than the communities of the western provinces. In the mid-third century AD Goths from the Black Sea region launched a series of devastating attacks on the Roman provinces in Asia Minor and the Balkans. Athens itself was sacked in 267/8, the first time that the city had been assaulted since the Mithradatic wars of the early first century BC. Nonetheless, under the leadership of an ageing historian and intellectual by the name of Herennius Dexippos, the Athenians assembled a scratch force of 2,000 men in a remote rural district of Attica, which succeeded in ambushing and destroying the greater part of the Gothic raiding band. It is tempting to explain the remarkable Athenian popular resistance of 267/8 through the deep emotional and cultural ties which bound them to the heroic Athenian past. The survival of a strong Athenian civic identity, still focused around the great days of Marathon and Plataea, may well have contributed to the Athenians' ability to mount an effective civic defence against the Gothic invasion. A telling contrast could be drawn with the cities of the Roman west, very few of which managed any such resistance to the (ever more frequent) barbarian invasions of the third and fourth centuries.

The world which the Greeks of the second century AD harked back to was, above all, the pre-Roman – and, indeed, pre-Macedonian – Greek world of the fifth and fourth centuries BC. It is hardly surprising that the problematic Hellenistic age, an era of uneasy collaboration and, at times, violent resistance to Roman imperialism, was quietly erased from Greek history. From the perspective of the Roman ruling power, the Greeks' obsessive nostalgia for a safely distant past was something to be encouraged. Athens, in particular, was ostentatiously favoured by Roman emperors as a cultural centre of the east Roman world, and by the mid-second century AD, the city had attained a level of wealth and prosperity not seen since the days of the Athenian empire in the fifth century BC. In the early 130s the emperor Hadrian made Athens the centre of a new religious confederation of bona fide Greek cities, the Panhellenion ('All-Greeks'). The Panhellenion was a largely ceremonial body, and its actual functions are very obscure; the interesting thing from our perspective is the definition of 'Greekness' which Hadrian used in vetting potential members. The Spartans, of course, were admitted without hesitation. So too were cities which claimed to be descendants or colonists of the old Greek cities of the mainland: Magnesia on the Maeander, a small town near the west coast of Asia Minor, was waved through on the basis that they were 'colonists of the Magnesians in Thessaly, the first of the Hellenes to cross over into Asia and settle there'. In 135 the town of Ptolemais-Barca in Libya petitioned the emperor Hadrian for membership of the Panhellenic club. The Barcaeans had high hopes of success, since everyone agreed that Barca was an ancient colony of Cyrene, a city which already sent two annual delegates to the Panhellenion. However, the emperor pointed out that Barca had been renamed 'Ptolemais' by one of the Macedonian kings of Egypt (probably Ptolemy II Philadelphos, reigned 282–246 BC). It was quite unreasonable for the Barcaeans to claim the same status as their neighbours at Cyrene, 'whose ancestry is pure Greek, and specifically Dorian'; by way of compromise, the Barcaeans were permitted to send one delegate per year.

Some curious birds found their way into Hadrian's Panhellenic nest.

The obscure city of Eumeneia, lying high in the mountains of central Asia Minor, was not at first sight an obvious candidate for membership of the Panhellenion. The history of Eumeneia was short and not very eventful. Like Ptolemais-Barca, the town took its name from a Hellenistic monarch, the Attalid king Eumenes II of Pergamum, who had founded Eumeneia in the 160s BC as one of a string of military forts along the border with Galatian territory. But by the second century AD the Eumeneians had mysteriously acquired a past as respectable as any city of mainland Greece. They were, so they claimed, the descendants of colonists from Argos in the Peloponnese, who had migrated to Asia Minor late in the heroic age. The proof of their Argive ancestry lay in the town's name. During the exile of the children of Heracles (Heracleidae) from their ancestral home in the Peloponnese, one of Heracles' sons, Hyllos, had travelled to Eumeneia, where he had been 'happy to stay' (in Greek: *eu menein*). The Eumeneians were duly admitted to the Panhellenion on the basis of their Argive ancestry, and henceforth proudly declared themselves to be the 'Eumeneian Achaeans' on their inscriptions and coinage – no doubt to the extreme irritation of the citizens of Ptolemais-Barca.

We may well conclude from this that whoever vetted applications for the Panhellenion ought to have been sacked. But the episode is nonetheless revealing. There were good practical reasons why Hadrian should have wanted to support the Eumeneians' flimsy claims to a place in the history of the heroic age: Eumeneia was home to the main Roman military garrison in the province of Asia, and as such held a key position in the Roman administration of the province. In such cases, where Rome's favoured Greek allies lacked an appropriately distinguished history, a history was simply invented. The city of Aphrodisias, also located in western Asia Minor, had been founded at around the same time as Eumeneia. Thanks to her conspicuous loyalty to the Roman cause from the first century BC onwards, Aphrodisias held the privileged status of a 'free city', and was eventually made the capital (*metropolis*, literally 'mother-city') of the late Roman province of Caria. As one of Rome's staunchest allies in Asia Minor, the city required a correspondingly impressive pedigree. So, in the late first century AD a new Roman civic basilica at Aphrodisias was decorated with relief sculptures depicting the newly discovered mythological founders of the city; in pride of place stood an image of the Greek hero Bellerophon with his winged horse Pegasus, consulting the oracle of Apollo at Delphi, and presumably receiving divine sanction for the foundation of Aphrodisias. The 'discovery' of a pre-Trojan War origin for Aphrodisias allowed the Roman emperors to carry on favouring her above her neighbours with a clear conscience. The creation of a respectable early history for Eumeneia and Aphrodisias is closely reminiscent of the invention of Messenian history at the time of the foundation of the *polis* of Messene in the mid-fourth century BC (above, pp. 134–6).

It is clear that the eastern provinces of the Roman empire did not become 'Romanized' to anything like the same extent as the western provinces. In the west, becoming Roman involved a wholesale obliteration of local languages, local history and pre-Roman forms of settlement. By contrast, the dominant cultural force in the eastern provinces was classicism, conformity to a homogeneous and unthreatening model of Greekness. This culture of classicism, safely focused on the distant past, represents a different kind of response to the reality of Roman dominance.

'Romanization' in the west and 'classicism' in the east were only in very limited ways conscious articles of policy of the Roman government. Far more important, in both cases, were the needs and aspirations of the provincials themselves. Certainly there was resistance to these processes too, not least among the selfsame provincial elites. But the interesting question is not so much why the subject peoples of the empire resisted Roman rule, as why, by and large, there was so *little* open resistance. Native rebellions, like that of Boudica in AD 60, were rare, and usually fizzled out within a generation of the initial Roman conquest.

The question becomes particularly pressing when we consider the one subject people who did try repeatedly to throw off the Roman yoke: the Jews. In AD 66 the Jewish inhabitants of Jerusalem rose up in open revolt and massacred the city's Roman garrison. The whole of Judaea soon followed suit, and the entire region saw mass ethnic cleansing of the Gentile population. A Roman force under the governor of Syria, which came within an ace of recapturing Jerusalem from the rebels, was all but wiped out by Jewish partisans in the autumn of 66. The Roman response was brutal. After a five-month siege, led by the future emperor Titus, Jerusalem fell in September AD 70. The entire population of the city was killed or enslaved, and the great Temple at Jerusalem, the centre of the Jewish faith, was burned to the ground. The second revolt in Judaea, in 132, seems to have been sparked by Hadrian's attempt to found a new

Roman colony, Aelia Capitolina, on the site of Jerusalem – just as Antiochus IV's attempt to turn Jerusalem into a *Greek* colony had kicked off the great Jewish revolt against Seleucid rule in the second century BC (above, p. 157). For three and a half years, the Jews, under the charismatic leadership of Shimon bar Kokhba, struggled to recapture Jerusalem. By the time the rebels were finally crushed, in the autumn of 135, Judaea was a wasteland; the Roman historian Cassius Dio claims that more than half a million Jews had been put to the sword.

Why was resistance to Roman rule in Judaea so fierce? Josephus, our main source for the first Jewish revolt, argues that the uprising was the work of a few bad apples on both sides. Roman governors in Judaea had behaved in an unusually vicious and insensitive manner; on the Jewish side, the breach with Rome was caused by a few villainous brigands and religious fanatics. However, Josephus has an axe to grind. Himself a prominent member of the native ruling class of Judaea, he had fought on the Jewish side in the first year of the revolt, before being captured by Roman forces. He promptly switched sides, was granted Roman citizenship, and spent the rest of his life in Rome. In part, his history is an attempt to justify his own conduct in the revolt and afterwards. As an apologist for the Judaean upper classes – who were, in fact, profoundly implicated in the revolt – it suits him to present the revolt as the work of a few extremists; as an interpreter of the 'Jewish situation' for a Roman audience, he diplomatically places the blame for the revolt on individual wicked Romans, rather than the nature of Roman rule itself.

The problem with this view is that the revolts were not merely protests against Roman maltreatment, but aimed at the establishment of an independent, self-governing Jewish state centred on Jerusalem. On both occasions, the rebel Jewish state minted silver and bronze coinage with aggressively nationalist inscriptions in the Hebrew language: 'JERUSALEM IS HOLY', 'FREEDOM OF ZION', 'FOR THE REDEMPTION OF ZION'. One group of coins, struck in the early days of the second revolt (132), carries an image of the lost Temple – destroyed sixty-two years earlier – and the proud inscription 'YEAR ONE OF THE REDEMPTION OF ISRAEL' (see Plate 31f).

Jewish resistance clearly had deeper religious roots than Josephus is prepared to admit. Before the first revolt, Jews throughout the empire had paid a voluntary contribution of two drachmas per year for the upkeep of the Temple at Jerusalem. After AD 70 this voluntary payment was replaced by a special Jewish tax, once again levied on all the Jews of the empire, to pay for the cult of Jupiter Capitolinus on the Capitol at Rome. The interesting point here is that Rome chose to respond to the revolt in Judaea with collective punishment of the Jewish race as a whole. The humiliating 'Jewish tax' was imposed not only on the Judaean rebels, but also on the large diaspora communities in Egypt, Asia Minor and Rome itself, which had taken no part in the revolt. All too clearly, Rome saw the uprising as a Jewish problem, not a Judaean problem. The Romans had a point: the Jews of the diaspora were no better integrated into the imperial system than the Jews of Judaea. In 116–17, Egypt, Cyrenaica and Cyprus were rocked by a sudden and violent mutiny of the Jewish minority community, this time directed against their provincial non-Jewish neighbours rather than the Roman government. The Roman response was, once again, draconian; henceforth, no Jew was allowed to set foot on the island of Cyprus, and even Jews whom bad weather forced to land at a Cypriot harbour were to be put to death.

The fundamental problem was that the kind of religious assimilation to Roman rule which happened elsewhere in the empire was impossible for the Jewish people. The Celts of northern Gaul were happy to identify their local deities, gods like Camulus and Mullo, with the Roman Mars or Jupiter. But the Jewish God was simply incompatible with any kind of polytheistic system. There was one true and omnipotent God; He was *not* the same as the Roman Jupiter. Nor was the line which separated Jew from Gentile open to negotiation. Observation of even the most basic elements of the Mosaic law – circumcision, dietary restrictions, keeping the Sabbath – sharply restricted the extent to which Jews could associate with Gentiles. Finally, subjection to Rome was not just humiliating; it was *wrong*, a fundamental breach of God's promise to protect and deliver his chosen people from oppression.

Nonetheless, as we have already seen, the Roman empire was essentially a world of religious pluralism. The provinces of the empire were home to an astonishing number of local cults, most of which were tolerated by the Roman ruling power. Perhaps the most striking example of Roman religious toleration is that of the Mithras cult of the second and third centuries AD. The origins of the cult of Mithras are clouded in mystery. All we can say for certain is that very suddenly, at the end of the first and the beginning of the second century AD, Mithraic sacred buildings ('mithraea') and dedications to Mithras appear simultaneously in very widely dispersed parts of the empire (Judaea, the Rhine and Danube frontier, Rome, inland Asia Minor). The cult became widespread in the second and third centuries AD, particularly among the frontier garrisons of the Roman army; three mithraea have been found at forts on Hadrian's Wall, at Housesteads, Rudchester and Carrawburgh. The Mithras cult was a mystery religion, open only to male initiates, each of whom belonged to one of seven grades, 'raven', 'male bride', 'soldier', 'lion', 'Persian', 'sun-runner', 'father', each associated with one of the seven planets (the five which are visible to the naked eye, Mercury, Venus, Mars, Jupiter and Saturn, plus the sun and moon). A Mithraic initiate passed through the seven grades in order, and as he moved from planet to planet, each lying further away from the earth, his soul too travelled further away from the material world, towards the final aim of salvation after death. A bronze plaque from Virunum (near modern Klagenfurt in Austria), lists all thirty-four members of one particular Mithraic congregation as it stood in 183. Over the following eighteen years the congregation was swelled by between one and eight new members per year, but only six of the ninety-seven men who belonged to this particular Mithraic group in the period 183–201 seem to have attained the highest and most prestigious grade of 'father'.

It would be quite wrong to regard the Mithras cult as an 'underground' sect. Most of the adherents of the cult were soldiers, slaves and ex-slaves, but a few initiates came from the upper ranks of the army, including some of equestrian and senatorial status; some of the best-preserved Mithraic sacred buildings are those from the city of Rome itself. Nonetheless, the Mithras cult was radically different from other Graeco-Roman religions. Mithras himself, as represented in cult icons, was a visibly non-Roman figure, invariably being depicted wearing a 'Phrygian' cap, associated with the far eastern reaches of the empire and the Persian world beyond its borders. Mithraic cult practice, too, was wholly unlike Graeco-Roman ritual. Women were totally excluded; Mithraic worship took place in secluded, indoor locations (private houses, military camps, even caves); most striking of all, the central icon of the cult, located at one end of the Mithraic sanctuary, depicted the god Mithras slaying a bull. The idea of the god himself performing animal sacrifice is a deliberate and pointed reversal of the ordinary rules of Graeco-Roman cult practice, according to which animal sacrifice was performed by the worshipper in honour of the god. Finally, Mithras was, uniquely, a god whose home lay outside the bounds of the Roman empire, in a mythical cave somewhere in Persia. While Greek and Roman gods were almost always worshipped in their capacity as protectors or inhabitants of a specific place (the Capitoline Jupiter, Athena Polias on the Athenian Acropolis, the Ephesian Artemis), Mithras was a geographically floating deity, tied neither to a particular civic locale nor to the imperial centre.

The Mithras cult seems to have been especially popular among serving soldiers and slaves or ex-slaves, precisely those groups in the Roman empire who were most cut off from the civic world of Graeco-Roman religion. It is tempting to see the Mithras cult, with its rootlessness, its deliberate rejection of the cult practices of civic religion and its emphasis on internal hierarchies and self-advancement, as a response to the experience of military service on the imperial Roman frontier, the *limes*. For the men of the frontier garrisons, thousands of kilometres from the temples of their native cults and thrown together with soldiers drawn from all corners of the empire, the Mithras cult may have been a way of making sense of their common experience.

The imperial frontier was one of the most distinctive and novel features of Roman Europe. The *limes* took different forms in different regions. In the east and south, in Mesopotamia, Arabia and North Africa, the effective limits of the empire coincided with natural boundaries, at the point where cultivable territory shades into desert. In continental Europe, throughout the first and second centuries AD, the northern limit of the empire was conventionally marked by the course of the Rhine and Danube rivers: Tacitus speaks of an empire 'fenced in by the Ocean and by great rivers'. In the second century AD parts of the frontier were still more clearly defined with the construction of physical barriers of earth, wood or stone; the best known example is of course Hadrian's Wall in northern Britain, but large parts of the *limes* on the Danube and Rhine were similarly fortified.

It is tempting to think of the Roman empire of the first three centuries AD as a static, non-expansionist state, enclosed by linear, heavily defended frontiers. The first emperor, Augustus, is said to have advised his successor, Tiberius, 'to keep the empire within its boundaries'. However, the actual behaviour of Roman emperors hardly supports this view: in AD 15, within a year of Augustus' death, Tiberius himself authorized an advance further into Germany, and few emperors did not at least attempt to add new territory to the empire. It may be helpful to imagine Europe in the first three centuries AD as being divided into three distinct regions. The first and innermost region, the 'core empire', was made up of the provinces directly administered by Roman officials, whose inhabitants paid taxes to Rome and were subject to Roman law and jurisdiction. Beyond the core provinces lay a second zone of territory, an 'inner periphery' of subject territories (the Latin word is *gentes*, 'tribes'), subject to Roman rule but not under direct Roman administration, controlled by client kings and native allies. The Roman emperor expected to be able to influence the succession of power from one client king to another; it was a rare privilege for King Herod of Judaea to possess the right of choosing his successor without reference to Augustus. This inner periphery separated the core provinces from the third region, the 'outer tribes' or *gentes externae*, who were not subject to Roman rule at all.

When we talk about the 'frontiers' of the Roman empire, then, we should really be thinking of the whole of the second zone: a broad, heavily militarized swath of territory, in places hundreds of kilometres in depth (in Britain, stretching from York to Newcastle upon Tyne). Actual lines of fortifications could stand either at the outer edge of this zone, as in the case of Hadrian's Wall, or at its inner edge, as in the case of the Danube frontier in Hungary. The fortifications built by the emperor Commodus (180–92) along the banks of the Danube south of Aquincum (modern Budapest) are a particularly interesting example. These towers and forts were certainly not built in order to protect the frontier from barbarian attacks: they were in fact constructed immediately *after* a peace-treaty with the barbarian kingdom on the far side of the Danube, the Iazyges. As part of the peace-treaty, the Iazyges were permitted to enter the Roman province to visit market towns on appointed days. Consequently, as we are informed by a series of building-inscriptions, Commodus 'fortified the whole river-bank with brand new towers and guard-posts, situated in opportune places for preventing the secret crossings of smugglers'. The Danube fortifications were needed precisely in order to regulate traffic between the province and the friendly barbarian kingdom outside it to the north. It is striking and appropriate that the only surviving map of the whole Roman empire, the Peutinger Table (a late medieval copy of a map of the fourth or fifth century AD), marks no frontiers at all; instead, roads continue smoothly beyond the nominal 'borders' deep into non-Roman territory.

The impact of the army on the societies of the frontier zones was immense. In second-century AD Britain, some 60,000 Roman soldiers were stationed among a total population of perhaps 4 million inhabitants, a ratio of one soldier to every sixty-five civilians. Britain was, of course, a heavily garrisoned frontier province, but even a peaceful 'core' province like Egypt, with a population comparable in size to that of Britain (4 to 5 million), may have had as many as 10,000 soldiers permanently stationed on its soil. In 238 the inhabitants of a village called Skaptopara in Thrace (modern Bulgaria) sent a desperate petition to the emperor Gordian III (238–44). Their village, they explained, was well situated: it possessed thermal springs with excellent therapeutic qualities, and once a year, a famous market-fair was held 3 kilometres from the village. Senior Roman officials, including the provincial governor, often came to stay at the village in order to enjoy the use of the thermal baths. (Delicate Italians often found the climate of the Balkans uncongenial: the poet Ovid, exiled to Tomis on the Black Sea in AD 8, suffered from indigestion, insomnia, fever and miscellaneous aches and pains.) However, Skaptopara also happened to lie just off the road connecting two military camps. Soldiers travelling between the two camps regularly descended on the village to use the hot springs; the villagers were required to house and provision them without compensation. As a consequence of this constant military traffic, the village, which had previously been prosperous, had been reduced to utter destitution. Attempts by the provincial governor to crack down on these abuses of power had made not the least difference, so that the villagers were now reduced to asking the emperor himself to step in. The emperor's unhelpful response was simply to refer them back to the governor.

The army was clearly a highly visible and unwelcome presence in the daily life of Skaptopara. Nor was this an exceptional case. In the militarized zone immediately to the south of Hadrian's Wall, in Co. Durham and North Yorkshire, no cities and very few rural villas have been located, and native sites have produced very few Roman coins and artefacts; most of the native population (the Brigantes) continued to live in traditional roundhouses, in increasingly impoverished conditions. To all appearances, the massive military presence in northern Britain had a parasitical effect on the people living in the frontier zone; native economic and cultural development simply ground to a halt.

A story in Apuleius' second-century AD Latin novel, *The Golden Ass*, makes the point about the relation between soldier and civilian as well as any. Somewhere in the northern Greek countryside, a legionary centurion comes across a market gardener riding a donkey. The soldier accosts the gardener, and demands, in Latin, to know where he is taking his donkey. The gardener, not knowing any Latin, rides on in silence; the soldier takes this as an insult and lands a vicious blow on the man's head with his staff. After striking the gardener to the ground, he asks the same question again, this time in Greek: where are you taking that donkey? The soldier is bilingual; he must have assumed that the gardener was a Greek-speaker. Nonetheless, he had chosen to address him in Latin, solely in order to have the opportunity to beat up a peasant for insulting behaviour. It is no surprise to read that the soldier goes on to demand that the gardener hand over his donkey for military use. That such arbitrary requisitions of locals' labour and livestock were a daily occurrence in first-century AD Judaea is clear from Jesus' advice in the Sermon on the Mount: 'And whosoever shall compel thee to go a mile, go with him twain' (Matthew 5: 41).

We have seen that the frontier 'zone' shaded off almost imperceptibly into the lands of the *gentes externae*. Among these neighbouring peoples, we can map a kind of 'ripple effect' of Roman cultural influence on their lifestyles and material culture. To the north-east, beyond the Rhine, Roman-style armour and weapons become steadily more popular over

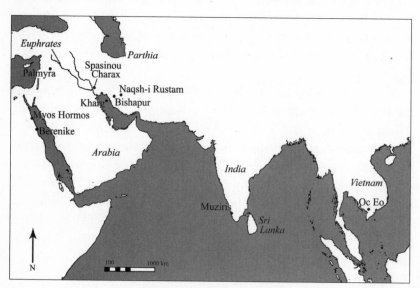

Map 32. Rome's eastern neighbours.

the course of the first three centuries AD. In the second century AD the first examples of the Runic alphabet, based directly on the Latin script, start to appear in Danish burials on weapons, tools and prestige objects. Most importantly, we start to see the emergence of local aristocratic dynasties, characterized by their ostentatious use of imported Roman luxury objects. At Himlingøje in eastern Denmark, the tombs of at least thirteen members of the same family have been uncovered, dating from the mid-second to the late third century AD. The grave goods from the Himlingøje burials are a mixture of high-quality Roman imports (bronze buckets and ladles, glass cups and drinking horns) and local prestige objects (gold finger- and arm-rings). It was through its Romanizing pretensions that the Himlingøje family chose to distinguish themselves from their lower-status neighbours.

The most powerful of the *gentes externae* lay beyond the river Euphrates frontier to the east. Roman relations with the great civilizations of inner Asia were far more intense and complex than with the barbarian peoples of northern Europe, for the simple reason that most of the essential luxuries of the Roman overseas trade – Arabian incense, African ivory, Chinese silk and Indian pepper – came from beyond the eastern frontiers of the empire. Most important of all was the Roman seaborne trade between Egypt and southern India, channelled through two great Roman trading stations on the Red Sea coast of Egypt, Myos Hormos and Berenikē. Recent excavations at Berenikē have brought this trade to life for us for the first time. Enormous quantities of Indian black peppercorns have been excavated there, including 7.5 kilograms of peppercorns still packed into a huge Indian storage jar which for some reason was never shipped onwards to the Mediterranean. Rome's Indian trade was dazzlingly profitable. Pliny the Elder, in his *Natural History*, claimed that the Indians received some 50 million Roman sesterces per year, in return for goods which were sold in the Mediterranean for a hundred times the price.

Pliny's figures have been routinely dismissed by modern historians as an absurd exaggeration, but a recently published Egyptian papyrus has provided a spectacular vindication of Pliny's statement. This document, dating to the mid-second century AD, records the transfer of a shipment of goods overland from the Red Sea coast of Egypt to the Nile valley. We learn that these goods had been shipped to the Red Sea from Muziris, in the south of India, on a single Roman merchantman called the *Hermapollon*. The journey of the *Hermapollon* can be reconstructed with some confidence: a thirty-day journey down the Red Sea to the gulf of Aden; twenty days across the Indian Ocean, with the monsoon winds at their backs; three to four months at Muziris, waiting for the wind to turn; and another fifty days back to Berenikē, making a round trip of almost eight months. The cargo carried on this ship on a single journey back from India to the Red Sea, including ivory, luxury fabric and spikenard (a perfumed oil) from the Ganges valley, is valued in the papyrus at around 7 million sesterces. To put that figure in context: 9 million sesterces would (on one estimate) have been enough to equip a city the size of Pompeii with *all* its necessary public buildings and amenities. The *Hermapollon* was a true floating treasure-chest.

At the eastern end of this particular channel of trade, staggering numbers of Roman coins have been found in Sri Lanka and southern India, along with transport jars, and Roman bronze- and glass-ware. The Peutinger Table (a fourth- or fifth-century AD map of the Roman empire, mentioned above) marks a 'temple of Augustus' in the vicinity of Muziris, which may suggest the existence of a permanent Roman trading post in southern India. Rome's connections in South Asia may have extended even further to the east: two Roman medallions, one of Antoninus Pius (138–61), the other of Marcus Aurelius (161–80), have been excavated at the trading post of Oc Eo, in the Mekong delta of South Vietnam, and there is some evidence that the builders of log-boats in Vietnam in the early first millennium AD were aware of Roman shipwrights' techniques.

By contrast to its seaborne trade, Rome's overland trade with its eastern neighbours is very poorly attested indeed. There is no doubt, for example, that Rome imported huge quantities of Chinese silk, the ultimate luxury fabric: the mistresses of the Augustan love poets shimmer around in translucent silk dresses, and fragments of silk clothing have been excavated as far north as Holborough in Kent. Whether this silk came to the Mediterranean by an overland 'Silk Road', however, is far more controversial. Evidence for direct Roman contact with China is very hard to come by. It was long believed that Roman glass was exported in large quantities to China. More recent research has shown that most of this glass was produced in China itself; sadly, one particularly spectacular example, a cast glass vase with engraved medallions of the goddess Athena, supposedly found in a Chinese tomb in Honan province, has now been recognized as the product of a nineteenth-century Bohemian glass factory. Similarly, a well-known hoard of sixteen Roman bronze coins from Ling-shih hsien in Shansi, ranging in date from Tiberius (AD 14–37) to Aurelian (270–75), has been shown to have been the private collection of a modern western missionary. Very sporadic Roman diplomatic contacts with China are known: Chinese sources record the arrival of a delegation from the emperor An-tun (Marcus Aurelius Antoninus) in AD 166, and in 226 a Roman merchant named 'Ts'in Lun' reached the court of the emperor Wu at Nanking. All this does not really add up to very much. The two greatest empires of the ancient world, imperial Rome and Han China, essentially proceeded on entirely separate paths, all but unaware of the other's existence.

Several Roman towns in the upper Euphrates region certainly grew rich from the overland trade with the east. Foremost among them was the great caravan city of Palmyra, lying deep in the Syrian desert between Antioch and the Euphrates, where fragments of Chinese silk have been discovered (Plate 22). However, this need not necessarily mean that there was an overland 'Silk Road' running directly between Syria and China. In AD 18/19, Germanicus, the nephew of the emperor Tiberius, sent a certain Alexandros on an official embassy from Palmyra to the head of the Persian gulf. To all appearances, Germanicus was attempting to formalize a caravan route between Palmyra and the harbour-towns at the mouths of the Euphrates and Tigris rivers. In the first and second centuries AD, Palmyrene trading colonies were established in several parts of southern Mesopotamia, and tombs of Palmyrene traders have been found as far south as the island of Kharg, off the Iranian coast in the Persian gulf; we have a long series of inscriptions from Palmyra honouring individuals who helped to conduct the camel caravans from Spasinou Charax (near the mouth of the Tigris) to Palmyra. It seems more likely, then, that Chinese silk reached Palmyra via the ordinary southern route from India, being carried by sea from the Indus delta to the head of the Persian gulf, where it was loaded onto Palmyrene camels for the overland journey up the Euphrates valley to Syria.

This crucial caravan route, from Palmyra down the Euphrates to the Persian gulf, was utterly dependent on stable relations with Rome's immediate neighbour to the east, the huge empire of the Parthians. The Parthians were originally a nomadic people, who migrated south from the steppes of central Asia into northern Iran in the early third century BC. Over the course of the third and second centuries BC, the Parthians expanded south and westwards into Seleucid territory; by the end of the reign of the Parthian king Mithradates II (124/3–88/7 BC), the whole of modern Iran and most of Mesopotamia, including Babylon, had fallen under Parthian control. The westward expansion of the Parthians inevitably brought them into conflict with Rome. Over the course of the first century BC Rome repeatedly provoked war with Parthia, with limited success and enormous loss of manpower; in 53 BC the Roman general Crassus lost 30,000 soldiers at the battle of Carrhae, in the course of an ill-judged invasion of northern Mesopotamia. Finally in 20 BC the emperor Augustus struck a treaty with the Parthians, fixing the Euphrates as the boundary between the two empires. As part of the deal, the Parthians agreed to return the military standards captured from Crassus thirty years earlier. For Rome, the treaty with Parthia was essentially a recognition of fifty years of military failure in the east. Nonetheless, Augustus cheerfully represented the treaty as a heroic Roman victory. A triumphal arch was erected in the Roman Forum, along with a temple of Mars the Avenger in Augustus' new Forum Augustum (see above, Figure 25); coins were struck depicting the Parthian king kneeling in submission, meekly handing back the Roman standards captured at Carrhae (see Plate 31e).

Augustus and his successors consistently represented their exploits against the Parthians, which were not especially glorious, as the continuation of the endless struggle between European civilization and the eastern barbarian. In AD 61/2 the Athenians set up a huge honorific inscription to the emperor Nero, in gilded letters, on the east wall of the Parthenon, to celebrate Nero's indecisive campaigns in the Parthian client kingdom of Armenia (AD 54–63). The location is significant: the Parthenon itself was a memorial to the Greek victory in the Persian Wars of the early fifth century BC, and Nero's inscription overlooked the late-third-century BC monument of Attalus I commemorating his victories over the Galatians (the 'New Persians' of the day: above, Figure 20). Similarly, at the Sebasteion of Aphrodisias in Caria, Nero was portrayed supporting a slumped personification of 'barbarian' Armenia, depicted in the character of an oriental Amazon.

In the second century AD a succession of Roman emperors attempted once again to push Rome's eastern borders beyond the Euphrates.

Septimius Severus (193–211) finally succeeded in creating two new Roman provinces beyond the Euphrates in northern Mesopotamia, the first lasting gains ever achieved by Rome against the Parthians. His son Caracalla (211–217), encouraged by these victories, entertained grand dreams of emulating the conquests of Alexander the Great in the east. In 214 he enlisted a phalanx of Macedonian soldiers, and set out to follow Alexander's path from Macedonia to Persia. The expedition began farcically and ended in disaster. Like Alexander, he crossed from Europe to Asia via the Hellespont; unfortunately, his boat capsized halfway across and the emperor had to be rescued by one of his officers. After tracing Alexander's route as far as Egypt, he provoked a gratuitous and humiliatingly ineffective war with Parthia (216–18); Caracalla himself was murdered by his own court in 217, and the war ended with Rome paying a huge indemnity to the Parthians, having won not a single inch of new territory.

It may ultimately have been the loss of northern Mesopotamia to Septimius Severus which led to the downfall of the Parthians. In the early third century AD the old Persian heartlands of southern Iran rose up against Parthian rule, under the leadership of an energetic new Iranian dynasty, the Sasanians. In AD 224 the Sasanian king Ardashir I slew the last Parthian king in battle, and by 226 the whole of the former Parthian empire was under Sasanian control. From the outset, the new Sasanian dynasty took a much more aggressive attitude towards the west. Ardashir promptly launched the first of a series of dramatic raids on the Roman fortresses of upper Mesopotamia; perhaps more significantly, his seizure of the ports at the head of the Persian gulf brought a sudden end to the profitable Roman overland caravan trade from Palmyra. His successor, Shapur I (240–72), continued his father's policy of uncompromising expansion in the west. Shapur swept the Romans out of northern Mesopotamia, and even captured the great city of Antioch, a stone's throw from the coast of the Mediterranean itself. In 243, a Roman emperor, Gordian III, was killed in battle against Shapur, and in 260, Shapur succeeded in capturing alive the Roman emperor Valerian. The Roman prisoners of war were set to work building a new royal city, Bishapur, high in the Zagros mountains of western Iran; the city's fine coloured mosaics were almost certainly laid by captured Roman craftsmen.

The Sasanian victories of the mid-third century were the most spectacular achievements of a foreign power against Rome since the wars with Carthage almost half a millennium previously. It is particularly striking that Ardashir and Shapur chose to commemorate their victories in ways which linked them explicitly with Iranian memories of the Achaemenid Persian world empire of the sixth and fifth centuries BC. The most dramatic monuments of the Persian imperial era to survive into the Sasanian period were the royal tombs at Naqsh-i Rustam, near modern Shiraz. The colossal tombs of the Achaemenid kings Darius I, Xerxes, Artaxerxes I and Darius II are still visible today, carved into a huge cliff-face overlooking the Marv Dasht plain. Both Ardashir and Shapur added rock-cut reliefs of their own, slotted in neatly between the Achaemenid royal tombs, commemorating Ardashir's accession to the throne (the re-establishment of the true Achaemenid royal line) and Shapur's defeat of the emperor Valerian (the modern counterpart of the Achaemenid conquest of the west). In front of the cliff with the royal tombs stands a great stone tower, the Ka'aba-i Zardusht, probably an early Persian fire-temple. It was on the base of this Achaemenid-era monument that Shapur carved a long trilingual inscription in Parthian, Middle Persian and Greek, recounting his victories in the west. Shapur's victories over three successive Roman emperors are thus set on a level with the conquests of his Achaemenid ancestors. It is still very unclear exactly how much the Sasanians actually knew about the Achaemenids and their empire, but there is some evidence that they went so far as to lay claim to all the lands once ruled by the Persians. Shapur II (309–79), in a letter to the Roman emperor Constantius II (337–61), declared that 'my ancestors' empire stretched to the river Strymon and the borders of Macedonia, as even your own historical records attest; it is right that I should demand these lands, inasmuch as I surpass even those ancient kings in magnificence'. The Sasanian empire, no less than the Roman empire, was profoundly shaped by its memories of the past.

By the time of the accession of Constantius II in 337, the Roman world had undergone a full-scale religious revolution, with momentous consequences for the history of Europe down to the present day. For Constantius' empire was now a Christian empire. In AD 326, Constantius' father, Constantine I (306–37), had written to the young Shapur II to commend the Christian faith to him, and to ask him to protect the Christians living under his rule. After three centuries of persecution and martyrdom, the tiny Messianic movement born under Tiberius among the fishermen on the shores of lake Galilee could now claim the public adherence of the Roman emperor himself.

The Church began as a reform movement within Judaism. Jesus' own ministry in Galilee and Jerusalem (c. AD 28–30) was directed primarily at the Jewish people, and long after the crucifixion many Jewish converts remained deeply hostile to the idea of 'gentile Christianity'. The crucial turning point, which set Christianity on a different path from other Jewish Messianic sects, came in AD 48 or 49, with the decision of the apostolic conference at Jerusalem that while gentile converts to Christianity must refrain from idolatory and unchastity and observe the main Jewish dietary laws, they need not undergo circumcision. This decision set the early Church firmly on a path of openness: gentiles who were unwilling to accept the rigid limits of Rabbinic Judaism were nonetheless welcomed into the Christian religion.

Over the second half of the first century AD the boundaries between Jew and Christian gradually became sharper. By AD 112, when the provincial governor Pliny the Younger wrote to the emperor Trajan to report the measures he had taken against a group of Christians brought to trial before him in Pontus (north-central Asia Minor), Christianity was clearly recognized by the Roman state as a sect distinct from Judaism. It is significant that Christians seem always to have been exempt from the Jewish tax, which had been imposed on all the Jews of the empire after the fall of Jerusalem in AD 70. Indeed, it is hardly surprising that some early Christians – most famously the adherents of the heretical bishop Marcion (c. AD 85–160) – came to reject Jewish scripture altogether. For the Marcionites, Christ was the son of a previously unknown god, quite different from the Jewish God of the Old Testament. Christianity, on this line, was an entirely new religion, with no past stretching back earlier than Jesus' lifetime. Unsurprisingly, this radical denial of the Church's Jewish roots met with ferocious opposition among ordinary Christians. Most Christians recognized the authority of the Jewish scripture; their attitude to the Old Testament differed from that of the Jews only in their belief that the scriptural prophecies had now been fulfilled in the person of Christ.

One of the key debates within the early Church was the question of how far the Christian faith was compatible with the Roman world order. The First Epistle of Peter, composed at an uncertain date in the late first century AD, is quite clear on the matter: 'Be subject for the Lord's sake to every human institution, whether it be to the emperor as supreme, or to governors as sent by him to punish those who do wrong and to praise those who do right . . . Fear God. Honour the emperor.' There was, it is true, a more militant strand in the Church, best represented for us by the Revelation of St John of Patmos. John's vision of Rome as the whore of Babylon, soon to be laid low by pestilence and mourning and famine, was hardly designed to promote friendly relations between Christians and pagans. This militant vision was fuelled by the increasingly fierce persecution of Christians in the second and third centuries AD by the imperial authorities. It is clear from Pliny's prosecution of the Christians of Pontus in 112 that profession of Christianity was a capital crime; it is equally clear that both Pliny and Trajan were fairly relaxed about enforcing the law. In the second and early third centuries, only the most outspoken fanatics could expect to face the death penalty. It therefore came as a real shock to the empire's Christians when, in 249, the emperor Decius (249–51) passed an edict requiring all the inhabitants of the empire to offer sacrifice to the pagan gods. The persecution which followed led to the execution of the bishops of Rome and Alexandria, among many others. Although the mass trials and martyrdoms eased off in the 260s, the experience of centrally directed persecution had shown quite how difficult it was to be a good Christian and a good Roman at the same time.

Those aspects of the third-century Church which seem strangest and most foreign to us today – the rejection of marriage and embrace of perpetual virginity, martyrdom, asceticism and self-abasement – can be seen in large part as an attempt to reject, as violently as possible, all the established norms and values of Roman society. Some of the internal conflict and anguish this provoked for individual converts can be seen in the remarkable account which has come down to us of the martyrdom of a Christian woman by the name of Perpetua, executed at Carthage in 203. Perpetua was, in most respects, a model member of provincial Roman society: a Roman citizen of the local Carthaginian nobility, married with a young child. The night before her death, Perpetua dreamed that she was wrestling with a black Egyptian in the amphitheatre at Carthage; the bout was presided over by a man clad in a purple robe, holding a branch with golden apples as a prize for the victor. On waking, she realized that her Egyptian opponent represented the devil, and the purple-clad master of ceremonies Christ. Perpetua's dream gives us a precious insight into an early Christian martyr's subconscious. From our perspective, the interesting thing is that she subconsciously interpreted her martyrdom in purely civic and pagan terms: the amphitheatre, the games, the master of ceremonies with his prize of golden apples (the chief prize at the pagan festival of the Pythia at Carthage in the early third century AD). The early Christians could not help but conceive their faith in terms of the Roman world they claimed to have put aside. At the very moment of her death, Perpetua 'pulled down her tunic, which was torn down the side, to cover her thighs, thinking more of her modesty than her pain'; one of her last acts was to ask for a hairpin to fasten her loosened hair. Before the crowds in the amphitheatre at Carthage, Perpetua's first instinct was still to try to look and behave like an appropriately modest and decorous Roman wife.

By the third century the Church had become a highly organized, empire-wide state within the Roman state. As a result of the struggle with heretical sects such as the Marcionites, the Church had developed a strict internal hierarchy, its own legal system, and a procedure for deciding doctrinal problems through universal (ecumenical) Church councils. Christians' relations with their non-Christian neighbours also showed an increasing sophistication and openness. Alongside the use made by the Church of the Jewish past, particularly in terms of Old Testament exegesis, Christians also began to negotiate with and tap into the civic cults and ideology of the cities of the Roman provinces. From the reign of Septimius Severus (193–211) onwards, the city of Apamea in Phrygia minted large numbers of bronze coins depicting the Judaeo-Christian story of Noah and the Ark. Apamea had long been informally known as Apamea 'Kibotos', the Chest, thanks to its status as the main Roman trading post in inland Asia Minor. However, the Greek word *kibotos* also means 'Ark'. The Noah coins of Apamea are apparently the result of a highly subtle and effective act of negotiation between the Christian and pagan communities at Apamea. The Christians of Apamea had successfully argued that Apamea's nickname derived from its status as the resting place of the Ark of Noah after the Flood, the true location of Mt. Ararat being unknown at this point. We have seen already in this chapter that the cities of inland Asia Minor were desperately keen to present themselves as communities of great antiquity, founded deep in the legendary past before the Trojan War. The claim that the city of

Apamea was the first city to be founded after the biblical Flood pushed all the right buttons for the pagans of Apamea; the town's Christian community had found the perfect way of legitimizing and publicizing their religion in terms which could be easily understood and appreciated by non-Christians.

We have no way of telling how many Christians there were in the Roman empire in the first three centuries AD. Most probably, the size of the Christian community differed radically from one region, even from one city, to another. According to a reliable source (Eusebius' *Church History*), there were 155 members of the Christian clergy in the city of Rome in AD 251; by this point the Christian population of Rome must have numbered in the thousands. The only area where we have real evidence for the spread of Christianity is, once again, the Phrygian highlands of inland Asia Minor. Christianity struck deep roots in Phrygia at an early date. This isolated rural area had had a large Jewish population since the Hellenistic period, and the Phrygian brand of paganism had strong monotheistic tendencies even before the coming of the Church. In the upper Tembris valley, a remote part of northern Phrygia, around 20 per cent of the population was openly professing the Christian faith on their tombstones by 230; by the end of the third century the proportion has risen to more than 80 per cent. In the late third and early fourth centuries AD Egyptian papyri show a sudden explosion of characteristically Christian personal names like David, Matthew, Johannes. The proportion of identifiably Christian names in Egypt rose from around 10–15 per cent of the population in AD 280 to *c*. 50 per cent at the death of Constantine in 337. By 425, a century later, the proportion had reached 80 per cent. At least in the eastern provinces, then, the late third and early fourth centuries mark the crucial turning point; by the end of Constantine's reign, the victory of the Church was assured. It is this new, Christian empire of the fourth century AD which will be the subject of our final chapter.

9

The Later Roman Empire:
AD 284–425

In the middle of the fourth century AD, the owner of a modest country house in south-east England, at Lullingstone, Kent, decided to decorate the reception room with a new mosaic floor. In the centre was a depiction of the ancient Greek hero Bellerophon riding the winged horse Pegasus, attacking the Chimaera, a monster that was part lion, part goat and part snake. The floor of an apsidal dining room built out at one side of the reception room was decorated with an even more remarkable mosaic (Plate 29). In the centre is Europa riding on the back of the bull, that is, Jupiter. These two stories were ancient by this time, a version of the Bellerophon story appearing more than a thousand years previously in Homer's *Iliad*, and they were widely known among the educated classes of the Roman empire. But the level of education presupposed by the Europa mosaic is hugely increased by a Latin verse couplet set above it: 'If jealous Juno had seen the swimmings of the bull, most justly would she have gone to the halls of Aeolus.' This allusion to Juno plotting against Aeneas, partly in order to gain vengeance on her faithless husband Jupiter, assumes a detailed knowledge of Virgil's *Aeneid*, which refers specifically to Juno asking the wind-god Aeolus to wreck Aeneas' ships. The mosaic cleverly, and humorously, brings together the conventional visual reper-toire of antiquity with a reading of Virgil's classic text. A decade or two after the mosaics were laid, a room in the house was converted into a Christian chapel, and was decorated with figured scenes, including six praying figures, who may represent the family of the house, and three large monograms XP, the first two Greek letters of 'Christ'.

These snapshots of Lullingstone encapsulate the themes of this chapter: the extraordinary stability and success of Greek and Latin culture, which was still the path to success in the western parts of the Roman empire; and the relation of this culture to the newly emerging Christianity.

After the emperor Constantine had converted to Christianity in AD 312 Christians moved from being a persecuted group to being supported by Constantine and subsequent emperors. The issue of how far Christianity was compatible with the inherited culture of the past continued to be, and still is, contested. We shall begin by looking at how central government became highly interventionist, which brought about great changes to civic life.

A map of the Roman empire in AD 284 would look much like a map of the empire 200 years previously. Roman rule stretched from Britain to the Euphrates, from the Rhine and Danube to the deserts of North Africa. But in the middle of the third century AD, the state faced a conjunction of major problems. The northern and eastern frontiers were not secure, with threats from the Sasanians in the east and 'barbarians' in the north. There was very serious inflation. And central leadership was weak: between 235 and 284 there were twenty-two emperors, most of whom died violent deaths. Diocletian, on becoming emperor in 284, built on the achievements of some of his immediate predecessors, and succeeded in creating a new, and relatively durable, imperial system. But by

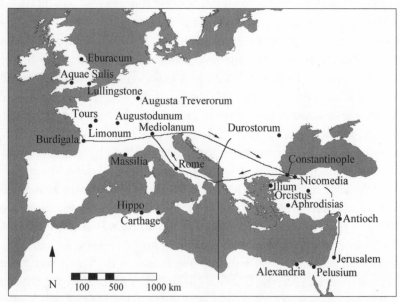

Map 33. The Roman empire c. AD 400. The vertical line marks the division of the empire in AD 395 between east and west, along the old line between the Greek- and Latin-speaking regions. The route of a pilgrim travelling between Burdigala and Jerusalem illustrates two of the overland arteries of the empire.

the end of our period the state had begun to lose control of some territory. The Romans pulled out of Britain in AD 409, and at around this time the Lullingstone house was destroyed by fire and abandoned.

Emperors had to carry on fighting on the northern and eastern frontiers. The state suffered some disasters: in 363 the emperor Julian invaded Sasanian territory, where he died. But emperors did retain almost all the old territory in the fourth century. A speech delivered in Augustodunum (modern Autun) around 298 records how the young men there used a map of the world in a portico to understand the scope of imperial successes, from Britain to the Euphrates. Emperors were shown as busy at war throughout the world, and as always victorious.

The army was reorganized, with many smaller units, though probably around the same number of men under arms. During the fourth century the processes of recruitment changed, with large landowners expected to supply men, or to pay cash in lieu. Later in the fourth century, to replace soldiers lost in battle, emperors recruited large numbers of Germans to serve in the army and even to form an officer class. Under Diocletian, military forces were concentrated along the frontiers, but subsequently, with the development of flexible response forces, many troops were billeted in cities and towns when not on active service. The impact on the life of those communities was vast. According to a pious Christian account, a Christian soldier in the legionary city of Durostorum (modern Silistra in Bulgaria) who declined to play the role of Saturn during the Saturnalia was put to death. The setting of the martyrdom is significant: during the thirty days of the Saturnalia festival, the soldiers regularly ran amuck in the city in a riot of licentiousness. This sort of abuse of power by soldiers remained an endemic problem in the Roman empire (above, pp. 288–90).

Partly to meet the needs of military leadership, Diocletian formalized the idea of an imperial team, of two emperors, titled 'Augusti', and two deputies, titled 'Caesars'. This system had some precedents at Rome, but a contemporary imperial panegyric also managed to find a precedent rather further back, in the unique dual kingship at Sparta. The initial intention of the new scheme was to ensure the unity of the Roman empire in the face of continued threats. By the end of the fourth century, the consequence was the division of the empire into eastern and western spheres, with one 'Augustus' in charge of each. This political division corresponded to, and reinforced, the linguistic division between Greek and Latin (see above, pp. 272–3): Italy and middle Europe were Latin-speaking zones, and Greece, Asia Minor and the Levant Greek-speaking, a pattern that would endure for centuries to come.

Diocletian's aspirations in tackling the problems facing the Roman state were deeply traditional, but the methods he used were not. He wanted to stabilize the situation by calling on traditional values, but in ways that were highly interventionist. Worried about the spread of Manichaeism, a religion founded in Persian Mesopotamia in the previous generation, Diocletian issued a ruling to the governor of Africa that adherents of Manichaeism should be severely punished: the gods had providentially ensured that true principles should be established and preserved by the judgement and deliberation of many wise men, but this new sect sought to undermine what had been fixed by the ancients. On much the same grounds, he next took action against Christians. Between 303 and 304 a series of increasingly severe measures were enacted, ending with an order that the whole population of the empire sacrifice to the traditional gods. Diocletian wanted everyone to pull together at this time of crisis, as did his predecessors Decius and Valerian in the mid-third century: only universal sacrifices would ensure the support of the traditional gods for the Roman state. As in the past, and the future, religion was primarily state-centred.

Diocletian also established a new administrative system, building on the piecemeal changes of some of his immediate predecessors. In the early empire, the state operated a somewhat laissez-faire system. Neither emperor nor governors went out looking for trouble. They wanted to maintain good order, but assumed that individual cities would provide the basic fabric of life. The problems facing the empire in the third century made the old system look weak. Diocletian and his successors felt that they could not stand by, and intervened much more widely than had previously been the case. Diocletian undertook various measures to tackle inflation, which had been a feature of the Roman economy for the previous century. These included the setting of maximum prices for goods and salaries throughout the empire, worried as he was that his soldiers were being defrauded by high prices. The price edict is the most widely attested imperial edict on any subject, but it was a complete failure and was probably repealed within a year. Diocletian was able, however, to protect his troops from the worst effects of inflation by paying them in rations, levied as taxation, and in semi-regular gifts of gold and silver coins.

Diocletian divided the provinces into smaller areas, more than doubling the total number of provinces from forty-eight to more than a hundred. For example, the old province of Thrace (north-east Greece and Bulgaria) was divided into four provinces, including 'Europa', which contained just twenty-two cities: the name of this tiny area, just west of the Bosporus, harks back to Homer's usage of the name. The provinces were then grouped into twelve large districts: for example, Galliae (covering central-northern France, Belgium, the Netherlands and part of Germany), Africa (central North Africa) or Oriens (all the way from the Tigris to the Red Sea). In addition, both the provincial governors and the officials in charge of the new districts came to have large staffs, 100 and 300 respectively. This creation of new provinces and of a new layer of Roman administration greatly increased the number of officials on the Roman payroll. The recurrent cost was deemed worth bearing, given that the Roman authorities, or so they believed, would now be able to run things better than the cities had done in the old laissez-faire system.

Military pressures on the empire demanded new imperial centres. In the course of the third century AD, largely because of military problems to the north and east, emperors had come to spend long periods of time outside Rome, in Augusta Treverorum (modern Trier; Plate 26), Mediolanum (modern Milan), Antioch on the Orontes (modern Antakya) and Nicomedia (modern İzmit, both in Turkey). The emperor, and his immediate troops, were thereby enabled to respond much more quickly than if he had resided at Rome. The emperor Constantine also wished to found a new eastern imperial centre, to commemorate his victory over his rival Licinius in 324. He toyed with the idea of placing it at Ilium (that is, Troy), but was deterred by a divine vision, that he should not found another Rome on the origin of the old Rome. Instead, he chose Byzantium, an ancient but minor Greek city on the Bosporus, where the land routes between Europe and Asia converged. The new city of Constantinople (modern Istanbul) was intended to rival, though not replace, Rome; indeed, at c. 430 hectares it was only a third the size of Rome within its walls. But in the long run the foundation of Constantinople was a major event in European history, ultimately restructuring the region as a bipolar entity with centres in the east and west, and further institutionalizing the Latin–Greek linguistic and cultural divide.

The founding of Constantinople was highly controversial. Was it a new Christian city? The public position of Christianity had certainly

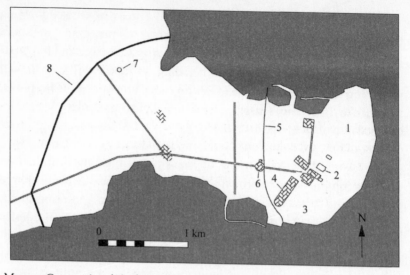

Map 34. Constantinople in the mid-fourth century AD. 1: location of ancient acropolis; 2: St Sophia; 3: palace; 4: hippodrome; 5: Old Severan wall; 6: forum of Constantine; 7: mausoleum of Constantine – Holy Apostles; 8: Constantinian walls.

changed dramatically with the conversion of Constantine. Constantine claimed that a decisive victory in 312 over a rival for power in the west was due to the Christian God. Within a month or two of the battle, Constantine joined with the eastern emperor Licinius to permit Christian meetings and the rebuilding of churches. In early AD 313 he restored Church property in the west, made huge donations to the Church from the public treasury and granted exemption to the clergy from compulsory civic duties. These were revolutionary moves, which made a public statement that the Christian Church was of benefit to the Roman state. Imperial favour from now on was behind Christianity and not the traditional cults. At Constantinople, Constantine's treatment of the traditional cults is controversial. Did Constantine leave alone the ancient temples on the acropolis, or did he erase the old cults, creating a new Christian city? Eusebius, the emperor's contemporary Christian biographer, certainly claimed that Constantinople was wholly Christian, with former pagan idols placed in the city as merely decorative features. And epigrams of Palladas, which seem to have been written here in the 330s, note that statues of the Greek gods in the city were now Christian, and, unlike other temple fixtures, would not be melted down to make new coins, and they also refer to the city as 'Christ-loving'. At least some people believed that Constantine created a high-profile position for Christianity in the new city.

Constantine built a palace and hippodrome in the city, where the people assembled for racing and shows, and acclaimed the emperor when he appeared in person. The central spine of the hippodrome was adorned with memorials of the Greek and Roman past, now placed in a new context: the bronze serpent column erected at Delphi to celebrate the Greek victory over the Persians in 480–479 BC; or statues from Rome of the sow with her piglets and of the she-wolf suckling Romulus and Remus, which recalled the dual stories of the foundation of Rome by Aeneas and by the twins. Only the serpent column survived: turned into a fountain in late antiquity, it was not pillaged by the Crusaders in 1204, and came to be seen as a talisman against poisonous snakes; it stands to this day in Istanbul in its original location. In addition, the Lupercalia, at which the crown had been offered to Julius Caesar, was celebrated in the new city, the racing conducted not through the streets, but by charioteers in the hippodrome. It was now a movable festival, held just before the start of Lent. The precise date depended on the date of Easter, but it still took place close to the original date of 15 February.

Constantine also built churches in Constantinople. He may have started the first church of St Sophia, which his successor Constantius finished, and which was eventually replaced by the surviving church in the sixth century AD, but he built fewer churches than in either Palestine or Rome. He also built a Christian mausoleum, the shrine of the Holy Apostles, where he himself was buried. In the course of the fourth century, the Christian presence in the city grew. Constantius transferred to the shrine of the Holy Apostles the bodies of three famous martyrs, Timothy, Luke and Andrew, who was said to have been active in the initial Christianization of Byzantium. This is the first time that relics were moved from their original places of burial, in Asia Minor and mainland Greece, a practice that was to become widespread; by the fifth century Constantinople itself acquired a huge collection of relics. The innovation shows the pressing need to furnish Constantinople with a rich Christian past.

The overall number of cities in the empire was unaffected by the reorganization of provinces and the creation of districts. In the Greek east, there were about a thousand cities, mostly with quite small territories. By contrast, in the area of Gaul that had been conquered by Julius Caesar there were only seventy-eight cities, all with large rural territories, over ten times the size of those in the Greek east. In both cases, there was continuity back to the early empire, and beyond. The Gallic cities of the fourth and fifth centuries AD corresponded in general to the tribes identified by Caesar at the time of conquest. The size and prosperity of individual cities did, however, change in comparison with previous centuries, with some winners and some losers. For example, Massilia in the late Roman period regained its role as a major port for inter-regional trade, and recovered the prosperity lost in the first century BC, when it had backed the wrong side in the civil war between Pompey and Caesar.

The key overall issue affecting the prosperity of individual cities was changes to the structure of Roman government. Because the new imperial bureaucracies were recruited locally, made hereditary and given exemption from civic office-holding, they drew upwards the talents and resources of local families. Those families had previously been the mainstays of their native cities. The effects are very clear in the public sculpture of Aphrodisias, an important city in south-west Asia Minor. In the first to third centuries AD local politics had been strongly contested by leading members of local families, who had memorialized themselves in hundreds of portrait statues, in local Greek dress. But from the fourth century onwards the old practice of competitive donations to the city by local dignitaries ended. Public statues were now mostly not of local citizens, but of emperors and high-ranking Roman officials. The ending of civic munificence is visible in large areas of the western empire, in Iberia, Gaul and Britain. Local elites diverted their wealth from cities to grand houses in the countryside, and also into church-building. In Britain, where cities had been of relatively new creation, there was widespread loss of civic spaces and amenities in the fourth century; of fifteen major public baths built in the first or second century AD, nine were still in use in 300, but all had gone by 400.

On the other hand, those cities that were or became the seats of provincial or regional governors benefited from the attention and wealth of the governor. Carthage, the seat of the regional governor of Africa, reached its greatest ever size by the early fifth century, some 320 hectares, with buildings displaying great wealth. Aphrodisias, which lost the civic munificence of its local citizens, became the seat of the governor of the new province of Caria. The governor was responsible for extensive building works in the fourth and early fifth centuries. These works had the aim of supporting the traditional image of the city. A fortification wall was built round the city, probably to enhance the city's prestige. Major public and civic buildings (baths, theatre, stadium) were repaired or redesigned, and two monumental gates were entirely restored.

As a result of these changes to the governance of the empire there emerged new elites, operating not at a civic, but at a regional or supra-regional level. Those who held imperial office at court had the highest prestige. Some families succeeded in maintaining their position over several generations, others had more rapid rises and falls. The career of Ausonius of Burdigala (modern Bordeaux) illustrates the latter pattern. For many years he taught literature and rhetoric in his home city, which had taken over from Augustodunum the reputation for the best centre of higher education in the west. Aged nearly 60, he was summoned to the imperial court by the emperor Valentinian to teach his young son Gratian. With Gratian's accession in 375, Ausonius obtained high imperial offices both for himself and for members of his family, which became the most important family in the western empire. On the murder of Gratian in 383, Ausonius moved back to his estates near Burdigala, and his family returned to relative obscurity. Ausonius also had renown for his poetry. He was interested in the period of the Trojan War, writing epitaphs on the heroes of the day. But he also wrote about the present. His twenty poems on famous cities rank them in order of importance, with Rome and Constantinople at the head, proudly including among five Gallic cities his native Burdigala. His most successful poem, the *Mosella*, united the classical and the contemporary by talking about the river Moselle in terms of Virgil's *Georgics*. Like other classically educated people, Ausonius was rooted both in the classical past and in the contemporary world.

Another change affecting cities of the empire was the system of Roman roads. Major arteries linked together the whole empire, from Eburacum (modern York) overland via Mediolanum and Constantinople all the way round to Alexandria in Egypt. These major arteries had been developed in the first instance for military and state purposes, going back to the early empire, but they were also used by private citizens. In 333 a wealthy pilgrim travelled from Burdigala to Jerusalem and back, along these roads, and the surviving record of the journey gives precise details of the route, which is shown on Map 33. There were three types of stop: cities or towns, hostels for overnight stays and places for changes of horse. The longest gap between any of these is about twenty Roman miles (30 kilometres), and mostly there was one or other type of stop every eight to ten miles. The travelling time from Burdigala to Jerusalem and back, at about twenty Roman miles per day, was about eight months. Such a long journey was unusual, but the major routes did provide an extraordinary degree of connection within the Roman empire. The cities lying on these routes had extra reasons to prosper, from the transit of people and goods.

A final issue that might affect cities was their relation to Christianity. Around 325 the small town of Orcistus in central Asia Minor (150 kilometres south-west of modern Ankara) petitioned the emperor Constantine for the reinstatement of the community's civic status. The Orcistans claimed that their town used to enjoy the splendour of a city, with proper magistrates, town councillors and a large number of citizens; that it lay at the junction of four roads, offering a hostel for those travelling on public business; that there was abundant water, and a forum decorated with statues of leading citizens of the past. These were not very strong claims: Orcistus was on only the lesser of the two main roads running through Asia Minor, and it did not have any notable buildings. Very strikingly, the Orcistans do not make any play with the ancient history of the city, that it was founded by Heracles or the like, claims which had been the mainstay of diplomatic arguments by Greek cities for more than seven hundred years. Instead, the Orcistans pointed out that the whole population of Orcistus were 'followers of the most holy religion', that is, Christianity. That Constantine accepted this as the clinching argument is a token of the new world created by the newly prestigious religion of Christianity.

Christianity was growing in strength, but it was not yet the official religion of the empire. The main way of understanding developments in the course of the fourth century is in terms of the relationship between Christianity and the traditional cults, each embodying different views of the past. Traditional cults continued to be practised in the fourth century, and into the fifth century in some places. Constantine himself was responsible for very few destructions of traditional temples, only those associated with Apollonius of Tyana, a first-century AD wonder-worker who had come to be seen as a rival of Christ. Subsequent emperors issued legal protection of temple structures, though they were not to be used for rituals after 389. In 391 and 392 the emperor Theodosius prohibited all sacrifices and closed all temples. Even these bans were not the end of the story, because Theodosius no longer had control of the west in 392, and the western emperor Eugenius restored some elements of the traditional cults. In 408–9, when Rome was under siege from the Goths, the Prefect of the City consulted Etruscan diviners and celebrated the ancestral rites with the Senate on the Capitol. But zealous bishops sometimes instigated direct action against temples. In 392 the great sanctuary of Serapis in Alexandria in Egypt was stormed and sacked, following provocative actions taken by the local bishop. This sack was a particular success for hardline Christians, as the sanctuary had considerable importance as a cultural centre. Only in the fifth century were more temples destroyed, and others, such as the Athenian Parthenon or the temple of Aphrodite at Aphrodisias, converted into churches; at Rome, the Pantheon was the first temple to be converted into a church, as late as 609. In the course of the fourth century, the scales were increasingly weighted against the ancient cults. In 420, a Christian priest, Isidore of Pelusium (near modern Suez) could write: 'The religion of the Greeks, made dominant for so many years by such pains, by the expenditure of such wealth, and by such feats of arms, has vanished from the earth.'

The sense of the past held by traditionalists was very different from that of Christians in the fourth century. Traditionalists continued to promote a vision of Rome's history familiar already to Cato the Elder or Virgil. An anonymous treatise on the *Origin of the Roman People* started with the earliest times, with Picus and Faunus, early kings of Latium, before reaching Aeneas, Ascanius, the kings of Alba Longa and kings of Rome. Then the treatise continued with Roman *dictatores*, and a list of Roman emperors down to Licinius (AD 324). Like Tacitus, it assumed that Rome was always ruled by autocrats. The work listed the length of each reign: for example, Aeneas 30 years; Romulus 38 years; Augustus 56 years, 4 months and 1 day. But it did not attempt any overall chronology. We might note here that counting 'ab urbe condita', from the foundation of the city, though used by scholars in the nineteenth century, was not much used by the Romans, partly because of disputes about precisely when Rome was founded. A second fourth-century AD anonymous treatise on the same subject focused entirely on the earliest times, from the kings of Latium down to Romulus' foundation of Rome. En route, it told the story of Hercules, Cacus and the Ara Maxima, and of Aeneas in Italy. Such a view of the past was very familiar, but also extremely narrow, suffering from real tunnel vision in its focus on just one city, even though that city was Rome.

Christian views of the past, by contrast, were far broader and more inclusive, though of course equally tendentious. Eusebius' *Chronicle* is one of the most remarkable intellectual achievements of the period. It became the standard account of world chronology from the birth of Abraham down to the present day. The first edition probably ended *c.* AD 311, the final went down to the twentieth year of Constantine (325/6). The original Greek text is lost, but part was translated by Jerome into Latin in the 380s, and part into Syriac and from that into Armenian. The first part of the *Chronicle* was a *Chronography*, which discussed the sources of evidence for world history. Its objective was to date Moses and the Jewish prophets in relation to the birth of Christ, and to correlate this story-line with that of the Chaldaeans, Assyrians, Medes, Lydians, Persians, Egyptians, Greeks, Macedonians (including the Successors of Alexander the Great) and Romans; unsurprisingly, given the obliteration of the history of western people conquered by Rome, there is no separate story-line for the west. The second part consisted of a *Chronological Canon*, which tabulated the various chronologies, noting all sorts of historical dates and events. It stood in the tradition of Greek chronological writing, going back to Hellanicus of Lesbos, and subsequent dating by Olympiads, but it was novel in two ways. Following the work of an earlier Christian author, Julius Africanus, it added Jewish and Christian history to the Greek chronological tradition, and for the first time in a work of chronology it used tabular form to set out the story-lines of different peoples, allowing the reader to see what happened simultaneously in different traditions. Eusebius used the birth of Abraham as the starting date of his chronology. The story-line from the birth of Abraham, via Moses and the Prophets, to the birth of Christ was the spine against which all other events were set; Eusebius worried about the seemingly earlier chronologies of the Near East and Egypt, but made them conform to his Abrahamic spine. Eusebius included the era of the sack of Troy, as established by Eratosthenes, but for Eusebius some Jewish history was much, much earlier. Cecrops became king of Athens 375 years before the sack of Troy, but the creation of the first king of Athens occurred in the thirty-fifth year of Moses, and no less than 460 years after the birth of Abraham. Similarly, 'Europa, daughter of Phoenix, had union with Zeus' 572 years after the birth of Abraham. The primacy of the biblical story-line had obvious apologetic implications in favour of Christianity in a world where religious traditions were valued in terms of their antiquity. Europa and Zeus, a primordial event for many Greeks, happened long after the start of history. And Christianity, Eusebius argued elsewhere, was of extreme antiquity, going back to the time of Abraham, and was therefore older than Judaism as reformed by Moses.

Chronologies of the past

We now call Eusebius' date for the birth of Abraham '2016 BC', and the union of Europa and Zeus '1444 BC', but Eusebius does not use this method of calculation. Counting backwards from the birth of Christ ('Before Christ') was established only in the seventeenth century, and did not come into common use before the late eighteenth century. Eusebius counts forward from the birth of Abraham to the present day. Though he noted the birth of Christ, he had no need to count forwards from it as we do ('Anno Domini'); 'AD' dates were invented only after our period. In what we call AD 526, Dionysius Exiguus, writing in Alexandria in Egypt, set out a new basis for the calculation of the correct dates for Easter. Wishing to avoid the local, Alexandrian era, which began with Diocletian, the 'impious persecutor' of the Christians, he noted years since the Incarnation, linking them to Roman chronology. But Dionysius' work was not historical. Dates from the Incarnation of Christ, one year earlier than modern AD dates, began to be used for general chronological purposes only with Bede's *Ecclesiastical History of the English People* in the eighth century.

Scaliger, one of the great scholars of the Renaissance, stood in the tradition of scholarship developed by Eusebius. His *New Work on the Correction of Chronology* (1583) discusses the main calendars, ancient and modern (Books 1–4), gives key days from the Creation to more recent times (Books 5–6), prints texts and translations of medieval Jewish, Ethiopic and Byzantine calendrical treatises (Book 7), and draws implications for contemporary calendar reform (Book 8). The book stood on the shoulders of the previous century's work on these subjects, but was extremely original and acute. For example, on the basis of a lunar eclipse before the defeat of the Persian king Darius III by Alexander the Great at Gaugamela, Scaliger argued that the battle followed the eclipse of 20 September 331 BC, rather than Eusebius' date of 328 BC (or rather,

Scaliger offered a date in his own complex dating system, which corresponds to our 331 BC). This date still stands, and is an important underpinning of our Greek chronology. In 1606 Scaliger also edited the Latin translation of Eusebius' *Chronological Canons*. Drawing on humanism, Hebrew and mathematics, he was able to show, against Eusebius and his followers in Scaliger's day, that chronology could not rest on the authority of the Bible, and that all authorities, including the Bible and Eusebius, must be subject to criticism in the search for truth. Scaliger's methods exemplify the great achievements of Renaissance humanism.

Eusebius was also responsible for establishing a new sort of historical writing. Josephus, our main source for the Jewish revolt of AD 66–70, later also wrote the *Jewish Antiquities*, a history of the Jewish people from the Creation down to the outbreak of the revolt. Inspired in part by Josephus, Eusebius wrote the first ever history of the Christian Church, from the birth of Christ 'in the forty-second year of the reign of Augustus, and the twenty-eighth after the subjugation of Egypt and the death of Antony and Cleopatra, with whom the dynasty of the Ptolemies in Egypt came to a final end', and ending with the unification of the whole empire under the Christian emperor Constantine. Eusebius, though beginning his account in what we call 2 BC, claims that Christianity is as old as the world, being foretold in the Hebrew Bible, and being a restoration of the religion practised before Moses. But this history is of Christianity as an institution, with established sequences of bishops in the major sees, and an inherent orthodoxy seeing off challenges from heresies and schisms. The manner in which he presents the history is quite different from the style of earlier Greek or Roman historians. They generally paraphrase the sources in their own words, much as we have done in this book, but large chunks of Eusebius' *Church History* consist of verbatim quotations of earlier authors and documents. The validity of the evidence was an important justification of the truth of the Church.

Emperors after Constantine were all Christians, with the exception of Julian (360–63). While a prince and still publicly a Christian, Julian was instructed in 354 by the emperor Constantius to leave Nicomedia and join him in Mediolanum, but he made a detour off the main road to visit the historic site of Troy. He was shown round by Pegasius, who despite being the local Christian bishop supported the worship of the goddess

Athena, and of the heroes Achilles and Hector 'just as we worship the martyrs'. This willingness by some Christians to favour elements of the pre-Christian past persisted, but Julian on becoming emperor declared himself a committed pagan. He promoted the traditional cults, somewhat reformulated so as to offer greater resistance to Christianity. Though he did not revive persecution of Christians, he banned them from teaching: Christians were unsuitable because such people expounded the works of Homer and Hesiod, while rejecting the gods whom those works honoured. Christian attempts to assimilate the classic literary heritage without accepting its religious values were, for Julian, absurd and unacceptable. In terms of religious practice, Julian was enthusiastic about large-scale animal sacrifices, for example at Antioch on the Orontes before the start of a campaign against the Sasanians. He even sought to bring about the rebuilding of the Temple in Jerusalem, so that the Jews could again sacrifice there, perhaps in order to drive a wedge between the Christians, who would not sacrifice, and the Jews, who would if they had a chance and would do so in a manner quite similar to traditional Greek and Roman sacrifices. According to Cyril, the contemporary bishop of Jerusalem, laying the foundations of the new Temple was halted by a disastrous earthquake that struck the region. When Julian died on his eastern campaign his dream of a revival of pagan practices died with him. In addition, Jews found themselves increasingly circumscribed by imperial legislation.

Despite the failure of Julian's policies, some aspects of traditional paganism might seem to be alive and well at the end of the fourth century AD. Take, for example, the sculpture being worked on in a sculptor's workshop at Aphrodisias at the time of its destruction, perhaps in an earthquake, in the late fourth or early fifth century. A statuette of Europa and the bull was in process of being carved, in a virtuoso fashion, from a piece of two-tone marble, so as to create a white Europa riding on a dark blue bull. Small-scale versions of other standard mythological figures were also in production: the gods Artemis, Asclepius and Aphrodite. Sculpture like this had been carved for centuries, and its display in houses and public buildings formed an important element in the historic memory of the Greek east. Scenes of classical mythology continued to feature in mosaics on the floors of houses in the Levant for the next two hundred years.

How far did such historic memories form part of a specifically religious identity at this period? How to conceptualize the issue is hotly debated. We have avoided the term 'paganism' in relation to previous periods, because it was only in the course of the third century AD, because of the growing strength of Christianity, that people came to see themselves not just as just as worshippers of Greek, Roman or other traditional gods, but also as being 'pagan'. At the same time some proponents of Christianity saw a conflict with paganism. So what sort of conflict was there between pagans and Christians? It seems that the so-called 'last pagans' of Rome in the late fourth and early fifth centuries were not hostile to Christianity, indeed some of them were in fact Christians, and their admiration for classical culture did not entail acceptance of the pagan gods. On the other hand, some Christians were responsible for serious acts of violence against pagan cults, but others attempted to find common ground. That is, there was both antagonism and assimilation.

Towards the end of the fourth century and into the fifth the classical past and its culture were much contested between pagans and Christians. Pagan senators in Rome were involved in the copying and correction of texts. For example, our texts of Livy go back to a project by the related families of the Nicomachi and Symmachi in the late fourth and early fifth centuries to edit the whole of Livy's *History*; later versions of the manuscripts preserved their 'signing-off' on sections of the *History*: 'I, Nicomachus Flavianus, senator, three-times Prefect of the City [of Rome], corrected the text at Enna'; Enna on Sicily was where his family had an estate. Such editing was not part of a co-ordinated propaganda move by the diehard pagans to preserve and transmit their culture to posterity, but equally it was not simply a private matter. Senators in Rome were known to possess large libraries. Even if critics alleged that few senators read the contents of their libraries any more, some certainly did. On their joint funeral monument, Paulina honoured her husband, Vettius Agorius Praetextatus, who died in AD 384, for his learning, that is, for his ability to improve the texts of the wise, by correcting manuscripts in Greek and Latin, prose and verse. Paulina went on to compare the transformation of texts with the much greater and more significant transformation of individuals through their initiation into mystery cults. Praetextatus was a notable pagan, and Paulina herself felt that she had been transformed by her husband, and so saved from death. That is, it was a culturally significant fact that members of the elite spent their time correcting classical manuscripts. It was also significant what texts they selected. Christians read both secular and Christian texts, but pagans read only secular texts, and could interpret them within their own religious framework.

Views of classical culture in the 420s and 430s remained highly charged. By this time all senators were Christians, but the reading of the classics remained problematic. Macrobius' *Saturnalia*, written in the 430s, was set back in AD 384, at the time of the struggles between paganism and Christianity. The work took the form of conversations between the leading pagans of the day, including Praetextatus, Symmachus and Nicomachus Flavianus, during the festival of the Saturnalia. They discuss frivolous and serious topics, such as the Saturnalia itself, and the Roman calendar, but devote most time to Virgil. Virgil is treated as the master of philosophical and religious knowledge, described as their *pontifex maximus*, the title which the Christian emperor Gratian had just repudiated. He was not just the author of a classic school text, but also the source of precise religious information. The *Saturnalia* has been seen as nostalgia for a lost age, when paganism might have been saved as an alternative to Christianity. In fact, it is more interesting than mere nostalgia. The author was no doubt a Christian, and he could not have circulated the work over his own name if it had been seen as anti-Christian, but the work, which never mentions Christianity, was a meditation upon the previous generation's dream of a revival of paganism.

Transmission of ancient texts

How do we know what ancient authors wrote? We have no ancient literary manuscripts in the authors' own hand. For Greek authors the library in Alexandria attempted to establish authoritative texts (above, pp. 159–61). The Nicomachi and Symmachi did the same for Livy, with much success: their text is far superior to an independently surviving manuscript of the same period, the early fifth century AD. How, though, do we know what these texts were? In some cases, texts, or more commonly, parts of texts, survive from antiquity: papyri from Egypt, mostly of Greek authors; or writing tablets from Vindolanda, which include odd lines of Virgil. But if we were dependent on such finds, we would be able to piece together very little classical literature. Two texts survive largely complete in antique manuscripts. Virgil survives in three manuscripts of the fifth–seventh centuries AD (see also Plate 28). And the Greek Bible, both the Old and New Testaments, is known in copies of the fourth century AD: a manuscript preserved until the nineteenth century in the Monastery of St Catherine's on Mt. Sinai, the Codex Sinaiticus, most of which is now in the British Library, and a manuscript in Rome, the Codex Vaticanus. It is no accident that two of the greatest classics of antiquity are so well preserved in antique manuscripts; oddly, the *Iliad* and *Odyssey* do not survive complete from antiquity. For other texts, we are mostly dependent on what was transmitted after antiquity. Sometimes, the transmission is a matter of translation into other languages, into Syriac and Armenian, as we saw with Eusebius, or into Arabic, as we saw with Greek scientific works (above, Chapter 5). Mostly, it is a matter of copying, and recopying, of the original in cathedrals and monasteries. The Carolingian period (751–887), notable for its interest in the classical past, was crucial: the royal court had an outstanding classical library, from which abbots and bishops could take copies. Manuscripts rarely survive from this period, but they formed the basis for the more plentiful surviving copies after around AD 1000. For Livy, we are fortunate that the edition by the Nicomachi and Symmachi was copied in the Carolingian period, and is thus the origin of our medieval manuscripts. But the line of transmission is sometimes very thin, even for major authors. Most of Tacitus' historical works are lost: of the *Annals*, Books 1–6 survive only in a single manuscript of *c.* AD 850; Books 11–16 and *Histories*, Books 1–5, survive only in another single manuscript, of the mid-eleventh century.

Against this impression of stability in paganism, we must emphasize the growing prominence of Christianity. From 312 onwards imperial patronage was put behind Christianity and not paganism, pressure was put on senators to convert to Christianity, and imperial legislation gradually defined more and more aspects of pagan religious rituals as illegal. But religious festivals continued, reinterpreted by the Christian authorities as 'amusements' and hence acceptable, though in 389 they lost their formal status as 'holidays'. The Lupercalia, for example, continued to be celebrated at Rome. It had been stripped of its accompanying sacrifices, and those who ran naked through the streets of Rome to the Forum were no longer senators, as in the time of Caesar, but hired people of low status. Gelasius, bishop of Rome (492–96), as part of a polemic against spiritual adultery on the part of Christians, criticized the leading Romans for believing that the festival brought them salvation. The Christian supporters of the festival, on the other hand, felt that the Lupercalia was an innocent carnivalesque festival, part of the heritage of Rome, tying the present back to the ancient days of Evander and Romulus.

Christian festivals in the meantime began to take over from the traditional ones. From 321 onwards Sunday possessed the status of a 'holiday', and in 389, when pagan festivals lost their protected status, the Easter period was added to Sundays as times when courts could not be held. The timing of Christian festivals sometimes also competed with paganism. In the fourth century the birth of the Sun was widely celebrated on 25 December; according to one Greek calendar, this was when 'light increases': 25 December was the winter solstice in the Julian calendar, after which the days get longer again. In the fourth century 25 December was also chosen as the date for the birth of Christ by the Church of Rome. Previously, this event had been assigned to various dates, but in an attempt to assert the theological importance of Christ, against eastern Christians who argued for the subordination of Christ to the Father, the Roman Church settled on 25 December; from Rome the festival spread to other western churches, and eventually to most eastern churches. This date had some biblical support: a prophet, Malachi, had foretold the coming of the Sun of Righteousness; and the new Christian festival would counter the popular pagan festival.

Another pagan festival at around the same time also had to be countered. The festival of the Kalends of January (1 January) was celebrated with great fervour throughout the Roman empire. The date marked the start of the Roman year, and was accompanied by the exchange of gifts, competitive feasting and drinking. Christian bishops often inveighed against it. Augustine once preached a sermon that lasted for over two and a half hours, in order to distract his congregation from the potentially corrupting festivities outside the church.

Christianity had spread rapidly during the fourth century, in comparison with the third century, increasing both its geographical coverage and the number of its adherents. A fourth-century curse tablet from the sacred spring at Aquae Sulis (modern Bath) appealed for help to 'you, lady goddess', that is, Sulis Minerva, against the thief who took six silver coins from a purse, 'whether pagan or Christian, whosoever, whether man or woman, whether boy or girl, whether slave or free'. The last three alternatives are standard in earlier curse tablets. As the purpose of the alternatives was to cover all possible categories to which the thief might belong, the novelty of the first alternative, 'whether pagan or Christian', is striking, indicating the pervasiveness of Christianity in Britain in the fourth century.

One of the mechanisms by which Christianity spread was by active, and now legal, evangelism. Martin of Tours (in central France) offers an extreme case of what was possible. Martin (died 397) was a contemporary of Ausonius, but unlike Ausonius he was an outsider to Gaul. Born in Pannonia (modern Hungary) and brought up in northern Italy, he served in the Roman army; it was while still a soldier, in his simple military dress, that he divided his cloak and gave half to a beggar. On being discharged from the army, he became a wandering Christian monk and finally bishop of Tours. He was famous for his miraculous cures, even raising people from the dead, and for his destruction of rural pagan cults. For example, in the territory of the Aedui, when attempting to destroy a pagan temple, he had to face down an angry and violent mob. Several cults in this area did indeed end in the time of Martin, with the deliberate destruction of cult images. Later local tradition even associated Martin with the site of Bibracte, the old centre of the Aedui; at the end of the fourth century, a chapel there to St Martin was built on the ruins of a temple, whose statues had been smashed. His biographer, Sulpicius Severus, writing towards the end of Martin's lifetime, was faced with a problem of how to describe such a remarkable person. Even if Homer were to reappear, he would not be able to put the life of Martin into adequate words. Martin's miracles, and his dialogues with saints and demons, were genuine, just as the miracles and dialogues with demons ascribed to Christ in the Gospels were genuine. Sulpicius was a man of classical learning, but for him the past against which Martin should be set was that of the Bible. Martin was another Apostle, whose dramatic actions fitted within an established narrative for the spread of Christianity.

By AD 400 each city in the Roman empire had its own bishop and at least one church. Huge regional councils of bishops met from time to time to decide matters of doctrine: more than three hundred mainly eastern bishops at Nicaea in 325, nearly two hundred at Constantinople in AD 381 and more than two hundred at Ephesus in 431. There were similar gatherings in the west: thirty-three western bishops at Arelate (modern Arles) in 314, but more than four hundred at Ariminum (modern Rimini) in 359, in each case including three bishops from Britain. These bishops had become prestigious figures in their own cities. It was increasingly common for them to be drawn from local aristocracies: Hilary of Limonum (modern Poitiers), the most important bishop in Gaul and a highly educated man from a good family, was more typical than Martin in this respect. Bishops also came to take on themselves the role of representing their cities to the central government. In 387, when the people of Antioch on the Orontes faced fearsome imperial retribution for a riot and the destruction of statues of the emperor, it was the bishop and monks, not the magistrates and council, who succeeded in obtaining an imperial pardon for the city. This pattern of widespread and powerful bishops would endure for centuries to come.

Monasteries were also becoming widely established by 400. The monastic movement began in Egypt under Antony (251–356) and then Pachomius. By the time Pachomius died in 346 his followers were said to number 3,000, and as many as 7,000 by the early fifth century. From Egypt the idea spread first to Palestine and then to inland Asia Minor, but it was slow to catch on elsewhere. In the west, the pioneer was Martin. He tried, but failed, to found a monastery in northern Italy soon after he ceased to be a soldier, but he did found one at Ligugé outside Hilary's city of Limonum, and another at Marmoutier outside Tours in 372, just after he became bishop there. Martin lived an ascetic life at Marmoutier with eighty monks, who were dressed not in local wool, but in rough camel hair imported from Egypt, the home of monasticism. The monks had no personal possessions, and undertook no work except for the copying of texts. Though there was debate about whether monks should do no more than pray and transcribe texts, the practices of monasticism would prove to be extremely durable.

Christian communities in the fourth century created Christian pasts for themselves through the cult of saints. Initially, the key people were those who had been martyred at the hands of the authorities in the time before Constantine. The calendar of the Church of Rome in 354 consisted almost entirely of commemorations of the deaths of third-century Roman martyrs. Apart from the birth of Christ at Bethlehem in Judaea and the anniversary of Peter becoming first bishop of Rome, all other entries were anniversaries of martyrs. Fifty-two people were commemorated on twenty-two occasions throughout the year. All died and were buried at Rome, apart from three North African martyrs, Cyprian (bishop of Carthage), and Perpetua and Felicitas, martyred in 203. There are no first- or second-century martyrs in the calendar, except for Peter and Paul, whose cult was reorganized in 258. The vision of the past implied in the calendar extended back to the beginnings of Christianity in Rome, but focused mainly on the events of the third century.

Tertullian, writing in Carthage around the time of the martyrdom of Perpetua and Felicitas, had ended his *Defence* of Christianity with a warning to the authorities that the blood of those killed was the seed of Christianity. This was a debating, and debatable, point. The prospect of bloody death in the arena was hardly a good advertisement for a minority sect. Christian leaders were not in favour of people seeking martyrdom, and indeed established proper forms of penance for Christians who had complied with orders to sacrifice. Only after the ending of persecution did cults of those put to death develop. The first Christian saints were all martyrs, but in the fifth century the cult of saints extended to include charismatic Christians who died peacefully.

Martin is an early example of this new type of saint (see Plate 30 for an eastern example). After Martin's death, Sulpicius Severus wrote letters and dialogues which retold stories about the miracles, anti-paganism and ascetic ideals of Martin. In one of the letters he claimed that Martin, with his endless sufferings, had endured a non-bloody martyrdom. At the monastery at Ligugé, soon after the death of Martin, a new shrine was built just west of Martin's original church, and at Tours his successor as bishop in 430 built a small chapel over Martin's grave. But the real growth in the local cult of Martin occurred more than fifty years after Martin's death, from the 460s onwards, and only in the sixth century did his cult become widespread, Martin being adopted by the Frankish king Clovis as his patron saint.

The building of churches in the fourth century constructed new religious topographies, and hence new readings of the past. By the time that the anonymous Burdigala pilgrim visited Palestine, as it was then known, in 333, the region had already been transformed. Constantine, in the nine years since he gained control of the east, had poured imperial resources into the region. Only two hundred years after Hadrian had transformed Athens, imperial interest had moved elsewhere, despite the memorable episode in the Acts of the Apostles of St Paul preaching in Athens.

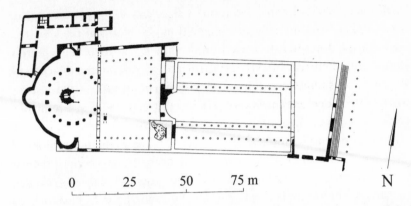

0   25   50   75 m   N

Figure 31. Floor plan of the Church of the Holy Sepulchre, Jerusalem, as built by Constantine. At the left is the monument built to enclose the shrine built over what was believed to be the tomb of Christ; in the centre was an open courtyard; and at the right a basilica, whose plan is uncertain because of later buildings.

Constantine destroyed the temple of Jupiter Capitolinus, built by Hadrian at Jerusalem after the Bar Kokhba revolt, and he built no fewer than four churches: one at Bethlehem, where Christ had been born; one on Golgotha, the place of Christ's crucifixion and also burial (see Figure 31); one on the Mount of Olives, from where Christ had risen to heaven; and one at Mamre (near modern Hebron), where Abraham had entertained three angels unawares and received the prophecy that he would be the father of a multitude of nations. Constantine's choice of locations for these churches was guided by existing Christian traditions about these places. In the case of Mamre, he took one of the three angels to be Christ, the first appearance of God to the world; he had also been warned by Eutropia, his mother-in-law, that she had seen the spot defiled by pagan ceremonies, but his decision to build a church here reminds us of how the birth of Abraham was the starting point of world chronology for Eusebius.

The record made by the Burdigala pilgrim shows how Palestine was seen at this early date. The description of the journey to and from Palestine consists largely of a bare list of the staging posts, but in Palestine the text gives instead a very rich account of the historical importance of the places visited. The pilgrim was interested in the entire run of biblical history, mentioning thirty-two places linked to the Old Testament, and twenty-one to the New. In Jerusalem, the text talks about the pools by the Temple of Solomon, Solomon's palace (above, p. 56), and within the Temple of Solomon an altar marked by the blood of the Christian Zacharias; it notes that Jews were allowed each year to anoint a pierced stone here, mourn and rend their garments. In Jericho, the pilgrim saw the house of Rachel the harlot, which plays an important part in Joshua's story of the falling of the walls of Jericho (above, p. 54). The pilgrim also commented, very favourably, on Constantine's four churches, but was also interested in landmarks not flagged by buildings: the tree which Zacchaeus climbed in order to see Christ, or the place where Christ was baptized in the river Jordan and where the prophet Elijah was taken up to heaven. The author is barely interested in contemporary Jews, and not at all in the non-biblical history and cults of the region: there is no mention at all that there had been a temple of Jupiter Capitolinus in Jerusalem. As was true for many later pilgrims, the past of the Burdigala pilgrim was entirely biblical, but from the perspective of Christianity. The land the Jews regarded as their holy land was now a Christian holy land.

In Palestine, because contemporary Jews were very weak politically, the creation of new topographies of the past was rapid and unproblematic. Elsewhere, there were real struggles over memory, for example at the temple and oracle of Apollo at Daphne outside Antioch on the Orontes. The local story about the origins of this shrine was that Seleucus I (308–281 BC), out hunting one day, came upon a tree, which he believed was the one into which Daphne, daughter of the local river-god, had transformed herself in order to escape the clutches of Apollo. The unearthing by the hoof of Seleucus' horse of a golden arrowhead with Apollo's name on it confirmed that the god continued to frequent the place. The story of Apollo and Daphne, known all over Greece and beyond, was still being told in Antioch in the third and fourth centuries AD. Here it was made to relate to a local cult, as had long been done in Greece with other stories about the gods and heroes. In the mid-third century AD one Babylas was martyred at Antioch, and was buried there. But in 353, Gallus, Caesar to the emperor Constantius and living at that time at Antioch, transferred the remains of Babylas the 9 kilometres from Antioch to Daphne. Here he built a mausoleum for Babylas, which became a centre for Christian worship.

In 362, Julian, Gallus' brother, now emperor, was horrified at the lack of piety at Antioch, blaming the city for neglecting the festival of Apollo.

He took it upon himself to restore the temple and statue of Apollo at Daphne, and attempted to revive the oracle and to cleanse the sacred spring, which had long since ceased to flow. The spring did not restart. When he was told that this was because of pollution caused by the presence of the body of Babylas, he had the remains taken back to their original burial spot in the city. However, as soon as the body re-entered the city, the temple roof mysteriously caught fire, and the ancient statue of Apollo was destroyed. Julian was furious. When a tribunal failed to identify the culprits, he punished the Christians collectively, shutting their principal church and confiscating its goods.

This whole story was much contested between pagans and Christians: the pagan Libanius and the Christian John Chrysostom, both locals of Antioch, had very different takes on it. Libanius, immediately after the events, wrote a dirge-like lament on the destruction of the temple, and its dreadful consequences for traditional religion. John Chrysostom, twenty years later, took the burning of the temple as divine retribution on Julian and his pro-pagan policies, but also talked about how the presence of Babylas at Daphne improved the moral climate of the place, the dissolute and depraved becoming restrained, as under the gaze of their teacher. The case of Babylas and Daphne is a wonderful example of conflicting attempts to memorialize religious places, and hence to emphasize different pasts.

The religious changes, accommodations and conflicts of the fourth century AD need to be seen in the context of major differences between Greek and Roman religion on the one hand, and Christianity on the other. Greek and Roman religion did not have sacred texts, or congregational temples, but did have both male and female deities, and both male and female priests. Christianity had had both male and female martyrs, and female prophets, but by the fourth century AD there were only male priests and bishops. The change in gendered authority aligned Christianity with Judaism as a (male) religion of the Book.

Augustine in the late fourth and early fifth century offers us a Christian perspective on the religious and cultural changes that had been taking place for the previous hundred years and more. Standing at the tipping point between the ancient and the medieval western worlds, he developed especially influential views on the classical past and present. His writings were arguably the most important Latin texts in the west for the next thousand years. Not long after the laying of the Lullingstone mosaic, with which this chapter opened, the young Augustine (born 354) was following the traditional educational curriculum in North Africa. As boys had done for centuries, he studied with *grammatici*, and loved reading Virgil. He wept for the death of Dido, and first made his mark at school with a speech that the jealous Juno might have made when watching Aeneas leave Carthage for Italy. He went on to study rhetoric, and began a meteoric rise, teaching rhetoric in Carthage and Rome, before becoming professor of rhetoric at Mediolanum (Milan) in 384. Augustine's mastery of Latin, and the standard curriculum, was clearly extraordinary. Not that such knowledge was easy to acquire, even for the most able: Augustine found that after he had been in Mediolanum for two years the Italians still mocked his African pronunciation. And in North Africa, some of the more remote towns remained primarily Punic-speaking in the early fifth century AD.

Following his very successful career in rhetoric, Augustine came to a new understanding of Christianity, was ordained priest at Hippo (modern Annaba in Algeria) in 391, and then bishop in 395. As bishop, his rhetorical skills remained important, and his Latin sermons became famous, which is why hundreds of them survive. Quite a few have only recently been discovered in libraries, first appearing in print between 1981 and 2009. Many were addressed to his existing flock on matters of doctrine or practice. Two of his recently discovered sermons were delivered on the feasts of African martyrs, Cyprian, and Perpetua and Felicitas. The latter pair was honoured, according to Augustine, not just as women, but as wives and, in the case of Perpetua, as mother, in which roles they were exemplars to everyone. Augustine talked about the vision of Perpetua of a black Egyptian, which was fulfilled in her victory over the devil; both Perpetua and Felicitas were triumphant despite their weakness as women. Some sermons dealt with the need for unity in the Church, following an imperial ruling that sought to suppress a long-standing breakaway Church. Others offered arguments designed to attract adherents of paganism over to Christianity. Augustine sometimes left Hippo to preach in the region of northern Tunisia and north-eastern Algeria. Christianity had only recently spread to some areas that he visited. Preaching at Tignica (modern Ain Tounga in Tunisia), Augustine noted that the whole congregation was made up of children of pagan parents. Elsewhere, he had to admit that he had been unable to convert educated pagans, and that the problem was the greater the more educated they were. At Boseth (in the Medjerda valley of Algeria–Tunisia), he preached twice to a congregation that included educated pagans, presumably specially invited for the occasions. The pagans held that the soul needed purification through pagan rituals, which placated the traditional gods and made possible ascent to the supreme deity. How could Christians object to this, as they ascribe a mediating role to Christ and the martyrs, who have an important place in their calendar? Augustine responded that the pagan philosophers' view of the soul needed to be modified, in that the soul, as they saw it, was less than divine, and that their purificatory practices depended on human pride. In other sermons, he had to face Christians who thought that paganism offered an alternative, and acceptable, path to God. This was the argument which some pagans had developed when arguing for the legitimacy of continued pagan practices in Rome, but Augustine would have none of it. There was only one path to the true God, and that was via the one Church.

In 397, two years after he became bishop, Augustine decided to write a spiritual autobiography outlining his progress towards Christianity. The *Confessions* is strikingly modern, and remains a gripping work. It deals with the facts of his life, down to his conversion to Christianity, ending with the death of his mother Monica in 387, as they waited to return home. It includes his successive conversions, to philosophy, thanks to reading a treatise by Cicero, to Manichaeism, a religion inspired in part by Persian ideas, which propounded an eternal struggle between Good and Evil, and which Diocletian had tried to stamp out, and to a version of Christianity much influenced by the thought of Plato. But having recounted events in Books 1–9, in Book 10 he develops an original theory of memory. The first books offered his memory of the failings of his past life and of his movement towards God, but the point of the work was to point the reader too towards God. How was it possible for anyone to seek God, and hence the happy life, which lay beyond ordinary sense perceptions? Augustine argues that it is through remembrance of something he has lost. Memory of God is like remembering joy, which all humans once knew, before Adam and the Fall. Augustine's theory of memory links together his past, present and future. As a condition for knowledge and understanding, memory explains his past, reveals his full identity, and mediates God's presence to him and his readers. The idea that the full meaning of memory could be seen only in a religious context would be important also for Augustine's handling of cultural memory.

At the same time as he was writing the *Confessions*, Augustine also turned his thoughts to classical education. The young Augustine may have wept for Dido, but he came to argue in the *Confessions* that this passion had blinded him to his true spiritual position. He was therefore ambivalent about Virgil, despite the fact that he knew the text by heart, and that he considered it to be written in far better Latin than the existing Latin Bible. In *On Christian Doctrine*, he handles at length the relationship between Christians and classical culture. The Bible was, of course, primary. Like other books, it was also complex, requiring sophisticated techniques of interpretation, not simply acceptance of authority. It also required a breadth of knowledge in Hebrew and the history of the Near East not possessed by those educated merely in the classics. But Augustine does not argue that the Bible alone should be studied, nor that extra-biblical education is unnecessary for a good Christian. Instead, he argues that culture is a social phenomenon, the extension of language. Even pagan religion is a social construct, with sacrifices a means of communication between humans and demons. In literature, religion is not a source of danger to Christians. Contrary to the view implied in Macrobius' *Saturnalia*, Virgil in describing sacrifices does not inspire religious feelings on the part of pagans, and need not inspire horror on the part of Christians. The pagan gods are simply 'traditional forms, laid down by humans, adjusted to the needs of human society, with which we cannot dispense in this life', and as such can be put to Christian use. Virgil and the other Latin classics were at a stroke made unthreatening, and could thus continue to serve as the basis for European education in a Christian age.

Augustine also began to think about Rome and the Roman empire, and its relationship to the Christian faith. He might have reacted to Rome as the whore of Babylon, as did St John of Patmos (above, p. 298). Or he might have treated the empire as the work of divine providence and the emperor as the vice-regent of God on earth, as Eusebius had argued. In fact, he did neither. His interest in the biblical theme of the two cities, the divine and the human, was already established when the actual city of Rome was sacked by the Goths in 410. It is one of the ironies of history that Augustine could look at the troubles afflicting Rome and Italy from the stability of North Africa, seemingly remote from invasions; a further irony is that the Vandals, a tribe originating in Poland, which had fought its way down through Gaul and Iberia, invaded North Africa in 429 and conquered Carthage in 439. In the course of AD 410–11, Augustine preached four sermons on the sack of Rome, but was faced with a challenging audience of refugees from Rome, who were Christian in name but classical in allegiance. The need to address waverers like these was the precipitating factor that led him to start writing the *City of God*, which appeared in sections between 413 and 425.

The *City of God* turned out to be the longest work of argumentative Latin ever written, excluding narrative histories like Livy, or codes of law. It has a complex structure, summed up by Augustine in a letter written to accompany a copy he was sending to a pagan friend, Firmus. The first five books were written against those who maintain that the worship of the gods, or rather demons, leads to happiness in this life. The next five books were written against those who think that such worship brings happiness in the next life. Then three groups of four books each describe the origin of the heavenly city, its development and the ends in store for it. The argument required that Augustine spend much time on Roman culture and history. In the first section, denying that paganism leads to happiness in this life, he writes at length on the material ills of Rome before the coming of Christ. The gods had no good reason for allowing the destruction of Troy. They did not avenge Romulus' murder of his brother Remus. Under the kings, Rome's lust for power, at the price of so much blood, resulted in the expansion of Rome's border only twenty Roman miles from the city, which would hardly stand comparison with the territory of a contemporary North African city. On the period after the sack of Carthage in 146 BC, Augustine stresses the violence in Rome from the Gracchi down to Augustus, and the massacre of Romans in Asia by Mithradates. All these disasters occurred while the pagan gods were worshipped at Rome. Subsequently, Augustine admits that some ancient Romans, such as Julius Caesar, possessed virtues, a point claimed strongly by contemporary pagans, but he argues that their virtues were unable to control the forces of moral corruption, and that they were not real virtues in comparison with those of the saints.

The second half of the *City of God*, on the origins, history and ends of the two cities, outlines human history from the Creation down to the time of David and Solomon, on the basis of the biblical accounts. The work then pauses to sketch the history of the human city, in opposition to the heavenly city, down to the coming of Christ, with the Assyrians and then the Romans as the principal examples of the human city. Augustine adopts the chronological framework established by Eusebius, as known to him in the Latin translation by Jerome, which as we have seen pegged other civilizations to a biblical story-line. So it was in the period after the departure of Israel from Egypt that cults of the false gods were introduced to Greece, and Europa was carried off from Phoenicia to Crete, though, according to Augustine, the contemporary pagans held that she was carried off by a king of Crete and that the story about Zeus and the bull was a mere popular fable. Augustine dates the arrival of Aeneas in Italy to the time when Menestheus was king of Athens, Polyphides king of Sicyon, Tantanes king of Assyria, and Labdon judge of Israel, just as Eusebius had done. This meticulous writing of the parallel histories of the two cities ended with the coming of Christ and the Church. Now the two are intermixed, and will be so until they are separated by the Last Judgement. Very remarkably, Augustine presents Rome as just another purely human institution, whose role could in principle be taken over by other states. How this came to pass is the subject of volume 2 of the Penguin History of Europe, *The Inheritance of Rome*.

Memories of the past within Classical antiquity have been the main recurrent theme within this book. Such memories of course do not start then, as we saw in relation to Bronze Age memories of the past, but from the early first millennium BC onwards two main sets of memories were, or became, important. The dominant one, first for Greeks and then for Romans, related various present days back to the time of the Trojan War and beyond. As peoples once peripheral to the Greek world sought to secure a place for themselves in that world, they related their pasts to the remote Greek past. Aeneas' journey from the burning Troy, via Carthage, to Italy became a repeated point of reference for people throughout the Roman world. The narrative of the rise of Rome, starting with Aeneas and Romulus, which was treated by Augustine as the main earthly city, formed part of the new ideological package transmitted to a Christian Europe. The other set of memories was that of the Israelites, consolidated in the sixth century BC, as a result of the experience of exile in Babylon. These memories were a defining force for the Jews, partially responsible for their revolts from Rome, but they remained particular to the Jews until they were partially adopted also by Christians, and so formed part of Augustine's history of the heavenly city.

Memories defined, united and divided peoples in the ancient world, but other factors were also important. Languages were key. Greek became the dominant language in the eastern Mediterranean, no doubt explaining why the first Christian texts, including the New Testament, were written not in Aramaic, the language of Jesus, but in Greek. Similarly, Latin became the dominant language in the west. In the early empire, the Roman elite prided itself on being seriously bilingual in Latin and Greek, but such bilingualism was limited to the elite, and did not endure. Christian texts were translated into Latin from an early date, and even someone as highly educated as Augustine knew little Greek. The division of the empire between east and west, first under Diocletian, and again from the end of the fourth century, followed this deeply rooted linguistic division between the two languages.

In the east, the imperial government retained control and cities prospered until the seventh century AD. The Sasanians continued to be a threat in the east, and in the early seventh century they succeeded in gaining control of much of the imperial east, though they were beaten back. In their weakened state, the Sasanians succumbed to a new coalition of Arab tribes led by Muhammad from 622 until his death in 632. The rapidly growing power of the Arabs marks a new stage in the history of the Near East, and of Europe.

The changes in the east are encapsulated in the building of the Dome of the Rock at Jerusalem. Arab control of Jerusalem began in around 640. The new Ummayad caliph Abd al-Malik in year 72 of the hegira (Muhammad's migration to Medina), the equivalent of AD 691–2, ordered the construction of the Dome of the Rock, as part of his proclamation of Islam as the ideological basis of Arab rule. This extraordinary building, not a mosque as it is not designed for prayer, is essentially an octagonal shell round an exposed piece of bedrock of the Temple Mount. This was the same piece of rock that the Burdigala pilgrim had reported as being sacred to Jews lamenting the destruction of the Temple; since at least the third century BC, Jews had also believed that Abraham's binding and near-sacrifice of his son Isaac had once taken place on this hill. Dominating the skyline of Jerusalem, the building marked the symbolic takeover of Jerusalem by the new rulers. But it also had particular meaning for Muslims. From the outset, they recognized Jerusalem as an important religious spot. According to early traditions, Muhammad was taken on a mystical Night Journey from Mecca to Jerusalem. At the Rock, the angel Gabriel told him that this was where God had ascended to heaven having created the earth, leaving behind him traces of his feet. This would also be the spot for the Last Judgement. Because of the position of Jerusalem in Jewish and Christian thought, the city in general, and the Rock in particular, had special significance for the beginning and end of things. Only in later traditions, from the eleventh century onwards, but usually repeated today, was the Rock the place from which Muhammad himself, on his Night Journey to Jerusalem, ascended to heaven to contemplate the universe, leaving *his* footprints behind.

The Dome of the Rock displays two huge mosaic texts, 240 metres long, on the inside and outside of the octagonal arcade inside the building. Dating to AD 691–2, they are almost the earliest datable Muslim texts. Both select and combine verses from the Qur'an to make powerful statements of the new religion. The text on the inside of the arcade begins: 'In the name of God, the Merciful, the Compassionate. There is no god but God. He is One. He has no associate . . . Muhammad is the servant of God and His Messenger.' The target of this claim was not just pagan polytheism, but more pressingly Christianity. 'The Messiah, Jesus son of Mary, was only a Messenger of God, and His Word which He conveyed unto Mary, and a spirit from Him. So believe in God and His messengers, and say not "Three".' Jesus was respected as a Messenger, and the days on which he was born, died and *will be* raised again were also respected, but 'it does not befit God that he should take unto himself a son'. These are vigorously polemical statements. The Dome of the Rock illustrates how earlier traditions of Jews and Christians, the earlier people of the Book, were adapted and incorporated into Islam, but it also demonstrates Islam's claim to radical novelty.

In the west, the fragmentation of imperial control was beginning already by AD 425. Britain had been lost, the Vandals were about to overrun North Africa, Gaul and Iberia would soon include areas controlled by barbarian allies of Rome. When Rutilius Namatianus sailed home from Rome to Gaul in 417 he wrote a poem praising the greatness of Rome and congratulating the general Constantius for defeating the Goths in Iberia. Rutilius, a pagan, noted that thanks to Rome's temples he was not far from heaven, and acknowledged the dual origins of the Roman race in Venus and Mars — mother of the sons of Aeneas, father of the descendants of Romulus. As he sails up the west coast of Italy, Rutilius notes with pleasure the continued performance of pagan rituals, and inveighs against both monks and Jews. He comments, in somewhat melancholy fashion, on the change and decay in the places which he passes, such as Pyrgi or 'desolate Cosa's ancient and unguarded ruins and dreadful walls', but the remote past remains a firm point of reference. At Pisa, where he had once served in the imperial palace, he recalls fondly the antiquity of the city: as a colony of Elis, which was the home of the Olympic games, the foundation of Pisa predated the arrival of Aeneas from Troy. Rutilius still conceives of himself leaving the centre (Rome) to return home to the periphery (Gaul). That is, he still thinks of himself as living in the world covered in this history of Classical Europe. In fact he is at the brink of the new world. Here the peripheries were becoming centres in their own right, with Gaul doing much better than Rome by the turn of the fifth century AD.

Views of the past in this new world varied in different parts of the west. In southern Gaul a remote monastery, now known as Saint-Guilhem-le-Désert, was founded in 804 by Count Guilhem. He had gained great glory in fighting back the Arabs from Gaul, but decided to retire as a monk. His cousin, the emperor Charlemagne, gave the monastery a fragment of the True Cross. In the twelfth or thirteenth century, at the time when a cult of Guilhem was developing, a fourth-century Christian sarcophagus was restored to hold the relics of the founder, a sixth/seventh-century sarcophagus was reused for his sisters Albane and Bertrane, and Roman busts were built into the façade of the main door of the church. Despite massive changes in political systems, this region could connect itself back to the Roman past. In Britain, things were different. Here, Romanization was more limited than in Gaul, in both extent and depth. Claims did come to be made about the Trojan origin of the Britons, but urbanization was collapsing even before the end of Roman rule. By the eighth century AD an Old English poet could reflect upon the ruins before him, probably those of Bath, that encapsulated complete collapse, and imagines the lives that had once been lived there:

> Splendid this rampart is, though fate destroyed it,
> The city buildings fell apart, the works
> Of giants crumble. Tumbled are the towers,
> Ruined the roofs, and broken the barred gate,
> Frost in the plaster, all the ceilings gape,

Torn and collapsed and eaten up by age . . .
Resolute masons, skilled in rounded building
Wondrously linked the framework with iron bonds.
The public halls were bright, with lofty gables,
Bath-houses many; great the cheerful noise,
And many mead-halls filled with human pleasures,
Till mighty fate brought change upon it all.
Slaughter was widespread, pestilence was rife,
And death took all those valiant men away.
The martial halls became deserted places,
The city crumbled, its repairers fell,
Its armies to the earth. And so these halls
Are empty, and this red curved roof now sheds
Its tiles, decay has brought it to the ground,
Smashed it to piles of rubble, where long since
A host of heroes, glorious, gold-adorned,
Gleaming in splendour, proud and flushed with wine,
Shone in their armour, gazed on gems and treasure,
On silver, riches, wealth and jewellery,
On this bright city with its wide domains.
Stone buildings stood, and the hot stream cast forth
Wide sprays of water, which a wall enclosed
In its bright compass, where convenient
Stood hot baths ready for them at the centre.
Hot streams poured forth over the clear grey stone,
To the round pool and down into the baths.

(trans. R. F. Leslie)

17. Statue of a richly clad woman making an offering, from sanctuary of Cerro de los Santos (south-east Iberia), early third century BC (p. 212). The hair-style and clothing are local, but the carving of the drapery and the head borrows from Greek sculpture of 250 years previously.

18. A reconstruction of the third-century BC harbours at Carthage (cf. p. 214). On the right is the commercial harbour. A narrow passage through a double wall, which could be shut off by chains, led to the circular military harbour. Two hundred warships were docked round the outside and round the central circular island; on top of the island was the admiral's headquarters, affording a good view out to sea.

19. The rugged landscape of Sphakia, south-west Crete, was exploited differently throughout antiquity: large Bronze Age site on the plain in the foreground (1); hilltop site in the Early Iron Age (2); Greek site on a lower hill (3); and Roman farms on the plain (p. 59).

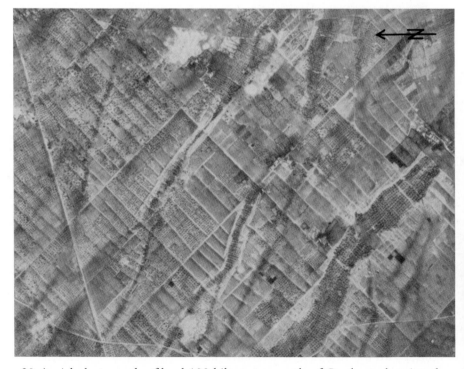

20. Aerial photograph of land 100 kilometres south of Carthage showing the Roman division of land (centuriation) into squares with sides of 710 metres. The straight line of a Roman road cuts across the direction of the centuriation.

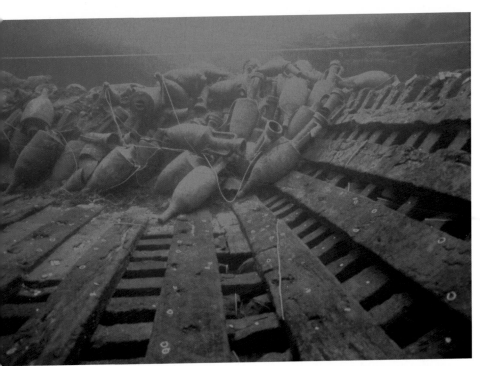

21. Roman trading ship wrecked at Madrague de Giens (off southern France), *c.* 75–60 BC. Its cargo of 600 wine jars came from just south of Rome (pp. 235–6).

22. Palmyra in the Syrian desert, in an oasis of date palms (p. 293). The main street, unpaved because it was for camels, not wagons, leads up to the colossal square sanctuary of Bel. The rebuilding of the city in the first century AD was paid for from the profits of the caravan trade.

23. Procession of priests and the imperial family, including women and children, from one side of the Ara Pacis, Rome, 13 BC. Note how Augustus, the third main figure from the left, does not stand out (p. 244).

24. *Boadicea and her Daughters* by Thomas Thornycroft, placed near the British Houses of Parliament in 1902 (pp. 260–61).

25. Aphrodisias, south-west Asia Minor. In the first century AD a grand approach to the local temple to Augustus was built (p. 255). Three-storey colonnades were adorned with relief sculpture.

26. The Porta Nigra at Augusta Treverorum (Trier, Germany), *c.* AD 160–180, a defensive show piece (p. 305).

27. Education, crucial to the Roman empire, is here caricatured on a terracotta relief lamp (first century BC/ first century AD): a donkey, seated in a high-backed chair, with a wax tablet in his left hand and a stick in his right, is surrounded by three monkey pupils; six more monkey pupils are seated, with their wax tablets on their knees.

28. An illustration of the *Aeneid* in the Vatican Virgil, dating to the fourth century AD (pp. 317–18): Aeneas sails away from Carthage, leaving Dido distraught, at an upper window.

29. Mosaic of Europa and the Bull from a house at Lullingstone, south-east England, mid fourth century AD. The verse couplet along the top alludes to Virgil's *Aeneid*: 'Invida si ta[auri] vidisset Iuno natatus, Iustius Aeolias isset adusque domos' (for translation see p. 301).

30. Church of St Simeon, Syria (see p. 322). Simeon lived for 37 years (AD 422–459) on top of a tall pillar. After his death a huge church was built round the pillar, whose stump is seen here.

31a. Alexander the Great, with ram's horn (alluding to Alexander's special relationship with Zeus Ammon), on a coin of Lysimachus, ruler of Thrace, 297/6–282/1 bc (p. 151).

31b. Flamininus, Roman conqueror of Macedonia, on a gold coin struck in Greece, 196 bc: a mixture of Hellenistic royal portraiture and Roman traits (p. 171).

31c. The Italic bull goring the Roman wolf, on coinage of Italic rebels, *c.* 90 bc, with the legend (in Oscan) 'víteliú' and mint control letter 'A' at top (pp. 221–2).

31d. The portrait of Mithradates (89/8 bc; p. 232) echoes the image of Alexander (Plate 31a), part of his self-fashioning as a traditional Hellenistic monarch.

31e. Kneeling Parthian (in un-Roman trousers) returns the Roman standards captured at Carrhae (p. 246). The legend reads: 'Caesar Augustus received the standards'.

31f. The Temple at Jerusalem, as imagined on coins of Jewish rebels, AD 134/5, with the legend in Hebrew 'Shimon' (p. 284).

Further Reading

In what follows, we do not list the sources or the works of scholarship, in many languages, which underpin what we have written. Instead, we offer a guide to relevant works in English, including some modern historical novels, that we hope will interest and excite readers. We also include translations of some key ancient texts, and give pointers to memorable places to visit. Where possible, we have included online resources.

INTRODUCTION

How societies think about and use their pasts has been explored in a number of important works. Paul Connerton, *How Societies Remember* (Cambridge: Cambridge University Press, 1989), and James Fentress and Chris Wickham, *Social Memory* (Oxford: Blackwell, 1992) are pioneering general studies. The place of monuments in the construction of social memory has been explored by Susan E. Alcock, *Archaeologies of the Greek Past: Landscape, Monuments and Memory* (Cambridge: Cambridge University Press, 2002); Ruth M. Van Dyke and Susan E. Alcock (eds.), *Archaeologies of Memory* (Oxford: Blackwell, 2003); and Lucia F. Nixon, 'Chronologies of Desire and the Uses of Monuments: Eflatunpınar to Çatalhöyük and Beyond', in David Shankland (ed.), *Anthropology, Archaeology and Heritage in the Balkans and Anatolia, or The Life and Times of F. W. Hasluck (1878–1920)* (Istanbul: Isis, 2004; freely available online at: http://tinyurl.com/qo87mc).

Stimulating introductions to the various uses of the classical past in more recent epochs are offered by: Mary Beard and John Henderson, *Classics: A Very Short Introduction* (Oxford: Oxford University Press, 1995); Simon Goldhill, *Who Needs Greek? Contests in the Cultural History of Hellenism* (Cambridge: Cambridge University Press, 2002), and his *Love, Sex and Tragedy: How the Ancient World Shapes our Lives* (London: John Murray, 2004). Richard Jenkyns, *The Victorians and Ancient Greece* (Oxford: Blackwell, 1980), and *Dignity and Decadence: Victorian Art and the Classical Inheritance* (London: HarperCollins, 1991), explore Victorian literature and art. Anthony Pagden (ed.), *The Idea of Europe from*

Antiquity to the European Union (Cambridge: Cambridge University Press, 2002) examines changing ideas of Europe down to the present.

CHAPTER 1: THE AEGEAN WORLD: MINOANS, MYCENAEANS AND TROJANS: *c.* 1750–1100 BC

Barry Cunliffe, *Europe Between the Oceans: 9000 BC–AD 1000* (New Haven and London: Yale University Press, 2008), ch. 7, outlines the Bronze Age, from Britain to the Near East, with great lucidity. For clear histories of the discovery of the Greek Bronze Age, see William A. MacDonald and Carol G. Thomas, *Progress into the Past: The Rediscovery of the Mycenaean Civilisation*, 2nd edn. (Bloomington: Indiana University Press, 1990); and J. Lesley Fitton, *The Discovery of the Greek Bronze Age* (London: British Museum Press, 1995; Cambridge, Mass: Harvard University Press, 1996). Cynthia W. Shelmerdine (ed.), *The Cambridge Companion to the Aegean Bronze Age* (Cambridge: Cambridge University Press, 2008), is the best single volume covering Crete and mainland Greece in this period.

The excavations of Heinrich Schliemann at Troy are described by Hervé Duchêne, *The Golden Treasures of Troy: The Dream of Heinrich Schliemann* (London: Thames and Hudson, 1996). The work of Sir Arthur Evans is best approached in the well-illustrated, brief account by Ann Brown, *Arthur Evans and the Palace of Minos* (Oxford: Ashmolean Museum, 1983); Alexandre Farnoux, *Knossos: Unearthing a Legend* (London: Thames and Hudson, 1996), is also attractively produced. J. A. MacGillivray, *Minotaur: Sir Arthur Evans and the Archaeology of the Minoan Myth* (London: Jonathan Cape, 2000), offers more details.

Modern responses to Knossos can be approached through Pierre Vidal-Naquet, *The Atlantis Story: A Short History of Plato's Myth* (Exeter: University of Exeter Press, 2007), a critical analysis of responses to Plato's myth of Atlantis, and Theodore Ziolkowski, *Minos and the Moderns: Cretan Myth in Twentieth-Century Literature and Art* (Oxford: Oxford University Press, 2008).

Two online resources offer introductions to the Aegean Bronze Age: Jeremy B. Rutter, *Prehistoric Archaeology of the Aegean*, http://projectsx.dartmouth.edu/history/bronze_age/ (2000), is a systematic introduction to the whole of Bronze Age Greece; Lucia Nixon and Simon Price, *Archaeology for Amateurs: The Mysteries of Crete*, http://crete.classics.ox.ac.uk/ (2002: created for an online course, but now freely available), covers the whole history of Crete from the Bronze Age to the end of the nineteenth century.

For the Near Eastern context, Marc Van De Mieroop, *A History of the Ancient Near East, ca. 3000–323 BC*, 2nd edn. (Malden, Mass., and Oxford: Blackwell, 2007), chs. 6–9, provides an excellent introductory account of the whole Near East. John Baines and Jaromir Málek, *Atlas of Ancient Egypt* (Oxford: Phaidon, 1980), is an illustrated and authoritative history of Egypt. Trevor R. Bryce, *The Kingdom of the Hittites*, 2nd edn. (Oxford: Oxford University Press, 2005), is the best starting point on the Hittite kingdom of Asia Minor. William L. Moran, *The*

Amarna Letters (Baltimore and London: Johns Hopkins University Press, 1992), translates the letters between the Egyptian pharaoh Akhenaten and various rulers in the Near East. The late director of the current excavations at Troy, Manfred Korfmann, outlines his views on an old question, 'Was there a Trojan War?', *Archaeology*, 57 (2004), online at http://www.archaeology.org/0405/etc/troy. html.

There are many wonderful Bronze Ages sites to visit. The 'Blue Guide' to Crete is the most detailed guidebook on the Bronze Age archaeology of the island (7th edn., London: A. & C. Black, 2003). For Sphakia in particular, see the website by Lucia Nixon, Jennifer Moody, Simon Price and Oliver Rackham, *The Sphakia Survey: Internet Edition*, http://sphakia.classics.ox.ac.uk (2000). For mainland Greece, including Mycenae, Tiryns and Pylos, the best guidebook is Christopher Mee and Antony Spawforth, *Greece: An Oxford Archaeological Guide* (Oxford: Oxford University Press, 2001). For Troy, there is an official excavation website: http://www.uni-tuebingen.de/troia/eng/index.html. The director and staff of the excavations, Manfred Korfmann and Dietrich Mannsperger, have written their own guidebook: *A Guide to Troia* (Istanbul: Ege Yayınları, 1999).

CHAPTER 2: THE MEDITERRANEAN, THE LEVANT AND MIDDLE EUROPE: 1100–800 BC

For the Near East in this period, see Marc Van De Mieroop, *A History of the Ancient Near East, ca. 3000–323 BC*, 2nd edn. (Malden, Mass., and Oxford: Blackwell, 2007), chs. 11–12. The best modern introduction to the Phoenicians is Maria Eugenia Aubet, *The Phoenicians and the West: Politics, Colonies and Trade*, 2nd edn. (Cambridge: Cambridge University Press, 2001). The history and archaeology of Israel are highly controversial topics. Kathleen M. Kenyon, *The Bible and Recent Archaeology*, revised edn. by Roger Moorey (London: British Museum Publications, 1987), chs. 4–5, is a classic, older account. A clear analysis of the biblical texts is offered by J. Maxwell Miller and John H. Hayes, *A History of Ancient Israel and Judah*, 2nd edn. (London: SCM, 1999). William G. Dever, *What did the Biblical Writers Know and When Did They Know It? What Archaeology Can Tell Us About the Reality of Ancient Israel* (Grand Rapids, Mich., and Cambridge: Eerdmans, 2001), uses archaeological evidence in a very well-informed way, in support of the biblical outlines of early Israelite history. Israel Finkelstein and Neil A. Silberman, *The Bible Unearthed: Archaeology's New Vision of Ancient Israel and the Origin of its Stories* (New York and London: Simon and Schuster, 2001), are also well informed on archaeological evidence, but argue that it does not support the biblical narratives; their claim that the strata of some key sites should be down-dated from the period of Solomon (on the basis of new radiocarbon dates) has not yet been supported.

The best introductions to the Greek world in this period are: Robin Osborne, *Greece in the Making, 1200–479 BC* (London and New York: Routledge, 1996;

2nd edn. 2009), ch. 2, and Jonathan M. Hall, *A History of the Archaic Greek World ca. 1200–479 BCE* (Oxford: Blackwell, 2007), ch. 3. On Lefkandi, the first publication of the 'Toumba' excavation remains informative: Mervyn Popham, E. Touloupa, and L. H. Sackett, 'The Hero of Lefkandi', *Antiquity*, 56 (1981), pp. 169–74, available as free pdf file at: http://antiquity.ac.uk/ant/056/Ant560169. htm. The site as a whole is presented by Christopher Mee and Antony Spawforth, *Greece: An Oxford Archaeological Guide* (Oxford: Oxford University Press, 2001), pp. 337–41.

On Italy, Rome and the Etruscans, see: T. J. Cornell, *The Beginnings of Rome: Italy and Rome from the Bronze Age to the Punic Wars (c. 1000–264 BC)* (London: Routledge, 1995), ch. 2, and Graeme Barker and Tom Rasmussen, *The Etruscans* (Oxford: Blackwell, 1998), ch. 2. There are two excellent introductions to middle Europe: Anthony Harding, 'Reformation in Barbarian Europe, 1300–600 BC', in Barry Cunliffe (ed.), *Prehistoric Europe: An Illustrated History* (Oxford: Oxford University Press, 1994), pp. 304–35; and Barry Cunliffe, *Europe Between the Oceans: 9000 BC–AD 1000* (New Haven and London: Yale University Press, 2008), pp. 228–69.

The fine remains of Ugarit, just outside modern Lattakia in northern Syria, are well worth visiting. Within Israel there are many notable sites. An excellent guidebook is Jerome Murphy-O'Connor, *The Holy Land: An Oxford Archaeological Guide from Earliest Times to 1700*, 5th edn. (Oxford: Oxford University Press, 2008). On the subsequent history of the Temple at Jerusalem, see Simon Goldhill, *The Temple of Jerusalem* (London: Profile, 2004). Goldhill explores memories of the whole city in *Jerusalem: City of Longing* (Cambridge, Mass., and London: Belknap Press of Harvard University Press, 2008), ch. 2. The relevant books of the Bible are Joshua, Judges, Samuel and Kings.

For Etruria, including Veii, see under Chapter 3. Sardinia has many Nuraghic sites; Nora, a Phoenician site, is also worth visiting.

CHAPTER 3: GREEKS, PHOENICIANS AND THE WESTERN MEDITERRANEAN: 800–480 BC

The best starting point for the history and archaeology of the Greek world in this period is Robin Osborne's *Greece in the Making, 1200–479 BC* (London and New York: Routledge, 1996; 2nd edn., 2009); for another good recent overview, see Jonathan Hall, *A History of the Archaic Greek World, ca. 1200–479 BCE* (Oxford: Blackwell, 2007). The Orientalizing culture of the eighth and seventh centuries BC is discussed by Walter Burkert, *The Orientalizing Revolution: Near Eastern Influence on Greek Culture in the Early Archaic Age* (Cambridge, Mass.: Harvard University Press, 1992).

On the Greek and Phoenician adventure in the western Mediterranean, the classic studies are John Boardman, *The Greeks Overseas: Their Early Colonies and Trade*, 4th edn. (London: Thames and Hudson, 1999), and Maria Eugenia

Aubet, *The Phoenicians and the West: Politics, Colonies, and Trade*, 2nd edn. (Cambridge: Cambridge University Press, 2001).

The most famous guide to ancient Etruria is that by George Dennis, *The Cities and Cemeteries of Etruria* (1848); it was edited in 1985 by Pamela Hemphill (Princeton: Princeton University Press). D. H. Lawrence, *Etruscan Places* (1932, often reprinted) is also evocative. The impact of the Greeks on Etruscan civilization is well traced by Graeme Barker and Tom Rasmussen, *The Etruscans* (Oxford: Blackwell, 1998), with good practical advice on locating sites (pp. 297–328).

An attractive introduction to the history and culture of the Persians is provided by the British Museum exhibition catalogue edited by John Curtis and Nigel Tallis, *Forgotten Empire: The World of Ancient Persia* (London: British Museum, 2005).

There are numerous translations of the *Iliad* and *Odyssey*. Many readers find the verse translations of Richmond Lattimore and Robert Fagles most satisfying; there is a good prose translation of the *Iliad* by Martin Hammond in the Penguin Classics series (1987). The prose translations of both epics by E. V. Rieu, also in the Penguin Classics series, are the smoothest and most readable of all, but give little sense of Homer's poetry.

A vivid sense of aristocratic Greek culture in the seventh and sixth centuries BC can be gained from the poetic fragments collected by M. L. West, *Greek Lyric Poetry*, in the Oxford World's Classics series (Oxford: Oxford University Press, 1999), and from the remarkable novel by Mary Renault, *The Praise Singer* (London: John Murray, 1978). For the visual arts, see Robin Osborne, *Archaic and Classical Greek Art* (Oxford: Oxford University Press, 1998).

Many of the sites mentioned in this chapter are well worth a visit. Eretria, on the island of Euboea, is easily accessible from Athens: there is an up-to-date guide to the site by Pierre Ducrey *et al.*, *Eretria: A Guide to the Ancient City* (Fribourg: École Suisse d'Archéologie en Grèce, 2004). Both Eretria and the dramatic site of Corinth are covered in the excellent guidebook by Christopher Mee and Antony Spawforth, *Greece: An Oxford Archaeological Guide* (Oxford: Oxford University Press, 2001). In Italy, the Etruscan sites of Tarquinii, Veii (Isola Farnese), Cerveteri (Caere) and Volsinii (Orvieto) are highly recommended: apart from the general books mentioned above, see Robert Leighton, *Tarquinia: An Etruscan City* (London: Duckworth, 2004). For the intrepid, the site of Persepolis, near Shiraz in south-western Iran, is one of the ancient world's finest: the guidebook by A. Shapur Shahbazi, *The Authoritative Guide to Persepolis* (Tehran: Safiran, 2004) is widely available in Iranian bookshops.

CHAPTER 4: GREECE, EUROPE AND ASIA: 480–334 BC

The best one-volume history covering this period is Simon Hornblower's *The Greek World 479–323 BC*, 3rd edn. (London: Routledge, 2002); Robin Osborne (ed.), *Classical Greece: 500–323 BC* (Oxford: Oxford University Press, 2000) is also helpful. For charm, wisdom and sheer readability, Herodotus' *Histories* (spanning the entire Greek world, and far beyond) remain matchless: there is a good modern translation by Robin Waterfield in the Oxford World's Classics series (Oxford: Oxford University Press, 1998, reprinted 2008). The Polish journalist Ryszard Kapuściński's *Travels with Herodotus* (London: Allen Lane, 2007) is an absorbing and provocative personal response to Herodotus' work. Tom Holland, *Persian Fire* (London: Abacus, 2005) is an up-to-date narrative history of the Persian Wars.

On Classical Athens, there is an accessible collection of papers in Deborah Boedecker and Kurt A. Raaflaub (eds.), *Democracy, Empire, and the Arts in Fifth-Century Athens* (Cambridge, Mass., and London: Harvard University Press, 1998). The Parthenon and the Acropolis are brilliantly dissected by Mary Beard, *The Parthenon* (London: Profile, 2002); more scholarly, but also very readable, is Jeffrey M. Hurwit, *The Athenian Acropolis* (Cambridge: Cambridge University Press, 1999). Thucydides' *History of the Peloponnesian War* can appear less immediately attractive than Herodotus' *Histories* (as Thucydides himself acknowledges in the introduction to his work), but many readers ultimately find its intellectual rewards to be deeper and more satisfying. The best English translation, that of Richard Crawley in the Everyman series, is out of print, but widely available; the recent translation by Martin Hammond in the Oxford World's Classics series (Oxford: Oxford University Press, 2009) is also recommended.

The most helpful introduction to the history of Sparta is Paul Cartledge, *The Spartans: An Epic History* (London: Channel Four Books, 2002); the afterlife of the Spartans is traced by Elizabeth Rawson, *The Spartan Tradition in European Thought* (Oxford: Clarendon Press, 1969, reprinted 1991). On the Greeks' northern neighbours, John Wilkes, *The Illyrians* (Oxford: Blackwell, 1992), is particularly good; the Thracians are discussed by R. F. Hoddinott, *The Thracians* (London: Thames and Hudson, 1981). Among numerous books on Classical Macedon, we would single out Eugene Borza, *In the Shadow of Olympus: The Emergence of Macedon* (Princeton: Princeton University Press, 1990).

A visit to the British Museum to see the Parthenon sculptures is a must. In Greece, although the Parthenon itself is currently undergoing an extensive programme of restoration, a visit to the Athenian Acropolis is still an overwhelming experience, and the Archaeological Museum and new Acropolis Museum at Athens are both superlative. The sacred island of Delos, the centre of the Delian League, is easily accessible from the Cycladic island of Mykonos; finally, Vergina, the old Macedonian capital of Aegae, is well worth a visit, primarily for the finds from the Macedonian royal tombs (including Tomb II, almost certainly the tomb of Philip II of Macedon).

CHAPTER 5: ALEXANDER THE GREAT AND THE HELLENISTIC WORLD: 334–146 BC

For the life and campaigns of Alexander the Great, there is still nothing to match the superb biography by Robin Lane Fox, *Alexander the Great* (London: Allen Lane, 1973). The fictionalized 'Alexander trilogy' of Mary Renault, *Fire from Heaven* (1970), *The Persian Boy* (1973) and *Funeral Games* (1981), takes the story down into the early Successor period.

The best general account of the Hellenistic kingdoms is that of Frank Walbank, *The Hellenistic World*, 2nd edn. (London: Fontana, 1992), now complemented by the useful collection of essays in Andrew Erskine (ed.), *A Companion to the Hellenistic World* (Oxford: Blackwell, 2003). An accessible introduction to Hellenistic science and mathematics is provided by Geoffrey Lloyd, *Greek Science after Aristotle* (New York and London: W. W. Norton, 1973).

Art and architecture are well treated (and lavishly illustrated) by Peter Green, *Alexander to Actium: The Hellenistic Age* (London: Thames & Hudson, 1990). The definitive study of ruler portraiture is R. R. R. Smith, *Hellenistic Royal Portraits* (Oxford: Clarendon Press, 1988); see also, more briefly, the same author's *Hellenistic Sculpture* (London: Thames & Hudson, 1991).

The culture of the La Tène celts and the history of the Celtic migrations are discussed by Barry Cunliffe, *The Ancient Celts* (Oxford: Oxford University Press, 1997).

The arrival of Rome in the Hellenistic east (which receives only brief treatment in Walbank's *Hellenistic World*) is explored in more detail by Erich Gruen, *The Hellenistic World and the Coming of Rome* (Berkeley, Los Angeles and London: University of California Press, 1984).

Of sites mentioned in the text, the most dramatic is undoubtedly the great fortress of Pergamum (modern Bergama), the Attalid royal capital, in western Turkey. There is a helpful guide to the site in George Bean, *Aegean Turkey*, 2nd edn. (London: John Murray, 1989), pp. 45–69. An excellent sense of the layout and fabric of a small Hellenistic city can be gained from a visit to the lovely site of Priene, also in western Turkey: see Frank Rumscheid and Wolf Koenigs, *Priene: A Guide to the 'Pompeii of Asia Minor'* (Istanbul: Ege Yayınları, 1998).

CHAPTER 6: ROME, CARTHAGE AND THE WEST: 500–146 BC

There are various full narratives and analyses of the period. T. J. Cornell, *The Beginnings of Rome: Italy and Rome from the Bronze Age to the Punic Wars (c. 1000–264 BC)* (London: Routledge, 1995), is the fullest modern account of the early history of Rome. *The Cambridge Ancient History*, 2nd edn., vol. 8: *Rome and the Mediterranean to 133 BC* (Cambridge: Cambridge University Press, 1989), is especially valuable on the subsequent history. Harriet Flower (ed.), *The Cambridge*

Companion to the Roman Republic (Cambridge: Cambridge University Press, 2004), provides a good introduction to a wide variety of topics. For an analysis of Roman religion down to the mid-second century BC, see Mary Beard, John North and Simon Price, *Religions of Rome*, 2 vols. (Cambridge: Cambridge University Press, 1998), vol. 1, pp. 1–113. On the Latin language, see James Clackson and Geoffrey Horrocks, *The Blackwell History of the Latin Language* (Malden, Mass., and Oxford: Blackwell, 2007), pp. 37–76. On the ways that Romans in historic periods talked about Romulus, see Augusto Fraschetti, *The Foundation of Rome* (Edinburgh: Edinburgh University Press, 2005).

Polybius, *The Rise of the Roman Empire*, Book 6 (translated by Ian Scott-Kilvert in the Penguin Classics series, 1979), is the classic account of the strengths of the Roman constitution. Ursula K. Le Guin, *Lavinia* (New York: Houghton Mifflin Harcourt, 2008), is an attractive imagining of early Latium, through the eyes of Lavinia and a time-travelling Virgil.

On the Roman calendar, see Mary Beard, John North and Simon Price, *Religions of Rome*, 2 vols. (Cambridge: Cambridge University Press, 1998), vol. 2, pp. 60–77 (some key documents in translation). Bonnie Blackburn and Leofranc Holford-Strevens, *The Oxford Companion to the Year* (Oxford: Oxford University Press, 2003), pp. 669–92, and Leofranc Holford-Strevens, *The History of Time: A Very Short Introduction* (Oxford: Oxford University Press, 2005), ch. 3, are masterly guides.

On the Etruscans, see under Chapter 3. For excellent introductions to middle Europe in this period, see Barry Cunliffe, 'Iron Age Societies in Western Europe and Beyond, 800–140 BC', in his *Prehistoric Europe: An Illustrated History* (Oxford: Oxford University Press, 1994), pp. 336–72, and the same author's *Europe Between the Oceans: 9000 BC–AD 1000* (New Haven and London: Yale University Press, 2008), pp. 317–63.

On the city of Rome, Claudia Moatti, *In Search of Ancient Rome* (London: Thames and Hudson, and New York: Abrams, 1993), offers an illustrated introduction. The best guidebook is that by Amanda Claridge, *Rome*, Oxford Archaeological Guides (Oxford: Oxford University Press, 1998); pp. 3–9 specify the sites in Rome relating to this chapter. Key finds from Etruria, including the gold plaques from Pyrgi, are in Rome, in the Museo Nazionale Etrusco di Villa Giulia; for good Etruscan sites to visit, see under Chapter 3. At Carthage, UNESCO-sponsored international excavations have resulted in much to be seen (despite the modern city): http://www.municipalite-carthage.tn/en/visiter.htm.

CHAPTER 7: ROME, ITALY AND EMPIRE: 146 BC–AD 14

For authoritative narratives and analyses of the period, see *The Cambridge Ancient History*, 2nd edn., vol. 9: *The Last Age of the Roman Republic 146–43 BC*, and vol. 10: *The Augustan Empire 43 BC–AD 69* (Cambridge: Cambridge University

Press, 1994 and 1996). On the religious history, see Mary Beard, John North and Simon Price, *Religions of Rome*, 2 vols. (Cambridge: Cambridge University Press, 1998), vol. 1, pp. 114–210. Denis Feeney, *Caesar's Calendar: Ancient Time and the Beginnings of History* (Berkeley: University of California Press, 2007), brilliantly explores the Romans' systems of chronology and hence sense of the past. Claude Nicolet, *Space, Geography, and Politics in the Early Roman Empire* (Ann Arbor: University of Michigan Press, 1991), is a pioneering account of the relations between Roman imperialism and concepts and organization of space. Andrew F. Wallace-Hadrill, *Rome's Cultural Revolution* (Cambridge: Cambridge University Press, 2008), is a wonderful analysis of the 'cultural bilingualism' of the late Republic. For arguments concerning the deaths of Tiberius Gracchus and Caesar, see T. P. Wiseman, *Remembering the Roman People: Essays on Late-Republican Politics and Literature* (Oxford: Oxford University Press, 2008), pp. 177–234.

For contemporary analysis of the tensions that broke Rome apart, see Sallust, *The Jugurthine War* and *Catiline's War*, translated by A. J. Woodman in the Penguin Classics series (2007). Virgil's *Aeneid* has been translated countless times. Perhaps the best are the verse translations by John Dryden or Robert Fagles; there is also a recent prose translation by David West (all in Penguin Classics).

The political life of the early first century BC is splendidly evoked by Robert Harris, *Imperium* (London: Hutchinson, 2006), on the young Cicero and his prosecution of Verres, a corrupt governor of Sicily.

Visitors to Rome should use Amanda Claridge, *Rome*, Oxford Archaeological Guides (Oxford: Oxford University Press, 1998); pp. 9–14 specify the sites in Rome relevant to this chapter. Bibracte (Mont Beuvray, in southern Burgundy) is an evocative site, with a fine Museum of Celtic Civilization at the foot of the hill (http://www.bibracte.fr/en). There is also a good museum at Autun (ancient Augustodunum). Entremont (just north of Aix-en-Provence) and Mailhac (near Béziers) are fine *oppida* of the second century BC: Henry Cleere, *Southern France* (Oxford: Oxford University Press, 2001), pp. 75, 126–9. The 'Druid' burial from Stanway can be seen in the Colchester Castle Museum (http://www.colchestermuseums.org.uk/), itself built on the foundations of the temple of the emperor Claudius. For Pompeii, there are several good archaeological and historical introductions to the site: Joanne Berry, *The Complete Pompeii* (London: Thames and Hudson, 2007); Roger Ling, *Pompeii: History, Life and Afterlife* (Stroud: Tempus, 2005); Alison E. Cooley, *Pompeii* (London: Duckworth, 2003); and Filippo Coarelli (ed.), *Pompeii* (New York: Riverside, 2002), though the translation, from Italian, is poor. A useful website is: http://www.pompeiisites.org/. But the outstanding book is Mary Beard, *Pompeii: The Life of a Roman Town* (London: Profile, 2008).

On Virgil in the Middle Ages, Domenico Comparetti, *Vergil in the Middle Ages* (London: Sonnenschein; New York: Macmillan, 1895; reprinted Princeton: Princeton University Press, 1997), which first appeared in Italian in 1872, remains exciting.

Quentin Skinner, *Machiavelli: A Very Short Introduction* (Oxford: Oxford

University Press, 2000), emphasizes Machiavelli's debt to classical humanism (not uncontroversially).

On Shakespeare's Rome, the best books are by Robert S. Miola, *Shakespeare's Rome* (Cambridge: Cambridge University Press, 1983), and Coppélia Kahn, *Roman Shakespeare: Warriors, Wounds, and Women* (London: Routledge, 1997).

Freud's collection of antiquities can be explored in Lynn Gamwell and Richard Wells (eds.), *Sigmund Freud and Art* (London: Thames and Hudson, 1989). Even better, many of them can be seen in the Freud House in London (http://www.freud.org.uk/). His house in Vienna is also a museum (http://www.freud-museum.at/).

CHAPTER 8: THE ROMAN EMPIRE: AD 14–284

The best single-volume introduction to the Roman empire is that of Colin Wells, *The Roman Empire*, 2nd edn. (London: Fontana, 1992). Authoritative narratives and analysis will be found in the *Cambridge Ancient History*, 2nd edn., vol. 10: *The Augustan Empire 43 BC–AD 69*, vol. 11: *The High Empire AD 70–192*, and vol. 12: *The Crisis of Empire AD 193–337* (Cambridge: Cambridge University Press, 1996, 2000 and 2005). Fergus Millar, *Government, Society, and Culture in the Roman Empire* (Chapel Hill, NC, and London: University of North Carolina, 2004), is a fine collection of essays on the administration and culture of the Roman provinces.

Tacitus' *Annals* are available in two good modern translations, by A. J. Woodman (Indianapolis: Hackett, 2004) and John Yardley in the Oxford World's Classics series (Oxford: Oxford University Press, 2008). The *Agricola* and *Germania* are available in a single Oxford World's Classics volume, translated by Anthony Birley (Oxford: Oxford University Press, 1999).

The whole question of 'Romanization' in the western provinces is explored by Greg Woolf, *Becoming Roman: The Origins of Provincial Civilization in Gaul* (Cambridge: Cambridge University Press, 1998). The problem of the survival of the native languages of the western provinces is studied in magisterial fashion by James Adams, *Bilingualism and the Latin Language* (Cambridge: Cambridge University Press, 2003).

There is an authoritative recent history of Roman Britain by David Mattingly, *An Imperial Possession: Britain in the Roman Empire* (London: Allen Lane, 2006). On Boudica and her posthumous reputation, Richard Hingley and Christina Unwin, *Boudica: Iron Age Warrior Queen* (London and New York: Hambledon Continuum, 2005) is a good starting point. The Vindolanda tablets from Hadrian's Wall, on display in the British Museum, are also available online: http://vindolanda.csad.ox.ac.uk/.

The history of Rome's wars with the Jews is traced by Martin Goodman, *Rome and Jerusalem: The Clash of Ancient Civilizations* (London: Allen Lane, 2007). On the Parthians and Sasanians, there is much of interest in Maria Brosius, *The Persians: An Introduction* (London and New York: Routledge, 2006).

The most imposing Roman monument in Britain is of course Hadrian's Wall (http://www.hadrians-wall.org/). A visit to Fishbourne is also highly recommended (http://www.sussexpast.co.uk/); see Barry Cunliffe, *Fishbourne Roman Palace* (Stroud: Tempus, 1998). In France, Bibracte and Autun are well worth a visit (see under Chapter 7); the Roman remains at Reims are described in J. Bromwich, *The Roman Remains of Northern and Eastern France: A Guidebook* (London and New York: Routledge, 2003), pp. 312–23, and there is a short guide to the site at La Graufesenque in Henry Cleere, *Southern France* (Oxford: Oxford University Press, 2001), pp. 45–7. The finds from Himlingøje are in the National Museum in Copenhagen (http://www.nationalmuseet.dk). Finally, the beautiful site of Aphrodisias (with its extraordinary sculpture museum, including the relief sculptures from the Sebasteion) is unmissable: see http://www.nyu.edu/projects/aphrodisias/.

CHAPTER 9: THE LATER ROMAN EMPIRE: AD 284–425

The study of late antiquity was pioneered by Peter Brown, *The World of Late Antiquity: From Marcus Aurelius to Muhammad* (London: Thames and Hudson, 1971; reprinted in 2004 as *The World of Late Antiquity: AD 150–750*), which remains a stimulating (and beautifully illustrated) essay. The best short introduction is Averil Cameron, *The Later Roman Empire: AD 284–430* (London: Fontana, 1993). For full documentation of this period, see the *Cambridge Ancient History*, 2nd edn., vol. 12: *The Crisis of Empire: AD 193–337*, and vol. 13: *The Late Empire: AD 337–425* (Cambridge: Cambridge University Press, 2005 and 1998). For a sketch of the religious changes in the fourth century AD, see Mary Beard, John North and Simon Price, *Religions of Rome*, 2 vols. (Cambridge: Cambridge University Press, 1998), vol. 1, pp. 364–88.

For the importance of Eusebius as chronographer and historian, see A. D. Momigliano, *The Classical Foundations of Modern Historiography* (Berkeley: California University Press, 1990), ch. 6, and Anthony Grafton and Megan Williams, *Christianity and the Transformation of the Book: Origen, Eusebius, and the Library of Caesarea* (Cambridge, Mass., and London: Belknap Press of Harvard University Press, 2006). On chronological eras more generally, see the excellent works by Bonnie Blackburn and Leofranc Holford-Strevens, *The Oxford Companion to the Year* (Oxford: Oxford University Press, 2003), pp. 762–90, and Leofranc Holford-Strevens, *The History of Time: A Very Short Introduction* (Oxford: Oxford University Press, 2005).

Peter Brown, *Augustine of Hippo: A Biography* (New York: Dorset Press, London: Faber and Faber, 1967; reprinted with epilogue 2000), is the classic biography. It would be hard to praise too highly Augustine, *Confessions*, translated by Henry Chadwick (Oxford: Oxford University Press, 1991), or Augustine, *City of God*, translated by Henry Bettenson (Penguin Classics series, 1984).

On the transmission of texts, L. D. Reynolds and N. G. Wilson, *Scribes and Scholars: A Guide to the Transmission of Greek and Latin Literature,* 3rd edn. (Oxford: Clarendon Press, 1991), is a lucid account of how ancient texts survived antiquity. For the Codex Sinaiticus: http://www.codexsinaiticus.org/en/; this website makes available online images of the 800 surviving pages of this bible, physically dispersed between the British Library, the National Library of Russia, St Catherine's Monastery Sinai and Leipzig University Library.

For Rome, once again we recommend Amanda Claridge, *Rome,* Oxford Archaeological Guides (Oxford: Oxford University Press, 1998); pp. 22–7 specify the sites in Rome relating to this chapter. In Germany, Trier is the best-preserved Roman city: Edith M. Wightman, *Roman Trier and the Treveri* (London: Hart-Davis, 1970), pp. 71–123. For sites in northern Germany, see Joachim von Elbe, *The Romans in Cologne and Lower Germany* (Düsseldorf: Ursula Preis Verlag, 1995). In France, there are some grand rural villas: Montaurin (Midi-Pyrénées); Loupian (south-west of Montpellier); see Henry Cleere, *Southern France,* Oxford Archaeological Guides (Oxford: Oxford University Press, 2001). On Saint-Guilhem-le-Désert, see the short guide by Frédérique Barbut, *Saint-Guilhem-le-Désert* (Rennes: Éditions Ouest-France, 2001); for practical information, see the website of the commune: http://www.saint-guilhem-le-desert.com. In Spain, some cities have important early Christian buildings: Tarragona, Mérida, Ampurias; and there is a grand rural villa at Carranque; see Roger Collins, *Spain,* Oxford Archaeological Guides (Oxford: Oxford University Press, 1998). On the Lullingstone villa, see Michael Fulford, *Lullingstone Roman Villa, Kent* (London: English Heritage, 2003); for information on how to visit the site, see: http://www.english-heritage.org.uk/server/show/nav.14714; the paintings are in the British Museum.

For Constantinople/Istanbul, see Hilary Sumner-Boyd and John Freely, *Strolling through Istanbul: A Guide to the City* (London: Kegan Paul, 2003); the remains of the serpent column are visible to this day. For Palestine, see under Chapter 2; and also Oleg Grabar, *The Dome of the Rock* (Cambridge, Mass., and London: Belknap, 2006). On the wonderful late mosaics in the Levant, see the imaginative book by Glen W. Bowersock, *Mosaics as History: The Near East from Late Antiquity to Islam* (Cambridge, Mass.: Harvard University Press, 2006).

For the next part of the story there are several excellent books. On the east, see Mark Whittow, *The Making of Orthodox Byzantium, 600–1025* (London: Macmillan, 1996). On the west, see Peter Brown, *The Rise of Western Christendom: Triumph and Diversity, AD 200–1000,* 2nd edn. (Oxford: Blackwell, 2003). Bryan Ward-Perkins, *The Fall of Rome and the End of Civilization* (Oxford: Oxford University Press, 2005), argues for major disruption in this period. Julia Smith, *Europe after Rome: A New Cultural History 500–1000* (Oxford: Oxford University Press, 2005), stresses the dynamism of the Early Middle Ages. Chris Wickham, *The Inheritance of Rome: A History of Europe from 400 to 1000* (London: Allen Lane, 2009), ranging from Ireland to the Levant, explores both the turbulence and the achievements of this period.

Date Chart

All dates before around 700 BC are both hypothetical and approximate. There is much controversy about Aegean dates of the second millennium BC between those favouring a 'high' and a 'low' chronology; we have picked what may be the emerging compromise.

Western world	Aegean world	Near East
1900 BC	1900–1750 First Palace period on Crete	
1800 BC	1750–1430 Second Palace period (or Neopalatial period) on Crete	
1500 BC		1550–1070 Egypt: New Kingdom
		1530–1155 Kassite state in Lower Mesopotamia
	1430–1350 Mycenaeans involved in dominance of Knossos	1420–1200 Hittite 'New Kingdom' in central Asia Minor
1400 BC	after 1400–1200 Palaces in mainland Greece (Mycenae; Tiryns; Pylos; Thebes)	1400–1050 Assyrian state in Upper Mesopotamia
	1350 Ending of palatial administration on Crete, though	

	Western world	Aegean world	Near East
1400 BC (cont.)		Khania continued down to 1200	
		1350–1300 Troy Level VIh	
1300 BC	1300–700 Late Bronze Age in western Europe: Urnfield period	1300–1210 Troy Level VIIa	
1200 BC		1200–1070 Post-palatial period in mainland Greece	1200 Israelite 'conquest' of Canaan (traditional date)
1100 BC		1070–900 'Early Iron Age' period in Aegean	1070–712 Egypt: Third Intermediate period (lack of unitary government)
1000 BC			1010–970 David, king of Israel
		950 Lefkandi 'Toumba' monument	970–930 Solomon, king of Israel
			969–936 Hiram I, king of Tyre
900 BC	900–700 'Early Iron Age', or Villanovan, period, in central Italy		883–610 Neo-Assyrian empire
800 BC	800–750 Earliest Phoenician and Greek colonies in western Mediterranean	800–700 Emergence of *poleis* in mainland Greece; 'Orientalizing' period in Greek world	
	770 Foundation of Pithecoussae (bay of Naples)	776 Traditional date of first Olympic games; 775 Earliest Greek alphabetic writing	775 Foundation of Al Mina (Syria)
	753 One traditional date for foundation of Rome by Romulus		

	Western world	Aegean world	Near East
800 BC (cont.)	730 'Nestor's Cup' at Pithecoussae		
700 BC	700–475 Etruscan civilization in central Italy	700 Hesiod, *Theogony*	
		700–650 *Iliad* and Odyssey are written down	
			c. 620 Hebrew Bible, first version
			616–608 Fall of Assyrian empire to Babylonians and Medes
600 BC	600 Foundation of Massilia (Marseilles)		605–539 Neo-Babylonian kingdom
	600–500 Hellenizing West Hallstatt chiefdoms in western Europe		
		582–573 Establishment of Panhellenic games at Delphi (582), Isthmia (c. 582) and Nemea (573)	586 Capture of Jerusalem by Nebuchadnezzar; Jews in captivity in Babylon
			550–330 Persian empire in the Near East: Cyrus (550–530); Cambyses (530–522); Darius (522–486); Xerxes (486–465)
			c. 550 Hebrew Bible, second version

	Western world	Aegean world	Near East
600 BC (cont.)			539 Persian conquest of Babylon
			525 Persian conquest of Egypt
	507 Expulsion of last king of Rome; foundation of the Roman Republic	508/7 Democratic reforms of Cleisthenes at Athens	
500 BC	500 Vix burial (Châtillon-sur-Seine)	499–494 Ionian revolt against Persia	
		490 Battle of Marathon	
		480–478 Xerxes' invasion of Greece	
		478 Establishment of Delian League	
		461 Athenian alliance with Argos	
	450 La Tène culture of middle Europe begins (ends around 50 BC)	458 Aeschylus' *Oresteia*	
		447–433 Construction of the Parthenon at Athens	
		431–404 Peloponnesian War between Athens and Sparta	
		420s Herodotus' *Histories*; Hellanicus' *Priestesses of Argos*	
		415–413 Athenian expedition to Sicily	
400 BC	396 Capture of Veii by Rome	c. 400 Thucydides' *History of the Peloponnesian War*	401 Xenophon's 'March Up Country' (*Anabasis*)
	386 Gauls attack Rome	386 King's Peace in mainland Greece	

Western world	Aegean world	Near East
400 BC (cont.)	382 Spartan seizure of Theban Kadmeia	
	371 Thebes defeats Sparta at battle of Leuctra	
	369 Foundation of Messene	
	359–336 Reign of Philip II of Macedon	
338 Rome's settlement imposed on the Latin states	338 Philip defeats Athens and Thebes at battle of Chaeronea	
	336–323 Reign of Alexander III ('the Great') of Macedon	
	335 Destruction of Thebes by Alexander	
		334 Alexander's invasion of Asia
		332 Foundation of Alexandria
		331–330 Capture of the Persian royal capitals
		327–325 Alexander's invasion of India
c. 320 Journey of Pytheas of Massilia		323 Death of Alexander at Babylon
	310 Death of Alexander IV	
	306 Antigonus the One-Eyed proclaimed king	
300 BC	301 Battle of Ipsus; death of Antigonus	305–282 Reign of Ptolemy I (Egypt)
	c. 287–211 Archimedes of Syracuse (mathematician)	c. 285–194 Eratosthenes of Cyrene (head of the

	Western world	Aegean world	Near East
300 BC (cont.)			library at Alexandria)
	264–241 First Punic War; Sicily becomes Rome's first overseas province	279 Celtic invasion of Greece	279/8 First celebration of Ptolemaieia at Alexandria
		c. 240–197 Reign of Attalus I (Attalid kingdom: Pergamon)	223–187 Reign of Antiochus III (Seleucid kingdom: Asia)
	218–202 Second Punic War (also known as the Hannibalic War)	221–179 Reign of Philip V (Antigonid kingdom: Macedon)	
200 BC		197–158 Reign of Eumenes II (Attalid kingdom: Pergamon)	
		190 Battle of Magnesia; end of Seleucid rule in Asia Minor	
		179–168 Reign of Perseus (Antigonid kingdom: Macedon)	175–164 Reign of Antiochus IV (Seleucid kingdom: Asia)
		168 Battle of Pydna; end of Antigonid kingdom in Macedon	167 Suppression of Jewish religion by Antiochus IV; beginning of Jewish resistance (context of writing of Book of Daniel, and 1–2 Maccabees)
	149–146 Third Punic War	148 Establishment of Roman province of Macedonia	
	146 Sack of Carthage; province of Africa created	146 Sack of Corinth; province of Macedonia extended to southern Greece	
	133 Tiberius Gracchus tribune		

	Western world	Aegean world	Near East
200 BC (cont.)	123–122 Gaius Gracchus' two tribunates		
100 BC	91–89 'Social War'; Italians become Roman citizens		
		89–63 Roman conflict with Mithradates VI of Pontus; 86 Roman sack of Athens	
	55, 54 Caesar invades Britain		
	52 Caesar completes conquest of Gaul		
	49–44 Caesar dominant at Rome; 44 Caesar assassinated		
	31 BC–AD 14 Augustus emperor (he was called 'Caesar Augustus' only from 27 BC onwards)		
	19 Death of Virgil		37–4 Herod king of Judaea
AD 1			6 Census of Quirinius
	14–68 Julio-Claudian dynasty: Tiberius (14–37), Caligula (37–41), Claudius (41–54), Nero (54–68)		c. 30 Crucifixion of Jesus
	43 Roman invasion of Britain	Late 40s and 50s Paul's missionary journeys round Greek world	
	60–61 Boudica's revolt in Britain		66–70 Jewish revolt in Judaea; destruction of Temple
	69 Year of the Four Emperors: Galba,		

	Western world	Aegean world	Near East
AD 1 (cont.)	Otho, Vitellius, Vespasian		
	69–96 Flavian dynasty: Vespasian (69–79), Titus (79–81), Domitian (81–96)		80s? Acts of the Apostles written
	78–84 Agricola governor of Britain		
	96–8 Nerva emperor		
AD 100	98–117 Trajan emperor		
	98 Tacitus' *Agricola*		
	c. 110–20 Tacitus' *Annals*		
	117–38 Hadrian emperor	131/2 Establishment of Panhellenion	132–5 Bar Kokhba revolt in Judaea
	138–92 Antonine dynasty: Antoninus Pius (138–61), Marcus Aurelius (161–80), Lucius Verus (joint reign, 161–6), Commodus (180–92)		
	192–235 Severan dynasty: Septimius Severus (193–211), Caracalla (211–17), Elagabalus (218–22), Alexander Severus (222–35)		
AD 200	249 Persecution of Christians under Decius		240–72 Reign of Shapur I (Persia)
		267/8 Sack of Athens by the Goths	260 Roman emperor Valerian captured by Shapur I

	Western world	Aegean world	Near East
AD 200 (cont.)	284–305 Diocletian emperor		
AD 300	303–4 Great Persecution (of Christians)		
	306–37 Constantine emperor		
		324 Foundation of Constantinople	
	337–61 Constantius II emperor		
	354–430 Augustine (bishop of Hippo, 395–430; writes *Confessions* 397/400; writes *City of God*, 413–25)		
	360–63 Julian emperor		363 Julian dies on campaign in Persia
	c. 371–97 Martin bishop of Tours		
	379–95 Theodosius I emperor		
AD 400	410 Sack of Rome		

Index

ab urbe condita, Roman dating 311
Abbasid caliphate 161–2
Abd al-Malik 331
Abraham 331, 333; in Eusebius'
  Chronography 312–13, 323
Abydos: *Map 16*; 113
Acamas 129
Achaea, Achaeans: in Homer –
  36–7, 100–101, 108, 133, 144;
  claims to Achaean descent by
  Eumeneia 282; Troy, attack on
  40–42; Metapontum, settlement of
  Achaeans at 93; League, Achaean
  172–3
Achaemenids, *see* Persia
Acharnae 124–5
Achilles 11, 101–3, 104; later uses of:
  by Alexander 147, by Julian 315;
  see also Homer; Trojan War
Acrocorinth, *see* acropolis
acropolis: at Athens: *Figs 10, 17,
  20*; Mycenaean: 61; Classical:
  Plate 12, 116, 124–6; Hellenistic
  167–8; written into the *Iliad* 105;
  nineteenth-century reinvention
  125–6; at Byzantium: built over
  by Constantine: *Map 34*, 306; at
  Corinth (Acrocorinth) 81; at Eretria
  77; at Mycenae 25, 43; at Thebes
  (Kadmeia) 134, 350
Actium (Punta): *Map 27*, 218–19, 243,
  246
Acts of the Apostles 273, 322; *see also*
  Bible
Aden, Gulf of 292
Adonis 207

adoption: at Rome 244, 253
Adriatic: *Map 23*; Byron's visit 114;
  Greek interest in 133, 138; Roman
  interest in 169, 173
Aeclanum: *Map 26, 222*
aedile 188–9
Aedui: Bibracte: *Maps 28, 29, Fig. 27,
  Plate 14*; pre-Caesar, at Bibracte
  234, 236, *see oppidum*; post-Caesar,
  at Augustodunum 263–4, 267
Aegean: *Map 9*; defined 18; fragmented
  geography of 122–3; Hittite
  influence in 16, 36, 39; and
  Mediterranean history 5–6; Bronze
  Age: *Map 3*, 12–14, 18, 35–6; Iron
  Age: *Maps 4, 10, 45, 62–8, 76*;
  Classical: *Map 16*, 112–13, 119–23,
  132–3, 139; Hellenistic 152, 158,
  204; in Roman Civil Wars 239, 243;
  nineteenth century 155–6; society,
  interpretation of by Lafitau –
  118–19; trade 38–9, 74, 84, 88
Aegina 105
Aegisthus 25
Aelia Capitolina – 284; *see also*
  Jerusalem
Aeneas: *Plate 28*, 175, 177, 180–83;
  in literature: Ennius 213; Fabius
  Pictor 213; Livy 195; Naevius 210;
  Virgil, *Aeneid* 180, 210, 247–8, 301;
  other uses of: Durocortorum 276–7;
  Geoffrey of Monmouth 183, 333;
  Julii 214–15; Latin League 193–4;
  Segesta 209–10; Titus Flamininus
  170; reception of, in the later
  Roman empire 311,

357

Augustus (*cont.*)
under 243–4, 257; *limes* 287; month
186; chronology, used for 311, 314;
see also Horace; Maecenas; Strabo;
Virgil
Aulis: *Map 16, 133; see also* myth,
political use of; sacrifice
Aurelian 293
Ausonius 309, 320; *see also* Burgidala
auspicium 191
autochthony: Athenian 120, 182; *see
also* ethnicity; identity
Averroes 162
Avicenna 162

Ba'al 206
Babylas, *see* martyrdom
Babylon, Babylonia: *Maps 1, 6, 7,
15, 17, 18*; in second millennium
BC 16–17, 37, 52–3; Jewish
exile at 54, 158, 330, 349; Neo-
Babylonian kingdom 109, 349; in
Persian empire 109, 111, 266; and
Herodotus 117; and Alexander
III of Macedon 145, 148, 266,
351; Seleucus I Nikator 150; in
Parthian empire 293–4; whore of
Babylon, Rome as 298; *see also*
Berossos; Chaldaeans; Euphrates;
Mesopotamia
Bacchus 265; *see also* Dionysus
Bactria: *Maps 15, 17, 18, 146, 152*;
camels, 110–11, *Fig. 15; see also*
tragedy, Athenian; Ai Khanoum
Balkans 5, 138–9, 142; *see also* Epiros;
FYROM; Illyria; Paeonia; Thrace
Bantia (Banzi): *Map 20, 201*
Bar Kokhba revolt 284, 322–3, 354
barbarians: Greek conception of
117, 133, 140, 144; Trojans not
barbarians 108, 182–3; Celts
166–8; Romans 170–71; Parthians
294; Goths 280–81, 288;
'barbarian' northern Europe 173–4,
291, 302, 332; Boudica 261
Barnabas 273
basileus (plural *basileis*) 26, 49, 77
basilica: at Aphrodisias 282; at Pompeii

224; at Rome 204
battles: turning points in history,
perceived as, *see* past, uses of;
past, views of; *see also* Actium;
army; Carrhae; Chaeronea;
Cynoscephalae; Gaugamela; Ipsus;
Leuctra; Magnesia; Marathon;
Pharsalus; Philippi; Plataea; Pydna;
Salamis; Thermopylae; war
Beauvais *see* Caesaromagus
Bellovacorum
Bede 313
Belgae: *Map 28, 237*
Bellerophon: at Aphrodisias 282–3,
Fig. 26; at Lullingstone 301
Beneventum (Benevento): *Map 23*
Berenikē: *Map 32; 291*
Bernal, Martin 89–90
Berossos 156
Bessus 146
Bethlehem 321, 333
Bible: Israelite history 53–5, 76, 206;
Old Testament 53–5, 297, 299,
323, 348, 349; New Testament
273, 323, 331; textual transmission
of 318; chronology of 313–14;
classical tradition 320, 328; *see
also* Acts of the Apostles; Daniel,
Book of; Gospels; Luke; Maccabees;
Matthew; Peter, First Epistle of;
Revelation
Bibracte (Mont Beuvray), *see* Aedui
bilingualism: in Hellenistic kingdoms
152–3; in Italian peninsula 225;
Romans bilingual in Greek 213,
290, 331; in Roman provinces 273,
290
Al-Birūni 162
Bishapur: *Map 32, 295*
bishops 314, 318, 320–21, 325; New
Year, opposition to 319; persecution
of 298; persecution by 310
Black Athena, see Bernal, Martin
Black Sea: *Maps 27, 31, 116, 138–9,
155, 236*; exile, place of 289; Goths
280; trade 39, 123
Boadicea, *see* Boudica
Boeotia, Boeotians: *Maps 4, 8; 37, 87*;

tragedy, Athenian: 'Classical' literature
in Hellenistic period 160–61;
indication of Greek culture in
Bactria 152; political function of
120, 128, 136
Trajan 258, 280, 353; attitude to
Christians 297–8
Transylvania 166
Treasury of Atreus, *see* tholos tombs
Trevelyan, Charles 269
tribune of the people, *see* Gracchi;
Livia, attained rights equivalent to
244
tribute: Athenian 121, 123–4;
Carthagian to Tyre 205; Persian
110; Ptolemaic 159; Roman 173,
195; *see also* tax
Trier, *see* Augusta Treverorum
Triptolemus 121
Troad 11–12, 39, 115, 144, 169–70
Trojan War: chronology, Eratosthenes,
precisely dated by 160, 181, 213,
312; universal date-horizon 64, 183;
views of 7, 67, 330; Alexander III
144; Artyactes 114–15; Asia Minor,
cities of 282–3, 299; Athens 105,
138; Ausonius 309; Constantine
305; Cyprus 63; Etruscan Dardanii
202; Mehmed the Conqueror 147;
paralleled with Persian Wars 115;
Rome and 171, 175, 180–81, 193,
195, 210, 277; Sparta 106–8, 133;
Thebes and 65; historicity of 12, 25,
43, 53, 40–42; Homeric tradition:
Cypria 62; *Iliad* and *Odyssey*,
genesis of 101–5; Nestor's Cup
100–101; *see also* hero-cult
Troy (Hisarlık): *Maps 3, 33, Fig. 7, 5,*
11, 18, 39–42, 348; excavations of
11–12, 40–42; *see also* Trojan War
(historicity of)
True Cross 333
Tudhaliya IV 37
Tullus Hostilius 186, 194
Tunisia, *see* Carthage; Utica
Turks, *see* empire (Ottoman)
Tuscan language (medieval) 179
Tusculum: *Map 22*

tyranny: accusations of: by Founding
Fathers 192; against the Gracchi
228–9; against Julius Caesar
241–2; against Mithradates 232;
in archaic Greek world 79, 137;
Brutus and Cassius as tyrannicides
241–3, 258–9; in Persian empire
110; tyrannicides at Athens, *see*
Peisistratids; *see also* aristocrats;
magistrates, civic
Tyre: *Maps 6, 7, 9, 56, 86*; Carthage
and 176, 205–6; myth 4, 205; trade
of 53, 62, 76, 100; *see* Hiram of
Tyre; *see also* Carthage, Phoenicia
Tyrrhenian Sea: *Map 23*
Tyrrhenians, *see* Etruscans
Tyrrhenos, *see* Etruscans
Tyrtaeus 107

Ugarit (Ras Shamra): *Map 1, 38, 41*
Uluburun: *Map 1, Plate 4, 38, 44*
Umbria: *Map 20, 199; see* Oscan-
Umbrian language
Umm el-Jimal: *Map 31, 265–6*
Uni-Astra, *see* Astarte
United Kingdom, *see* Britain
Urartu: *Map 6, 51*
urbanization: Etruscan 73, 97–100;
in Gaul 232–3, 262–4, 275; Greek
62–3, 81–2, 93, 138; in Iberia 92,
95, 211; in Illyria and Thrace,
absence of 139–40; in Levant 262;
in Macedonia, under Philip II 142;
in middle Europe 233–4; Rome
183–4, 250; *see also* polis
Urnfield: defined 69, 348;
Mediterranean and middle Europe
compared 74, 76; in middle Europe
71–2; late Urnfield, *see* Hallstatt
culture
Ussher, Archbishop, *see* Creation
Utica: *Map 12; 91; see also* Phoenicia
Uzbekistan 146; *see also* Bactria;
Sogdiana

Valentinian 309
Valerian 295–6, 304, 354
Vandals 328, 332